Global Strategic Management

Philippe Lasserre

First published 2003 by
PALGRAVE MACMILLAN
Houndmills, Basingstoke, Hampshire RG21 6XS and
175 Fifth Avenue, New York, N.Y. 10010
Companies and representatives throughout the world

PALGRAVE MACMILLAN is the global academic imprint of the Palgrave
Macmillan division of St. Martin's Press, LLC and of Palgrave Macmillan Ltd.
Macmillan® is a registered trademark in the United States, United Kingdom
and other countries. Palgrave is a registered trademark in the European
Union and other countries.

ISBN 0–333–79374–9 hardback
ISBN 0–333–79375–7 paperback

This book is printed on paper suitable for recycling and made from fully
managed and sustained forest sources.

A catalogue record for this book is available from the British Library.

Library of Congress Cataloging-in-Publication Data
Lasserre, Philippe.
  Global strategic management / Philippe Lasserre.
      p.   cm.
  Includes bibliographical references and index.
  ISBN 0–333–79374–9—ISBN 0–333–79375–7 (pbk.)
  1. International business enterprises—Management.   2. Strategic planning.
  3. Globalization—Economic aspects.   I. Title.

  HD62.4 .L37 2002
  658.4'012—dc21

                                                        2002074813

10   9   8   7   6   5   4   3   2
12   11   10   09   08   07   06   05   04   03

Printed and bound in Great Britain by
J.W. Arrowsmith Ltd, Bristol

Contents

List of figures

List of tables

List of mini-examples

List of abbreviations

ABB	Asea Brown Boveri
APV	Adjusted Present Value
ASEAN	Association of South East Asian Nations
ATT	American Telegraph and Telephone
B2B	Business to Business
BT	British Telecom
B.O.T	Build Operate and Transfer
BPI	Bribe Payers Index
CEO	Chief Executive Officer
CIA	Central Intelligence Agency
CIF	Cost Insurance Freight
CPI	Corruption Perception Index
EDI	Electronic Data Interchange
EIU	Economist Intelligence Unit
FDI	Foreign Direct Investments
FOB	Free on Board
GATT	General Agreement on Trade and Tariffs
GDP	Gross Domestic Product
GDP/Cap	Gross Domestic Product per Capita
GE	General Electric
GNP	Gross National Product
GNP/Cap	Gross National Product per Capita
GRI	Global Revenue Index
GCI	Global Capability Index
HQ	Headquarters
ILO	International Labour Organisation
IMD	International Institute for Management Development
IMF	International Monetary Fund
IPR	Intellectual Property Rights
IRR	Internal Rate of Return
JV	Joint Venture

LIBOR	London Inter Bank Offering Rate
M&A	Mergers and Acquisitions
NAFTA	North American Free Trade Agreement
NPV	Net Present Value
NYSE	New York Stock Exchange
OECD	Organisation for Economic Cooperation and Development
PCN	Parent Country National
PPP	Purchasing Power Parity
RFQ	Request for Quotation
R and D or R&D	Research and Development
SME	Small and Medium Sized Enterprises
SNECMA	Société Nationale d'Études et de Construction de Moteurs d'Avions
SRI	Socially Responsible Investing
TCN	Third Country National
TI	Transparency International
UNCTAD	United Nation Centre for Trade and Development
UK	United Kingdom
UN	United Nations
USA	United States of America
US	United States
WACC	Weighted Average Cost of Capital
WTO	World Trade Organisation

Preface and acknowledgements

I want to thank particularly my colleagues at INSEAD, from whom I have borrowed much material and many ideas. Amelia Ho contributed to the bibliographical search as well as to the summary at the end of each chapter, and to the text editing. Michelle Gauthier, Joan Lewis and Magdalene Khng also helped me with the manuscript editing.

Singapore

PHILIPPE LASSERRE

Introduction

This book is about global firms and global management. Its objective is to help graduate and undergraduate students, as well as company executives, to understand the main issues that companies and their managers confront when they 'go global' or 'manage globally', and to cope with them.

The book has been designed as a support for specialised courses on Strategic Management for Global Firms, equivalent to a series of course notes to be read in preparation for a class or afterwards. Students will normally be assigned a case study for each of the topics covered in the book. It can also be used as a reference guide for managers and executives.

WHY ANOTHER BOOK ON GLOBAL STRATEGIC MANAGEMENT?

There are a number of excellent textbooks on international business already available.[1] So why do we need another one?

First, the focus of the book is on business firms and their employees. It has eliminated from the text the macroeconomical and political factors that traditional international business textbooks cover, such as international trade and investment flows, the problems of economic development in emerging countries, the analysis of international and regional institutions such as the World Trade Organisation (WTO), the United Nations (UN), the World Banks and other Development Banks, the European Union (EU), the North American Free Trade Agreement (NAFTA), the Association of South East Asian Nations (ASEAN) and the like, or the geopolitical analysis of diplomacy and defence. It is assumed that students interested in those topics will read specialised books or attend courses taught by economists or political scientists.

Second, the book takes the view that the traditional international business paradigm based on the study of foreign investments in 'foreign' countries by 'home'-country firms is no longer valid for studying global firms. As will be argued, international and multinational firms, controlling a vast array of 'foreign subsidiaries', have been in existence for a long time. Global firms that progressively abandon their original nationality to manage a network of firms in an integrated and coordinated way out of 'centres' that are no longer necessarily located in their country of origin are a recent phenomenon. Scholars like Chris Bartlett, Sumantra Ghoshal, Yves Doz and C.K. Prahalad, and more recently Peter Williamson and José dos Santos[2] have studied this evolution: they came up with the terms still 'transnational' or 'metanational' corporations to describe these new entities. Earlier, George Yip analysed what he called 'Total Global Strategy'.[3] This book is inspired largely by their theoretical and empirical work. Obviously, classical issues such as entry strategies or expatriate management will not be forgotten, but the overall tone of the book looks at how, ultimately, international or multinational firms become global and managed globally.

Third, the book aims at describing and analysing the key strategic and managerial challenges for firms, but does not pretend to be exhaustive or encyclopaedic. As Michel Montaigne said, it is better *'d'avoir une tête bien faite qu'une tête bien pleine'* (a well-rounded brain rather than a full one). A lot of theoretical developments have been deliberately omitted: transaction costs theory, locational theory and agency theory, for instance, have been left out. The quotation of a multitude of articles published in academic journals and collections of papers in the field of international business such as the *Journal of International Studies*, the *Strategic Management Journal* or the *Academy of Management Journal* has been strictly limited. Those who want to know more are invited to look at the list of References and further reading at the end of each chapter as well as the works quoted during the text.

Fourth, several mini-examples have been inserted in many chapters in order to illustrate the points made in the text. Those are not case studies. Appendix I.1 (p. 4) lists selected relevant cases.

Finally, the book borrows considerably from the work done by professors or ex-professors at the European Institute of Business Administration (INSEAD), and has favoured their works rather than others. This has been a deliberate choice, given the long-standing involvement of the author in the intellectual life of this institution.

THE STRUCTURE OF THE BOOK

As the diagram below shows, the book is organised in three parts of unequal length: The Process of Globalisation, Managing Globally and Broad Issues in Globalisation.

HOW CAN THIS BOOK BE USED?

This book can be used in three ways:

(1) As background reading for a course based on case studies. To that end Appendix I.1 (p. 4) lists potential cases that the author has used to support each chapter of the book. Those cases are available in international clearing

I THE PROCESS OF GLOBALISATION

	Chapter
Why globalisation?	
Globalisation of Markets and Competition	1
How to Globalise?	
Designing a Global Strategy	2
Designing a Global Organisation	3
Global Strategic Alliances	4
Global Mergers and Acquisitions	5
Assessing Countries' Attractiveness	6
Entry Strategies	7

II MANAGING GLOBALLY

Global Marketing	8
Global Operations	9
Global Innovation	10
Cross-Cultural Management	11
Global Human Resource Management	12
Global Financial Management	13

III BROAD ISSUES IN GLOBALISATION

Globalisation and the Internet	14
The Social Responsibility of the Global Firm	15
Global Trends	16

houses such the Harvard Business School Clearing House or the European Case Clearing House.[4] There are also some excellent casebooks available.[5]

(2) As a stand-alone textbook for a course based on lectures and exercises. At the end of each chapter there are questions that can serve as learning assignments to prepare for such lectures, or to follow them.

(3) As a reference book, particularly in executive programmes or for individual readers who want to get acquainted with global strategic management without being burdened by too much theory and background reading.

Appendix I.1   List of potential case studies to be used to support the book

(HBS = Harvard Business School, IMD = International Institute for Management Development, INSEAD = Institut Européen d'Administration des Affaires)

Chapter	Cases	Reference
1 **Globalisation of Markets and Competition**	▪ This session is not usually taught by cases. However, Mercedes-Benz can be used to discuss in general all issues surrounding globalisation for the firm	HBS, 1993
2 **Designing a Global Strategy**	▪ Royal Ahold NV: Shopkeeper to The Global Village.	HBS, 1997
	▪ The Benetton Group	HBS, 1995
	▪ TNT Limited's Logistics Services in Asia (A): The Strategy	HBS, 1997
	▪ AXA: The Global Insurance Company	HBS, 1993
	▪ Sony Corporation: Globalization	HBS, 1991
	▪ Ajinomoto Co., Inc.	HBS, 2000
	▪ The Acer Group: Building an Asian Multinational	INSEAD, 1997
3 **Designing a Global Organisation**	▪ Eli Lilly, 1998: Emerging Global Organization	HBS, 1999
	▪ Becton Dickinson: Managing the Global Enterprise, 1996	HBS, 1996
	▪ Thorsten AB 1	IMD, 1999
4 **Global Strategic Alliances**	▪ Advance Drug Delivery Systems: Alza and Ciba-Geigy	INSEAD, 1994
	▪ PixTech, Inc.	INSEAD, 1998
	▪ General Electric and Snecma	INSEAD, 1992
	▪ Renault–Nissan: A Marriage of Reason	INSEAD, 2001
5 **Global Mergers and Acquisitions**	▪ DBS: Thailand	INSEAD, 2000
	▪ Electrolux: The Acquisition and Integration of Zanussi	INSEAD, 1990
	▪ SmithKline Beecham	INSEAD, 1995
	▪ Nestlé-Rowntree	IMD, 1989
6 **Assessing Countries Attractiveness**	▪ Enron Development Corporation: The Dabhol Power Project in Maharashtra, India	HBS, 1997

Notes

1. Hill (2000); Raymond, Wells and Rangan (1996); Segal-Horn (1999).
2. Bartlett and Ghoshal (1989); Prahalad and Doz (1987); Doz, Santos and Williamson (2002).
3. Yip (1992).
4. Harvard Business School Publishing, 60 Harvard Way, Box-5C, Boston, MA 02163 USA <http://www.hbsp.harvard.edu/>; the European Case Clearing House, Cranfield University, Wharley End, Bedfordshire MK43 0JR UK <http://www.ecch.cranfield.ac.uk/>.
5. Bartlett and Ghoshal (2000); De la Torre, Doz and Devinney (2000).

References and further reading

Bartlett, Christopher A. and Sumantra Ghoshal, *Managing Across Borders: The Transnational Solution*. Boston, MA: Harvard Business School, 1989.

Bartlett, Christopher A. and Sumantra Ghoshal, *Transnational Management: Text, Cases and Readings in Cross-Border Management*, 3rd edn. Boston, MA: McGraw-Hill, 2000.

De la Torre, José, Yves L. Doz and Timothy Devinney, *Managing the Global Corporation: Case Studies in Strategy and Management*. Boston, MA: Irwin, McGraw-Hill, 2000.

Doz, Yves L., José dos Santos and Peter Williamson, *From Global to Metanational: How Companies Win in the Knowledge Economy*. Boston, MA: Harvard Business School, 2002.

Hill, Charles, *International Business: Competing in the Global Market Place*. New York: Irwin, 2000.

Prahalad, S.K. and Yves L. Doz, *The Multinational Mission: Balancing Local Demands and Global Vision*, 1st edn. New York: Free Press, 1987.

Raymond, Louis T. Wells, Jr and Subramanian Rangan, *The Manager in the International Economy*. Upper Saddle River, NJ, Prentice-Hall, 1996.

Segal-Horn, S. Faulkner, *The Dynamic of International Strategy*. International Business, London: Thomson Business Press, 1999.

Yip, George, *Total Global Strategy: Managing for World Wide Competitive Advantage*. Englewood Cliffs, NJ: Prentice-Hall, 1992.

Part I

The process of globalisation

Part I, The Process of Globalisation, looks at *why* and *how* a firm globalises.

Chapter 1 Globalisation of markets and competition

Chapter 1 defines what 'globalisation' means for a business enterprise, differentiates it from the traditional process of extending internationally and makes a distinction between a multinational and a global company. It also looks at the factors that have driven globalisation as well as the localisation factors restraining it. It ends by proposing a mapping of industries and firms according to the extent to which they are exposed to globalisation or localisation drivers.

Chapter 2 Designing a global strategy

Chapter 2 analyses the different components of a global strategy. It includes the formulation of objectives, the choice of countries and regions, the competitive positioning of the products and services, the design of and the investment in a global business system to create and sustain global competitive advantages and the choice of a global organisation.

Chapter 3 Designing a global organisation

Chapter 3 describes the advantages and disadvantages of various forms of global organisational designs, from pure geographical to global and matrix models. It ends by presenting the transnational organisational culture that is considered necessary to support the structure, processes and system of the global organisation.

Chapter 4 Global strategic alliances

Chapter 4 looks at strategic alliances as a recent and important form of reaching a global position. A framework for the analysis of global strategic alliances and recommendations for their implementations are given in this chapter.

Chapter 5   Global mergers and acquisitions

Chapter 5 focuses on mergers and acquisitions (M&As) as means of achieving globalisation. It offers an analysis of the various phases of global M&As, from the pre-acquisition phase, to valuation and post-acquisition.

Chapter 6   Assessing countries' attractiveness

Chapter 6 looks at the first step in the decision to develop a presence in a country, the analysis of opportunities and risks. It covers such aspects as country risk analysis, industry and competitive analysis, market opportunities and host government policies.

Chapter 7   Entry strategies

Chapter 7 discusses the various decision choices in entering a country. It considers the timing of entry and the various forms of entry, ranging from wholly-owned subsidiaries to joint ventures, licensing or other types, each form being analysed in terms of its advantages and disadvantages.

1

Globalisation of markets and competition

Chapter 1 defines what globalisation means for a business enterprise. It differentiates globalisation from the traditional process of setting up subsidiaries abroad and makes a distinction between a *multinational company* and a *global company*. Based on the example of the Otis Elevator Company, it looks at how a company having multiple international subsidiaries can move towards a global competitive configuration by which its international activities can be strongly co-ordinated and integrated across borders. This transition from a multinational to a global posture was driven by various social, political, economical, technological factors that are described in the chapter. The benefits of globalisation are described, as well as the constraints. Some factors are still pushing towards a local approach to management, on a country-by-country basis, and the factors inducing this localisation are analysed.

Finally the global integration/local responsiveness grid is presented as a tool to position industries, companies and businesses according to the relative importance of global versus local competitive pressures. The chapter ends by introducing some of the societal issues associated with globalisation.

At the end of the chapter one should be able:

- To define what is globalisation and what a global firm is, and how it differs from a multinational company
- To identify the forces pushing towards globalisation
- To identify the forces pushing for localisation
- To position an industry or a business on the global integration/local responsiveness grid.
- To spell out the benefits and pitfalls of globalisation.

THE PHENOMENON OF GLOBALISATION

In today's business world, managers, politicians, journalists and academics commonly use the concepts of 'globalisation', 'global industries', 'global competition', 'global strategies' and 'global corporations'. More and more companies are confronted with the need to globalise or die. While those concepts are widely used, their meaning is often not well understood. For some people, globalisation means to expand the company's presence abroad, for others it means standardising a product and selling it to the world, for yet others it denotes an approach to management in which decision-making is centralised at corporate headquarters. There are many reasons for this confusion; one is due to the fact that the concept of globalisation is relatively new. Before the 1970s almost no one talked about globalisation; the most frequently used terminology, when referring to companies operating in various part of the world, was 'multinational' or occasionally 'transnational'. **Multinational companies** have been around for many years. Even if we ignore the East India Company, which started in the early seventeenth century, modern corporations like Unilever, Nestlé, and Procter & Gamble were operating all over the world at the end of the nineteenth century. They are known as multinational companies, but nobody would have called them global. The global concept appeared in the early 1970s and progressively invaded boardrooms, classrooms and editorial offices. What happened, and why?

To illustrate the phenomenon of globalisation let us take the example of the elevator industry in Europe in the late 1960s as represented in Figure 1.1.

In each country of Europe, different firms fighting for a share of the market contested the elevator market. Competitors were either local companies or subsidiaries of large multinational companies like Otis or Schindler. Each competitor designed, marketed, manufactured, installed and serviced elevators for their respective markets. The subsidiaries of the multinationals had all the activities of the value chain (marketing, design, production, installation and service) under their control. The French subsidiary of Otis designed elevators for the French market, manufactured them in French factories, sold them with French sales forces and maintained them with a French after-sales organisation; the management was essentially French. In Germany, Otis designed, manufactured, sold, installed and serviced elevators for the German market; and so on in nearly every major country. In smaller countries products or components were exported from major countries' subsidiaries. The operations were *self-contained* in each country and the results were evaluated on a *country-by-country* basis. Such a situation had prevailed since the 1880s. It corresponds to what was referred as a multinational or multidomestic world, in which multinational companies like Otis were competing in each main market of the planet.

By the end of the 1960s several key elements played a role in changing this competitive structure. One country manager at Otis perceived that the European business context was changing. First, the Treaty of Rome in 1957 had created the European Economic Community (EEC), at that time called the Common Market. This meant that tariff barriers across Europe were coming down; it became possible to produce components in one country and export them to other countries. This allowed companies to concentrate on the production of components in one specialised factory and to have a network of specialised factories across Europe,

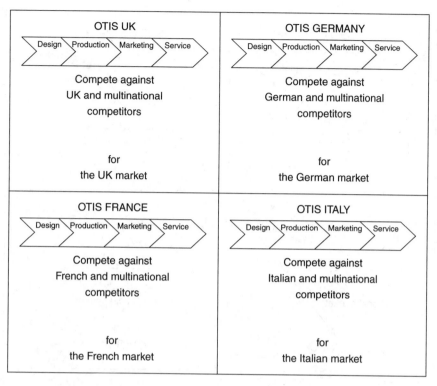

Figure 1.1 A multinational competitive configuration

each of them making one product category or one component. Components would be cross-shipped for ultimate installation in the various client countries.

The benefits of such a system were obvious – by concentrating production the company could benefit from economies of scale, some costs could be passed to the customers in the form of price reduction, leading to higher market share. Products could be designed for the whole market (standardised): instead of having country segmentation one would have pan-European segmentation based on utilisation, i.e. high-rise buildings, low-rise buildings, etc.

This would be possible only if customers in Europe – architects, engineers, real estate developers, housing departments, etc. – had a common view about what an elevator should be. Despite the differences in housing organisation across countries, elevators were essentially technical products with very little cultural content and therefore able to be standardised. Only selling methods would vary from country to country. The Otis manager perceived this as an opportunity to gain market share in Europe and engaged in the pan-European strategy depicted in Figure 1.2 in which design centres and factories were specialised and interdependent.

From a management point of view this was a radical change: country managers were no longer responsible for the whole value chain as before, but only for part of it. They were obliged to co-ordinate with other countries and they were dependent on a co-ordinating organisation called the European headquarters. This led to a

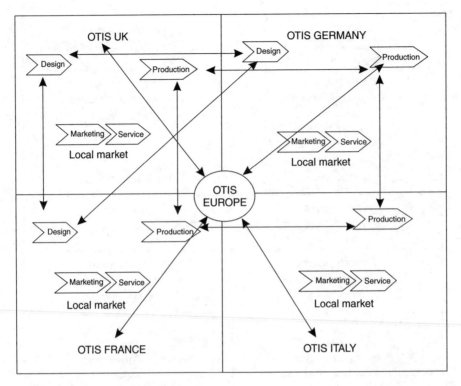

Figure 1.2   A global competitive configuration

very successful story. By 1975, Otis had captured 40 per cent of the European market, containing Japanese penetration, and competitors if they wanted to survive were obliged to adopt a similar strategy. This concept was further expanded and today Otis is organised by product lines on a worldwide basis. There are still country subsidiaries, which take care of installation, maintenance, public relations and personnel, but otherwise product development, and manufacturing is co-ordinated globally by product lines. From being a 'multinational', Otis has become a 'global' company.

This phenomenon of an *active co-ordinated and integrated presence* in the main regions of the world is what 'global company' means. It is important to observe that this change gave Otis a competitive advantage and that competitors were obliged to adopt a similar approach if they wanted to survive. Globalisation is neither a consultant's fad nor a management buzzword; it is a competitive imperative in an increasing number of industries (see Mini-Example 1.1 for some definitions).

WHAT ARE THE FACTORS THAT PUSH FOR GLOBALISATION?

Globalisation became a necessity at the beginning of the 1970s because of the convergence of several political, technological, social and competitive factors.[1]

Mini-Example 1.1 Some global definitions

Global industries are industries in which, in order to survive, competitors need to operate in the key world markets in an integrated and co-ordinated way. Industries like aerospace, computers, telecommunication equipment, appliances, power generation, large industrial projects, insurance and re-insurance and corporate data transmission are examples of what a global industry means. In these sectors it is difficult to sustain competition if one does not cover the whole world (or nearly) as a market, and if one does not integrate operations to make them cost and time effective.

Global companies are the companies that operate in the main markets of the world in an integrated and co-ordinated way. Companies like Coca Cola, Asea Brown Bovery, Sony and Citibank are global companies.

Globalisation is the phenomenon of the transition of industries whose competitive structure changes progressively from multinational to global. Industries such as telecommunications, processed food, personal care and retail are in the process of globalisation.

Global integration and co-ordination are the organisational structure and management processes by which various activities scattered across the world are made interdependent on each other. As examples, global manufacturing integration implies the specialisation of factories and the cross-shipment of parts between different production sites; global product development requires the co-ordination of various research centres and marketing teams; global account management demands that different country subsidiaries provide a service according to a plan negotiated centrally, etc.

Political factors: liberalisation of trade and investments

The main political factor has been the development of *free trade* among nations. Two main organisations have been the source of trade liberalisation: the General Agreement on Tariffs and Trade (GATT) (now replaced by the World Trade Organization, WTO) and the EEC, to which one may add the progressive opening of emerging nations to foreign investments.

The GATT, which was founded in 1946 by 23 nations, initiated a series of negotiations, called 'rounds', aimed at reducing tariff concessions to create liberalisation of trade. The GATT became the WTO in 1995.

The Kennedy Round in the mid-1960s, and the Tokyo Round in the early 1970s created an environment that fostered international trade, as shown in Figure 1.3.

The European Community (EC) was established on 25 March 1957 by the Treaty of Rome, signed by Belgium, France, Italy, Germany, Luxembourg and the Netherlands, with the aim of creating a common market and economic and political integration among the six member states. As a result goods, people and financial flows could move freely across countries. During the 1970s, the EC was enlarged

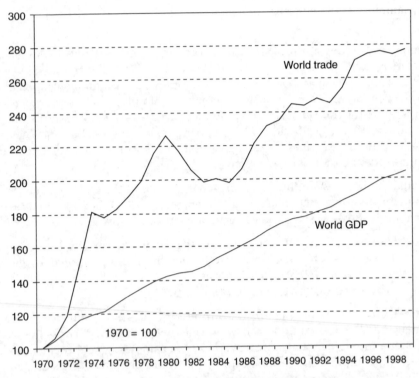

Figure 1.3 World trade has grown faster than world output, 1970–98

Source: IMF <http://www.imf.org/external/pubs/ft/weo/1999/02/data>.

with the entry of the United Kingdom, Ireland and Denmark, followed by Spain, Portugal and Greece in the 1980s and by Sweden, Austria and Finland in the 1990s. Companies like Otis could take advantage of European integration to create their own integrated trading network.

Finally, in parallel with what was happening in the industrialised countries, third-world nations progressively adopted more positive attitudes towards foreign direct investments (FDI). At first, investment laws were designed to attract foreign investors in order to induce them to produce locally, but over the years the legislation has evolved toward a more open stance, favouring cross-border investments.

Technological factors: transport, communication and economies of scale

Another set of 'push factors' for globalisation is related to *technological progress* that lowered the cost of transport and communication as well as the unit cost of production through economies of scale or the localisation of productive capacities and sourcing in low-cost economies.

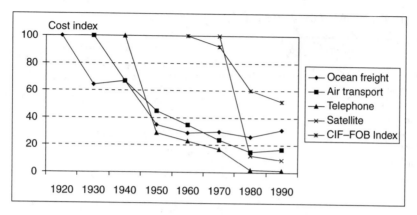

Figure 1.4 International transportation and communication costs, 1920–90

Source: World Bank, *World Development Report*, 1995.

Air, rail and road transport and the use of containers in maritime transport have reduced the cost of shipping goods from country to country as well as, in the case of air transport, favouring the travel of managers. The development of telecommunications has reduced the cost of information exchange between business units scattered around the globe. Between 1950 and 1990, the transportation costs of air transport, ocean freight and transatlantic phone calls decreased by some 56 per cent, 14 per cent and 29 per cent, respectively. For satellite charges, there was an approximate decrease of 90 per cent between 1970 and 1990 (Figure 1.4).

Progress in manufacturing technology gave a tremendous impetus to the need to concentrate production in world-class factories benefiting from huge economies of scale, thus encouraging the rationalisation and integration of production systems.

Besides manufacturing concentration, companies have been able to source components or services from low-cost countries, either by setting up their own operations or by purchasing locally.

Another source of economies of scale comes from the need to quickly amortise research and development (R&D) expenditures. Companies are confronted with a dual pressure: R&D budgets are increasing and product life cycles (PLCs) are reducing (Table 1.1). Companies need to launch products and services at the same time in all major markets in order to be able to recoup their investments.

Social factors: convergence of consumer needs

International air transport and the diffusion of lifestyles by movies and TV series have increased the *brand awareness* of consumers worldwide. Brands like Sony, Nike, Levi or Coca Cola are known nearly everywhere. Kenichi Ohmae,[2] in his book *'Triad Power'*, has discussed the 'Californisation of society' – teenagers in São Paolo, Bombay, Milan or Los Angeles listening to the same music, using the same walkman and wearing the same pair of blue jeans. Convergence of customer behaviour and needs is also facilitated by urbanisation and industrialisation of

Table 1.1   Illustrations of the shortening of product life cycles

General product category	Time of invention to commercial exploitation (years)
Electric motor	65
TV	52
Vacuum tube	33
Zip-fastener	30
X-ray tube	18
Frozen foods	15
Nuclear reactors	10
Radar	5
Solar batteries	3
Appliance category	*Average length of introductory stage*
Period 1922–42	12.5
Period 1945–64	7
Period 1965–79	2
Intel microprocessor products	*Duration of life cycle*
286	7
386	6
486	5
Pentium	5

Sources: Baker and Hart (1999, p. 115); Michaels, Olshavsky and Qualls (1981, pp. 77–8); Michel, Salle and Valla (1996, p. 178).

societies. The less cultural and the more technical is the product, the more likely it can be standardised and appeal to masses of consumers in all countries: VCRs, PCs, mobile phones or elevators, cranes and robots are products for which national differences do not matter much.

Competitive factors

The 1960s saw the emergence of Japanese competitors in markets that traditionally had been dominated by American or European competitors. Japanese firms, and later on Korean firms, adopted a global approach at the very beginning of their international expansion. One of the reasons is that they did not have many national subsidiaries and their international expansion was occurring at the time of the opening of trade barriers. Right at the beginning they designed products for the world market, creating *global brands* such as 'Sony' or 'Panasonic', and their efficient production system gave them a cost advantage in electronics and automotive parts. Competitors had to adopt a similar strategic posture if they wished to survive.

Another competitive force that pushed companies to globalise is the *globalisation of customers*. During the 1970s, Citibank created a Global Account Management Unit to service those corporate customers who had international subsidiaries.

Figure 1.5 summarises these 'push factors' in favour of globalisation.

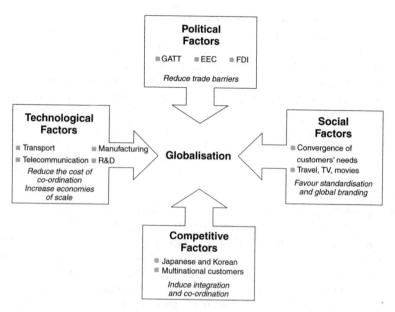

Figure 1.5 Globalisation push factors

THE BENEFITS OF GLOBALISATION

The benefits of globalisation can be assessed from two points of views: the business and competitive point of view and the macro socio-economical point of view. In this chapter we will focus only on the business and competitive point of view. A more general discussion on the socio-economic benefits and costs of globalisation will be included later in the chapter, while this part focuses on the benefits for a corporation to adopt a global strategy.

The business and competitive benefits can be grouped into four categories: cost, learning, timing and arbitrage.

(1) *Cost benefits*. These come, on the one hand, from economies of scale owing to products/processes standardisation as well as increased bargaining powers over suppliers of raw materials, components, equipment and services and, on the other hand, from the ability to organise a logistic and sourcing network based on location factors. Examples of economies of scale through standardisation are numerous; in the example mentioned earlier, Otis was able to lower the cost of elevators in Europe by 30 per cent after introducing a pan-European manufacturing system.

(2) *Timing benefits*. These are due to the co-ordinated approach in product launching in the early stage of the product life cycle. In a multinational setting, each subsidiary is more or less free to adopt products for its own market. This is sometimes called 'the shopping caddy' approach to product adoption. Such an approach generates inefficiencies in the management of the product life cycle

since the optimal volume is obtained only after a lengthy process of product adoption by all subsidiaries. A classic example of the deficiency of the 'shopping caddy' approach is the refusal of Philips America to adopt the video system, the V2000, developed by Philips' mother company in the Netherlands. In the late 1960s a theory of multinational product introduction, known as the **'International product life cycle'** theory, postulated a progressive adoption of products over time according to the level of economic and scientific develop- ment of countries (see Figure 10.1, p. 264). Such a theory is no longer valid when industries globalise: waiting too long to launch a product can be fatal, particularly if the product has a short life cycle, which is more and more frequently the case. Microsoft launched Window 2000 at the same time every- where in the world.

(3) *Learning benefits.* These accrue from the co-ordinated transfer of information, best practices and people across subsidiaries. Such transfer eliminates the costly 'reinvention of the wheel' and facilitates the accumulation of experiences and knowledge. In Thailand, Unilever formulated and implemented an innovative strategy to produce and market ice creams. The Thai experience served as a template for other countries in the Asia Pacific region, giving to the company a first-mover advantage. This example illustrates the benefits that can be gained from a co-ordinated transfer of best practices.

(4) *Arbitrage benefits.* These come from the advantages that a company managing globally can gain in using resources in one country for the benefit of another country subsidiary. These advantages can be direct competitive advantages or indirect cost advantages. A competitive advantage can be gained by playing a 'global chess game': for instance, engaging in a price war in one country in order to mobilise the resources of competitors in that country, depriving them of cash flow which could be used elsewhere. This strategy was used by Goodyear, the US tyre giant, when in the early 1970s, Michelin from France moved to North America. Goodyear, who had a small market share in Europe, engaged in a price war that Michelin was obliged to counter by lowering its prices, and de facto reducing its financing scope for its American expansion. Another type of arbitrage comes from differential cost elements such as taxes, interest and possibly risk reduction though the pooling of currencies.

Those four benefits are real but achieving them is subject to certain conditions, and their adoption has to be measured against the real competitive advantage they provide to the firms adopting them.

The benefits in costs reduction obtained by economies of scale are contingent upon the market responsiveness to standardisation and whether customers are price sensitive. If, on the contrary, customers are not responsive and prefer tailored products and services to standardisation, a global approach is less appropriate. A similar reasoning applies to the benefits of timing. As for purchasing power, it may be limited for culturally sensitive services such as advertising.

The benefits of learning are positive if the experience gained in one country is applicable to another. If it is not the case, there is a *timing deficit*: the time of realis- ing that one has made a mistake plus the time to learn the new environment. At Euro Disneyland near Paris, two years were lost because the transfer of knowledge from Florida or California did not help the European operation.

The benefits of arbitrage can be offset by the cost of managing the arbitrage and the legal barriers that may exist in order to prevent such arbitrage. In the case of tax arbitrage, governments are very careful to make sure that global companies do not abuse their arbitrage power.

Despite those limitations, more and more companies recognise the competitive benefits of globalisation. However, one should be aware there are still some factors that work against globalisation and this is what the next section will consider.

WHAT ARE THE FACTORS THAT WORK AGAINST GLOBALISATION? THE LOCALISATION PUSH

As mentioned earlier, globalisation is associated with some degree of standardisation of products and practices plus a high level of co-ordination and integration of activities in the companies' value chain. Factors that defeat standardisation, co-ordination and integration are working against globalisation. One can group those factors into four main categories: cultural, commercial, technical and legal.

(1) Cultural factors: attitudes, tastes, behaviour and social codes
When the consumption of a product or a service is linked to traditions and national or religious values, global standardisation is not effective. Some products – for instance, Kretek (tobacco and clove) cigarettes in Indonesia, or the Pachinko (pinball) game in Japan – are unique to one society and their globalisation is nearly impossible, although one can argue that with innovative marketing it may be possible to do so. The example of the arrival of 'Beaujolais nouveau' wine, typically a Burgundy and Parisian bistro event before the 1970s, can be now available in Tokyo, Paris, New York on the same day, 'Halloween' (trick or treat) masquerades, a typical US festivity, are now celebrated in Europe. This shows that even some highly cultural goods can be appreciated by customers all over the world, but it remains that food and drink tastes, social interactions in the process of negotiating a sale, attitudes towards hygiene, cosmetics or gifts varies from culture to culture, thus hampering a global product design or approach. In the Asia Pacific region, for instance, personal relationship building more than legal contracts is the normal way to conduct business. One has to spend time and effort to build these personal ties, which in a US context would be considered as a waste of time.

(2) Commercial factors: distribution, customisation and responsiveness
In some sectors, distribution networks and practices differ from country to country and as a consequence the ways of managing the network, motivating dealers and distributors, pricing, and negotiation are hardly amenable to global co-ordination. For instance, the marketing and distribution of pharmaceutical products differs according to the country's health system. In some countries, like Japan, doctors sell medicine, while in other countries pharmacists are selling to patients who get a refund (or not) from their insurance company, while in yet other cases pharmaceutical products are delivered freely to the patient.

Responsiveness to customers' demands, as well as customisation are other factors which almost by definition defeat standardisation. Private saving or current accounts to individuals, loans to small and medium-size enterprises (SMEs), mortgages, consulting activities and individual architectural designs are activities in which a local presence and a fast reaction to customers' requirements are needed for competitive success. Although some practices, processes or methodologies can be standardised on a worldwide basis (consultants, engineering, architects or auditors for example), it remains that specific customer requests have to be taken into consideration, thus limiting globalisation.

(3) *Technical factors: standards, spatial presence, transportation and languages*
Technical standards in electrical, civil, chemical or mechanical engineering can create a burden for global companies. Scale economies and cost benefits of global integration and standardisation cannot be exploited fully when technical standards vary greatly. In certain cases, standards can be changed without major modification – as, for instance, in consumer electronics where creating multi-standard products with PAL, SECAM and NTSC does not represent a major hurdle for global manufacturing. In other instances, standards are not that easy to accommodate and require specific local production lines; that is mainly the case for beer, for instance.

Spatial presence is needed in those industries which need to occupy a physical space in order to create and distribute their products and services: retail banking, retailing, hotels, local telephones services, hospital, entertainment, car dealers, etc. are example of industries where the services have to be produced locally. In those industries there are still some advantages in globalising certain functions such as back office functions (accounting, data processing, global sourcing, transfer of best practices, etc.) but the location constraint still limits globalisation benefits. In the future, E-commerce is likely to reduce the spatial constraint considerably, particularly when it comes to immaterial services such as banking or movies on demand. E-commerce with physical products can also eliminate the spatial constraint as far as the customer interface is concerned but is still hampered by the logistical constraints. The example of Amazon.com demonstrates that it is possible for a customer in Paris or in Rio de Janeiro to order a book through Amazon but the same customer will have to bear shipping costs that will eliminate the basic cost advantage of the E-bookstore. This is the reason why Amazon is looking for local partnerships outside the United States, thus moving toward a more multinational business design.

The impediments of transportation are important if the cost of transport cancels out the benefits of concentration of production. Bulk commodities like cement or basic chemicals are more economically produced in local plants rather than in global centralised units, despite the scale economies that could be gained: the cost and the risks of transport cancel out the benefits of centralised production. Similarly, when production systems are not scale-intensive and small productive units can achieve similar costs to large plants – in plastic moulding, for instance – there are no major benefits in building a global productive system.

Finally, languages can add additional constraints to global approaches. Those constraints can be significant when it comes to services to individual customers: training services, personal banking and personal telecommunication or retailing are possible examples. However, there are two major trends that can reduce language constraints. English has become more and more a 'global language' and industries such as graduate business training or high-level consulting can use English without bothering with translation.

(4)   *Legal factors: regulation and national security issues*
Governments impose regulatory constraints that often work against globalisation, either because they limit the free flow of personnel (regulation on working permits), cash (exchange control, tax), goods (custom duties, quotas), data (censorship, the Internet and EDI control) or because they impose localisation constraints (local content policies, local ownership and joint venture policies).

Over the years, thank to the GATT and now the WTO and also multilateral agreements (European Union (EU), ASEAN, NAFTA, etc.) or International Monetary Fund (IMF) requests, government legislation is leaning towards more open legislative contexts that favour globalisation. However, some constraints still exist. Some sectors such as telecommunications, media, banking and insurance are still tightly controlled and some countries, (such as China and India) or regional blocks (EU), still impose local content requirements.

Finally, governments are much concerned with national security and will prevent foreigners gaining too much control of their defence or strategic sectors industries. In the defence sector, for instance, where R&D costs are huge and economies of scale significant, globalisation would be fully justified, but is in fact limited because of national security constraints. Figure 1.6 summarises the localisation push.

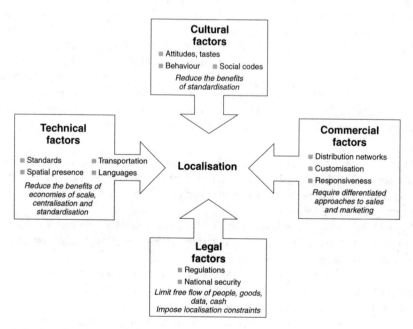

Figure 1.6   Localisation push factors

THE BENEFITS OF LOCALISATION

The benefits of localisation, instead of a global integrated and co-ordinated approach, are essentially customer-oriented benefits that give firms an increased market power and ultimately an increased market share. Those benefits are flexibility, proximity and quick response time.

- **Flexibility** is the capability to adapt to customer demands in the various dimensions of the marketing mix: product/service design, distribution, branding, pricing and services. Ultimately flexibility leads to *customisation*.
- **Proximity** is the capability to be close to the market, to understand the customer's *value curve*.
- **Quick response time** is the ability to respond at once to specific customers' *demands*.

Flexibility, proximity and quick response time are very much related to each other: proximity provides the basis for flexibility and flexibility provides the basis for quick response time. All three give a competitive advantage when local cultural, technical, commercial and legal contexts vary so much from country to country.

THE GLOBAL INTEGRATION/LOCAL RESPONSIVENESS GRID

The two sets of forces – globalisation and localisation forces – are shaping the competitive structure of industries and inducing companies to configure their worldwide business systems with the right mix of co-ordination, integration or decentralisation. The Global Integration/Local Responsiveness[3] grid is a mapping tool that has been developed to position industries and industry segments according to the relative importance of each set of forces. Figure 1.7 represents a Global Integration/Local Responsiveness grid for various industries, while Figure 1.8 represents a similar grid for various segments of the telecommunication industry.

The mapping in Figures 1.7 and 1.8 reveals that industries and segments can be broadly positioned into three types of competitive situations:

- **Type I**: *Global forces* dominate and there are few advantages to push for local adaptation and responsiveness. What matters is efficiency, speed, arbitrage and learning. These industries are global, as in the case of microchips, bulk chemicals or civil aircraft.
- **Type II**: *Local forces dominate* and flexibility, proximity and quick response are determining capabilities for competitive advantage. Food retailing, consumer banking or voice telephony fall in this category.
- **Type III**: In these industries there is a *mix of global and local forces at play* and competitiveness cannot be achieved without achieving the benefits of global integration and co-ordination and, at the same time, the benefits of flexibility, proximity and quick response time. This positioning is increasingly becoming the dominant competitive battleground for a vast majority of sectors.

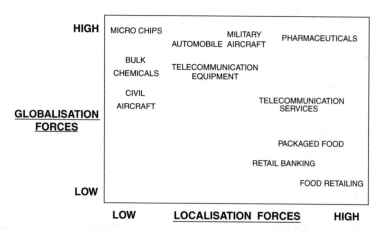

Figure 1.7 Global Integration/Local Responsiveness Grid: different businesses have different competitive requirements

Source: Prahalad and Doz (1987).

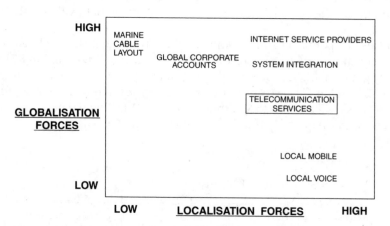

Figure 1.8 Global Integration/Local Responsiveness Grid: different segments have different competitive requirements – example of telecom services

The Global Integration/Local Responsiveness Grid can be used for assessing a situation at a point in time or to anticipate evolution over time. It can also serve as mapping for the various activities of the value chain. As it will be seen in Chapters 2 and 3, a good understanding of industry positioning will help the formulation of business and country strategies, as well as the implementation of an effective organisational design.

In Appendix 1.1 there is a questionnaire that will help managers to position their business on the Global Integration/Local Responsiveness Grid.

GLOBALISATION: THE MACRO PICTURE

In 1817, David Ricardo in his *Theory of Comparative Advantage*[4] showed that it was beneficial to nations to specialise and trade goods in which they had a *comparative advantage*. This laid the foundation of trade theory, which itself is the underlying foundation of globalisation: in a perfect global setting where goods, people, data and money flow freely, companies can adopt an integrated and co-ordinated approach to their operations and the competitive battlefield would be the world. Since Ricardo's time, partisans and adversaries of free trade have exchanged heated debates about the pro and cons of globalisation for society.

Table 1.2 summarises those arguments.

This debate gained political visibility during the 1990s. In Europe, the Treaty of Maastricht (signed in 1992) adopted the Euro as a single currency, generating a heated debate on the loss of sovereignty and the advantages of further political and economical integration. In North America, the NAFTA agreement (1995) created similar discussion. In Asia, after the 1997 financial crisis, globalisation was put in question and, at the end of that decade, the WTO at the Seattle ministerial conference could not set up an agenda for launching another trade round because of public criticism of the whole concept of globalisation. Since 2001, there has been a growing debate about the future of globalisation. Some, like Alan Rugman, have announced the 'end of globalisation',[5] an issue that will be discussed in Chapter 16.

Despite all this political turmoil, some analysts think that the world is becoming progressively more integrated. According to the consulting firm McKinsey,[6] by 1997, truly global markets represented approximately $6 trillion out of a total world output of $28 trillion (21 per cent). The firm anticipates that by 2030 the proportion of global markets will amount to $73 trillion out of $91 trillion (80 per cent). However, as will be seen in Chapter 15, this forecast may be challenged.

Table 1.2 The societal benefits of globalisation

Arguments in favour of globalisation	Arguments against globalisation
Creates overall wealth for all nations because specialisation increases trade	Imposes massive strain on labour force both in developed countries (job destruction) and developing countries (sweatshops, child labour)
Reduces inflation because of cost efficiencies	Standardises customer tastes. Reduces diversity
Benefits customers because of price reduction owing to cost efficiencies	Induces concentration of power in a few global corporations
	Introduces a 'jungle' leading to the domination of the strongest multinational
Better allocation of natural, financial and human resources	Harms the environment because of unrestrained exploitation of natural resources such as forests
Reduces corruption because of free market trade	Reduces capacity for nations to protect their national interests, cultures and values

Source: Ricardo (1967).

Pragmatically, companies adopt a competitive positioning which tends to foster further globalisation. The development of information technologies, the fluidity of capital markets, the creation of mega mergers in the telecoms, computer, oil, pharmaceutical, power and car industries demonstrate that business firms are increasingly behaving as if they were already living in a global world.

SUMMARY AND KEY POINTS

1. A global company:
   - Can be defined as a company that operates in the main markets of the world in an integrated and co-ordinated way
   - Is different from a multinational company since it operates in the main markets of the world in an integrated and co-ordinated way
   - Is one which carries out one activity (e.g. manufacturing) or a component of the activity (e.g. manufacturing one sub-part only) of the value chain in one country which serves the company's worldwide market.

2. Globalisation:
   - Is the phenomenon of the progressive transition of industries from a multi-national to a global competitive structure
   - Has four factors in its favour which are:
     - *Political*: reduces trade barriers
     - *Technological*: reduces the cost of co-ordination and increases economies of scale
     - *Social*: encourages standardisation and global branding
     - *Competitive*: induces integration and co-ordination
   - Has four competitive benefits:
     - *Cost*: economies of scale and increased bargaining powers
     - *Timing*: reaches the optimal production volume and increases the reach of a product with a short product life cycle
     - *Learning*: facilitates best practices to be adopted across subsidiaries through the experience effect and the transfer of knowledge
     - *Arbitrage*: is derived when a global company uses resources in one country for the benefits of a subsidiary in another country.

3. Localisation
   - Has four driving forces:
     - *Cultural*: reduces the benefits of standardisation
     - *Commercial*: requires differentiated approaches to sales and marketing
     - *Technical*: reduces the benefits of economies of scale, centralisation and standardisation
     - *Legal*: limits free flow of resources and imposes localisation constraints
   - Has three benefits:
     - *Flexibility*
     - *Proximity*
     - *Quick response time* to customers.

4. A Global Integration/Local Responsiveness grid:
   - Is used for identifying the competitive requirements of an industry or a business segment
   - Can assist companies in formulating business and country strategies.

Appendix 1.1 Positioning a business on the Global Integration/Local Responsiveness Grid

Assign a score for each question from 1 to 5

			1	2	3	4	5	
	GLOBAL FACTORS							
A	To what extent customers have similar demands for functionalities and design across countries	Very different						Very similar
B	To what extent products or services have a high proportion of standard components across countries	Low proportion of standard components						High proportion of standard components
C	To what extent customers (or distributors) are themselves operating in different countries and are buying centrally your products or services	Buying locally						Buying centrally
D	To what extent significant economies of scale in your industry are important for the cost of the product (i.e. one needs very high volume to obtain low cost)	Low economies of scale						High economies of scale
E	To what extent the speed of introducing new products worldwide is important for competitiveness	Speed is not that important						Speed is very important
F	To what extent the sales of your product or service are based on technical factors or alternatively on cultural factors	Highly cultural						Highly technical

			1	2	3	4	5	
G	To what extent experience gained in other countries by a 'sister' subsidiary can be successful if applied in other countries	No great benefits						Yes, highly beneficial
H	To what extent competitors in your industry operate in a 'standardised' way across countries and are successful in doing so	Competitors are localising						Competitors are successful in standardized approaches
I	To what extent customers 'behave' the same way across countries	Customer behaviour is very different						Customers behave in the same way
J	To what extent innovative activities (R&D, design) require concentration of expertise in order to be effective (critical mass)	Low critical mass						High critical mass

GLOBAL INTEGRATION SCORE
Sum of A to J / 10 = ...

			1	2	3	4	5	
K	To what extent pricing can be different from country to country without introducing dysfunctionalities	Pricing has to be coherent across borders						Pricing can be very different
L	To what extent distribution channel management differs from country to country	Not so different						Yes, very different
M	To what extent business regulations and contexts differ from country to country requiring a high degree of local practices	Not too different						Highly different
N	To what extent products or services require a high degree of interaction with customers (customisation)	Low customisation						High customisation
O	To what extent transportation costs or customer interface are such that local operations are needed	Not so different						Local operations are essential

LOCAL RESPONSIVENESS SCORE
Sum of K to O / 5 = ...

One obtains scores between 1 and 5 and one can position the business on the Grid below.

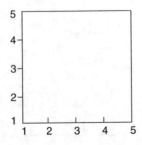

Learning assignments

1 Among the enterprises that you know, can you identify one that can be qualified as a global company? Why?
2 Why, in Figure 1.8, is voice telephony positioned low on global forces and high on local forces while global corporate accounts is high on globalisation forces and low on localisation forces?
3 In Figure 1.7, food retailing is positioned as a local business, with a very low globalisation score. However, in the press companies like Tesco, Wal-Mart or Carrefour are qualified as 'global retailers'. Explain this discrepancy?
4 What are the social factors that have been pushing for globalisation and which have been pushing against?
5 What are the benefits of not being global and having a local approach?
6 When the Otis Elevator Company introduced the change described at the beginning of the chapter, there was a lot of resistance from the various heads of the European subsidiaries. Why? What arguments do you think the people hostile to globalisation used?
7 Can Intel be qualified as a global firm? Why?

Key words

- Arbitrage benefits
- Comparative advantage
- Global companies
- Global industries
- Global Integration/Local Responsiveness grid
- Globalisation
- International product life cycle
- Multinational companies

Web resources

<http://knowledge.insead.fr/category.cfm?catid=8>
A link to the database of INSEAD Knowledge under the category of Globalisation

<http://www.businessweek.com/mediacenter/specials/globalization.html>
Business Week – Globalisation

<http://www.mckinseyquarterly.com/category_archive.asp?tk=86032::&L3 =33>
McKinsey Quarterly – Globalisation

<http://www.nato.int>
Provides information on North Atlantic Treaty Organization (NATO), including its 19 member countries, its organisation and values.

<http://www.wto.org/>
Provides information about the WTO

<http://www.imf.org/>
Provides statistics and papers from the International Monetary Fund (IMF).

Notes

1. George Yip (1992) gives four globalisation drivers: cost, market, competition and govern-ment. These are similar to those presented here.
2. Ohmae (1985).
3. Prahalad and Doz (1987).
4. Ricardo (1967).
5. Rugman (2000).
6. Lowell and Fraser (1999, pp. 68–81).

References and further reading

Books and articles

Baker, Michael and Susan Hart, *Product Strategy and Management*. London: Prentice-Hall, 1999.
Bartlett, Christopher A. and Sumantra Ghoshal, *Managing Across Borders: The Transnational Solution*. Boston, MA: Harvard Business School Press, 1989.
Fraser, Jane N. and Jeremy Oppenheim, 'What's New about Globalization?', *McKinsey Quarterly*, 2, 1997, pp. 168–79.
Harvard Business School Global Strategies: Insights from the World's Leading Thinkers. Boston, MA: Harvard Business School Press, 1900. (This book contains a collection of *Harvard Business Review (HBR)* articles.)
Humes, Samuel, *Managing the Multinational: Confronting the Global–Local Dilemma*. London: Prentice-Hall, 1993.
Lowell, L. Bryan and Jane N. Fraser, 'Getting to Global', *McKinsey Quarterly*, 4, 1999, pp. 68–81.
Michaels, R.E., R.Z. Olshavsky and W. Qualls, 'Shortening of the PLC – An Empirical Test', *Journal of Marketing*, 4, 1981.
Michel, D., R. Salle and J. Valla, *Marketing industriel*, Paris: Economica, 1996, *from Nouvel Economiste*, 1026.
Micklethwait, John and Adrian Wooldridge, *A Future Perfect: The Challenges – And the Promise – of Globalization*. London: Heinneman, 2000.
Mirza, Hafiz (ed.), *Global Competitive Strategies in World Economy: Multilateralism Regionalization and the Transnational Firm*, New Horizons in International Business. London: Edward Elgar, 1998.
Ohmae, Kenichi, *Becoming a Triad Power*. New York: McKinsey & Co., 1985.
Porter, Michael E. (ed.), *Competition in Global Industries*. Boston, MA: Harvard Business School Press, 1986.
Porter, Michael E., *The Competitive Advantage of Nations*. New York: Free Press, 1998.
Prahalad, C.K. and Yves L. Doz, *The Multinational Mission: Balancing Local Demands and Global Vision*, 1st edn. New York: Free Press, 1987.
Rangan, Subramanian and Robert Z. Lawrence, *A Prism on Globalization*. Washington, DC: Brookings Institution, 1999.
Ricardo, David, *The Principles of Political Economy and Taxation*. Homewood, IL: Irwin, 1967.
Rugman Alan, *The End of Globalization: A New and Radical Analysis of Globalization and What it Means for Business*. London: Random House, 2000.
Yip, George, *Total Global Strategy: Managing for World Wide Competitive Advantage*. Englewood Cliffs, NJ: Prentice-Hall, 1992.

Journals

Business	Semi-academic	Academic
■ Business week	■ Multinational Business	■ Journal of International
■ Fortune	■ Harvard Business Review	Business Studies
■ Economist	■ California Management Review	■ Strategic Management Journal
■ International	■ Columbia Journal of World Business	■ International Human
Management	■ Sloan Management Review	Resources Management
■ Financial Times	■ European Management Journal	

2

Designing a global strategy

The globalisation of industries discussed in Chapter 1 was led by some precursor companies that identified early the opportunities of designing and implementing global strategies. In this chapter, on the basis of the experience of leading global companies, a framework for the formulation of global strategies is proposed.

The chapter starts by defining what *business strategy* is about, and gives an example of how SONY Corporation has developed its global strategy. The framework for strategy consists of:

- *Global ambition*: stating the relative importance of region and countries for a company
- *Global positioning*: choice of countries, customer segments and value proposition
- *Global business system*: investments in resources, assets and competence to create a global value chain and global capabilities through alliances and acquisitions
- *Global organisation*: global structure, processes, co-ordination and human resources (HR) management.

The chapter details all those elements and provides some tools:

- The *Global Revenue Index* and the *Global Capabilities Index*, measuring the extent to which a company can be considered as a global, a regional player or simply a global exporter or a global sourcer
- The classification of countries according to their *strategic importance* (key countries, emerging countries, platform countries, marketing countries)
- The definition of *global positioning* according to the scope of markets, value proposition and of competitive approach based on cost leadership or differentiation

- *Business system* design
- *Competitive advantages* analysis
- *Sustainability* of competitive advantages.

It then describes three stages in the process of globalisation: export, multinational and global

The chapter ends by sketching the various forms of organisational structures found among multinational and global firms.

At the end of this chapter one should be able:

- To identify out a global strategy by decomposing all its elements
- To contribute meaningfully to the formulation of a global strategy
- To describe a global business system
- To identify the sources of competitive advantages in a given company.

A COMPANY BUSINESS STRATEGY

A company business strategy is a set of *fundamental choices* which define its long-term objectives, its value proposition to the market, how it intends to build and sustain a competitive business system and how it organises itself (see Mini-Example 2.1 for a more detailed definition of strategy).

A business strategy is global when a company competes in the key markets of the world and when the business system is made of integrated and co-ordinated activities across borders.

The case of Sony Corporation presented below illustrates how a global strategy has been developing over time.

Mini-Example 2.1   Origin and content of strategy

Strategy (from the Greek, *stratos*: an army and *agein*: to lead) has traditionally been a military art. The ancient Chinese military theorist, Sun Tzu (circa 500 BC) stated that 'the supreme art of war is to subdue the enemy without fighting'.

Strategy as an art of war was transferred into a business context in the early 1960s. This does not mean that there was no 'strategy' behind business decisions earlier; but there were no formal theories of business strategy.

There are several schools of thought about what business strategy is, but all schools recognise that business strategy has to do with *choice* and *investments*. A business strategy will generally cover the following:

- **Ambition:** Choice of *long-term objectives* for the business
- **Positioning:** Choice of *customer segments* and of a *value proposition* to customers

Mini-Example 2.1 *(Continued)*

> ▪ **Investment**: Choice of investments in order to create business system able to *deliver value to customers competitively*
> ▪ **Organisation**: Choice of *people, structure, processes* and *systems*.
>
> The concept of strategy may apply at various types of corporation. The most frequent distinctions are:
>
> ▪ **Business strategy** (also called Competitive strategy) applies at the level of a business operating in a particular industry segment. It defines the way this business wants and is able to compete in his segment.
>   If the market in which the firm operates is global, its business strategy will be a **Global business strategy** that defines the way to compete across the world.
> ▪ **Corporate strategy** applies at the level of a company engaged in different business segments: the multi-business corporation. It essentially defines the portfolio of businesses in which the corporation wants to be and the resource allocation pattern among those businesses.
>   If the corporation operates globally, the Corporate strategy will be a **Global corporate strategy** which will incorporate the choice of regions and countries in the corporate portfolio.

SONY CORPORATION GLOBALISATION[1]

Foundation and expansion

In 1953, Akio Morita, the co-founder of Tokyo Tsushin Kogyo KK (TTKKK), a company making tape recorders and magnetic tape, visited the United States. Morita bought a licence for a new electronic component, the transistor, from Bell Laboratories. The purchase of this licence allowed TTKKK engineers to develop a transistorised radio in 1955 and a pocket-sized radio in 1957.

During his trip to the United States, Morita realised the importance of the American market. He decided that his company needed to market its products outside Japan, and first in the most important market of the world, the US market. One of the first decisions taken in 1953 was to invent a name for the firm that could be recognised and appreciated by American consumers. TTKKK became SONY, and its name became the brand name of its products. In 1960, SONY opened its first office in America to control the exports and the distribution of its products. It concluded distribution agreements in other countries as well but the United States initially remained the focus of its internationalisation effort. According to Morita, SONY needed to succeed first in the United States in order to increase its reputation in Japan and then to spread it to Europe and other parts of the world. During the 1960s the company exported radios, magnetic tapes and black and white television sets; exports represented more than 50 per cent of its revenues.

In 1971, the first overseas plant, manufacturing colour TVs, was built in the United States, followed during the decade by a progressive expansion of manufacturing operations in America, Europe and Asia Pacific. By 1990, SONY had manufacturing operations in 17 countries and by 2000, 43 subsidiaries outside Japan including movie and TV studios in the United States, component manufacture in Malaysia, Taiwan, Thailand, Korea and Singapore, and finished product assembly factories in Europe, North America, Brazil and Australia. Outside Japan, R&D centres were located in West Germany, England and Australia.

By 1988, SONY's management had coined the term 'global localisation' to define their world operations. The intention was to balance sales and production according to the respective weight of North America, Asia and Europe. Three regional headquarters – in New York, Cologne and Singapore – were set up in the mid-1980s to co-ordinate the activities in North America, Europe and Asia (outside Japan). *Product groups* are in charge of developing products and setting up global strategies while *regional groups* are in charge of developing markets. Both products and regions work in a co-ordinated fashion.

By 1999, 32 per cent of SONY's revenues were generated in North America, 37 per cent in Asia and 25 per cent in Europe.

Analysis of SONY's global strategy

Looking at the example of SONY, one can observe some key characteristics of the strategy developed by the company:

- First, was the decision taken very early by Morita that the Japanese market was not the right battlefield for consumer electronics business; for him, the world market was the right battlefield. SONY had the *ambition* to become a global player in the key world markets. Based upon this initial ambition, SONY implemented a *strategy* that ultimately gave a significant market presence in the key major regions of the world.
- Second, even if the world was the right competitive arena, some markets like the United States in the 1960s were considered as *key markets*, to be developed as a priority.
- Third, Morita was thinking not only in terms of market conquests but was looking at the *interactive positive effects* of success in one market, the United States, on other markets in Japan and in Europe. This interactive thinking, linking together markets over the world is characteristic of global thinking: the world is not a collection of markets but a set of *interacting markets*.
- Fourth, *localisation* of marketing, manufacturing and later on R&D activities were put in place in order to achieve a balance between sales and production on a worldwide basis. Production centres were designed for serving the world and their location selected according to the comparative advantages of each country. Production centres in Asia were built to produce low-cost components, while factories in the United States and Europe were built in order to be close to consumers. SONY built up an *integrated network* of production and, later on, research centres worldwide.

- Fifth, as early as 1953, SONY realised that to succeed in the world market it was necessary to have a *global name*: hence 'SONY', that can be understood every-where and that can become a very important competitive asset. At the end of the 1990s SONY was among the brands that were the most recognised in the world.
- Sixth, attached to its global image, SONY's value proposition to the custom-ers across the world was to offer innovative, miniaturised audio and video products that enhanced customer's satisfaction thanks to their functionality and quality. Such differentiated *global positioning* was consistent in all markets.
- Seventh, in 1972, the Head of SONY America was an American whose salary was higher than the equivalent SONY executives. Foreigners were brought on to the main board in 1989. In order to support its global strategy Morita developed a *global management* team.
- Eighth, the globalisation process was *progressive* and spread over time, as shown in Figure 2.1.

Based on SONY's example it is now possible to describe more formally the components of a global strategy.

FRAMEWORK FOR GLOBAL STRATEGY

A *global strategy* is the way a company defines its long-term objectives for the world market; selects its value proposition for the world market; builds, integrates and

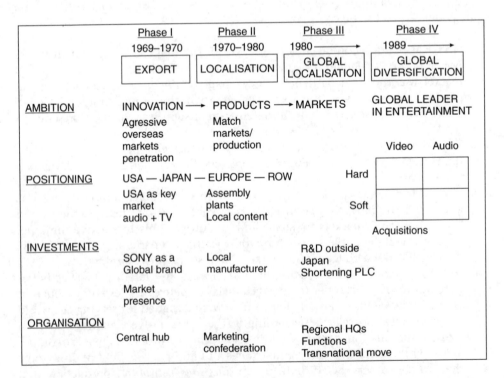

Figure 2.1 SONY's global development

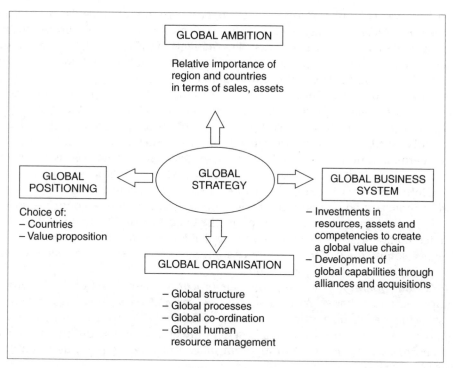

Figure 2.2   Global strategy framework

co-ordinates its business system to gain and sustain a global competitive advantage and puts in place an organisation to manage its operations worldwide.

A global strategy is made up of four major components (see Figure 2.2):

- A global strategic *ambition*
- A global strategic *positioning*
- A global *business system*
- A global *organisation*.

Global ambition

The global strategic ambition expresses the role a company wants to play in the world marketplace and how it views the future distribution of its sales and assets in the key regional clusters of the world. One can identify five types of role:

- Global player
- Regional player
- Regional dominant global player
- Global exporter
- Global operator.

A company whose ambition is to be a **Global player** aspires to establish a *sustainable competitive position in the key markets of the world* and to build an integrated business system of designs spread over those key markets. SONY would qualify for such a description of its role, as would Unilever, Ericsson, Nokia, Alcatel, Motorola, Shell, Xerox, Canon, Procter & Gamble and Citibank.

A **Regional player** defines its role as to capture a *strong competitive advantage in one of the key regions of the world* – North America, Europe or Asia – and to be a marginal or relatively weak competitor in the other parts. Peugeot or Fiat in automobiles, NEC or Barclays would be examples of such an ambition.[2]

A **Regional dominant global player** is a company whose role is more than a regional player but it is not yet selling across the *key markets of the world.*

A **Global exporter** is company whose role is to *sell across the key markets of the world* products manufactured or services operated in its home country and who builds foreign operations only to support the export drive. The major aerospace or defence companies like Boeing, Airbus and Raytheon can be classified into this category despite the fact that they have some supporting assets (maintenance, sales offices, etc.) outside their home region.

A **Global operator** is a company that procures a large fraction of its product components in factories[3] located outside its base market and which concentrates its sales in its *domestic market.* In such a case the ambition would hardly qualify as a global: however, many managerial issues of integration and co-ordination of activities, both in-house factories or long-term subcontracting, would be quite similar to those that a global company would have to face.

In order to assess the degree of global ambition exhibited by companies, one should look at their distribution of sales, assets and personnel.

In 1999, the world economy produced $30,000 billion of goods and services, 33 per cent in North America, 27 per cent in Asia and 31 per cent in Europe, the rest being spread over Africa, South America, the Middle East and Eastern Europe.

In certain industries the distribution of markets can differ from the distribution of GDP, and growth differentials will make the future distribution of world market different from what it is today.

Table 2.1 gives a distribution of world markets by regions.

Ideally, one can imagine that a pure global company would exhibit three major characteristics:

- First, it would have a distribution of its sales proportional to the distribution of markets in its industry.
- Second, it would have a distribution of its assets and work force proportional to the distribution of markets in its industry.
- Third, it would manage its activities on an integrated and co-ordinated way across the globe.

Obviously, this may not apply to all industries since no industry has the same degree of global pressure towards globalisation, as has been discussed in Chapter 1. In a global industry like the consumer electronics industry, in which the distribution of market is 32 per cent in North America, 30 per cent in Europe, 30 per cent in Asia

Table 2.1 Distribution of world market, by region, selected industries, 2000 (percentage of US$ value)

Industry	North America (%)	Europe (%)	Asia (%)	Rest of the World (%)
Automobiles and light trucks	28.0	39.1	18.3	14.6
Beer	26.0	33.5	10.8	29.7
Biotechnology	31.0	27.6	28.2	13.2
Building products and materials	19.6	30.5	33.9	16.0
Canned foods	11.5	33.8	19.8	34.9
Clothing	19.5	33.4	17.0	30.1
Drugs	33.3	26.9	24.7	15.1
Electrical power systems and equipment	12.2	26.3	49.2	12.3
Financial services	13.9	45.7	23.2	17.2
Home computers	59.2	14.7	11.9	14.2
Household consumer goods	20.6	34.7	21.7	23.0
Machine tools	15.0	43.2	24.9	16.9
Mobile phones	27.4	34.5	23.0	15.1
Petrol	28.0	30.1	22.5	19.4
Plastic materials and resins	24.2	33.2	27.7	14.9
Retail trade	27.5	36.6	21.6	14.3
GDP US$ billion (1999)	9,600	9,300	7,800	3,300
GDP % (1999)	33	31	27	7

Source: Data bases from ICON Group International Inc. <http://www.icongrouponline.com/>.

Table 2.2 Distribution of markets and revenues in consumer electronics

Company	North America (%)	Europe (%)	Asia (%)	Rest of the World (%)
Industry	32	30	30	8
SONY	32	25	36	7
Matsushita	13	8	76	3
Philips	18	56	22	3
Thomson Multimedia	64	25	10	1

and 8 per cent in the rest of the world, the distribution of revenues of the four major players differs substantially from the industry distribution as shown in Table 2.2. SONY's ambition to be a tri-legged competitor in the world market (North America, Europe, Asia) is reflected in its distribution of revenues. Of all the players, SONY is the one that can be qualified as a global player, at least from the point of view of the distribution of its sales; Thomson is an American dominant global player, Philips an European dominant global player and Matsushita is an Asian dominant player.

The globalisation indices

In order to evaluate the extent to which a company has followed a global ambition, one can usefully utilise two globalisation indices: the Global Revenue Index and the Global Capability Index.

The **Global Revenue Index** (GRI) is calculated by taking the ratio of the company distribution of sales in the major world regions to the industry distribution of demand in the same regions.[4] It is calculated with the formula:

$$GRI = \sum 1^n \left[Ix_n (\text{cum}RX_n + \text{cum}RX_{(n-1)}) \right]$$

Where:

n is the number of regions taken into consideration.

In practice $n = 4$, since there are four major clusters: North America, Europe, Asia and the Rest of the World

Ix_n is the industry demand in the region as a proportion of world demand, $\text{cum}RX_n$ is the cumulative proportion of sales achieved by the company in region n in ascending order; for instance, if SONY's TV sales are 25 per cent in Europe, 32 per cent in North America, 36 per cent in Asia and 7 per cent in the rest of the World, SONY's cumulative proportion (cumRX) is 7 per cent for the rest of the world, 32 per cent for Europe, 64 per cent for North America and 100 per cent for Asia.

The calculation of SONY's GRI is shown in Table 2.3.

A company whose sales distribution matches the exact distribution of its industry market would have a GRI of 100 per cent.

A company that concentrates its sales to one region and sells nothing elsewhere would obtain a GRI corresponding to the percentage of demand in this region. For instance, if SONY's sales were entirely concentrated in Asia, SONY's GRI would have been 30 per cent.

GRI is by definition used for measuring how *global* a company is. For firms engaged in an industry which is local in nature, the GRI will favour the firms that

Table 2.3   SONY: calculation of the Global Revenue Index

Distribution of sales	Rest of the World (%)	Europe (%)	North America (%)	Asia (%)
Industry	8	30	32	30
SONY RX	7	25	32	36
CumRX	7	32	64	100
Cum RX − n	0	7	32	64
Cum RX + cum RX−n	7	39	96	164
Ix *(cum RX + cum RX − n)	0.56	11.70	30.72	49.20
Then SONY's GRI (%) = 0.56 +11.70 + 30.72 + 49.20 = 92.18				
Similar calculations will derive the following results for the other players:				
Philips GRI =	70			
Thomson GRI =	61			
Matsushita GRI =	52			

are in countries/regions with the biggest consumption for that industry. For example, in the restaurant business, which is local in nature, US restaurants would have had a higher GRI than that of Asian restaurants during the Asian Crisis simply because US people visited restaurants more often than Asians during that period. In this case, the higher GRI of the US restaurants should not be interpreted as the US restaurants being more global than their Asian counterparts, as the majority of both the US and Asian restaurants are local players.

Also, for companies which implement globalisation by competing in small markets (e.g. South America, Eastern Europe), the GRI does not reflect the extent of global sales the company has. This is owing to the fact that the company's sales are in world markets that the other industry major global players have not yet fully explored. For example, ACER, the Taiwanese PC company, had a relatively low GRI at the early stage of its globalisation strategy where it began to capture the South American markets. Nonetheless, the low GRI score correctly reflects the fact that the company did not closely resemble the industry's demand pattern. This type of company will further expand to the major world markets after establishing itself in smaller foreign markets. Once the company has established itself in the major world markets, it will have a higher GRI.

The **Global Capability Index** (GCI) is calculated in a similar way, but instead of taking the distribution of sales, one takes the distribution of *assets for capital-intensive industries* or else of *personnel*. The 'capability' described here is in-house capability, not capability which a firm can acquire through external sourcing like outsourcing, sub-contracting or strategic alliances with overseas companies in which the firm has no ownership in the alliance partner(s) and/or alliance venture. For strategic alliances in which a firm has ownership interest, one can theoretically include in the GCI calculation the proportional amount of assets which the company owns or has control over. When gathering data for the calculation of GCI, care should be taken, and an attempt should be made, to account for off-balance sheet assets such as asset finance by sales and leaseback arrangements.

Companies which rely heavily on external sourcing will have a low GCI score. This is because the company cannot deploy resources and capabilities at will but relies on external parties to supply the capability. This reliance on external parties also means that the company can face potential problems such as product/service unavailability, time delays in delivery, or price pressure from the overseas suppliers.

If one combines the GCI and the GRI in one chart, we obtain a mapping of the *global ambition of players* (Figure 2.3).

A company low in both GRI and GCI would be a **Regional player**, a company low in GRI and high in GCI would be a **Global operator**, a company low in GCI and high in GRI would be a **Global exporter** while a company high in both dimensions would be a **Global player** and a company with an average score in both dimensions would be a **Regional dominant global player**. Figure 2.4 shows the mapping of the four leading companies in the consumer electronic industry.

A dynamic utilisation of the global indices

As part of the strategy formulation process, companies can use the global indices to analyse their position and set their global ambition. To illustrate, we will take the example of Whirlpool and the global appliance industry. In 1980, Whirlpool

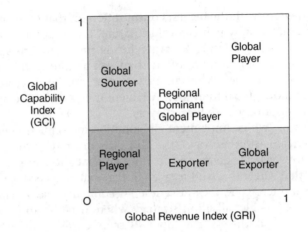

Figure 2.3 Mapping of global ambition

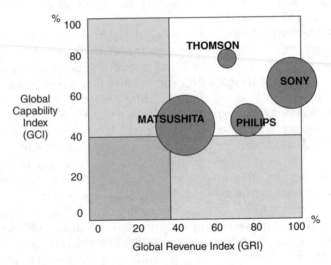

Figure 2.4 Mapping of the consumer electronics industry

was essentially a regional operator. Its sales and assets were concentrated in the United States. Its GRI was 0.35 and its GCI 0.40. The white goods industry (refrigerators, washers, cookers) was at that time primarily a regional industry. For instance, American refrigerators tended to be very big and would not fit easily in European or Japanese homes. Progressively, however, the industry moved towards globalisation because of the huge economies of scale to be gained in components manufacturing, branding and R&D. The Swedish company, Electrolux, moved aggressively in Europe to become a pan-European company and invested in the United States and Asia to become a global player. The Whirlpool management realised that its future would be at stake if it did not follow a globalisation path. The first step of this process was an alliance with the Philips appliance business which was transformed into a straight acquisition. From a single regional player, Whirlpool moved into the position of a dual regional player (GRI 0.55, GCI 0.90) with a strong

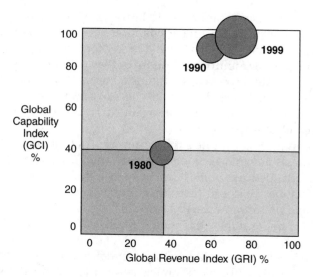

Figure 2.5 The evolution of Whirlpool globalisation

delocalisation of its factories, particularly in Latin America. Then, in the early 1990s, Whirlpool realised that the Asia Pacific region was going to represent 40 of world sales for refrigerators, washers and cookers. It set up its ambition to gain a significant position in Asia. By the year 2000, Whirlpool had become a global player (GRI 0.68, GCI 0.84) (see Figure 2.5).

Global positioning

Global positioning consists of two types of choices:

- First, the *choice of countries* in which the company wants to compete and the role that those countries have to play in the global country portfolio.
- Second, the definition of the various *value propositions* for the product or services of the company, corresponding to the type of segments and countries in which the company wants to compete.

Choice of countries

Depending on the industries, countries differ in the opportunities they offer to companies for their strategic development. Some countries, given their size, growth or the quality of their human, natural or locational resources, are critical for companies' long-term competitiveness. Those countries are qualified as **Key countries**. Not to be present in these countries is a serious handicap for companies who want to be global players. As mentioned earlier, Europe, North America and Asia are the three regional clusters that a global player would consider, but within those clusters some countries are more important than others, and should be given priority. In Asia, for instance, in the automobile sectors, Japan, Korea and, in the future, China can be considered as key. In Europe, Germany and, to a certain extent, the United Kingdom or France are also key countries.[5] In the pulp and paper industry, in which natural resources are a key component of competitive advantage, countries like Indonesia can be considered as key, while California (Silicon Valley) would be key for Internet players.

The second category of countries is countries that exhibit a high growth rate, making them strategically attractive in the near future. Those are the **Emerging countries**. China, India, Brazil, Poland in the early twenty-first century would generally qualify for that definition but, again, it is difficult to generalise since opportunities are industry-specific.

The **Platform countries** constitute a third category. These are the countries which, because of locational advantage, good logistical, financial, regulatory and legal infrastructure or qualified personnel, can serve as a 'hub' for setting up regional centres, global factories that are 'platforms' for further development. Singapore, Hong Kong, Ireland or Taiwan present these characteristics. Carrefour, the French hypermarket giant, for example, has used Taiwan as a platform for its strategic development in Asia.

A fourth category would be the **Marketing countries**, where the attractiveness of the market is good, without being as strategically critical as for the key countries. The type of presence in such countries should be assessed on its own merits, depending on the political, economic and business context.

Countries with a strong resource base but limited market prospects would be classified as **Sourcing countries**; for instance, Malaysia for rubber or Saudi Arabia for petroleum.

Typically, a global company will control a portfolio of operations in these different categories of country. The benefit of such categorisation is to establish *priorities* in investments and to guide *entry strategies* (an issue that will be dealt with in Chapter 7).

Value proposition

The value proposition is the definition of a customer's *value attributes* that the company is offering to the market. It implies:

- Choice of value attributes
- Choice of customer segments
- Choice of degree of world standardisation of the product/service offering.

Value attributes are the elements of the products or services that customers value when making their purchasing decision. Those include the product design, functionality, performance, quality, customisation and price, as well as the related service, the brand, the availability and other features. The set of those attributes for a particular group of customers and a particular product or service is the customer's **Value curve**.

Professor Michael Porter, from the Harvard Business School, has identified two 'generic' strategies corresponding to two types of value attributes:[6]

(a) A proposition based on value-enhancing attributes such as performance, quality, service, customisation. Porter calls this type of value attribute *differentiated*.
(b) A proposition based on price for standardised products or services. Porter calls this type *Cost leadership*.

The same typology can apply to global positioning: the company can either position itself as a **Global differentiator** or a **Global cost leader**.

Customer segments are the groups of customers that have *similar value curves*. Those customer groups can be identified by income level, geographical location, age, socio-psychometric attributes in consumer goods and service industries or by industry, size, purchasing behaviour in business-to-business industries (B2B). The strategic choice at this level will be to decide whether the company concentrates its segmentation on one or two customer groups, a positioning that Michael Porter qualifies as *Focused*, or whether it attempts to embrace many or all customer segments, a positioning qualified as *Broad*.

The third component of a value proposition is the choice between a standardised versus an adaptive-value proposition across countries. If one adopts a similar or standardised value attribute to the same type of customer segments across the globe, the approach will be qualified as *Standard*; if one tries to differentiate value attributes and segments according to the country or regions, the approach will be qualified as *Adaptive*.

Then the company's value proposition will consist of trying to identify the customer groups it wants to serve (Focused or Broad), the type of value attribute it wants to offer (Cost versus Differentiation) to those customers, and whether it is homogeneous or not across country (Standardised versus Adaptive). Coca Cola, Swatch or SONY, for instance, have a standard value proposition across the globe and serve similar segments. Unilever and Procter & Gamble adjust their value proposition and their segmentation in different countries.

The combination of those three choices will lead to eight different positionings, which are illustrated in Table 2.4 with some examples.

The strategic choice of a value proposition dictates the type of capabilities that are needed to compete globally, and therefore the type of *business system* in which the company needs to invest.

Investment in a global business system

The third element of a global strategy consists of building and developing capabilities to compete successfully in the global marketplace, in accordance with the positioning that has been already determined. Global capabilities are embodied in a business system deployed in various countries. In order to be competitive the company should be able to leverage some of its competitive advantages across countries.

Competitive advantages

Competitive advantages are capabilities that are difficult to replicate or imitate and are non-tradable.[7] Generally one can distinguish two types of capabilities leading to competitive advantages, as illustrated in Table 2.5:

(a) Capabilities leading to an increase in customer value through performance, quality and brand services, leading to a *Differentiated* value proposition
(b) Capabilities leading to a lower cost base, such as low-cost labour, low-cost sourcing, economies of scale in production, efficiency, leading to a *Cost leadership* value proposition.

Table 2.4 Global positioning

Global niche players				Broad global players			
Standard		Adaptive		Standard		Adaptive	
Differentiated	*Cost leader*	*Differentiated*	*Cost leader*	*Differentiated*	*Cost leader*	*Differentiated*	*Cost leader*
Standardised niche differentiator	Low-cost standardised niche	Differentiated niche adapter	Low-cost niche adapter	Broad standardised differentiator	Broad standardised cost leader	Broad adaptive differentiator	Broad adaptive cost leader
Example: Swatch, Intel	**Example:** Acer	**Example:** McDonald	**Example:** Carrefour	**Example:** SONY	**Example:** Matsushita	**Example:** Unilever P&G Philips	**Example:** Electrolux

Table 2.5 Capabilities leading to competitive advantage

Capabilities leading to enhanced customer value *Differentiation*	Capabilities leading to low-cost position *Cost leadership*
▪ Superior technology	▪ Low-cost raw material
▪ Superior quality	▪ Low-cost labour
▪ Innovative design	▪ Economies of scale
▪ Better functionality	▪ Economies of scope
▪ Customisation	▪ Cumulative volume
▪ Better related services	▪ Customer base
▪ One-stop shopping	▪ Network externalities
▪ Solution selling	▪ Efficient process technology
▪ Brand image	▪ Time management
▪ Responsive distribution	▪ Productivity management
▪ Customer relationships	
▪ Customer services	
▪ Financing	

Table 2.6 Sources of competitive advantage

Resources-based	Access to unique raw materials or location Access to licence from regulatory authorities Privileged access to information Privileged (or first-choice) access to skilled labour Privileged access to low-cost labour force Privileged access to suppliers Privileged access to cheaper capital
Assets-based	Unique low-cost position owing to accumulated volume Unique low-cost/quality position owing to proprietary process technology Unique low-cost position owing to installed base Control of distribution network Well established brand/reputation Patents
Competencies-based	Proprietary scientific/technological know-how Superior ability to bundle know-how Superior ability in management of critical processes Superiority in time management Faster product development Better management of information

Those competitive advantages find their sources in the proprietary ownership or access to valuable resources, assets or competencies. These sources of competitive advantage are described in Table 2.6.

Sustainability of competitive advantage

Competitive advantage, in order to be valuable, needs to be long-lasting. From an economic point of view, a competitive advantage is similar to a monopoly that the company creates for itself and which gives the company a *profit advantage* (an economic rent). This happens only if this monopoly is not immediately destroyed by imitation.

One can generally distinguish three ways of achieving sustainability:

(a) Customer loyalty
(b) Positive feedbacks
(c) Pre-emption of capabilities.

Customer loyalty creates sustainability when customers keep coming back to a company by choice, because the product or service provided to them is *unique* or more valuable than competition. It can also be due to a *brand* that has imprinted an association of uniqueness to the product or service in the mind of the customer. It can also be due to *high switching costs* that customers would incur if they changed products or services: in that case the customer is *locked-in*. An example of uniqueness or superior value is provided by Schlumberger, which commands nearly 70 per cent of the world market for logging, a highly specialised service of control for oil exploration. Coca Cola or Louis Vuitton are among the most characteristic examples of sustainable competitive advantages coming from a strong brand. A high switching costs example is given by Microsoft, whose operating system is so dominant that a customer wishing to shift to a competitive system like Linux or Apple would have tremendous application software adaptation costs.

Positive feedbacks are advantages that follow the logic of 'success brings success' and produce *increasing returns*. There are two kinds of positive feedback: 'network externalities' and 'experience effects'.

Network externalities exist when the customer base of a product or service is such that it induces other products or services providers to adopt it in their own value proposition. In turn, the fact that other products or services use the original product increases the value for new customers to buy the original product or service. This *virtuous circle* creates a positive loop that reinforces the company's competitive position. The classic example of network externalities has been provided by the battle of standards between VHS and Betamax. Because JVC, the inventor of VHS, opened its licence to many consumer electronic manufacturers, it made VHS more readily available. This, in turn, induced video producers and distributors to put more movies on the VHS standard, inducing more consumers to buy VHS machines, given the large number of VHS movies available. Microsoft DOS and Windows or Microsoft Office followed the same path: more software available with Windows or more users of Microsoft Office attracts more customers to buy Windows personal computers and to become users of Microsoft Office which in turn induces more Windows-based software, thereby attracting more customers. Betamax cassettes disappeared, Macintosh computers were pushed into a small market niche and Lotus 123 or WordPerfect nearly collapsed. In the end, network externalities create a situation in which the 'winner takes it all', meaning that the company which has developed a competitive advantage based on network externalities has reached a quasi-monopolistic situation.

The war of *standards* that is taking place in emerging industries like wireless communications, Internet portals, etc. is a war which uses network externalities to build a customer base and ultimately lock them in by making switching costs too high for them. *Experience effects* exist when accumulated volume reduces costs or increases customer benefits in such a way that the competitors, being ahead in accumulated volume, can use their lower cost base or customer value advantage to eliminate weaker competitors, which in turn helps them to accumulate more volume which then helps them to eliminate more competitors, etc. The Boston Consulting Group (BCC) in the early 1970s developed the theory of the 'experience curve', a modern version of the 'learning curve' discovered in the 1930s by aerospace engineers, demonstrating that the cost of production in standard products or services decreases by a fixed percentage each time the accumulated volume of production doubles. Based on this law, they suggested that, for standard products, competitive strategies should be based on a race for accumulated volume that would ultimately lead the larger competitor to achieve a *sustainable dominant profitable competitive position*. Although the experience curve theory has been criticised for its simplistic assumptions (it applies mainly to standard products in price-sensitive markets), it has proven to be a powerful competitive advantage in many industrial or services sectors such as chemical products, electronic components or automotive parts. A more subtle experience effect exists when accumulated volume reinforces customer *value creation*. In the service sectors, which provide what economists, call 'experience goods' (a service whose quality can be tested only by consuming it), the more customers that have experienced the services, the more comfortable it is for would-be customers to know that the service has been 'experienced' by many people. The same effect applies in professional services where word-of-mouth 'references' are a strong marketing factor.

Pre-emption of capabilities is a type of competitive advantage based on the appropriation by one company of key resources or assets that competitors will find difficult to access, or to the development of competencies that are 'time incompressible' (see below). Appropriation of resources or assets applies to the privileged access to natural resources such as location or mining concessions. It may apply to access to skills and talents when they are in limited supply, as is the case in many emerging markets such as the Internet-related sectors. It may apply to the right to do business, such as the obtaining of licences, as in telecommunications, or landing rights in air transport. *Patenting* is a form of pre-emption since it gives the patent holder a period during which it has the proprietary right to exploit the patent. It applies to distribution networks, partnerships or access to favourable locations, as in the retail or hospitality industries. *Time incompressibility* is a competitive advantage based on competencies which are time-consuming to imitate. For instance, Toyota obtained a sustainable advantage by developing the '*kanban*' and the 'just-in-time' processes. Those processes have been built up over time, through trial and error. When Western automobile manufacturers discovered the power of such processes in the 1980s they also discovered that they were not so easy to imitate given the complexity of the social relationships involved. They had to take the time to go through the same type of trial and error that Toyota had experienced in the first place.

Building sustainability

One of the key elements of any strategy is to be able to *create* and *exploit* sustainable competitive advantages. For global firms, the central issue is to be able to utilise

Table 2.7 Sources of competitive advantage of global companies

Manufacturing	*Services*

■ **Access to a globally scarce resource**
  – Access to natural resources: agribusiness,
    mining, etc.
  – Access to low-cost labour: labour-intensive
    industry
  – Access to supplies network
■ **Critical mass built at home**
  – Efficient manufacturing system size
■ **'Network' effect**
  – Specialised network of production sites
■ **Established product performance, quality**
■ **Competences built over time**
  – Technology management
■ **Image, brands and reputation**
■ **'Piggybacking'**
  – Associated with the international development
    of another firm or industry
	■ **Access to a globally scarce resource**
	  – Access to financial resources: banking, insurance
	  – Access to qualified human resources: designers,
	    entertainment, etc.
	  – Access to information: consulting activities
	■ **Critical mass built at home**
	  – Credit cards, courier services, airlines, transport
	■ **'Network' effect**
	  – Consulting, engineering, financial services,
	    brokerage, buying services, shipping agency,
	    news agencies, hotel chains
	■ **Competences built over time**
	  – Consulting, engineering, hospital management,
	    legal, education, etc.
	■ **Image, brands and reputation**
	  – Hotel, fast foods, distribution, training, etc.
	■ **'Piggybacking'**
	  – Associated with the international development
	    of another firm or industry
	  – Some consulting activities, banking, engineering,
	    hotels

their existing advantages in multiple-country leverages in order to compete success-fully with local players and other global competitors. This can be done in two ways:

(a) By being among the first competitors to enter a given market: *first-mover advantages*.
(b) By exploiting capabilities already built up in other countries in order to displace and dominate existing competitors: *leveraging advantages*.

Table 2.7 describes the typical sources of competitive advantages of global firms and Table 2.8 shows how such global firms typically achieve sustainability.

Global chess

On the top of leveraging their intrinsic competitive advantages, global companies possess the ability to play a global 'chess game', meaning that they can *cross-subsidise* one country by another in order to compete more effectively. A company uses its cash flow in one country in order to subsidise the development of the business in another country or loses money in one country in order to gain a higher profit compensating the losses in another country. Finally, tax arbitrage through transfer pricing mechanisms allows global companies to optimise their overall return given the constraints imposed by the various regulatory authorities.

An example of global 'chess game' was provided in the 1970s, when Michelin of France entered North America with the radial tyre technology that American tyre producers did not control on a large scale. In order to delay Michelin's entry and

Table 2.8 Building global sustainable advantage

	Type of sustainability			
Mode of building advantages	*Customer loyalty*	*Network externalities*	*Accumulated volume*	*Pre-emption*
First mover	▪ Introduce new concept or product ▪ Create new brand	▪ Create standard in key countries right at the beginning of the product life cycle	▪ Build volume rapidly ▪ Use experience effect from global operations to be a cost leader	▪ Capture locations, distribution, available talents, partners, etc.
Leverage	▪ Use global brand ▪ Leverage R&D to innovate and differentiate	▪ Use existing global customer base to expand globally		

to make it more painful, Goodyear engaged in a price war in Europe where it had a relatively small market share, to oblige Michelin, leader in Europe, also to lower its prices and therefore to be deprived of a source of cash flow that could have been used to finance its expansion in the United States. Another example of cross-subsidisation is provided by Citibank and its Global Account Management Programme. A global marketing plan is negotiated by the Citibank parent account manager with the corporate client for its financial needs worldwide. Citibank may give 'sweetener' financing for a project in Argentina, for instance, but as a *quid pro quo* will get a large share of a securitisation in Hong Kong. In such a case, 'Argentina' subsidises Hong Kong for the overall benefit of the company.

Global business system

Business system design consists of decomposing the company value chain into elements that are spread and integrated across the world. A company *value chain* is the set of activities that a company employs in order to design, produce and deliver the value proposed to the customer.[8] Each company has a different value chain according to the type of industry in which it operates and the degree of vertical integration it has adopted.

However, one can distinguish three major generic components of a value chain:

(a) *Innovative activities*: R&D, knowledge, creation, design
(b) *Productive activities*: procurement, manufacturing, back office, operations, logistics
(c) *Customer relationship activities*: marketing, sales, distribution, customer services.

In each of these activities, the company deploys resources, assets and competencies.

Figure 2.6 represents a generic value chain, showing the key resources assets and competencies that one typically finds in each activity.

During the process of globalisation, companies progressively split their value chain by spreading their activities across the world. The typical path of globalisation of the value chain is described in Figure 2.7. The first stage is the *export stage* in which the only elements of the value chain which are set up in foreign countries are the sales, and even then not through direct investment but through local distributors, agents or licensing. The only possible direct investment at this stage, if the size of the market justifies it, is the creation of a representative office in one country or a regional office for a group of countries. Those representative offices are set up to seize opportunities, identify agents, distributors, partners, organise the trade flow and prepare future substantial investments.

The second stage is to invest in *marketing subsidiaries* actively to manage the marketing mix. Those subsidiaries are staffed with expatriates plus local recruits and their role is to co-ordinate the activities of the distributors, organise the promotion, set up logistics and service centres and, in some cases, some operational facilities, such as testing laboratories or assembling operations to support the sales effort. Those marketing subsidiaries may eventually take over the local distributors. When the market justifies or when local governments require a localisation of value adding activities, companies invest in manufacturing or operational facilities for the service sectors. Some R&D facilities may be localised as well, in order to adapt products or

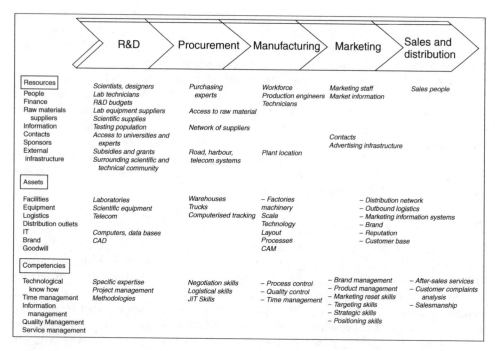

Figure 2.6   Generic value chain

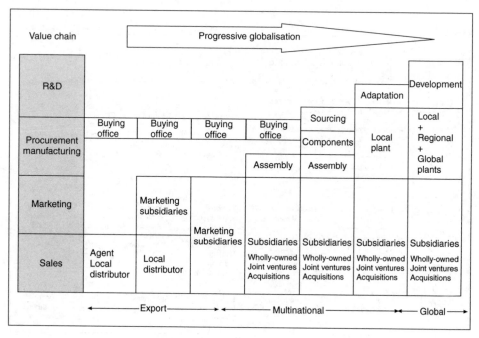

Figure 2.7   Typical globalisation of the value chain

services to local conditions. These foreign investments are made either as wholly owned subsidiaries or joint ventures or acquisitions of local firms. At this stage, as the number of those investments increases, the company is a multinational, managing a portfolio of relatively independent worldwide subsidiaries.

During the final stage of globalisation, multinational companies feel the competitive need to integrate and co-ordinate their worldwide operations to take advantage of economies of scale, transfer of know-how and resource optimisation. This leads to an interlocked set of value chain activities which falls broadly into three categories: the activities which have a global role to serve the whole world (*global activities*, such as global research centres, or global plants), those which have a regional role (*regional activities*) and those which are purely local (*local activities*). Figure 2.8 shows how these three categories interact.

The role of partnership and strategic alliances in building global capabilities

In the process of globalisation, companies may usually need to acquire and complement their capabilities by setting up *partnerships*. Although we will discuss global strategic partnership in Chapter 4, it is useful, at this stage, to note that partnerships are very often critical for achieving a global presence and building global competitive advantages, even for the most alliance-allergic firms, such as Michelin of France who tried to build a global presence by itself, was forced to make an acquisition in the United States (Uniroyal) and several joint ventures in Asia (Japan, Korea, Thailand). Strategic alliances for globalisation can take several forms:

(a) *Global alliances*, whose role is to pool complementing capabilities to reach world markets, or to achieve a critical mass in R&D. The most usual examples

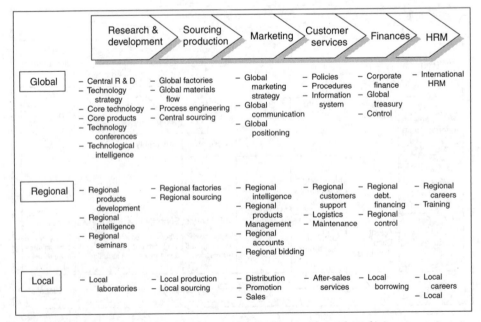

Figure 2.8 A generic global distribution of activities in the value chain

of world market partnerships are the airlines alliances such as Star or One-World, or Concert in the telecoms sector between BT and ATT. R&D global alliances are frequent in aerospace, life sciences, electronic defence industries or oil exploration.

(b) *Partnerships for market entry*, joint ventures, franchises or licensing, whose role is to comply with local government requirements (as has been the case in China) or to facilitate entry or minimise risks in a particular country.

(c) *Acquisitions* that, from an ownership point of view, are not partnerships, since one party takes over the other, but from a management point of view can be assimilated to an alliance since different national and corporate cultures have to be combined. Acquisitions may have either a global or a local scope.

Global organisation

The final element of a global strategy is the design of an *organisational architecture* which is able to support and implement the global ambition, global positioning and global business system already described. In Chapter 3, we will discuss more deeply the various types of global organisations and the issues associated with their implementation. Here, we will limit our comments to the key elements of choices that may be considered during the strategy formulation process.

Alongside the global development path described in Figure 2.7, Stopford and Wells (1972), Heenan and Perlmutter (1979), Prahalad and Doz (1987), and Bartlett and Ghoshal (2000) have identified different types of structures, systems and cultures in the management of global firms.[9] These are summarised in Table 2.9.

These different organisational choices have been mapped by Doz and Prahalad in what they call the Integration/Responsiveness Grid, which positions the various types of global structures according to the competitive requirements of global integration and local responsiveness, as in Figure 2.9.

The choice of an adequate organisational model is contingent upon the following factors:

(a) The nature of the *competitive context in the industry*. As discussed in Chapter 1, the more 'global' is the industry, the more integrated and co-ordinated the activities and the more the organisational structure should reflect this integration. The world functional, the global business structure or the matrix structure fulfils this requirement.

(b) The *strategic positioning* adopted by the firm. A standardised positioning using cost leadership as a competitive advantage will require a tightly integrated organisation such as the world functional or the global business structure.

Global strategies and the multi-business firm

In the previous sections of this chapter we developed a framework for the formulation of global strategies made up of four elements: ambition, positioning, investment and organisation. This framework applies when a company operates in a homogeneous industry environment. If the company is multi-business, and controls a portfolio of different business sectors, the framework applies at the level

Table 2.9 Organisational designs for global strategies

Phases of global development	Structure	Process	Culture
Early export	Export Department Within marketing and sales All activities at home Distributors, agents in foreign countries Export managers travel Possible foreign representative offices	Domestic Process plus: International data base (market research) International financing Instruments (trade financing)	Domestic corporate culture dominates Pioneering phase Export managers as missionary
Large export and early multinational subsidiaries	International Division as distinct from domestic activities Subsidiaries report to International Division on a country-by-country basis	Specific planning and control processes for international operations International careers distinct from domestic ones	Ethnocentric culture Expatriate domination High degree of operational autonomy in subsidiaries
Full multinational	Geographical structure The world is organised by region Country subsidiaries report to regional headquarters which report to corporate headquarters The company is a confederation of national units	Localisation Multiple processes fitted to national requirements Only a few central policies Careers essentially national except for a few international managers	Pluricentric Except for a few international managers each national entity reflects its national culture International diversity prevails
Global	Integrated structures Two types: (A) Global-functional structure: each key function is managed centrally	Global Standardisation Common processes and standard procedures across borders Activities co-ordinated centrally Synergies systematised Careers international	Global Mind Strong corporate values Common themes Corporate culture Corporate culture prevails above any national culture including culture of the mother company

(B) Single Matrix structure: dual line of reporting, geographical and functional

Dual information process:
Global and local but working in integrated manner
Transfer of people and knowledge
A large number of policies to define responsibilities and avoid conflicts

Negotiating culture
Ability to solve conflicts
Requires strong corporate values

(C) Transnational Network
Not really a structure but more a way of managing global companies in such a way that efficiency, responsiveness and innovation are optimised

Multidimensional information system: transfer of people and knowledge

Team Mind
Culture of sharing transfer and co-operation

Multi-business
Global product
When the company is at the same time multi-country and diversified

The business diversity adds another dimension of complexity in the organisation of global operations
Three types of structures, processes and culture may apply depending on prevailing competitive context of the industry:

(A) Multi-business geographical structure
The company is organised by region/countries which are in charge of managing multiple products' businesses in each country
Each country is in charge of formulating the appropriate strategy for each business line and is responsible for profits
Business managers support national policies but do not have profit responsibilities

(B) Global business structure.
Each business is integrated centrally
The country subsidiaries are implementors of centrally formulated strategies and policies
Profit responsibilities are assigned to global business managers who manage their global business according to competitive conditions

(C) Multi-business matrix structure
Dual-line business/geography
Profit responsibilities are in the hands of both business managers and country managers

Source: Adapted from Stopford and Wells (1972), Prahalad and Doz (1987), Bartlett and Ghoshal (2000), Heenan and Perlmutter (1979).

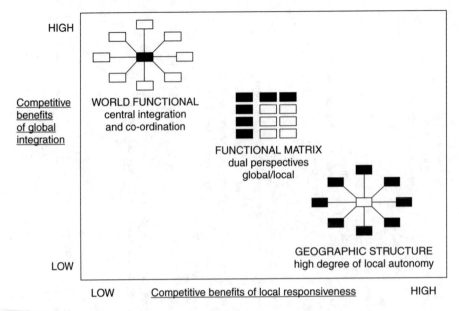

Figure 2.9   The Integration/Responsiveness Grid and global structures

Source: Adapted from Prahalad and Doz (1987).

of each business but not directly at the level of the total corporation. As is often the case, in a given corporation, some businesses are more global than others and the rules of competition differ from business to business. For instance, in the telecommunication industry, voice telephony and mobile telephony are essentially a local or national businesses, while corporate data is a global business. France Telecom's stated strategic ambition is to be a national player in France, a European player for mobile and a global player for corporate data.

However, the global corporate strategy of a multi-business corporation is more than the mathematical sum of the global strategies of each business it controls.[10] It may be defined in terms of the four elements described earlier, but with a modified content:

(a) *Corporate global ambition*: Overall strategic direction assigned to the group for its globalisation. Does the corporation wants to be a global player in all businesses it controls or does it assign different global profiles to different businesses? What is the overall mission for the group?

(b) *Corporate global positioning*: Which businesses does the corporation want to be in? Does the corporation view its business portfolio as homogeneous in terms of competitive positioning? Does it want to be a cost leader across the board? Does it want the businesses to share a common global brand?

(c) *Global business system*: To what extent do business units share resources, assets and competencies in order to optimise synergies? What are the corporate priorities in resource allocation among businesses?

(d) *Global organisation*: Is the global structure organised according to a geographical design, a global business design or a matrix design? What is the role of the corporate headquarters in the strategic and operational control of the business units? Does the corporation set up regional headquarters to co-ordinate activities at regional level? What kind of human resource management (HRM) has the corporation put in place? Are the key managerial functions managed globally for all businesses or at business level or at regional level?

All those questions boil down to the key consideration: What is the *value added of corporate activities* in fostering the global competitiveness of the business units?

In Chapter 3 we will give more details on that issue and some examples will be presented with the analysis of Asea Brown Boveri (ABB).

Global strategies and the small- and medium-sized enterprise (SME)

Does the framework presented here apply to SMEs or is it designed only for large multinational and global enterprises?

The answer to that question is 'yes and no'. 'No', because of SMEs' limited resource base; SMEs are not generally able to create global capabilities by deploying assets, resources and competencies in the 20–30 countries that represent 90 per cent of world demand. 'Yes', because if these companies are competing in sectors that are confronted with global competition and new market opportunities are located outside their national boundaries, they also need to 'think global'.

Obviously their global strategic design will probably not be as comprehensive and complex as the one that has been developed here, but the ambition, position, investment, organisation framework may be a useful tool for organising their thinking. Most SMEs will, most of the time, perceive themselves as 'Global exporters', relying on local distributors and agents for the sales and marketing of their products. Some more daring companies will set up representative offices in key countries in order to support their marketing efforts and control and co-ordinate their distributors. The most resourceful will establish operational subsidiaries either directly or through partnerships of resources to 'globalise'.

In all cases, they will have to address the question of their competitive positioning and the deployment of capabilities to capture the market opportunities. Some of them will use their own resources, some others will 'piggyback' on the efforts of global customers, some will use the various national government or national Chambers of Commerce 'schemes' for the promotion of SMEs.

In the late 1980s, the French company Gemplus, one of the first companies to enter the market for smartcards, immediately after its formation in Marseille in the South of France, created a subsidiary in Germany, a joint venture company in Singapore and a marketing company in the United States. This strategy reflected the nature of the industry: the technology of the smartcard is pervasive; it has numerous applications in banking, telecommunications, transport and Internet transactions; it has the potential to become global. National boundaries do not provide strong entry barriers, but national legislations and established infrastructures make national presence a competitive requirement. Network externalities, customer base and first-to-enter are competitive weapons in this industry. Gemplus, a middle-sized technology firm, realised this competitive imperative and, right at the beginning, devoted a large proportion of their limited resources to expanding globally.

SUMMARY AND KEY POINTS

1. A global business strategy consists of:

▪ Global *ambition*	Stating the relative importance of region and countries for a company
▪ Global *positioning*	Choice of countries, customer segments and value proposition
▪ Global *business system*	Investments in resources, assets and competences to create a global value chain and global capabilities through alliances and acquisitions
▪ Global *organisation*	Global structure, processes, co-ordination and HRM.

2. Global ambition:
   ▪ There are two global indices:
   - *Global Revenue Index (GRI)* is the ratio of the company distribution of sales in the major world regions to the industry distribution of demand in the same region.
   - *Global Capability Index (GCI)* is the ratio of the company distribution of assets or personnel in the major world regions to the industry distribution the same region. Distribution of assets is used when the company is engaged in a capital-intensive industry. Otherwise, the distribution of personnel is used.
   ▪ Types of global ambitions:
   Depending on the value of the GRI and GCI, there are five main global ambitions for different players:
   - A *Global player* aspires to establish a sustainable competitive position in the key markets of the world and to build an integrated business system of designs spread over those key markets. It has both a high GCI and a high GRI score.
   - A *Regional player* captures a strong competitive advantage in one of the key regions of the world (North America, Europe and Asia) and is a relatively weak player in the other parts. It has both a low GCI and a low GRI score.
   - A *Regional dominant player* sells in more countries than a regional player but it does not yet sell across the key markets of the world. It has a medium score for GCI and GRI.
   - A *Global exporter* sells across the key markets of the world products manufactured or services operated in its home country and builds operations only to support the export drive. It has a low GCI and a high GRI score.
   - A *Global sourcer* procures a large fraction of product components in factories located outside its base market and concentrates its sales in its domestic market. It has a high GCI and a low GRI score.

3. Global positioning:
   ▪ Global positioning involves:
   - *Choice* of countries
   - *Value* proposition.

■ There are five types of countries where global positioning occurs:

- *Key countries*   Countries critical for the long-term competitiveness of the company owing to its size, growth or resources available
- *Emerging countries*   Countries that exhibit high growth rate for a particular industry
- *Platform countries*   Countries which can serve as a 'hub' for setting up regional centres, global factories that are 'platforms' for further development
- *Marketing countries*   Countries with attractive markets without being as strategically critical as the key countries
- *Sourcing countries*   Countries with a strong resource base but limited market prospects

■ Value proposition:
- The value proposition comprises:
  (a) Choice of value attributes
  (b) Customer value curve
  (c) Degree of world standardisation of products/service offering
- *Value attributes* are the elements of the products/services that customers value when making their purchasing decision; examples include price, design, functionality, performance, quality and customisation
- The *customer's value curve* is the set of value attributes for a particular group of customers and a particular product/service
- Degree of world standardisation of products/services:
  (a) A *standardised value proposition* adopts a similar or standard value attribute to the same type of customer segments across the world
  (b) An *adaptive value proposition* tailors or customises the value proposition for different countries/regions

■ Choices of global positioning:

There are eight choices of global positioning, depending on the company's decisions on:
- *Scope* of targeted customer segments (broad/focused player)
- *Approach* of making a value proposition in different countries (standardised/adaptive)
- Choice of *generic strategies* adopted (differentiation or cost leadership).

4. Global business system:

■ *Elements*:
- A global business system decomposes the company value chain into elements which are spread and integrated across the world
- It involves building and developing capabilities to compete successfully on the global market space; global capabilities are embodied into a business system deployed in various countries

■ *Value chain*:

Each company has a different value chain according to the type of industry in which it operates and the degree of vertical integration it has adopted. One can distinguish three major generic components of a value chain:

- *Innovative* activities (R&D, design, knowledge)
- *Productive* activities (procurement, manufacturing, back office, operations, logistics)
- *Customer relationship* activities (marketing, sales, distribution, customer service)

■ *Capabilities*:
- Types:
  (a) Capabilities that lead to a *differentiation proposition*, such as superior quality, customisation, innovative design
  (b) Capabilities which lead to *cost leadership*, such as low-cost labour/raw materials
- Factor determining global competitive advantages: proprietary ownership or access to valuable assets, resources or competencies
- Types of sustainability in competitive advantage:

(a) *Customer loyalty*	Can be built on brand or high switching costs involved
(b) *Positive feedbacks*	Can result from network externalities and experience effects
(c) *Pre-emption of capabilities*	Based on the appropriation by one company of key resources or assets that competitors will find difficult to access or to develop since they require investment of resources and/or time

- Modes of building competitive advantage:

(a) *First-mover advantages*	Being among the first competitors to enter a given market
(b) *Leveraging advantages*	Exploiting capabilities already built in other countries

■ *Evolution of firms in globalisation process*:
- There are three stages of progress:
  (a) *Export*
     (i) Sales is the only element in the value chain which is set up in foreign countries and not through direct investment but through local distributors, agents or licensing; a representative office can be set up at this stage if the market size justifies it
     (ii) As the company progresses through the export stage, it invests in marketing subsidiaries actively to manage the marketing mix; their role is to co-ordinate the activities of the distributors, organise promotion and set up logistics and service centres: these marketing subsidiaries may eventually take over the local distributors
  (b) *Multinational*
     The company manages a portfolio of relatively independent worldwide wholly owned subsidiaries or joint ventures

(c) *Global*

A global company integrates and co-ordinates its worldwide operations to take advantage of economies of scale, transfer of know-how and resource optimisation; this leads to an interlocked set of value chain activities which falls broadly into three categories: the activities which have a global role to serve the whole world (global activities), those which have a regional role (regional activities) and those which are purely local (local activities)

- *Partnerships*:
  - Companies usually need to acquire and complement their capabilities by setting up partnerships; global strategic partnerships are often critical for achieving a global presence and building global competitive advantage
  - Forms of strategic alliances include:
    (a) Global alliances to pool complementing capabilities to reach world markets and achieve a critical mass in R&D
    (b) Partnerships – joint ventures, franchises or licensing for market entry
    (c) Acquisitions.

5. Global organisation (see Chapter 3):

- Organisation *choice* is dependent on:
  - The nature of the *competitive context* in the industry: Phases of global development include:
    (a) Early export
    (b) Early multinational subsidiaries
    (c) Full multinational
    (d) Global
    (e) Global multi-business
  - The *strategic positioning* adopted by the firm
- Organisational *dimensions* cover:
    (a) Structure
    (b) System/processes
    (c) Culture.

6. Global corporate strategy:

- For a multi-business corporation, the four elements of the global corporate strategies are extended in scope:
  - *Corporate global ambition* specifies the different global profiles for each business e.g. whether the corporation wants to be a global player in all of the businesses it controls
  - *Corporate global positioning* considers which businesses the corporation wants to be in: does it want the businesses to share a common global brand and/or standard competitive positioning?
  - *Global business system* describes how business units share resources, assets and competences to obtain synergies and what the company's priorities are in resource allocations among businesses
  - *Global organisation* explains the role of corporate headquarters and the company organisation by function/products/countries/region

■ For SMEs:
They still need to 'think global' if the industry in which they compete experiences global competition; with their limited resource base SMEs may not be able to create global capabilities and reach, but can still establish representative offices and/or operational subsidiaries.

Learning assignments

1 The distribution of sales and assets of General Motors, the US cars and trucks manufacturer, is shown below:

	Nafta	Europe	Asia	Rest of World
Unit sales	5,874,000	1,968,000	421,000	523,000
Personnel	217,000	87,000	10,000	23,000

What is GM's position on a GCI/GRI mapping?

2 In your opinion, in which industry could London (UK) be a 'key' country – Italy? Australia?

3 What could be the benefits of positioning oneself as a standardised global niche differentiator (see Table 2.4, p. 46)? What kind of competitive advantages does it require?

4 What are the capabilities needed to be a broad adaptive cost leader?

5 What are the ways to sustain competitive advantage?

6 What types of competitive advantages does being a first-mover provide?

7 Can you sketch the mapping of the value chain for:
   (a) A consulting firm
   (b) An airline
   (c) A trading firm
   (d) A corporate and investment bank?

8 For each of the entities in Question 7 (a)–(d), can you represent a possible global distribution of their value chain, as illustrated in Figure 2.8?

Key words

■ Business strategy
■ Corporate strategy
■ Cost leadership
■ Differentiation
■ Global business strategy
■ Global Capability Index
■ Global corporate strategy
■ Global positioning
■ Global Revenue Index
■ Network externalities
■ Time incompressibility
■ Value chain
■ Value curve
■ Value proposition

Web resources

<http://www.businessweek.com/globalbiz/index.html>
Business Week – Global business

<http://www.forbes.com/forbesglobal/>
Forbes Global Magazine online, with a section on companies and strategies

<http://harvardbusinessonline.hbsp.harvard.edu/>

<http://harvardbusinessonline@hbsp.harvard.edu/>

Notes

1. This section is based on the Harvard Business School case study 9–391–071, written by Thomas W. Malnight under the supervision of Michael Yoshino.
2. One should observe that the distinction between a global player and a regional player is more a function of the relative importance of each major region of the world in the company's portfolio than the published ambition of the company in its external communications. Many companies assert that they are 'global', although their accounts reflect a strong concentration of their sales in one region. However, this situation may change if there is a real strategic ambition to become a real global player supported by the appropriate investments. Renault, for instance, a traditional European player, has acquired controlling positions in Nissan and Samsung automobiles, transforming the company into a European, Asian and also North American player thanks to Nissan's operations in the United States.
3. Global sourcing applies also to some services sectors; for instance, a software company setting up a programming operation in India but limiting its sales to one country would be a global operator. Similarly, a domestic mass retailer that had purchasing offices across the world and long-term manufacturing contracts would also be a global operator.
4. A similar calculation could be done by taking the major countries, but it becomes more complicated. However, it is perfectly possible to apply a similar methodology by taking the 10 major world markets, for instance, or applying it at the level of a region (the distribution of sales in Asia Pacific, for instance, among the key countries of the region).
5. The European case presents the particularity of being a set of countries, but also a common market, with a free movement of people, capital and goods and having endorsed a single currency (the Euro). In theory Europe, from the point of view of global players, could be considered as a 'country' and therefore the concept of key countries should not apply. However, cultural, structural and political differences have led global companies carefully to assess each national context in making their global positioning and investment decisions. In the future, Europe will probably be like the United States, where foreign investors will compare the relative strategic importance of California versus Texas or Washington State.
6. Porter (1980).
7. One can find a more elaborate treatment of competitive advantage in Porter (1985, 1986).
8. The concept of the value chain was developed by Porter (1985, 1986).
9. Stopford, Wells, Doz and Prahalad (1987); Bartlett and Ghoshal (1989).
10. See Goold, Campbell and Alexander (1994).

References and further reading

Bartlett, Christopher A. and Sumantra Ghoshal, *Managing Across Borders: The Transnational Solution*. Boston, MA: Harvard Business School Press, 1989.

Bartlett, Christopher A. and Sumantra Ghoshal, 'Going Global: Lessons from Late Movers', *Harvard Business Review*, March–April 2000, pp. 132–42.

Davidson, William H., *Global Strategic Management*. New York: John Wiley, 1982.

Doremus, Paul N., Louis W. Pauly, Simon Reich and William W. Keller, *The Myth of the Global Corporation*. Princeton: Princeton University Press, 1999.

Doz, Yves L. and C.K. Prahalad, *The Multinational Mission*. New York: Free Press, 1987.

Goold, Michael, Andrew Campbell and Marcus Alexander, *Corporate-Level Strategy*. New York: John Wiley, 1994.

Hamel, Gary and C.K. Prahalad, 'Do You Really Have a Global Strategy?', *Harvard Business Review*, July–August 1985, pp. 139–48.

Heenan, David and Howard Perlmutter, *Multinational Organization Development*. Boston, MA: Addison-Wesley, 1979.

Ohmae, Kenichi, *Becoming a Triad Power*. New York: McKinsey & Co., 1985.

Porter, Michael E., *Competitive Strategy: Techniques for Analysing Industries and Competitors*. New York: Free Press, 1980.

Porter, Michael E., *Competitive Advantage Creating and Sustaining Superior Performance*. New York: Free Press, 1985.

Porter, Michael E., *Competition in Global Industries*. Boston, MA: Harvard Business School Press, 1986.

Prahalad, C.K. and Yves L. Doz, *The Multinational Mission: Balancing Local Demands and Global Vision*, 1st edn. New York: Free Press, 1987.

Rennie, Michael W., 'Global Competitiveness: Born Global', *McKinsey Quarterly*, 4, 1993, pp. 45–52.

Stopford, John and Louis Wells, *Strategy and Structure of Multinational Enterprises*. New York Basic Books, 1972.

Verdin, Paul and Nick van Heck, *From Local Champions to Global Masters: A Strategic Perspective on Managing Internationalisation*, London: Palgrave Macmillan, 2001.

Yip, George, *Total Global Strategy: Managing for World Wide Competitive Advantage*. Englewood Cliffs, NJ: Prentice-Hall, 1992.

3

Designing a global organisation

In Chapter 2 various models of organisational designs were introduced. It has been argued that those designs were contingent upon the nature of the global industry context as well as the strategic positioning and business system selected by corporations. In practice, whatever the type of design chosen, companies engaged in global business have to cope with a dual requirement:

(a) They need efficiently to introduce and leverage their competitive advantages across borders; consequently their organisational design demands a certain degree of *co-ordination and centralisation,*

(b) They need to adapt to local conditions; consequently their organisational design demands a certain degree of *de-centralisation and local autonomy.*

Organisational design reflects the way companies put this dual demand into action through the implementation of three interlocked elements:

(a) *Organisational structure*: how roles, responsibilities and power are assigned.

(b) *Organisational processes*: how decisions are made, resource allocation commitments decided, policies enacted and rewards, sanctions and control exercised. Organisational processes include information processes, decision-making processes, planning and control processes and performance evaluation processes.

(c) *Organisational culture*: the shared values and the dominant logic[1] of doing business'; the 'dos' and 'donts' and what kind of behaviour is rewarded or sanctioned'.

This chapter discusses the various organisational designs used by corporations in their international, multinational and global operations. Based on the work of prior research, three generic organisational models are identified:

- **Global hub**: a worldwide functional or global product structure
- **Confederation**: a multinational geographical structure
- **Multidimensional**: a matrix or transnational structure.

A variety of structures is derived from these three generic models. These are described and illustrated in turn, showing their advantages and disadvantages. It can be argued that there is no single best structure and that the adoption of a particular structure is contingent upon the competitive imperative. The chapter ends by advocating that global firms should develop a culture and management processes of the 'transnational' model.

At the end of the chapter one should be able:

- To identify the benefits and issues for each organisational type
- To participate in a meaningful way in designing an appropriate organisation in the context of a particular global firm
- To understand the characteristics of the transnational model and to be able to introduce its features in a particular firm.

STRUCTURE, PROCESSES AND CULTURE

The configuration and evolution of structure, processes and culture in different globalisation settings can be best illustrated by the example of two companies which operate in a similar industrial environment: NV Philips and Matsushita.[2]

Philips: evolution of global organisation

Founded in 1882 in Eindhoven, Holland, as a producer of light bulbs, Philips rapidly expanded into geographical internationalisation as well as product diversification. As early as 1899 it started to export its products, and by 1912 it had established subsidiaries in the United States, Canada and France. Philips' product line expanded to electronic vacuum tubes, radios, X-rays and later on to electrical appliances, TVs, videos, electronic components, medical equipment and telephony. By the year 2000, Philips was a $30 billion company involved in 150 countries with nine major product lines. Philips' global organisational design was based on the predominance of national subsidiaries called National Organisations (NOs). Each NO built its own technical and marketing activities in order to adapt products to local conditions. Countries initiated product development – as, for instance, in Canada where the first colour TV was created. Although 14 product divisions in Eindhoven were theoretically in charge of product development and global marketing, national subsidiaries had the real power of making strategic decisions, since they controlled the assets and reported directly to the Board. Except for a few high-flyers, most executive careers at Philips were built within NOs. This organisational design was the 'administrative heritage'[3] of Philips' early expansion in international markets at a time when political, economic and technological forces were in favour of strategic adaptation and responsiveness to local country-specific conditions; Philips' design was representative of a multi-business geographical model. Table 3.1 gives a summary of the traditional Philips global organisational system.

Starting in the early 1980s, this global geographically oriented organisation was challenged by the forces of globalisation and the emergence of strong Japanese competitors. The ability of Philips to bring products rapidly to market and to produce them at competitive costs forced top management to reconsider the organisation. During the 1980s and 1990s four different chairmen embarked on reorganisation with the aim of moving away from the geographical decentralised confederation in favour of a more globally efficient network of operations. The restructuring was not without resistance and led to a drastic reduction in

Table 3.1 Philips' global organisational design until the late 1980s

Organisational dimensions	Need for local adaptation	Need for global leverage and efficiency
Structure		
Design	Geographical Units (NOs)	Product Divisions (PDs)
Power	NOs control assets Marketing Product adaptation Production	Research direction supervises eight separate laboratories located in Europe and the United States
Responsibilities	Responsible for profit and return on assets	PD formally responsible for product development and global marketing
Reporting	NOs report to the Board	
Processes		
Planning	Mainly made within NOs	An International Council established in the mid-1950s to organise meetings with the principal managers of the NOs and the Board. Frequent visits to foreign affiliates by senior corporate management
Decision-making	Senior Management Committees of each NO ensure that Product Groups' directions fit with national strategies	PDs organise cross-functional co-ordination PDs set directions for product marketing
Careers	Mostly within NOs except for top managers	Top managers (the elite group) have career built through successive foreign tours of duty
Culture	Strong technological and commercial competencies embodied in national culture	Strong technological and commercial culture corporate-wide

Source: Bartlett (1992).

headcount and to the disposal of several business lines. In 1990 Philips posted a loss of $2.5 billion. Tom Timmer, appointed Chairman in 1990, and later Cor Boonstra, who replaced him in 1996, rationalised the global structure by shifting the power from the national reorganisation toward global business units.

Matsushita: evolution of global organisation

Matsushita, founded in 1918 by Konosuke Matsushita, was, after the Second World War, the dominant Japanese player in the appliances and later consumer electronics industries. Benefiting from a 40 per cent market share in Japan, Matsushita embarked on an internationalisation strategy in 1953 with the opening of its American subsidiary, Matsushita Electric Corporation of America. Over the years, the company controlled more than 200 subsidiaries outside Japan. Those subsidiaries are divided into two broad categories: wholly owned single-product plants reporting directly to the product divisions in Japan and sales, marketing and assembling subsidiaries producing and selling product lines for local markets reporting to Matsushita Electric Trading Company (METC) a legal entity supervising overseas operations. The 36 central product divisions headquartered in Japan had a strong control over the first category of operations, while METC subsidiaries were tightly controlled by the Japanese headquarters through the assignment of Japanese expatriates to key positions in local subsidiaries. These Japanese expatriates maintained strong relationships with corporate senior executives, and corporate managers frequently visited local operations. Matsushita's organisational design was representative of a 'global hub' form of organisation. See Table 3.2 for details of Matsushita's global organisational design until the late 1980s.

In the mid-1980s a newly appointed President launched a programme named 'Operation Localisation', with the objective of putting in place localisation of personnel, technology, material and capital. Local nationals were appointed to key positions, procurement of components with local suppliers was progressively implemented and products could be adapted to meet local requirements. METC became the sole co-ordinator of all foreign operations and regional headquarters were set up in North America, Europe and South East Asia. In spite of all these efforts, the product divisions still played a dominant role in company strategy and few senior foreign managers occupied a central position.

Philips and Matsushita: the search for global organisational fit

The two examples just described illustrate quite well the search for 'fit' between the strategic requirements imposed upon global companies and their organisational responses. This evolutionary search is represented in Figure 3.1.

The vertical axis of Figure 3.1 measures the requirements for efficiency and leverage demanded by the industrial competitive context while the horizontal axis measures the requirement for local adaptation and responsiveness; this represents the Global Integration/Local Responsiveness Grid introduced in Chapter 1.

Table 3.2 Matsushita's global organisational design until the late 1980s

Organisational dimensions	Need for local adaptation	Need for global leverage and efficiency
Structure		
Design	Marketing and local production subsidiaries (overseas companies) reporting to METC	Product Companies (PCs) Reporting to PDs in Japan
Power	Overseas companies in charge of marketing and local production when needed. Planning of sales and profit determined centrally by METC	PDs in Japan responsible for product development (R&D), global production and sourcing
Responsibilities	Local marketing	PDs responsible for product development, global manufacturing and marketing
	Responsible for return on sales	Responsible for return on assets
Reporting	Subsidiaries report to METC	Subsidiaries report to PDs
Processes		
Planning	Mainly made at headquarters between METC and Product Divisions (PDs)	PDs prepare global product strategies
Decision-making	Autonomy of local managers to achieve targets	
Careers	Main functions in the hands of expatriates	Expatriate managers sent to transfer products and process technologies and provide headquarters with market information
	Expatriate managers maintain relationships with 'mentors' at headquarters	Expatriate managers maintain relationships with 'mentors' at headquarters
Culture		Matsushita philosophy: 'The Seven Spirits of Matsushita' developed by the company's founder is spread throughout the world by expatriate managers

Source: Harvard Business School case study 9-392-156, written by Robert Lightfoot under the supervision of Christopher Bartlett (1992).

The Philips' organisational design up to the 1980s is positioned in the lower right-hand corner as a decentralised confederation: the corporate headquarters in the centre are linked to the various national subsidiaries on a one-to-one basis with very little integration across subsidiaries. Each national subsidiary is shown tinted to indicate that the locus of strategic decision-making is in their hands. Matsushita's design, on the other hand, is located in the upper left-hand corner as an integrated global organisation with the locus of power in the centre.

Both designs are the result of the historical development of the firm – their 'administrative heritage' from the time when their international expansion started. Philips created subsidiaries abroad early in the twentieth century at a time when technological, economic and, later on, political barriers (the First and Second World Wars) forced each subsidiary to operate independently. Matsushita, which globalised its operations after the Second World War during a period of increasing trade

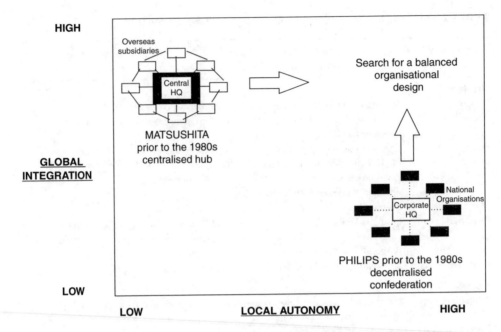

Figure 3.1   Philips and Matsushita: global organisational designs and their evolution

Source: Bartlett (1992).

liberalisation and technological development in transport and communication, could adopt a more centralised approach which favoured efficiency and transfer of product and manufacturing technologies across borders. Because the industrial context of the 1960s and 1970s was favourable to an global integrated approach, Matsushita's organisation was more appropriate than Philips'. As, for instance, in the case of the VCR technology, Philips' corporate headquarters was not able to persuade Philips North America, the US subsidiary, to adopt the V2000 system developed by Philips laboratories. Instead, Philips North America adopted the competitive VHS system. The successive reorganisations undertaken by various chairmen was an attempt to become more integrated. Those efforts are represented graphically by the West–East arrow in Figure 3.1. Matsushita, whose integrated design proved successful in the 1960s, 1970s and 1980s, felt on the other hand that an increased variety in market characteristics and sourcing opportunities demanded a more localised approach. This is represented by the South–North arrow in Figure 3.1. Both companies have tried to build on their strengths and compensate for their weaknesses by building an organisational design which simultaneously satisfies the requirements for global efficiency/leverage and local responsiveness.

By the mid-1980s both companies had undertaken some change in order to develop competencies in the dimension in which they were less strong. Philips attempted to gain efficiency and leverage while keeping its strong national respon-siveness, while Matsushita attempted to gain local responsiveness while preserving their strong global efficiency capabilities. Both companies tried to become 'multi-dimensional' in their organisation.

The organisational evolution of these two giants, Philips and Matsushita, is a good illustration of the constraints that globalisation puts on companies and the type of responses that are sought to solve the constraints of efficiency, leverage and responsiveness.

Since the 1990s, customer service has gained popularity among companies as part of their positioning and value proposition to customers. This strong customer focus has prompted some companies (e.g. Reuters and SingTel) to restructure their organisation and form departments which are based on *customer groups*. By having designated staff specialising in customer groups, customer needs and responsiveness can be better catered for.

With increased customer convenience and responsiveness, however, comes the trade-off of reduced technical competence among staff of the service provider. Since each person is now serving a customer group, their knowledge is spread across the wide range of products which are being offered to that particular customer group. One can argue that customers may not be expecting flawless technical advice (e.g. details of printer specification) or may not be able to discern that ineffective 'expert' advice is due to a lack of knowledge or underlying uncertainty surrounding the advice (e.g. bank's investment advice given to customers). The remaining part of this chapter will be devoted to describing and analysing different organisational models: the global functional model, the single and multi-business geographical models, the global product division model, the single and multi-business matrix models and the transnational model.

These models will be presented according to the respective contribution of the three dimensions of organisational design (structure, processes and culture) to the three value creation activities: innovation, operational efficiency and marketing impact.

THE GLOBAL FUNCTIONAL MODEL

The global functional design is based upon the worldwide centralisation of decision-making, co-ordination and control at the level of the key functional activities such as R&D, operations and marketing. All strategic decisions and operational policies are made at headquarters level. Country subsidiaries are local legal entities; the heads of country subsidiaries have responsibilities with the regard to the laws of the countries in which they operate, but in practice all the key business decisions relative to products, production, operations and marketing are activated from headquarters. The functional managers within the subsidiaries take their instruction from the corporate vice-president or director in charge of their function. The only autonomous decisions are those related to the practical implementation of policies, such as sales management, or those with a strong local legal content, such as tax reporting or personnel management.

This organisational model fits companies or business units of multi-business corporations operating in single business environments with strong demand for global integration and co-ordination.

The global functional organisational design is represented in Figure 3.2 and its characteristics described in Table 3.3. An example of global functional design is provided in Mini-Example 3.1

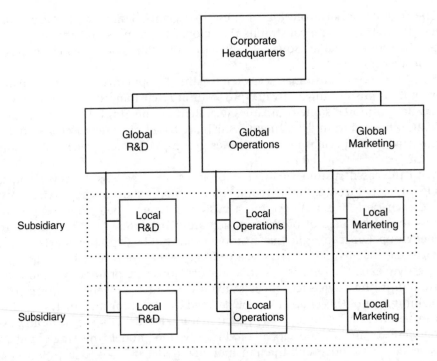

Figure 3.2 The global functional organisational design

Table 3.3 Characteristics of the global functional organisational design

Organisational dimension	Innovation	Efficiency of operations	Marketing impact
Structure Central functional executive exercises global power and responsibilities	■ Central R&D function ■ If various research centres, research policies are centrally lead ■ Subsidiaries' R&D managers report to central R&D	■ Central operational function such as VP manufacturing ■ Subsidiaries' operational managers report to central VP operations	■ Central marketing function ■ Subsidiaries' marketing managers report to central marketing vice-president ■ Country managers in charge of local interface with government and legal matters ■ Sales function quite autonomous
Processes	■ R&D strategy and budgets decided centrally ■ Control and reporting centrally organised ■ R&D worldwide policies ■ Global standardised products development	■ Global supply chain management ■ Global factories and operational centres ■ Central policies	■ Key marketing policies set globally ■ Global advertising ■ Global pricing ■ Global sales policies ■ Some local adaptation of sales practices depending upon authorisation by centre ■ Countries are nominally profit centres but without much power to influence profit

Culture			
	▪ Careers are managed globally	▪ Careers managed globally	▪ Marketing careers are managed globally
	▪ High level of transfer of personnel	▪ High level of transfer of personnel	▪ High level of transfer of personnel
	▪ Expatriates are key transferors of technology	▪ Expatriates are key transferors of best practice	▪ Expatriates are key transferors of best practice
	▪ Strong product/ technology identity	▪ Strong technology identity	▪ Strong brand identity

Mini-Example 3.1 Renault

Renault is a passenger car and light commercial vehicle company. Until the late 1990s it was essentially a regional player with operations mainly concentrated in Europe. In 1999 Renault acquired a controlling equity stake in Nissan automobiles in Japan, and in 2000 in Samsung's car division in Korea. Prior to those acquisitions Renault's organisational design was based on the global functional design in its two divisions: Renault passenger car division and Renault industrial vehicle division. The three major functions of R&D, manufacturing and marketing were driven from the centre. Local subsidiaries were in charge of operational management in the countries. Although technically local subsidiaries were profit centres, most of the parameters contributing to the profitability were set up centrally.

Source: Flament, Fujimura and Willes (2000).

Advantages of the global functional organisational design

The key advantages of this model are the efficiencies obtained through the coherence of decisions and policies, leading to the optimisation, concentration and specialisation of resources, which in turn produces economies of scale, avoids duplication of effort and favours rapid transfer of know-how from headquarters to the subsidiaries. The benefits of those efficiencies are best obtained when products are standardised and economies of scale and rapid transfer of central know-how are key determinants of competitive advantage – examples are commodities businesses such oil or basic chemicals, or industries in which manufacturing or operational systems demand size optimisation and complex supply chain logistics, such as car industries.

Disadvantages of the global functional organisational design

The disadvantages of this model are more visible when either the competitive context is fragmented into several segments, calling for distinct capabilities, or when the markets and business local environments are significantly different. In such cases a standardised, undifferentiated approach leads to inflexibility, local disfunctionalities and market rejection. Internally, it fosters bureaucracy and discourages initiative.

THE GEOGRAPHICAL MODEL

The geographical organisational design, unlike the global functional design, is based on the worldwide decentralisation of decision-making, co-ordination and control at the level of the subsidiaries. In such a model, central functions or product management roles are sometimes non-existent or, when they do exist, play an advisory, stimulating or co-ordinative role without much executive power. The relationships between the subsidiaries and the central functional directors or product managers are sometime referred as 'dotted-lines' relationships, to signify that there are no hierarchical links. Functional managers within business units report to the local country manager, who in turn reports either directly to the chief executive or to a central senior manager in charge of international operations. In many cases, intermediary executive powers are given to regional executives located at regional headquarters in the key region of the world. Country managers develop strategies and adapt or select products which fit with their local environment. Policies are set up locally. In many cases, country or regional managers sit on corporate executive committee. As in the case of Philips prior to the 1980s, the global strengths of the business come from its basic technological capabilities (products in particular) and from the global management of key expatriates who rotate from country to country.

The geographical organisational design is represented in Figure 3.3 and its characteristics described in Table 3.4. Mini-Example 3.2 provides an example of a geographical organisation.

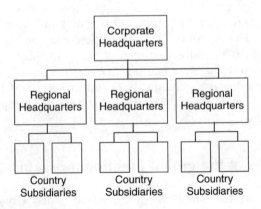

Figure 3.3 The geographical organisational design

Table 3.4 Characteristics of geographical organisational design

Organisational dimension	Innovation	Efficiency of operations	Marketing impact
Structure Countries or regional subsidiaries have strategic and operational responsibilities	■ R&D centres are distributed. ■ Central R&D centre focuses on fundamental research ■ Central R&D centre and product managers propose innovation but have no power to impose ■ Local companies have power to adapt products locally or have the discretion to choose from the corporate product portfolio the products they want to commercialise in their territory	■ Self-contained operations at the level of countries/regions ■ Scale efficiency obtained with country volume	■ Local brands and promotion ■ Local pricing ■ Local distribution and maintenance
Processes	■ Very little attempt to share and transfer best practices ■ Reliance on subsidiaries' self-interest ■ Regular information about corporate programmes through conferences and forums, but subsidiaries are free to decide what kind of innovation they adopt	■ Arm's-lengths transactions among subsidiaries and between central factories and subsidiaries ■ Transfer pricing issues ■ Very often information systems are not compatible	■ Marketing policies; subsidiaries' management have a high degree of discretion in implementation ■ Countries are profit and investment centres
Culture	■ Pride in local adapted products ■ Careers essentially local ■ Local identity ■ Autonomy	■ Careers essentially local ■ Local identity ■ Autonomy	■ Careers essentially local ■ Local identity ■ Entrepreneurship ■ Autonomy

Mini-Example 3.2 International Service Systems A/S (ISS)

Headquartered in Denmark, the ISS group specialises in cleaning services. It employs around 216,700 employees spread across some 120 companies and 34 countries. The group is organised around four major regional divisions: Asia/Pacific, Northern Europe, Western Europe and Southern and Eastern Europe. Poul Andreassen, who was the key architect of this organisational design, thought that the 'most profitable way to provide services is through small stand-alone companies led by a local manager who is encouraged to think of the business as his or her own. He intentionally erected a barrier around the operational units which he called "the Chinese Wall" to keep out top management'.[4] The role of the corporate centre is to provide financial and marketing expertise to the various countries.

Source: Ghoshal (1993).

Advantages of the geographical organisational design

The main advantage of this model is its flexibility and ability to incorporate local specificity into the company's competitive approach. Products tailored to consumer demands, advertising campaigns reflecting local culture, and investment practices fitting with national policies enable companies to make more appealing value propositions. The ability to adapt and change competitive parameters without involving lengthy negotiations with the corporate centre gives geographically structured companies a better chance to capture rising opportunities, or react rapidly to changing local conditions. Those advantages are more significant when customers' tastes and needs differ significantly across countries, for economic, cultural, social or political reasons and when scale economies can be attached easily within national boundaries. Traditionally foods, cosmetics, personal services and government-regulated industries are those in which geographical design has worked well.

Disadvantages of the geographical organisational design

Disadvantages arise when local autonomy creates too much duplication, erodes economies of scale or slows down the transfer of innovation. When customers become global and require a 'global' pricing or service, geographically structured companies may lose their competitiveness if they do not introduce some element of global co-ordination. As seen in Chapter 1, the overall competitive context in many industries has been pushing in favour of globalisation, and geographically managed companies like Philips have been disadvantaged.

THE SINGLE MATRIX MODEL

The single matrix model is an organisational design in which both functions and geography are given equal power and responsibilities. In such a case the R&D global vice-president would be responsible for the global R&D budget and would have some authority over the career of scientists and designers, but country managers would have some authority over the allocation of resources, local laboratories and the career of scientists or designers. A similar dual responsibility would apply for operations and marketing. The end result of that design is a shared executive power which puts middle-managers in a situation of having 'dual bosses'. This design is very often used by professional firms such as engineering companies, advertising or consulting firms.

The objective of such a design is to solve the requirements of efficiency, leverage and responsiveness through a dual structure. It aims to develop a culture of 'thinking globally, acting locally' by institutionalising the tensions arising from the two competitive imperatives.

The single matrix organisational design is represented in Figure 3.4 and its characteristics described in Table 3.5. An example of a single matrix structure is provided in Mini-Example 3.3.

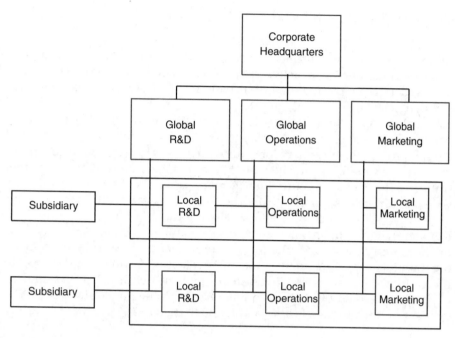

Figure 3.4   The single matrix organisational design

Table 3.5   Characteristics of the single matrix organisational design

Organisational dimension	Innovation	Efficiency of operations	Marketing impact
Structure Both functions and countries are given equal power and responsibilities	▪ Central R&D responsible for product innovation ▪ Local subsidiaries responsible for product adaptation	▪ Central operations responsible for global operations and optimisation ▪ Local subsidiaries responsible for local results	▪ Central marketing responsible for global marketing strategies ▪ Local subsidiaries responsible for local marketing strategies
Processes	▪ Global research strategic plan and budget drawn up by global vice-president ▪ Local budgets at subsidiaries level ▪ Conferences for transfer of best practices	▪ Strategic investment in global factories or operational centres by global vice-president ▪ Global best practices ▪ Local operational responsibilities	▪ Global marketing plan ▪ Local marketing plans ▪ Reconciliation through strategic planning meetings ▪ 'Think global, act local'
Culture	▪ 'Think global, act local' ▪ Dual identity ▪ Negotiation	▪ Local operating procedures ▪ 'Think global, act local' ▪ Dual identity ▪ Negotiation	▪ Dual identity ▪ Negotiation

Mini-Example 3.3   Citibank Global Account Management

Although, as a group, Citibank is structured along a multi-business geographical reporting line, one of its activities, the management of global accounts, is managed according to the single matrix design. Global accounts are the large corporate customers who themselves operate globally and who may need a coherent set of financial services across the world. The traditional geographical structure focusing on the individual maximisation of profits at country level did not provide the incentives for country managers to accept some low-profit deals in one country for the benefit of gaining higher-profit deals in another country. The global account management team, called World Corporate Group at Citibank, appoints a Parent Account Manager (PAM) in the country in which the customer's headquarter is located. Every year, this PAM negotiates a global financing plan with the customer's Chief Financial Officer. In the country subsidiaries the local account managers, who report both to the country manager and to the PAM, are in charge of providing local services to the customer's subsidiaries. This system, implemented in 1974, has allowed Citibank to become a global leader in global corporate financial services. (The system was discontinued in 1981 but re-established in 1985.)

Source: Malnight and Yoshino (1995).

The advantages and disadvantages of this model will be discussed together with the multi-business matrix model presented later.

THE MULTI-BUSINESS GLOBAL PRODUCT DIVISION MODEL

When a company has diversified in several business activities to become a multi-business corporation, it has the choice among three different organisational models to manage its global operations. Either it organises itself along the *product dimension* or along the *geographical dimension* or with a *matrix*. The first organisational model is known as the multi-business global product division organisation, which is represented in Figure 3.5 and its characteristics described in Table 3.6. Mini-Example 3.4 provides an example of a multi-business global product division organisation.

In this model, the company is divided into *business divisions*, each in charge of a product or service line. Each division chief executive is responsible for the global performance of its business and, as such, formulates his global strategy and puts in place the organisational design which fits best its competitive context. In some cases divisions act independently from each other and subsidiaries of one division in one country frequently do not interact at all with subsidiaries of another division. Within the division, the organisational design can be one of the three kinds described earlier: global functional, geographical or matrix.

If the competitive contexts of the division differ, one division can be organised geographically, for instance, and another use the global functional model. Country

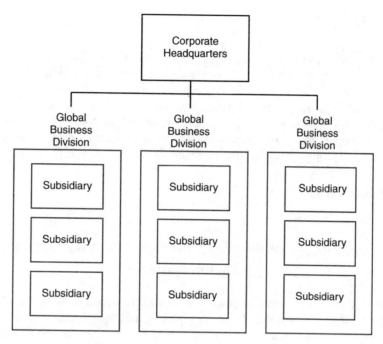

Figure 3.5   The multi-business global product division organisational design

Table 3.6   Characteristics of the multi-business global product division organisational design

Organisational dimension	Innovation	Efficiency of operations	Marketing impact
Structure Global strategic and operational power and responsibilities given to separate product divisions	▪ R&D initiated by product divisions ▪ Encourages global standardisation	▪ Encourages co-ordination of activities within divisions ▪ Strong efficiency and scale economies within divisions ▪ Poor co-ordination among divisions	▪ Each division develops its own marketing approach ▪ Marketing adapted to industry contexts
Processes	▪ Within divisions	▪ Within divisions	▪ Within divisions
Culture	▪ Careers and identity within divisions	▪ Careers and identity within divisions	▪ Careers and identity within divisions

subsidiaries managers report to division heads. In this model, the divisional global headquarters of one business can be located in one country while the headquarters of another division are based in another country and the corporate headquarters in another one. The corporate headquarters' role is limited to overall strategic planning, financial control and executive career management.

When potential synergies exist between divisions, the corporate headquarters play a more active role and provide some corporate support to subsidiaries such as training, logistics, legal matters and financing, either directly or through regional corporate headquarters.

Mini-Example 3.4 Tyco

Tyco International Ltd is a multi-business conglomerate controlling 150 subsidiaries grouped into four core businesses: healthcare and specialty products, fire and safety services, flow control and electrical and electronic components operating in 80 countries throughout the world. Corporate management gives complete strategic autonomy to the business units and does not interfere with 'managing' synergies. Subsidiaries report to the businesses and no attempt is made to co-ordinate their activities within countries.

Source: Kennedy *et al.* (2001).

Advantages of the multi-business global product division model

This model gives the global company the flexibility to adapt its structure to the competitive context of each business. By giving division executives the strategic responsibility for their business, this design provides the organisational mechanisms for global efficiency and co-ordination. This model tends to be favoured by the vast majority of multi-business corporations.

Disadvantages of the multi-business global product division model

The disadvantages of this model appear most clearly in countries or regions like China, or when customers demand a strong co-ordination among businesses, which is the case in information system integration or big engineering projects. If no organisational mechanisms compensate for the autonomy of product divisions, there are risks of duplication of commercial effort – as, for instance, when the same customer is approached by various sales persons coming from different divisions of the same company for the same project. The second obvious disadvantage of this model comes from the predominance given to *global efficiency* as opposed to *local responsiveness*.

THE MULTI-BUSINESS GEOGRAPHICAL MODEL

In the multi-business geographical organisational design, country subsidiaries are given full strategic and operational responsibilities for all product lines in their territory. In this design, the central global functions and product divisions have a 'support' or 'dotted-line' role. Countries or regional units are profit centres and act autonomously. The multi-business geographical organisational design is

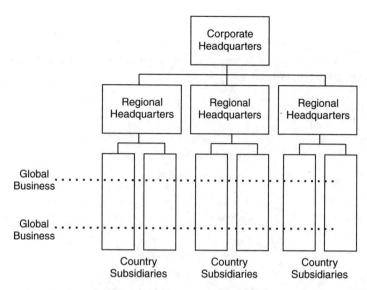

Figure 3.6 Multi-business geographical organisational design

Table 3.7 Characteristics of the multi-business geographical organisational design

Organisational dimension	Innovation	Efficiency of operations	Marketing impact
Structure Countries or regional subsidiaries have strategic and operational responsibilities Global products or functions have a 'support' role	▪ Adaptation of products to local conditions ▪ Optimisation of product lines at country level	▪ Adaptation of products to local conditions ▪ Optimisation of product lines at country level	▪ Full localisation of marketing mix conditions ▪ Optimisation of marketing activities at country level
Processes	▪ Country-specific	▪ Country-specific	▪ Country-specific
Culture	▪ Country identity ▪ Careers within countries	▪ Country identity ▪ Careers within countries	▪ Country identity ▪ Careers within countries

represented in Figure 3.6 and its characteristics described in Table 3.7. Mini-Example 3.5 gives an example of the multi-business organisational design.

Advantages of the multi-business geographical model

The main advantages of this design are its *flexibility* and *adaptiveness* to local conditions. It encourages the optimisation of the product and investment portfolio at country level, fitting with local tastes and regulatory conditions.

Mini-Example 3.5   Vodafone

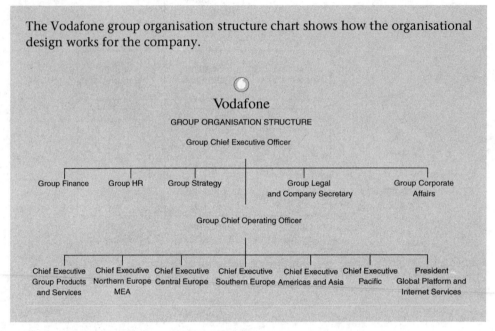

The Vodafone group organisation structure chart shows how the organisational design works for the company.

Source: Vodafone's website <www.vodafone.com>.

Disadvantages of the multi-business geographical model

Sub-optimisation of resources allocation and delays in new product introduction are the main pitfalls of this model. In industries in which the pressures for globalisation are high, this model leads to inefficiency and loss of competitive advantage. Over the past 20 years, this model has progressively been abandoned by many large global corporations and replaced either by the global product division or by the multi-business matrix (described later).

THE MULTI-BUSINESS MATRIX MODEL

As in the single matrix model, this design emphasises dual (and sometime triple) responsibilities. In the case of multi-business companies, the responsibilities are shared between the product divisions and the geographical units.

The multi-business matrix organisational design is represented in Figure 3.7 and its characteristics described in Table 3.8. Mini-Example 3.6 gives an example of the multi-business matrix organisational design.

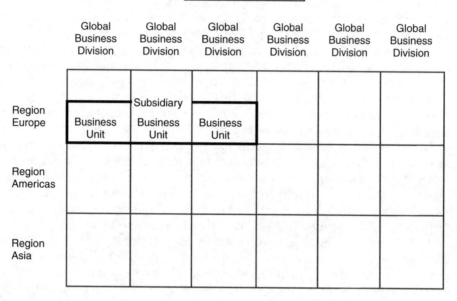

Figure 3.7   Multi-business matrix organisational design

Table 3.8   Characteristics of the multi-business matrix organisational design

Organisational dimension	Innovation	Efficiency of operations	Marketing impact
Structure Strategic and operational responsibilities shared by product and geographical units	▪ Global product divisions lead global product developments ▪ Country management adapt products and services locally	▪ Global factories and operational units ▪ Local factories ▪ Integration of supply chain	▪ Global marketing 'guidance' ▪ Local integration of product portfolio
Processes Dual systems Free flow of information Multidimensional data bases	▪ Dual strategic plans ▪ Shared information systems ▪ Transfer of 'best practices'	▪ Dual strategic plans ▪ Shared information systems ▪ Transfer of 'best practices'	▪ Dual strategic plans ▪ Shared information systems ▪ Transfer of 'best practices'
Culture 'Think global, act local'	▪ Sharing and negotiating culture	▪ Negotiating	▪ Optimisation

Mini-Example 3.6 BASF

The BASF Group is one of the world's largest chemical corporations, with manufacturing facilities scattered throughout 39 countries and customers in over 170 countries. In 1999, the company's sales reached 29.5 billion Euros with pre-tax profits of 2.9 billion Euros. The group's activities are divided into five segments containing 17 Operating Divisions that were further sub-divided into Strategic Business Units (SBUs). These products are organisationally balanced by 12 Regional Divisions and 14 Corporate and Functional Divisions. This provided BASF with a three-dimensional matrix. In the 1980s, most important business decisions were still taken in the Ludwigshafen headquarters; organisations with regional responsibilities remained sited in Germany, for the most part staffed by Germans. At the beginning of the 1990s, as part of a new globalisation drive, the BASF Group made a major effort to decentralise its international business, moving many of the company's operations and decision-making capabilities and key region-sensitive activities, such as marketing, as well as certain administrative functions into three principal geographical areas: Europe, NAFTA and Asia. As part of BASF's long-term strategy, manufacturing capabilities in each region were slated to receive major investments, with the eventual aim of increasing locally manufactured content to 70 per cent and above. Decision-making was to be non-confrontational; where possible, executives sought to forge a consensus through compromise, with the overall aim of maintaining the long-term health and profits of the BASF Group as a whole. In fact, the ability to compromise represented a crucial career skill within BASF culture; without it, few executives could hope to advance.[6]

Source: Crawford and Schütte (2000).

Advantages of the multi-business matrix organisational design

As Percy Barnevick, a former Chairman of Asea Brown Boveri, puts it, 'Matrix management is like breathing, whether you like it or not you are obliged to do it'.[5] The multi-dimensional matrix design is supposed to internalise the pressures for global efficiency, leverage and local responsiveness, as well as achieving synergies among businesses. The mechanism is twofold: at the business level, the global dimension is represented by the executive in charge of the worldwide product division, while the local dimension is in the hands of the business units in the countries. The synergies among businesses are achieved at the region or country level by the regional or country manager. Taking, for example, the case of a power-generation firm selling a large project to a public utility in Venezuela through international bids. The country sales persons will be in contact with the customer at the pre-bidding stage, discussing specifications and bidding modalities. To make an effective proposition, several divisions have to be involved: one for turbines, one for generators, one for transformation and one for regulation. A *bidding task force* will be gathered by the Venezuela country manager in order to co-ordinate the bids of the various divisions. Assuming that the company wins the contract, the country manager will be credited with the sales and the profit on these sales, while each product division will be credited for the sales and the profits for their respective product offering. The project manager in Venezuela will effectively report to the country manager as well as to the different divisions: she/he will be the one who will manage the tensions between her/his various 'bosses'. By forcing the project managers permanently to make the needed trade-off between the product divisions and the country management, the matrix structure is supposed to optimise the dual requirements of global efficiency and local responsiveness.

Disadvantages of the multi-business matrix organisational design

Matrix organisations are complex and may lead to power struggles that cancel out their expected benefits. There are five main pitfalls of matrix structures:

(a) *Role ambiguity*. Middle-managers living in matrix structures are more than often placed in situations where their 'dual bosses' put pressure on them to achieve conflicting objectives. While, theoretically, the matrix organisation is designed to force those managers to 'solve' those conflicts, in reality it does not. Managers will follow whatever instructions they consider come from the 'most powerful boss'. The matrix becomes an illusion.

(b) *Dilution of responsibilities*. In order to make a matrix work properly, numerous conflict resolution mechanisms have to be put in place, particularly committees, meetings and task forces. Decisions take a long time and, at the end of the day, it is very difficult to untangle who is responsible for what. In case of failure or mistake, it is always possible to find excuses for decisions made by an anonymous unaccountable committee.

(c) *Cost inefficiencies*. Co-ordination costs of matrix structures – such as travel, communication, time spent in meetings and delays in making decisions – tend to rise very rapidly without compensation in competitive benefits.

(d) *Turf battles*. By design, matrix structures encourage product divisions and country managers to assert their power, leading to numerous territorial conflicts. The worst scenario is when customers themselves become involved in the conflict; for instance, receiving different value propositions from different organisational units.

(e) *Costs of compromise*. The main danger of the dual tension resolution implied in the matrix design is the danger of compromise. In order to satisfy their 'two bosses', managers may adopt middle-of-the-road solutions, ultimately leading to mediocre decisions. To take an example of such an outcome, let us consider a lubricant company: the sales people in Japan ask for 11 different sizes of cans to serve the motorist market. The global product division has decided that five sizes of cans are sufficient to cover the market needs and that it is more cost effective to focus on those five types of cans. Here is a typical conflict between global efficiency (five sizes) and local responsiveness (Japanese market demands 11 sizes). A matrix structure may encourage the local lubricant manager to 'compromise' and propose seven sizes: a decision that will not satisfy the Japanese customer, and will increase costs.

These pitfalls have encouraged many corporations to abandon this type of structural design and return to a simpler product or geographical organisation structure. However, this does not overcome the fact that in a global company, the tensions between efficiency, leverage and responsiveness are permanent, like 'breathing'. If the matrix structure that is supposed to achieve a symbiotic reconciliation between various competitive requirements does not fulfil this reconciliation, how can it be achieved?

Some companies have implemented *hybrid structures* by which the global product dimension co-exists with a regional geographical structure but without forming a matrix, but the vast majority of global firms came to realise that structural answers were not sufficient and whatever the design, the global efficiency and innovation/ local responsiveness requirements could be achieved only by a cultural approach. The theory of this approach is provided by the *transnational model*.

HYBRID STRUCTURAL MODELS

Managers in such a structure follow a *single line of reporting*. Global products divisions act as suppliers of innovation, products and components to geographical units in charge of marketing, local production and product adaptation, if needed. One can distinguish two types of hybrid model:

(a) The traditional international division model described briefly in Chapter 2
(b) Complex dual structures.

The international divisions model

The international divisions model has been described as the first organisational structure adopted by firms at an early stage of internationalisation.[7] In this model, there is a clear distinction between the home-country business units managed by divisional executives in charge of product development, manufacturing and home marketing plus exports and the international subsidiaries who, under the leadership of an international division executive, develop their countries' strategic development. The overseas subsidiaries possess a high degree of autonomy, but are dependent upon the home-country divisions for products and technical support. To the extent that international sales represent a small proportion of total sales and transactions between home divisions and country subsidiaries are limited, this model fulfils the requirements of global efficiency and local responsiveness.[8] When international sales increase and represent a significant proportion of total turnover, the company begins to feel the need to integrate all activities in a global structure, either geographical, divisional or matrix. In their seminal work, John Stopford and Louis Wells have described this evolution as represented in Figure 3.8.

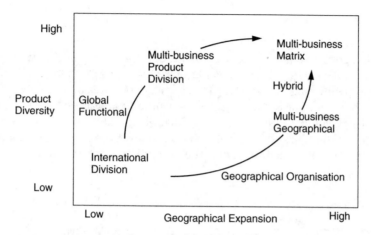

Figure 3.8 The evolution of global organisational models

Source: Adapted from Stopford and Wells (1972).

Complex dual structural models

As mentioned earlier, the logic of dual models is to create within the global organisation a mix of different designs. For instance, Citibank built an organisation in
which a global product division design (consumer banking and corporate banking),
a geographical design (country subsidiaries) and a single matrix design for global
account management co-exist. Another example is provided by 3M in Europe, which
has adopted a global product division design in the form of European Business Centres
(ECBs), which would be pan-European product line organisations reporting to the
US main product divisions in charge of R&D, manufacturing and technical services
to customers. The geographical dimension is represented by regional subsidiaries,
who are in charge of the operational results within the countries.[9] The ACER group
has similarly divided its global operations in two categories, SBUs which essentially
develop products and manufacturing components in world-class factories and
Regional Business Units (RBUs) which are locally based and in charge of assembling, marketing and sales (see Mini-Example 3.7). These dual complex designs
offer the flexibility to take care of the many specifics of contexts and businesses
without locking managers into the straitjacket of a unique organisational design.
The obvious pitfalls of these designs are their complexity, which requires from
managers a culture similar to that advocated by the 'transnational' model.

THE TRANSNATIONAL MODEL

Contrary to the other models presented earlier, the transnational organisational
design model does not focus on organisational structure but on *management
processes and culture.*[10] The transnational design does not prescribe any particular

Mini-Example 3.7   ACER

The ACER group, created in Taiwan in 1976, is one of the largest PC manufacturers. It employs personnel in 120 enterprises in 44 countries. Its Chairman, Stan
Shih, has organised it global operations according to the client–server principle.
The business units are divided into two broad categories: the SBUs which
essentially develop products and manufacturing components in world-class
factories and the RBUs which are locally based and are in charge of assembling,
marketing and sales. Each unit is at the same time client and server:

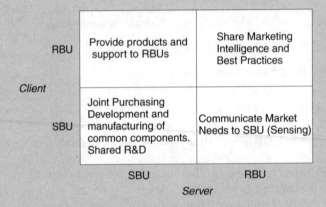

Stan Shih wants local company managers to own a local shareholding of
equity. 'At the heart of the client–server organisation lies a closely linked team
of mature and experienced managers committed to long-term success of their
own piece of the ACER group. Mutual understanding and trust, communication
and consensus are the cornerstone of ACER management'.[11]

organisational structure, but recognises that a global organisation is made up of
four types of differentiated managerial roles:

(a) *Global business managers* act as strategists, architects of assets distribution and
    competencies leveraging and co-ordinators of global activities
(b) *Country managers* act as sensors of local opportunities and threats, builders of
    national resources and contributors to global competitive development
(c) *Functional managers* act as specialists, looking after new developments
    and making sure that best practices are shared and transferred across the
    organisation
(d) *Corporate managers* act as overall organisational leaders and developers of
    talent.

These four roles can be distributed within a global product, a geographical or a matrix structure, the important thing being that managers develop a 'matrix in the mind'.

The seven key features of the transnational design are:

(a) Business units are part of a network, which follows the principle of *reciprocal dependencies*.
(b) A *non-dominant dimension*. All roles are important for competitive success and therefore no dimension, global, functional or geographical, predominates.
(c) A clearly defined and tightly controlled set of *operating systems*, and in particular of a transparent and multidimensional information system.
(d) Good *interpersonal relationships*.
(e) *Inter-unit decision forums* with active participation of global and functional managers in subsidiaries' boards.
(f) Strong *corporate values*.
(g) A culture of *sharing and willingness to collaborate*.

Mini-Example 3.7 discusses ACER, a Taiwanese computer manufacturer who has designed an organisational design based on a dual complex structure supported by an organisational culture similar to the transnational model.

Since 1990, global corporations have come to understand that the search for an ideal structure is vain, and that what matters more is the way managers behave. Most of them have now invested in the development of attitudes, skills and behaviour in line with the 'transnational' model (see Figure 3.9).

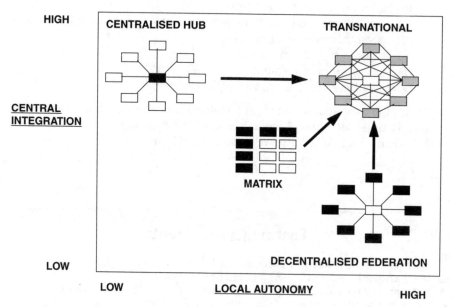

Figure 3.9 Convergence of global organisational designs

Source: Adapted from Bartlett and Ghoshal (1989).

SUMMARY AND KEY POINTS

1. A global business organisation should balance the following dual requirements:

    ■ efficiently maintain *competitive advantages* across borders
    ■ adapt to *local conditions*.

2. Organisational designs.

    ■ There are three main models of organisational design:
       -   *Global hub*:   a worldwide functional or global product structure
       -   *Confederation*:   a multinational geographical structure
       -   *Multidimensional*:   a matrix or transnational structure

    ■ There are three key elements of organisational design:
       -   *Organisational structure*:   assignment of roles, responsibilities and power
       -   *Organisational processes*:   decision-making, resource allocation, rewards and appraisal systems, planning and control
       -   *Organisational culture*:   shared values, reward system

    ■ Types of *organisational designs* (or models):
    (see also the summary of the common types of models in Table 3.9 on p. 93).

    ■ The *Transnational* model
       -   is different from the other organisational designs as it focuses on management processes and culture instead of organisational structures
       -   possesses seven main features:
          (a)   a network of business units
          (b)   a non-dominant dimension
          (c)   a clearly defined and tightly controlled set of information systems
          (d)   good interpersonal relationships
          (e)   inter-unit decision forums
          (f)   strong corporate values
          (g)   a willingness to share and collaborate

    ■ Most global companies have now realised that the search for an ideal structure is futile and have invested in the development of *attitudes, skills and behaviour* which are in line with the transnational model.

Learning assignments

1   Why have Philips and Matsushita changed their organisational design over time?
2   What are the benefits of having a geographical organisation?
3   What are the typical difficulties in implementing a matrix organisation?
4   What are the characteristics of the transnational model?
5   To what extent does the transnational model differ from the other organisational models?

Table 3.9 Types of organisational design

	Global functional model	Geographical model	Single matrix model	Multi-business global product division model	Multi-business geographical model	Multi-business matrix model	International divisions model	Dual complex structure model
Organisational structure	Centralised decision-making, co-ordination and control	Decentralised decision-making, co-ordination and control	Both functions and geography are given equal power and responsibilities	▪ Each business division is responsible for a product or a service ▪ Within the division, organisational design can be matrix or global functional or geographical	Country subsidiaries have full strategic and operational responsibilities for all products in their territories	Emphasises dual or triple responsibilities which are shared between product divisions and geographical units	Overseas subsidiaries have high autonomy but rely upon home country division for products and technical support	A mix of different designs with global product division and geographical subsidiaries
Supporting line(s)	Functional manager reports to vice-president or director in charge of their functions	Functional manager reports to local country manager	Middle-managers typically have two bosses	Country subsidiary managers report to division heads	Central global functions and product divisions have a 'dotted-line' role	Same as single matrix model	Division executives manage home country businesses and international division executives manager international subsidiaries	Reporting line is complex and depends on the choice of organisational design

Table 3.9 (Continued)

	Global functional model	Geographical model	Single matrix model	Multi-business global product division model	Multi-business geographical model	Multi-business matrix model	International divisions model	Dual complex structure model
Advantages	■ Efficiencies ■ Economies of scale ■ Rapid transfer of know-how	■ Flexibility ■ Can incorporate local needs ■ Can quickly adapt to market conditions	■ Global efficiencies ■ Local responsiveness	■ Flexibility ■ Global efficiencies ■ Global co-ordination	■ Flexibility ■ Adaptive to local conditions ■ Optimisation of product and investment portfolio at country level	■ Refer to the single matrix model	■ Global efficiencies ■ Local responsiveness	■ Flexibility
Disadvantages	■ Inflexibility ■ Local disfunctionalities ■ Market rejection ■ Bureaucracy ■ Discourages initiatives	■ Diseconomies of scale ■ Duplication ■ Lack of global co-ordination means poor at serving global customers	■ Potential power struggles ■ Role ambiguity ■ Dilution of responsibilities ■ Cost inefficiencies ■ Turf battles ■ Costs of compromise	■ Duplication of commercial effort ■ Lack of local responsiveness	■ Sub-optimisation of resources allocation ■ Delay in new product introduction ■ Inefficiencies and loss of competitive advantage for industries which require globalisation	■ Refer to the single matrix model	■ Inflexibility ■ Market rejection	■ Complexity
Potential application	Single business environment with strong demand for global integration and co-ordination	Businesses where customer tastes or needs differ significantly across countries	Professional firms such as consulting or engineering	Vast majority of multi-business corporations with relatively high product diversity and significant geographical expansion	Becoming less popular with large global corporations	Decreasing popularity	Other models will be used when international sales become a significant amount of turnover	Companies with sophisticated and diverse offerings

Key words

- 'Dotted-lines' relationship
- Global hub
- International divisions
- Matrix
- Organisational culture
- Organisational processes
- Organisational structure
- Transnational

Web resource

<http://www.mckinseyquarterly.com/category_archive.asp?tk=86032::&L3 =30>
McKinsey Quarterly – Organisational Design.

Notes

1. Prahalad (1986).
2. This example is derived from Bartlett (1999).
3. The concept of 'administrative heritage' was developed in Bartlett and Ghoshal (1989).
4. This quotation is taken from Ackenhusen (1993).
5. Quoted in Kets de Vries (1993).
6. Stopford and Wells (1972).
7. Franko (1976).
8. Ackenhusen (1994).
9. The transnational model was developed by Bartlett and Ghoshal (1989). See also Bartlett and Ghoshal (1990, 1992).
10. The case and quotations are taken from Clyde-Smith (1997).

References and further reading

Ackenhusen, Mary, 'ISS-International Service System A/S', INSEAD Case Study 11/93/4220, 1993a.

Ackenhusen, Mary, 'The 3M Company: Integrating Europe', INSEAD Case Study 06/94/4317, 1993b.

Bartlett, Christopher A., 'MNCs: Get Off the Reorganization Merry-Go-Round', *Harvard Business Review*, March–April 1983, pp. 138–46.

Bartlett, Christopher A, '"Philips and Matsushita": A Portrait of Two Evolving Companies', Harvard Business School, Case Study 9-392-156, 1992.

Bartlett, Christopher A., '"Philips vs Matsushita': Preparing for a New Round', Harvard Business School Case Study 9-399-102, 1999.

Bartlett, Christopher A. and Sumantra Ghoshal, *Managing Across Borders: The Transnational Solution*. Boston, MA: Harvard Business School Press, 1989.

Bartlett, Christopher A. and Sumantra Ghoshal, 'Matrix Management: Not a Structure, A Frame of Mind', *Harvard Business Review*, July–August 1990, pp. 138–45.

Bartlett, Christopher A. and Sumantra Ghoshal, 'What is a Global Manager?', *Harvard Business Review*, September–October 1992, pp. 124–32.

Clyde-Smith, Deborah, 'The ACER Group: Building an Asian Multinational', INSEAD Euro Asia Centre Case Study 01/98-4712, 1997.

Crawford, Robert and Hellmut Schütte, 'BASF: Working the Matrix in Asia', INSEAD Euro Asia Centre Case Study 04/2999-4845, 2000.

Davis, Stanley M., *Managing and Organizing Multinational Corporations*. Oxford: Pergamon Press, 1979.

Flamant, Anne-Claire, Sumie Fujimura and Pierre Willes, 'Renault and Nissan: A Marriage of Reason', INSEAD Case Study 10/2001-4928, 2000.

Franko, Larry, *The European Multinationals*. New York: Harper & Row, 1976.

Ghoshal, Sumantra, 'ISS-International Service System A/S', INSEAD Case Study 11/93/4220, 1993.

Kennedy, Robert E., Cynthia A. Montgomery, Lisa Cladderton and Harold Hogan, 'Tyco International (A)', Harvard Business School Case 9-798-061 (1998).

Kets de Vries, Manfred, 'Percy Barnevick and ABB', INSEAD Case Study 05/94/4308, 1994.

Malnight, Thomas W. and Michael Y. Yoshino, 'Citibank: Global Customer Management', Harvard Business School Case Study 9-395-142, 1995.

Prahalad, C.K., 'The Dominant Logic', *Strategic Management Journal*, 7(6), 1986, pp. 485–501.

Pucik, Vladimir, Noel M. Tichy and Carole K. Barnett, *Globalizing Management: Creating and Leading the Cooperative Organization*. New York: John Wiley, 1992.

Stopford, John and Louis Wells, *Strategy and Structure of Multinational Enterprises*. New York: Basic Books, 1972.

4

Global strategic alliances

While Chapters 1–3 looked at globalisation of industries, firms and organisational structure, Chapter 4 and Chapter 5 look at two main vehicles through which firms have globalised over the past 30 years: *global strategic alliances* and *global mergers and acquisitions* (M&As).

With increased pressures for globalisation, technological developments and compression of time to market, companies have increasingly searched outside their internal boundaries to build or reinforce their global competitive capabilities. Since 1980 there has been a dramatic increase of international strategic alliances, mergers and acquisitions.

In this chapter we will look at the strategic and managerial issues involved with global strategic alliances, while in Chapter 5 we will study more particularly global M&As.

Strategic alliances are not recent phenomena, but their pace of growth and the variety of their forms has been increasing. In the new economy, alliances are the normal way of doing business. We will first define what is a strategic alliance, discuss the various potential types of alliances and analyse the aspects of forming, analysing, negotiating and implementing global strategic alliances.

An **alliance** is the sharing of capabilities between two or more firms with the view of enhancing their competitive advantages and/or creating new business without losing their respective strategic autonomy. A *global alliance* is one in which the object is either to develop a *global market presence* (global reach alliance) or to enhance the *worldwide competitive capabilities* of the firm (global leverage alliance).

There is a variety of types of alliances: some of them have a global scope, with the perspective of enhancing the competitive presence of the partners across the world, some have a more local focus, the global firm wishes to penetrate a given country by setting up local joint ventures.

A framework to study the various steps of alliance formation and implementation has four main steps:

- Understanding the *strategic context* and spelling out the *strategic value* of an alliance
- Analysis of *partner(s)*: strategic fit, capabilities fit, cultural fit and organisational fit
- Negotiation and design of the alliance *structure*
- *Implementation*: integration, co-operation and evolution.

At the end of the chapter we shall present some criteria for successful alliances.

At the end of the chapter one should be able:

- To formulate a global alliance strategy
- To analyse the various fits among partners
- To structure an alliance negotiation
- To anticipate potential issues in alliance management and to set-up the proper mechanisms to solve them.

A STORY OF TWO PARTNERSHIPS: FUJI XEROX AND DAEWOO–GM

In 1962, Fuji Xerox, a 50/50 joint venture between Fuji Photo Film and Rank Xerox, was established to sell photocopiers and related products and services to the Japanese and some Asian markets. The Japanese government at the time refused the approval of a marketing joint venture and forced local manufacturing. Fuji Xerox was granted the right to exploit Xerox patents in Japan and the exclusivity of marketing products in Japan, Indonesia, Korea and the Philippines. Managed by a team of Japanese executives, Fuji Xerox progressively transformed itself from a pure local regional organisation to a global partner for Xerox, developing new products and leading the way in containing competition from Japanese firms such as Canon or Ricoh. Fuji Xerox, which during the 1970s and 1980s was at the forefront of Japanese competition, initiated a series of initiatives such as Total Quality Management (TQM) and new product development for small photocopiers. Thanks to those initiatives, Xerox was able to fight back against Canon. Today, Fuji Xerox is a global partner of Xerox, involved in R&D, manufacturing of global products and marketing over the whole Asia Pacific region.

In December 1991, Kim Woo Chong, Chairman of the South Korean conglomerate, Daewoo, and Jack Smith, Vice-Chairman of General Motors, started talks about ending their 15-year-old joint venture. Both partners had for some time been dissatisfied with various aspects of the relationship. The main problems revolved around quality, technology transfer, capital infusion, market access and sales support and management style. The joint venture was dissolved after each partner blamed the other for not fulfilling its contractual obligations.[1]

Those two examples show two different alliance paths, one successful and one unsuccessful. Both of them started with a local scope that very rapidly became global. In the case of Fuji Xerox, the alignment of objectives between partners and the mutual trust that was built up over time were a source of a fruitful partnership. In the case of Daewoo–GM, lack of alignment of objectives and trust led to the dissolution of the venture.

STRATEGIC ALLIANCES: TYPOLOGY AND FRAMEWORK

An alliance can be defined as the *sharing of capabilities between two or more firms* with the view of enhancing their competitive advantages and/or creating new business without losing their respective strategic autonomy. What makes an alliance *'strategic'* is that the sharing of capabilities, such as R&D, manufacturing or marketing affects the long-term competitiveness of the firms involved and implies a relatively long-term commitment of resources by partners.

According to economists, a joint effort involving the contribution of separate firms can be organised either through a *market contract*, such as a buyer–supplier contract, or through the *merger of capabilities* under a single management control, as in the case of a merger, an acquisition or an internal development. An alliance is somewhere in between when either full control is not feasible, for legal or practical reasons, or when a contract is difficult to draw up because of the uncertainties involved and none of the parties involved has the ability to develop the needed capability internally. As a consequence, a strategic alliance has been sometimes defined as 'a governance structure involving an incomplete contract between separate firms and in which *each partner has limited control'*.[2] An alliance is an incomplete contract to the extent that 'it cannot specify fully what each party should do under *every conceivable condition'* and, therefore, requires that both parties engage in some form of trusting open-ended relationship in which decision-making is shared in order to allocate resources and distribute the outcome of the joint activity according to the prevailing business conditions.

International business and the pressure for globalisation often make alliances necessary. One can distinguish four various types of alliances depending upon the scope (global or local) and the object (market access or capabilities enhancing), as in Figure 4.1.

A *local* alliance would be one in which either the object is for a foreign company to penetrate a local market (*alliance for market entry*) or to have access to a set of resources available in a particular country (*resource-based country alliance*). A *global* alliance would be one in which the object would be either to develop a global market presence (*global reach alliance*) or to enhance the worldwide competitive capabilities of the firms (*global leverage alliance*).

In Chapter 7, we will discuss the issues involved in country-based partnerships while here we will concentrate on global strategic alliances.

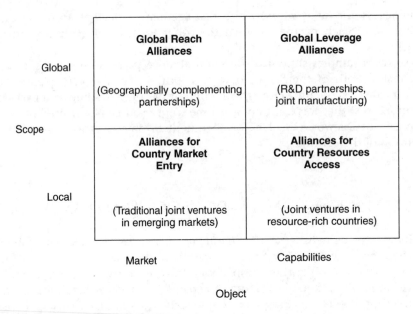

Figure 4.1   Various types of international alliances

Global versus local alliances

Local alliances under the form of *joint venture* companies have been traditional vehicles for market entry since 1945 in countries that aimed at bringing value adding productive activities to their economy, protecting their natural resources and also promoting the strategic development of national firms. Japan in the 1950s, Korea, China, Indonesia, India in the 1960s are among the countries that have systematically encouraged the formation of international joint ventures between foreign investors and local firms. Although in these countries the legal requirement for joint venture has been somewhat relaxed, a joint venture mindset subsists. The logic of these joint ventures is simple: it consists in an exchange of market or resources for technology. Foreign investors are invited to bring their products, processes and management technologies alongside their capital in exchange for an entry in the domestic market or an access to key natural resources. The value created by those local alliances is straightforward: the value for the foreign partner is an increase in market penetration, a set of profits coming from various sources – dividends, transfer prices, management fees. The value for the local partner is an increase in know-how, a flow of dividends and other indirect cash flow such as rental fees, local procurement, etc.

By contrast, *global* alliances are much more complex and subtle in their strategic and economic scope. Doz and Hamel (1998) distinguish three broad types of strategic alliances:

(a) **Coalitions** (what Doz and Hamel call 'co-option') are alliances of competitors, distributors and suppliers in a same industry putting together their capabilities with the view of spanning world markets ('the search for global reach') or to establish a common standard. Airlines alliances such as STAR represent a good example of such a coalition.

(b) **Co-specialisations** are alliances of firms that join their respective unique but complementary capabilities to create a business or develop new products or technology. What characterises this type of alliance is that each partner contributes to a unique asset, resource or competencies. Combined together, the capabilities of partners create the needed capabilities for business development. Airbus and GE–SNECMA in the aerospace industry are examples of such alliances.

(c) The primary purpose of **learning alliances** is to serve as a vehicle for know-how transfer between partners. A classical example is the alliance formed between Toyota and General Motors, called the NUMMI project, where the fundamental purpose for GM was to learn 'lean' manufacturing processes and for Toyota to learn how to operate in a highly unionised North American environment.

Strategic alliances differ from country-based joint ventures in five main aspects:

- First, they differ not only in their geographical scope – local versus global – but also in the complexity of their *strategic objectives*. While in the case of country-based joint ventures the objectives are straightforward; this is less obvious in the case of strategic alliances. Very often market objectives are combined with technological learning or strategic options. Hidden agenda are more present in strategic alliances than in joint ventures.
- Country-based joint ventures are based on a simple complementary scheme – market access against technology transfer – while strategic alliances have a more complicated *strategic architecture*. Often there is a mixture of complementary capabilities, consolidation of certain activities as well as technology transfer from both sides.
- The *valuation* of strategic alliances is more difficult than for joint ventures since they frequently involve contributions in intangible assets and know-how, and in most situations they take place in new and volatile products or processes.
- In joint ventures the value is created by the venture and distributed to the partner under the form of dividends or transfer pricing. In a strategic alliance value is created not only in the alliance but also outside the alliance through the *applied learning* that partners can utilise in other products of their own.
- Finally, partners in strategic alliances are frequently also *competitors*; this is less often the case in country-based joint ventures.

Framework for analysis

The study of strategic alliances can be divided in four major steps, as shown in Figure 4.2:

- Understanding the strategic context and spelling out the strategic value of an alliance
- Partners' analysis

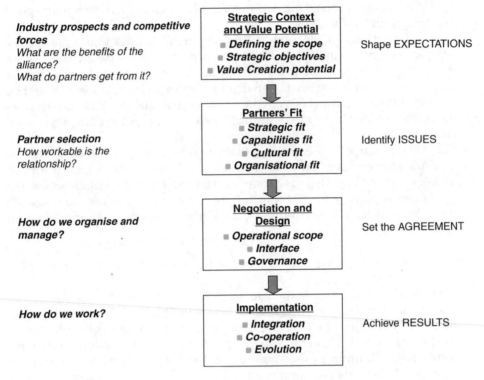

Figure 4.2 Framework for the analysis of strategic alliances

- Negotiation and design
- Implementation.

In order to discuss in detail these different steps, we will take the example of a long-lasting strategic alliance between an American company, General Electric (GE), and a French company SNECMA.

GENERAL ELECTRIC AND SNECMA: THE CFMI ALLIANCE[3]

In 1968, informal contacts began between GE's jet engine representative in France and SNECMA's commercial director about a potential collaboration for a 10-ton commercial aero-engine to be offered for civil aircraft in the 150-seat aircraft segment.

GE, the aero-engine division of General Electric, the US industrial conglomerate giant, and SNECMA, a state-owned firm engaged in designing and manufacturing engines for military jets, were both concerned by their lack of significant presence in the civilian market. This market, dominated by Pratt and Whitney from the United States and Rolls Royce from the United Kingdom, was booming, and its prospect for growth was appealing since a new competitor, Airbus, was entering the battlefield.

GE had some limited experience in civil engineering with a 2 per cent market share, but SNECMA's position was limited to only relatively small motors. Development of a new engine would typically last 10 years while the development of an aircraft would be only five years. This discrepancy obliged engine manufacturers to engage in R&D with a limited knowledge of future market needs, and to take enormous financial risks of around $1 billion. GE and SNECMA knew each other since SNECMA was already a sub-contractor of GE for a civilian version of a military engine. SNECMA, as a state-owned enterprise, was in a good position to obtain French government funding and some privileged relationship with the new-born Airbus consortium, a potential buyer of aero-engines. GE Aero-engine, as a division of a publicly traded firm, was having funding problems because of investment needs in other divisions. On the technical front, SNECMA had accumulated strong competencies in the low-pressure cold part of engine design and manufacturing, while GE could bring the original design of a military engine, the F-101, which could serve as the core element of a civilian 10-ton motor. GE's strengths were in the hot part of engine design and manufacturing. However, GE and the US government were concerned that some military secrets included in the F-101 would 'leak'. GE was also concerned by the fact that Pratt and Whitney, its main competitor, owned an 11 per cent shareholding in SNECMA, and GE also wondered if an alliance between a profit-oriented company would sit well with a state-owned enterprise. On its side, SNECMA was concerned about a potential 'short-termism' inherent in US listed companies, who are under the influence of financial analysts and could possibly abandon their involvement in a long-term project.

However, there was a strong desire by both firms to enter the civilian market, and neither of them, for whatever reason, was in a position, either technically or financially, to proceed by itself. On the top of that, both leaders had developed a mutual respect and the two companies had already some working relationship. Finally, the two companies agreed to collaborate, and formed a joint venture company named CFM International (CFMI) for the development and commercialisation of a 10-ton jet engine called the CFM56. The nine main features of the agreement were:

- ▪ 50–50 equity sharing.
- ▪ The joint venture company would act as 'project manager', leading the development, organising the work between partners and taking care of the sales. The work would be distributed among partners according to a physical distribution of tasks, GE being in charge of the 'hot' part and SNECMA of the 'cold' part. The distribution of work would be done so that each partner would have 50 per cent of the work.
- ▪ Each partner's work would not be shared so that no partner had access to the technological know-how of the other. It was the task of the joint venture project team to organise the minimum interdependences needed for the two parts developed independently to fit together.
- ▪ Partners would share revenues and not profits, meaning that whatever the price obtained on the market, the partner would get half of the selling price minus a commission for the joint venture and would manage its own part distinctively. If one company made more profit than another, it kept it for itself.
- ▪ The joint venture company would be staffed by a small group of people drawn from the two partners.

- The joint venture company would be headquartered in the United States but the CEO would be a SNECMA executive.
- An advisory committee chaired by the two chairpersons of SNECMA and GE Aero-engine would supervise the functioning of the joint venture and would act as a conflict resolution body in case of severe disagreement.
- In each company's major function, a person would be designated to serve as an interface with the joint venture, while within the joint venture, programme managers were placed in charge of co-ordinating with their respective mother companies.
- The working language would be English.

The programme was launched in 1972 and the first engine was certified in 1979. After a short period of uncertainty, Boeing decided to adopt the CFM56 for a new version of its 737 line. The following decade was highly successful, and by 1995 CFMI had sold 7,000 engines to 190 airlines. In the meantime, GE and SNECMA further extended their collaboration to new types of engines. By the mid-1990s GE, either directly or through CFMI, had 33 per cent of world sales in engines for more than 100-seat airplanes, while SNECMA controlled 19 per cent of this market.

UNDERSTANDING THE STRATEGIC CONTEXT AND SPELLING OUT THE STRATEGIC VALUE OF AN ALLIANCE

Strategic context

The starting point of any alliance analysis is a deep understanding of the *industry drivers* and *competitive forces* that shape the prevailing position of partners and the challenges they confront. For GE and SNECMA, both companies were interested in entering the market and neither of them was capable of doing it alone. The strategic context was favourable to an alliance. From there the second step consists in determining the *scope of the alliance*, setting the strategic *objectives* of the alliance and calculating its value creation potential.

The *scope* of the alliance has to do with the type of alliance one is looking for. As mentioned earlier, there are three types of partnership corresponding to different strategic contexts and needs: the coalition, the co-specialisation and the learning alliance.

In *coalition* alliances, partners looking to develop their market reach by co-ordinating their geographical assets, pooling their capabilities in order to reduce costs or enhance competitiveness, or integrating their product offering with the view of gaining market acceptance, as in the 'battle for standard' discussed in Chapter 2. SONY and Philips, for instance, have been co-allied for the development of the DVD; in the past there was an alliance between IBM, Apple and Motorola. The strategic scope of the alliance is to create a *bigger and stronger competitive player* in the global marketplace. The essence of the alliance is 'size'.

Co-specialisation alliances have a different scope: most of the time they aim at creating new products or at increasing competitiveness through the assembly of relatively independent capabilities. The benefits of co-specialisation alliances are

Table 4.1 Main strategic objectives pursued in various types of alliances

	Coalitions	Co-specialisation	Learning
Positioning	– Market reach – Enhance competitiveness through cost reduction or pooling of capabilities – Establish standards	– Create new business – Develop new products – Enhance competitiveness through specialisation – Complement strengths – Product line	– Access to technology
Capabilities			
Resources	– Financing – Sharing risks	– Complementarities of resources – Risk-sharing	– Research and marketing personnel – Financing
Assets	– Distribution – Manufacturing – Customer services – Code sharing (Airlines)	– Complementarities of assets	– Access to key tangible and intangible assets
Competencies	– Market knowledge	– Complementarities of know-how	– Technology – Know-how
Economic value	– Economies of scale – Economies of scope – Increased revenues – Increased customer responsiveness – Increased quality	– Maximisation of asset utilisation by each partner – Faster time to market – Product development (new revenues stream)	– Skills development

exactly the same as the benefits of specialisation of business units in an integrated company. Each party will concentrate on what it is good at, and as a consequence will deliver a product, a service or a component with the best concentration of resources and skills. The GE–SNECMA case falls into this category. Each party focuses on what it is good at and there is no attempt to extract joint learning.

The primary purpose of *learning alliances* is to set the mechanisms in place to transfer valuable competencies through a symmetric exchange of technological know-how. Learning alliances are also designed for co-learning in the sense that partners develop new competencies together. An example of learning alliance is described in Mini-Example 4.1. Strategic objectives are subordinated to the respective business strategies of the partners involved. The starting point, then, is for each partner to define what the contribution is of the alliance to her/his own strategy. Table 4.1 describes the main strategic objectives pursued in various types of alliances.

Value potential

The *value potential* of the alliance for the alliance partner is calculated on the basis of the potential benefits it brings to the respective company(ies) involved. In theory, it is a straightforward calculation done in two steps (see Figure 4.3):

■ **Step one**: value *created* by the *alliance*
■ **Step two**: value *captured* by each *partner*.

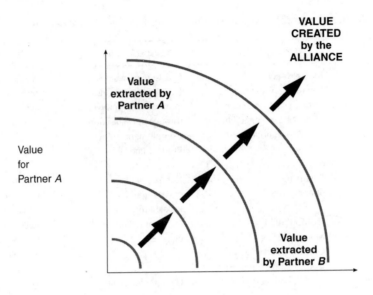

Figure 4.3 Value creation and extraction in alliances

The value created by the alliance is driven by four factors:

- Revenues generated by the alliance through volume of sales
- Revenues generated by the alliance through the ability to command a high-differentiated price
- Future revenues or costs benefits coming from joint R&D products or processes
- Cost benefits resulting from economies of scale and scope.

The value captured by partners comes from:

- Distribution of the alliance profits when the alliance is structured as an auto-nomous economic entity
- Profit generated by the sales of intermediary products, components or services to the alliance
- Profits derived from products or processes developed thanks to the alliance
- Increased revenues or costs reduction coming from the alliance because of increased market reach or economies of scale or scope
- Profits coming from other products whose sales are boosted because of the alliance.

However, whatever the type of alliance, the value created is more difficult to assess than for the traditional joint venture for market entry or natural-resource access. According to Doz and Hamel (1998), the reasons for these problems are:

(a) Partners bring hard to value non-traded resources, assets or competencies
(b) The relative contribution is often hard to assess

(c) Most of the time, much of the value accrues outside the alliance
(d) The relative value to each partner may shift over time
(e) Partners may not declare what real value they seek from the alliance:[4]

Despite these difficulties, it is advisable to try to measure the value expected from the alliance since it will serve as a yardstick to assess its success or failure.

In the case of GE–SNECMA, the value of the alliance came from the sales of engines to the marketplace, and the value for the partners came from the difference between the split revenues and their own costs plus the profit made on spare parts. Probably some intangible elements were present in this venture as well, and other products of each firm may benefit from the increased volume coming from CFMI. By design, the companies have denied themselves any value from reciprocal technology transfer.

PARTNER ANALYSIS

Partner analysis consists in determining the extent to which the relationship with the proposed partner is viable and valuable. It consists of four assessments (Figure 4.4):

(a) *Strategic* fit
(b) *Capabilities* fit
(c) *Organisational* fit
(d) *Cultural* fit.

Strategic fit

The purpose of strategic fit analysis is to assess the degree of *compatibility* among the partners, given their respective explicit or implicit strategic objectives. When stated objectives are explicit the analysis is simple, but when behind stated objectives there are implicit ones (a hidden agenda), the analysis requires an in-depth study of the partner's strategic context – competitive position and managerial power

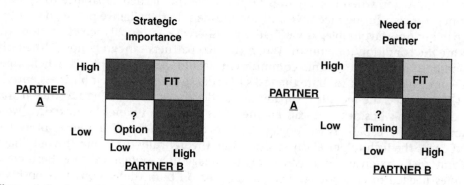

Figure 4.4   Assessing the strategic fit based on the criticality of the alliance for partners

structure – to unravel the 'real' expectations of the other party. An analysis of strategic fit implies the following assessments:

- *Criticality* of the alliance for the partners
- The relative *competitive position* of partners
- The compatibility in *strategic agendas*.

Answering two very simple questions will evaluate the criticality of the alliance for each partner:

- How important is the alliance for the partners?
- Do they need an alliance to achieve their objectives?

The answers to these two questions can be represented into two different matrixes, as in Figure 4.4, where one can assess the degree of commitment one can expect from partners to the alliance.

The importance of the alliance for partners is determined on the basis of the contextual analysis done earlier. If both partners have a strong strategic stake in the business, one can expect a high commitment that is favourable to a good fit. If the strategic importance is unbalanced (it is important for one partner but not for the other), there will be a divergence in commitment and the fit will be more questionable. When both partners have a low strategic stake, one may not expect a high degree of commitment from both partners, which by itself represents a fit, but not a favourable one for the future of the alliance. One may wonder, under such conditions why should they even consider a strategic partnership. The answer to that question can be found in the theory of real options:[5] partners may consider the alliance as a *forward option* for future decision. In such a case, the degree of commitment may be positive although one may wonder what will happen when the option has to be called in or forfeited.

In the case of GE–SNECMA, both partners had a strong motivation to enter the civilian markets, given their high dependencies on the military segment of aero-engines. The demand was there since no modern fuel-efficient engines were available.

The ability to 'go it alone' depends on the existing resources – *assets and competencies* that each partner possesses at the time – and the degree of time pressure put on them. Again, when both parties do not have the needed capability to venture alone, there is a strong incentive and commitment to the alliance provided that the capability fit is favourable, as we shall see. Otherwise, an unbalanced situation will create the condition for a misfit. When the two partners can 'go it alone', the only condition under which the commitment would be favourable is when time pressure obliges them to share the tasks in order to accelerate their business entry.

GE possessed the technical capabilities to develop a civilian engine since it was already in this business with an engine of its own, but financial constraints were hampering its capability to engage in the development of a new motor. For SNECMA, the technological capabilities were theoretically there, but it would have meant a very extensive and risky effort to engage in a *solitaire* venture. Both companies needed to collaborate. The strategic fit on both dimensions was positive, as far as the criticality was concerned.

The *relative competitive* position of partners is a second important parameter to investigate when assessing a strategic fit. Doz and Hamel (1998, Chapter 4) have developed a typology of competitive positions and postulated their mutual degree of fit depending upon the type of alliance.

They class competitors in three broad categories: *leaders* (dominant firm in the industry), *challengers* (second-tier firms in the industry) and *laggards* (firms which need to catch up). They conclude that alliances among leaders are plagued with problems.

GE and SNECMA are in the situation of two challengers pooling their specialised capabilities to obtain a complementary division of labour. GE could be tempted to play the father figure in the partnership given its already established business but will probably refrain from it, due to a small 2 per cent market share in the industry. Again, at this level the fit was favourable.

The last part of strategic assessment is the confrontation of the strategic agendas and their resulting expectations. One can distinguish four kinds of strategic agendas:

- *Venturing* agendas
- *Extractive* agendas
- *Sharing* agendas
- *Options* agendas.

In *venturing agendas* partners have a deliberate desire to engage in collaboration to create a business. Their prime motivation is to see the alliance grow and flourish, and they get their reward from the continuation of a successful partnership.

Extractive agendas have a different logic: the objective is to 'learn' or to 'acquire' capabilities from the partner or from the alliance. The prospects of a fit in such a case are short-term: as long as one get the necessary capabilities one sticks to the alliance; as soon as the learning or acquisition cycle is achieved, the strategic value of the alliance vanishes.

Sharing agendas are limited ones, their prime objectives being to maximise efficiency in certain elements of the value chain through economies of scale and scope. Airline alliances are of that nature: they share flight codes, lounges, frequent flyers programmes and sometimes aircraft maintenance.

Options agendas, as noted earlier, are based on the desire for partners to 'look and see' without committing vast amounts of resources, and using the alliance as an experimental platform for monitoring the business. As in any option, such an agenda has a time limit, at the end of which partners have to make up their mind: break the alliance and continue alone or continue and expand the alliance.

Figure 4.5 gives a graphical representation of those various types of strategic agendas and their combinations.

Both GE and SNECMA were on the venturing mode: first, because of the importance of the civilian engine business for them, their inability to 'go it alone' and the constraints placed by the US government for the protection of military technology embodied in the core engine provided by GE. An extractive approach by SNECMA was banned by design. The length of engine development also prevented GE from adopting an extractive attitude with regard to the financial subsidies made by the French government on behalf of SNECMA. The scenario of GE taking advantage of this money and later on dropping the alliance was an unlikely one. Once partners are engaged in development they have to stick to it, given the huge financial

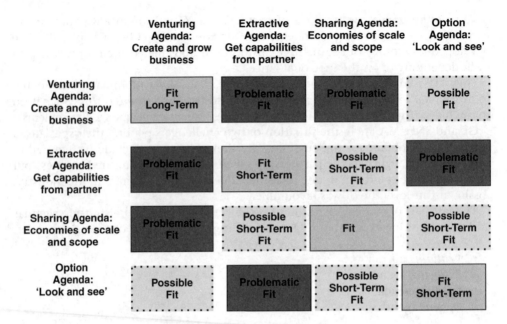

Figure 4.5 Strategic fit against partners' strategic agendas

commitment; a retreat by one partner would imply that either it loses its investment or it has duplicated the R&D on its own premises to be able to handle the project alone. GE was not in a financial position to do that, not to mention SNECMA.

Capabilities fit

The objective of a capabilities fit analysis is to assess the extent to which partners are capable of contributing to the necessary *competitive capabilities* of the business.

The framework for the analysis of capabilities fit is straightforward; it consists, first, in determining the required resources, assets and competencies needed in the value chain of the business as described in Chapter 2 (Figure 2.5). Then, for each partner, the specific contribution in each element of the value chain is drawn, based on exposed or supposed resource assets and competencies. The last phase of the analysis determines the *potential gap* to be filled by joint investment and an evaluation of whether the mutual contributions plus the additional investments make the future alliance effective is made.

This logical analysis is depicted in Figure 4.6 and an illustration of the GE–SNECMA case is presented in Figure 4.7. It shows that the complementarities of the contributions were a good fit in this alliance.

Cultural fit

Three types of cultural differences can be distinguished in global alliances – corporate, industrial and national – each of them likely to create a gap that may affect the

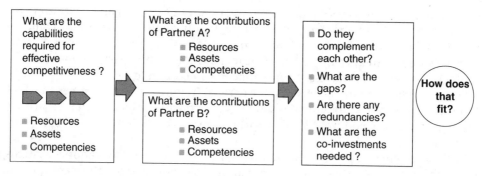

Figure 4.6 Method for assessing capabilities' fit

Source: Krishna (1990).

What is needed?	TECHNOLOGY	PRODUCTION	MARKETING
▪ RESOURCES	Financing Researchers	Production specialists Qualified personnel	Contacts with customers Sales people
▪ ASSETS	Testing facilities	Factories	Service centres
▪ COMPETENCIES	Hot and cold technology	Quality management	Salesmanship in a civilian environment
Who contributes to what ?			
GE ▪ RESOURCES	Researchers	Production specialists Qualified personnel	Contacts with Boeing and MD Contacts with airlines
▪ ASSETS	Testing facilities Hot	Factory in Evendale Quality	Service centres
▪ COMPETENCIES	technology	management	Salesmanship in a civilian environment
SNECMA ▪ RESOURCES	Financing researchers	Production specialists Qualified personnel	Contacts with AIRBUS
▪ ASSETS	Testing facilities	Factory in France	Some service centres
▪ COMPETENCIES	Cold technology	Quality management	

Figure 4.7 Capabilities' fit in the case of GE–SNECMA

future functioning of the partnership. The role of cultural fit analysis is to understand the nature of the differences, to anticipate their possible consequences in the functioning of the alliance and to take action in order to prevent negative effects.

In organisations such as companies, culture is the set of beliefs – values, assumptions and causal models – that influences the way individuals in that organisation think and behave. As mentioned earlier, one can identify three types of differences in organisational cultures:

▪ Differences in *corporate cultures*
▪ Differences in *industry cultures*
▪ Differences in *national cultures*.

Corporate culture differences come from the *history* of the company (start-up versus well-established firm), its *ownership* structure (family-owned versus public company versus government owned), its *managerial* style, (entrepreneurial versus bureaucratic) as well as the personality of its leaders. Good or bad past experiences with strategies and alliances have a strong influence on corporate cultures.

Industry cultures are the norms that are derived from the type of business in which firms are engaged: fast-moving consumer goods (fmcg) companies share a marketing mindset that would not fit particularly with a specialty chemical company, for instance.

National or ethnic cultures are the product of the history, educational systems, religions and social codes that each nation has woven over the centuries. In Chapter 11, we will analyse national cultures in more detail, but as far as alliances are concerned, we will take for granted the fact that firms are influenced by the national culture of their country of origin and the citizenship of their key executives.

All three differences can be present in global alliances, and usually atleast two of them: the corporate and the national cultural differences. Those differences may impact the alliance management in five main ways:

- On the *definition of objectives* of the alliance: growth versus profit, short-term versus long-term are the major trade-offs that cultural differences may exacerbate.
- On the way of *competing and doing business*: price competition versus differentiation.
- On the way partners *communicate*: formal versus informal, hierarchical versus horizontal, degree of openness, emphasis on interpersonal communications.
- On *financing and re-investing*: distribution of dividend versus reinvestment of profits, debt policy.
- On *human resources management* (HRM): criteria for recruiting, degree of autonomy and criteria for performance evaluation.

Organisational fit

Organisational fit is strongly correlated with cultural fit. The objective is to assess whether the partners' organisational structure *systems* and *procedures* differ significantly to the extent that the organisation of the work between partners within the alliance is affected.

The main dimensions included in organisational fit analysis are:

- The degree of decentralisation of *decision-making*
- The degree of *documentation* of policies and rules
- The *accounting* and *reporting* methods and systems
- The degree of *formalisation* of decision-making
- The kind of *incentives* used to motivate personnel.

In the case of GE–SNECMA, the cultural fit was not *a priori* ideal. On the three dimensions of culture – corporate, industry and national – only the industrial culture suggested a positive fit, since both entities were very focused on the development and manufacturing of aero-engines. In this industry, norms and working methodologies are very much the same across the globe and both companies had had a limited collaboration before. Corporate cultures were highly contrasted: SNECMA a state-owned enterprise, and GE the division of a listed conglomerate. One might fear that the motivation, the management style and the various organisational mechanisms would all conflict. For the national culture, France and the United States have a long history of rivalry based on their historical ambition to be a 'leading' nation. Given the intense competition in the aerospace industry, both civil and military, one might have feared that national pride and other cultural idiosyncrasies would disturb a potential relationship. This did not happen, for several reasons. First, the strong strategic stake made the partners more reasonable with regard to their national pride. Second, having worked together, GE and SNECMA engineers had learned about their cultural differences, had successfully managed them and had built mutual respect. Third, as will be seen later, the architecture of the alliance was such that interdependencies were minimised, so reducing the risks of too many operational encounters. Fourth, the governance structure was also built so that interactions were transacted by a group of engineers who could communicate with their own organisations as well as with the other partner organisation. Finally, English was adopted as a working language and it was agreed that the headquarters of the alliance would be based in the United States and managed by a French manager, forcing a mixture of cultures.

NEGOTIATION AND DESIGN

Operational scope

One of the first essentials is to agree on the *organisational design* and the *operational content* of the alliance. When deciding on the organisational design, one has to choose between two approaches according to the degree of operational capabilities one wants to give to the alliance structure. One can choose between four generic types of alliance design, depending on whether the structure has full operating capabilities or acts as a broker and also whether it is a coalition, a co-specialisation or a learning alliance (Figure 4.8).

In broker designs, the alliance structure acts as an intermediary between the two (or more) partners who keep their own operational capabilities (resources, assets and competencies). Broker structures can be either in the form of a project management or co-ordination structure, or alternatively can consist in a series of joint committees. When the alliance is a coalition or a co-specialisation, the alliance structure is generally similar to a project team or a co-ordination structure. GE–SNECMA adopted this design. The partners formed an independent legal entity named CFM International, headquartered in the United States, in which GE and SNECMA each owned 50 per cent. The role of this joint venture would be to co-ordinate activities between the two parties. Each company worked on its own R&D, manufacturing and servicing on the basis of a work-sharing plan decided upfront. The joint venture structure owned no assets and the people working in this structure were

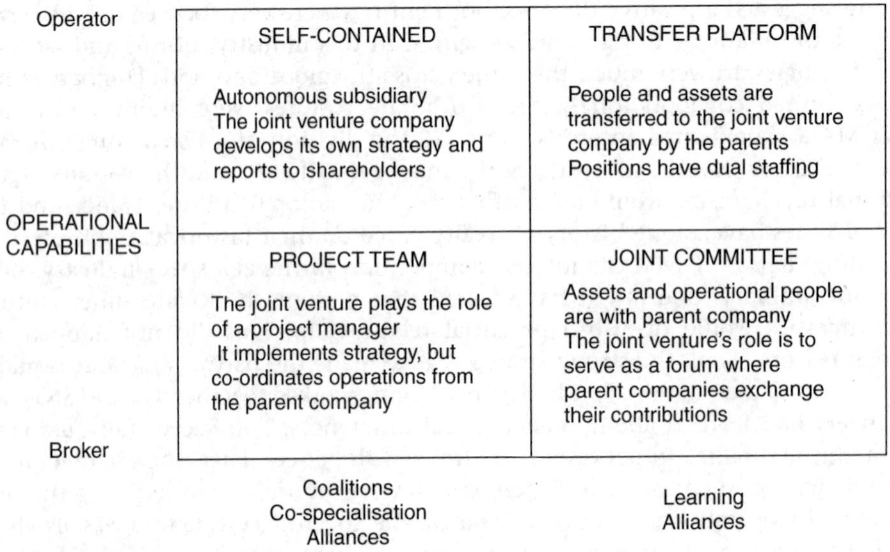

	SELF-CONTAINED	TRANSFER PLATFORM
Operator	Autonomous subsidiary The joint venture company develops its own strategy and reports to shareholders	People and assets are transferred to the joint venture company by the parents Positions have dual staffing
OPERATIONAL CAPABILITIES	**PROJECT TEAM** The joint venture plays the role of a project manager It implements strategy, but co-ordinates operations from the parent company	**JOINT COMMITTEE** Assets and operational people are with parent company The joint venture's role is to serve as a forum where parent companies exchange their contributions
Broker	Coalitions Co-specialisation Alliances	Learning Alliances

Figure 4.8 Organisational designs in alliances

essentially programme managers working in relationship. Figure 4.9 gives a schematic representation of the organisation of CFMI.

In the case of learning alliances, broker designs will consist generally of joint committees. For instance, in the case of the Alza–Ciba-Geigy alliance for advanced drug delivery systems, the design of the partnership was based on the regular meeting of three committees: an audit committee, a joint research board and a series of joint research conferences.[6]

The operator alliance structure owns and operates its own operational capabilities, which are transferred to it by the parent companies, or the alliance builds and develops with the capital injected by the parents. Again, an operator design can take two different forms: self-contained or transfer platform.

In *self-contained* designs, the alliance structure creates economic value by itself and distributes it to the parent shareholders, as in any company. An example of a highly successful alliance of this type can be found with Fuji Xerox, which develops products, manufactures them and markets them with a high degree of autonomy from the parents.

Transfer platform designs are structures in which the joint venture controls its own resources, assets and competencies and therefore is fully responsible for creating the value. But in such designs, partners allocate engineers and staff to the joint venture with the view of 'learning' from the other partner and from the alliance. A good example is the NUMMI 50/50 joint venture between Toyota and General Motors. General Motors has allocated a factory at Freemont, California, and transferred 2,500 workers plus around 25 engineers to the joint venture. Toyota brings managers and specialists in 'lean' manufacturing systems. NUMMI can be considered as a transfer platform for Toyota to learn how to operate in an American unionised environment, while GE learns how to implement 'lean' manufacturing systems.

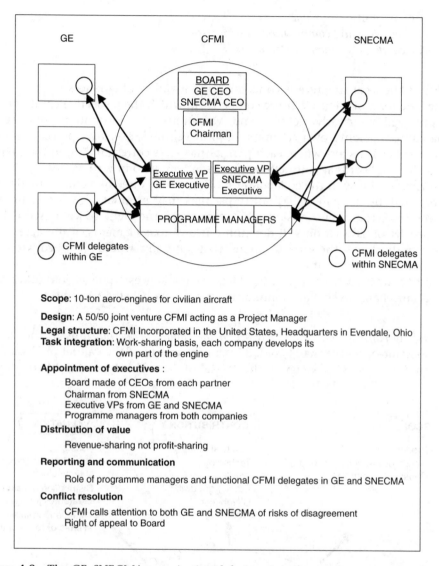

Figure 4.9 The GE–SNECMA organisational design, interface and governance

Source: Krishna (1990).

Interface and governance

Deciding on the interface and governance for the alliance is probably the most difficult part of the negotiation between partners. Six domains have to be agreed:

(a) The *legal structure* and the *decision-making* mechanisms
(b) The degree of *task integration*
(c) The appointment of *executives*

(d) The distribution of *value*
(e) The *reporting* and *communication* processes
(f) The *conflict resolution* mechanisms.

As far as the legal structure is concerned, the majority of alliances will be created under the form of a joint venture company, in which the respective equity participations will be clearly defined and valuations of contributions and results isolated from parent's own accounts. In joint ventures, executive power is granted to a Board of Directors where each partner has seats corresponding to their equity participation. Boards appoint operating executives, who in turn are responsible for producing results with the collaboration of personnel directly recruited by them or 'transferred' by the parents. Minority partners may negotiate some 'concurrence' clauses for certain key decisions that give them the right of veto (see below). The articles of association will determine the various elements of the agreement. Figure 4.10 shows the various items that typically would be negotiated and included in a joint venture.

Joint ventures are not the only legal form that alliances can take. Four other types of legal mechanisms that are commonly found in global alliances are:

- *Equity participation by one partner in the capital of the other*, as in the case of Renault–Nissan (Renault took 37 per cent equity of the capital of Nissan), or in the case of Ciba-Geigy in the capital of Alza. This type of legal structure is

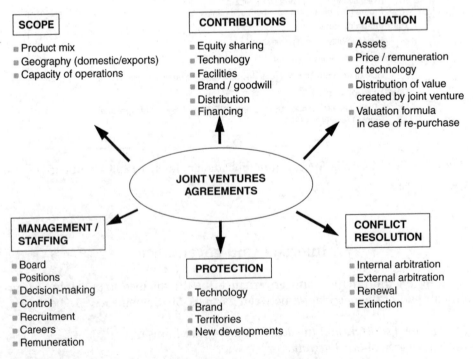

Figure 4.10 Typical items in a joint venture agreement

very close to an acquisition, but in reality, as long as the equity partner does not get full control of the operation it is still considered as an alliance.

■ *Joint equity participation*, in which one partner takes a shareholding in the other partner's capital. This kind of agreement has to be complemented by contractual arrangements that define the scope of the joint activities and their respective valuations. This was the case with the now-defunct alliance between Renault and Volvo. In that case, the joint equity was supposed to be the prelude to a merger that ultimately was refused by Volvo's shareholders.

■ *Long-term contract agreements*, such as distribution agreements or manufacturing agreements. Cisco, for instance, manufactures 75 per cent of its products with external suppliers with whom it has long-term relationships.

■ R&D joint projects.

Legal structure and decision-making mechanism

When negotiating an alliance agreement, a majority of executives insists on having 'control', meaning that they want to obtain the majority shareholding in a joint venture. Many academic studies have found that this is one of the requirements stated by most managers surveyed. However, research has also found that 'control' is not correlated with 'success'.[7] In fact, a legal majority control is only a fraction of the total control over a company or a set of operations. First, there is the possibility for a minority partner to activate 'concurrence' clauses that may limit the power of the majority and ultimately block decisions. One can perceive intuitively that control is real if, and only if, a person or a group of persons is able positively and negatively influence to behaviour. A majority shareholding does not guarantee that. Some authors have even argued that a 50/50 joint venture arrangement is even better than a majority arrangement because it forces partners to make all the necessary effort to make the alliance work.[8] This may be the reason why in the GE–SNECMA case, despite the differences in competitive capabilities between the two partners, it was agreed that it would be a 50/50 venture.

The degree of task integration

Task integration defines which activities are carried on by the alliance, which ones are carried separately, and the extent to which activities carried by each partner need to be integrated. For instance, when the task is jointly to develop a new product, R&D departments often need to be merged, at least partially, while if the alliance is only a sharing of distribution networks, the amount of interdependency between the two networks may be limited. Integration requires co-ordination and joint work and therefore is likely to demand *complex management approaches*. Alternatively, if integration is limited, each party fulfils its obligations separately, making co-ordination straightforward and simple. Limited integration is possible if tasks are defined precisely up front and the joint output is obtained by 'assembling' the separate outputs together with limited interactions. This is a 'plug-in' operation. This is the model that GE and SNECMA adopted. Because the technology of aero-engines could be technically separated into independent components, the role of engineers at SNECMA and GE was to define which part GE should do and which should be done by SNECMA, leaving the relatively limited management of the interface in the hands of the joint venture. When the task complexity is such that clearly separates job distribution is not possible, then a self-contained joint venture in which teams are temporarily merged is the best solution. Otherwise, co-ordination of interdependencies could prove to be a hurdle.

Appointment of executives

Whom to appoint as the alliance leader is often a major issue for the success of the venture, as well as a subject of contention between partners when they negotiate the agreement. Two key issues arise: the amount of parents' transfers and the skills of alliance managers.

Parents' transfer refers to the allocation of managers and staff from each parent to the venture as opposed to the independent staffing of the alliance structure. When the alliance is a co-specialisation or a reciprocal learning one, partners' transfer is expected to be high since the whole purpose is to activate the unique capabilities of partners. Alternatively, when the alliance is a coalition or co-learning (both partners want to learn from the alliance but not necessarily from each other), people transfer is less of an issue.

In the case of transfer, the problem arises of the distribution of *functions* and *roles*. One technique, known as the 'shadow' organisation, consists of putting a manager from one partner in charge of a function with a manager from the other partner as his or her deputy, and so on and so forth. This technique seems appealing because of its apparent fairness, but it is not necessarily effective, since it reinforces a 'them and us' attitude and leads to a long decision-making process or to many conflictual situations. In the case of GE–SNECMA, as Figure 4.9 shows, the staffing of CFMI was based on this principle, but the shadow approach was not implemented.

The second important consideration is to select managers with the appropriate skills to manage the alliance. An interesting work by Robert Spekeman and Lynn Isabella (2000, Chapter 8) has identified different roles and skills of alliance managers; Figure 4.11 gives a summary of their findings. Other authors have stressed the critical importance of the managerial, communication and negotiation skills of managers in the alliance.[9]

Distribution of value

As mentioned earlier, *an alliance creates value* and this value has to be distributed to the partners according to an agreed scheme. Owing to the fact that valuation is complex, alliance negotiators often have difficulty in finding a 'fair' mechanism taking into consideration all the elements that contribute to value. The simplest form is the distribution of profits in a joint venture. This works only if the entire profit is created by the joint venture without any significant input apart from the initial capital from the partners. When profit is dependent on inputs provided by the parents, there is a high risk of *transfer pricing disputes*. This is the reason why GE and SNECMA adopted a 'revenue-sharing' scheme instead of 'profit-sharing'.

Alliance Manager Role: Visionary

Stage: Anticipating

■ Searching for partners
■ Planning an alliance

– Serve as driving force behind the alliance's creation
– Paint picture of the possibilities that forming an alliance might create
– Initiate contact with potential partners
– Understand company's strategic intent and recognise similarity
  of intent in potential partner companies

Alliance Manager Role: Strategic Sponsor

Stage: Engaging

■ Evaluating partners
■ Identify value-creation
  opportunities

– Have authority to commit resources and key personnel to the alliance
– Define and promote the dream on which the alliance is based
– Actively promote and sell the alliance internally
– Help the company identify synergies and imagine possibilities
– Create an atmosphere of high energy, personal compatibility and strategic
  complementarity

Alliance Manager Role: Advocate

Stage: Valuing

■ Building business plans
■ Negotiating

– Spend a significant amount of time convincing others within the company
  of the value of the alliance
– Be responsible for developing support for the alliance
– Constantly push the dream forward
– Rally the right people at the right time
– Make things happen 'deep' in the company
– Act as champion for the alliance

Alliance Manager Role: Facilitator

Stage: Investing

■ Demonstrate commitment
■ Leveraging synergies

– Encourage open, honest and straightforward communication among
  all parties to the alliance
– Facilitate effective 'no-blame reviews'
– Interact with diplomacy, tact and objectivity
– Create bridges between diverse parties with different interests
– Resolve conflicts
– Exhibit sensitivity to the needs of all parties

Alliance Manager Role: Networking

Stage: Co-ordinating

■ Creating teams
■ Aligning work processes
  across partners

– Rely on frequent contacts to expedite alliance business
– Know whom to ask for help and when to ask
– Put the right people together
– Access resources quickly and efficiently through others
– Create links between the partner companies' internal networks
– Put in face-to-face time in order to cultivate trust in key relationships

Alliance Manager Role: Manager

Stage: Stabilising

■ Consolidating
■ Managing

– Shoulder responsibilities for sustaining the alliance
– Ensure that the alliance follows its prescribed path
– Maintain relationships critical to alliance success
– Communicate frequently with all partners
– Maintain the alliance's momentum
– Actively develop future alliance managers

Figure 4.11   Alliance stages and alliance managers' skills

Source: Spekeman and Isabella (2000).

In a revenue-sharing scheme each partner receives the revenues generated by the alliance on the market proportionately to their share of work. Then it is up to each partner to manage its costs and to generate profit. This method implies that there is an up front agreement on work-sharing. That was the case in CFMI, since both companies were already familiar with engine development and had a pretty good awareness of the relative importance of the work to be completed by each party. Corrective mechanisms were included in case a work discrepancy appeared during the implementation of the alliance.

Reporting and communication processes

Alliance agreements should provide *communication platforms* so that partners remain informed about the development of the venture. Academic research has stressed the importance of communication in the success of alliances.[10] The legal forum for communication is the Board of Directors in a joint venture, but this is not enough. Communication needs to be organised horizontally and vertically *among* partners and *within* partners, as shown in Figure 4.12.

In the case of GE–SNECMA, communication is mediated by programme managers detached from the parents of CFMI, who serve as an interface to the different functional activities inside the parents. Within the parent organisations, CFMI interface managers are appointed within their respective functions to communicate with their CFMI counterparts. Frequent inter-functional meetings are held to monitor and discuss developments.

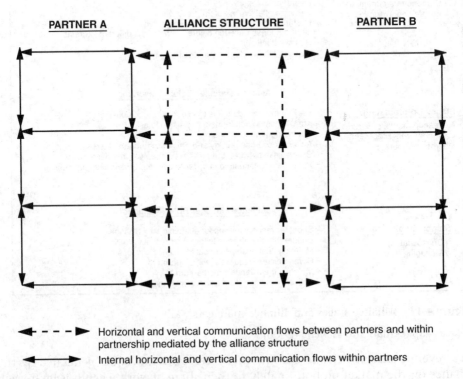

Figure 4.12　Communications flows in alliances

Source:　Adapted from Doz and Hamel (1998, p. 190).

Conflict resolution mechanisms

Friction and conflict is almost inevitable. As will be seen later, disenchantment, frustration and conflict of interests may surface rapidly after the deal is consumated (the 'death valley' problem[11]) or during the life of the alliance.

All contracts include legal provision for conflict management between shareholders in joint ventures by *arbitrage clauses*. The real problem is not these legal mechanisms – which in many cases are employed when the two parties have more or less already decided to terminate their agreements – but the difficulty of creating the *internal mechanisms* for solving problems. In the case of GE–SNECMA, for instance, major operational disagreements were to be directed to the Executive Committee made up of the two CEOs of GE Aero-engines and SNECMA plus the CFMI Chairman. Managers in both organisations were encouraged to solve conflicts among themselves and a right of appeal to the Board was supposed to be exceptional. Both parties stimulated a culture of permanent negotiation through which managers were supposed to look at the benefits of the joint effort (the success of the venture) before looking at the benefits for their mother company.

IMPLEMENTATION

The last stage in alliance management, but not the least, is the implementation stage. Two different aspects of implementation have been identified as critical: integration and co-operation and learning.

Integration and co-operation

Once the alliance has been formed the immediate implementation phase is to put the respective companies and the alliance structure to work so that the teams allocated to the alliance achieve the planned output. This phase is frequently operationalised by 'integration teams'. *Integration teams* are functional working groups made of managers from the different partners who are assigned the task of identifying the practical ways of implementing the alliance. This covers items such as which processes to adopt, which IT platform, the kind of measurements to adopt, how to manage relationships with third parties, which accounting system to use, etc. Integration teams are important because they offer the first opportunity to work together in a concrete fashion. Cultural differences are discovered, as well as practical issues that were not anticipated during the negotiation phase. The ways these unanticipated issues are handled sets the initial tone of relationships and demonstrates the actual mindset of partners. Since integration teams are staffed with operational people, of whom a large majority did not participate in the alliance negotiations, their attitudes and perspectives have to be 'shaped' by their respective management teams. An 'internal selling job' is often needed to erode fears or misinterpretation of the alliance's value; trade unions have to be convinced

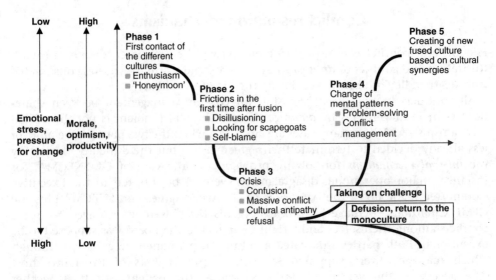

Figure 4.13 The 'death valley' spiral

that the alliance is not designed to eliminate jobs and cultural stereotypes have to be challenged through internal training sessions.

Despite all these preparatory efforts, what it is called the 'death valley' issue-often arises. This model inspired by many global alliances, is based on the fact that surprises and unanticipated events or behaviour occur frequently during alliance implementation. If not properly prepared, managers may retreat into blaming and stereotyping – particularly cultural stereotyping – instead of coping with the stress and anxiety provoked by any 'surprises'. A vicious spiral then develops (see Figure 4.13) in which communications are shut off and the viability of the alliance is put in question. Since such a 'death valley' is almost inevitable, companies engaged in global alliances should prepare their managers to cope with the situation, to avoid blaming and stereotyping and look for win-win solutions.

Learning[12]

As we have seen earlier, some types of partnerships are specially designed as learning alliances, but all alliances in practice involve some kind of learning. One can distinguish two forms of learning:

- Learning from the alliance, or *co-learning*: what the partners learn *within the alliance,*
- Learning from the partners, or *captured learning*: what the partners learn *from each other.*

Learning from the alliance

In implementing alliances, partners can learn:

- About the *business*
- About the *tasks*
- About partners' *expectations and capabilities*.

Partners discover jointly the characteristics and trends of markets, the industry and its competitive drivers. This kind of learning is normal in any venture, whether joint or not. The specific issue in the case of a partnership is to put in place the organisational mechanisms for such learning to take place and to be *distributed* to partners. This is done by setting up and using common data-bases, and possibly with the advent of E-business platforms to integrate the joint venture data-base to the partner's Intranet software. In addition, the alliance structure should organise reflective and analytical forums for joint planning, seminars, conferences and review sessions.

Partners should also be able to redefine their mutual contributions and work processes in the light of new events and changes in business context. Functional committees and operational reviews can make such mutual adjustments. In the case of GE–SNECMA, production and development engineers were meeting regularly to adjust the various technical procedures and also to redefine, if needed, the work-sharing scheme to maintain the 50/50 balance.

Over time, partner's expectations may change and imbalances in the value distribution may appear. This kind of change is obviously one of the most difficult to handle since change in expectations may undermine the initial alliance's foundations. A constant observation of change in partner's internal context, such as a new CEO, modification of strategic direction, analyst opinions, etc., helps to predict the likelihood of a shift in expectations. In the mid-1990s, the GE–SNECMA alliance entered a period of tension when, because of market depression and a slow process of internal cost-cutting measures, SNECMA was losing money while GE was still profitable. SNECMA felt that this imbalance could not last and considered renegotiation of the partnership. The accumulated trust and communication mechanisms plus a resurgence in market growth allowed the collaboration to continue. In fact, because of learning from its partner, SNECMA was able to restructure faster.

Learning from the partner

In 1986 Reich and Mankin published an explosive article named 'Joint Ventures with Japan Give Away Our Future'. In a more moderate rein, Doz, Hamel and Prahalad argued in 1989 that Western partners could use alliances to regain competitiveness against Japanese competitors. They gave as an example the case of Thompson Multimedia, who gained expertise in the design and manufacturing of VCRs thanks to its alliance with JVC.

In both cases, the arguments were based on 'learning from the partner' in an alliance context. In practice a 'learning from the partner' approach implies two key capabilities: clarity of objectives and organisational receptivity.

Clarity of objectives implies that the company engaged in an alliance for learning should identify clearly what it wants to learn and set up a *learning agenda* defining

Table 4.2   Receptivity in learning

Weak learning capabilities	Strong learning capabilities
No systematic collection of information	Organised intelligence
No sharing of information	Networked internal information exchange
'Not invented here' attitudes	'Why' attitude, curiosity, search for benchmarking and outside best practices
No 'organisational memory'	Planned approach to skill acquisition
Pressure to achieve only operational/ financial results	Internal training
Recruitment of people based only on technical professional skills	Allocation of time and budgets to 'learn'
	Recruitment of people based on 'social' as well as professional skills

the learning sequence. All capabilities cannot be learned at once. Thomson embarked on a step-by-step approach to learn first the assembly of VCR components, and then the ability to design and manufacture next-generation products such as handheld mini video cameras.

Receptivity is the second type of learning capabilities. It consists of the various internal organisation mechanisms that companies engaged in alliances may use to accumulate, retain and transfer knowledge. Table 4.2 gives a list of such weak and strong learning mechanisms.

GLOBAL MULTILATERAL ALLIANCES[13]

Most of the discussions in this chapter have been centred around dyadic alliances involving only two partners. In practice, global companies are often engaged in a multiplicity of alliances, some of them domestic, but the vast majority with 'foreign' partners.

Each product division of multi-business corporations is engaged in *multiple alliances*, so that if one counts the total number of strategic partnerships for the whole corporation, one may find several hundred as in the case of IBM, Motorola or Siemens.

Gomez-Casseres (1995) has qualified these alliances as 'constellations' in which partners are co-operating in one business segment but possibly compete in another.

Doz and Hamel (1998) identify three types of constellations (see Figure 4.14).

- Alliance *networks*
- Alliance *portfolios*
- Alliance *webs*.

Alliance networks are those to which partners contribute to increase reach, adopt a common standard or promote a new technology. VISA (credit card), SWIFT (banking), STAR (airlines) are alliances of this nature. Like in a club, several partners contribute and benefit from the alliance as long as they subscribe to the rules and discipline of the network. It is a 'one alliance, multiple partners' design.

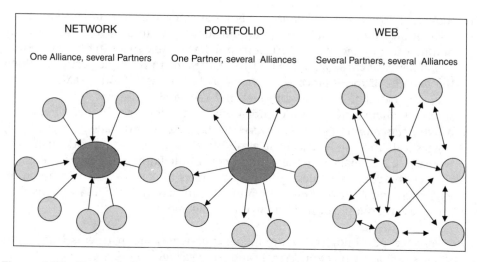

Figure 4.14   Types of alliance constellations

Source: Adapted from Doz and Hamel (1998).

Alliance portfolios are those where a company enters into a partnership with multiple companies, with different products, technologies or markets. The company deals with its partner as a portfolio, or on a one-to-one basis. There is no interaction among partners, only between partners and the 'core' parties. This is a 'one partner, several alliances' design. Corning Glass is a good example.

Alliance webs are constellations in which partners contribute and benefit inter-dependently, a 'several partners, several alliances' design. Airbus, during the last 20 years of its existence, functioned as a 'global web'. In an alliance web, one can find some characteristics of alliance networks (a common platform) or of alliances portfolios (one company in the web may have a central nuclear position, as Aerospatiale did for Airbus) but the relationships among partners are more equal and interdependent than in alliance portfolios and even more than in alliance networks.

Constellations of global partners put a high degree of constraint on companies, because of their complexity and diversity. Managerial challenges can arise at two levels:

- At the *alliance* level: how to make it work?
- At the *partners'* level: how to cope with multiple alliances, and in each alliance how to manage the relationships with other parties?

ALLIANCE CONSTELLATION MANAGEMENT

Depending upon the type of alliance, the managerial challenges vary. In an alliance network one will typically find two kinds of issues: first, alliance *creation and mobilisation* and second, alliance *governance and maintenance*.

(a) *Alliance creation and mobilisation.* Both alliance creation and mobilisation depend on core companies or on an outsider (this can be a government body or a new technology developer). Someone has to take the initiative to identify the benefits of those alliances and to 'sell' them to multiple partners. When the benefits of the alliance are obvious, as in the case of airline alliances, the task may be relatively easy, although the key element in that case is to make sure that alliance members are sufficiently compatible among themselves.

(b) *Alliance governance and maintenance.* As Lorenzoni and Baden-Fuller (1995) suggest, alliance networks must establish a centre or a 'network manager', whose role is to make sure the partners contribute fairly to the partnership and respect the common rules. Alliance managers also serve as an information exchange and clearing house for mutual transaction. The VISA organisation serves as an example of such 'network management'.

In an alliance portfolio, the main managerial issues are partner *selection* and *attraction* as well as partnership *leverage* and *relationships*.

(a) *Partner selection and attraction.* In an alliance portfolio, the prime objective for the 'nodal' firm (the portfolio manager) is to utilise a multiplicity of co-specialised, co-allied and learning alliances in order to foster its global competitive capabilities.

In selecting partners, the 'nodal' firm will look at firms bringing the necessary complementary capabilities but which are not likely to take advantage of the alliance in order to build their own competing capabilities. Corning, for instance, in its alliances with Siemens to develop, manufacture and sell optic fibres for communication, selected a partner who was not interested in building a competitive position in the design and production of fibres, but only in their utilisation.

(b) *Managing partner leverage and relationship.* The 'nodal' firm will make sure that the 'relevant' capabilities are obtained from the alliance, but also that it contributes positively and significantly to the partner's expectations. By keeping partnership as a one-to-one relationship, the 'nodal' firm builds a set of *converging capabilities* that are not shared by the whole constellation of partners.

In alliance webs, in contrast, the task of the 'nodal' firm is to build an interdependent set of mutual relationships to which each participant contributes but gains from all the others. Pixtech, for instance, has built a web of partners for the development of Field Emission Display (FED) technology for flat panel displays to be used in a variety of applications.

Partners entering the alliance have to demonstrate their commitment by opening their R&D labs (the LED-related technology) to other partners. Each party has to host meetings in its own facilities for alliance members to exchange their research progress. Reciprocal patent licensing is also involved in this type of alliance.

CRITERIA FOR SUCCESSFUL ALLIANCES

In this chapter we has tried to describe and analyse the various issues relevant to the management of global strategic alliances. In the business world today one can make two observations: first, more and more cross-border alliances are needed as a

Table 4.3   Eight criteria for successful alliances

▦ Individual excellence	– Both partners are strong
	– Have something to contribute
	– Have positive intent
▦ Importance	– Fits strategy of both partners
	– Long-term view
▦ Interdependence	– Partners need each other
	– Complementary capabilities
	– Nobody can 'go it alone'
▦ Investment	– Partner shows commitment
	– Investment/re-investment
▦ Information	– Reasonable open communication
	– Sharing of operational information
▦ Integration	– Shared operating procedures
	– Numerous connections
	– Teachers/learners
▦ Institutionalization	– Clear responsibilities
	– Clear decision processes
▦ Integrity	– No abuse
	– Willingness to enhance trust

Source: Moss Kanter (1994).

result of globalisation and with the advent of the 'new economy' (see Chapter 14) and second, most of the alliances fail to achieve their expected results. Probably two reasons can explain this poor record. First, a 'control' mindset – executives have difficulty shedding the hierarchical model of management inherited from vertically integrated business activities. Partnership requires a set of skills and mindsets on the part of the manager involved giving them the capacity to work in a network.[14] The second reason relates to the difficulty in building trust between organisations coming from different cultures: mistrust is probably the one single factor that explains partnership failure.[15] Building trust requires competencies that are not necessarily those taught in engineering and business schools; it requires the mastery of techniques belonging to social sciences such as 'negotiation analysis', the art of 'signalling' and the practice of 'credible commitment'.

Rosabeth Moss Kanter (1994) summarised the factors that can be found in successful alliances. Table 4.3 reproduces a valuable checklist for use when considering the design and implementation of particular global strategic alliances.

SUMMARY AND KEY POINTS

1. An *alliance*:
    - ▦ is the sharing of capabilities
    - ▦ between two or several firms
    - ▦ with the view of enhancing their competitive advantages and/or creating new business
    - ▦ without losing their respective strategic autonomy.

2. A *strategic alliance*:
   - is the governance structures
   - involving an incomplete contract between separate firms
   - in which each partner has limited control.

3. Types of strategic alliance depending on the scope (global/local) and object (market access or capabilities-enhancing):
   - A *local alliance*
     - is one in which either the object is for a foreign company to penetrate a local market (alliance for market entry) or to have access to a set or resources available in a particular country (resource-based country alliance)
     - Benefits of a local alliance are:
       (a) For the *foreign investors*: can increase market penetration and make profits in dividends or transfer prices of products/technologies introduced or management fees
       (b) For the *local partner*: can increase know-how, receive a flow of dividends and other indirect cash flow
   - A *global alliance*
     - is one in which the object would be either to develop a global market presence (global reach alliance) or to enhance the worldwide competitive capabilities of the firm (global leverage alliance)
     - There are three broad types of global strategic alliance:
       (a) *Coalition*: alliances of competitors, distributors and suppliers in the same industry pooling their capabilities to reduce cost or establish standards with the ultimate goal of developing market reach
       (b) *Co-specialisation*: alliances of firms that join their respective unique capabilities (resources, assets and competencies) to complement each other in order to create a business or to develop new products/technology
       (c) *Learning alliance*: for partners to transfer know-how and develop new competencies together
     - The eight criteria for successful global alliances are:
       (a) Individual excellence
       (b) Importance
       (c) Interdependence
       (d) Investment
       (e) Information
       (f) Integration
       (g) Institutionalisation
       (h) Integrity
     - Global multilateral alliances:
       (a) can potentially create constellations in which partners co-operate in one business segment but could possibly compete in another
       (b) There are three types of alliance constellations and each has their own managerial challenges:
         (i) *Alliance networks*: partners contribute to increase reach, adopt common standards or promote new technology – i.e. 'one alliance, multiple partners'

(ii)   *Alliance portfolios*: one company enters into a series of partnerships with multiple companies with different
products/technologies or markets – i.e. 'one
partner, several alliances'

(iii)   *Alliance webs*:   partners contribute and benefit interdepend-
ently – i.e. 'several partners, several alliances'.

4. There are four major steps for analysis of strategic alliances:

- Understanding the *strategic context* and spelling out the *strategic value* of an alliance:
  - Scope definition
  - Strategic objectives
  - Value creation potential
- Analysis of *partner(s)*:
  - Strategic fit
  - Capabilities fit
  - Cultural fit
  - Organisational fit
- *Negotiation* and *design*:
  - Operational scope
  - Interface
  - Governance
- *Implementation*:
  - Integration
  - Co-operation
  - Evolution.

5. Strategic context and strategic value of an alliance:

- *Strategic context*
  - Depends on the objective of the alliance partners whether the alliance is a coalition, co-specialisation or a learning alliance.
- *Strategic value*
  - For each alliance partner, strategic value of the alliance is determined based on:
    (a) The value created by the alliance:
        (i)   Revenues generated from the alliance through sales volume or high price resulting from differentiation
        (ii) Revenue or cost benefits coming from joint R&D products or processes
        (iii) Cost benefits from economies of scale/scope
    (b) Value which will be captured by the alliance partner:
        (i)   Share of the value created from the alliance
        (ii) Additional profit resulting from sales boosted by the alliance (e.g. increased company reputation)
  - Valuation of alliance is difficult due to:
    (a) Inherent difficulty of valuing non-traded resources, assets or compe-tencies brought in by partners
    (b) Assessment of relative contribution by partner
    (c) Much of the value accrues outside of the alliance

      (d) Relative value of each partner may shift over time

      (e) Lack of knowledge of partners' intention in value they are seeking from the alliance.

6. Partner analysis involves four assessments:

- *Strategic fit analysis*
  - Can predict longevity of alliance and requires an assessment of the criticality of the alliance for the partners, competitive position of partners and compatibility of strategic agendas
  - Four agendas are possible for each alliance partner:

      (a) *Venturing agenda*: intention to engage in a collaboration to create a business

      (b) *Extractive agenda*: aim of 'learning' or 'acquiring' capabilities from the partner or alliance

      (c) *Sharing agenda*: Goal of maximising efficiency in certain elements of the value chain through economies of scale and scope

      (d) *Options agenda*: Using the alliance to explore without committing vast amount of resources and need to decide whether to terminate or continue the alliance

- *Capabilities fit analysis*
  - Involves assessment of capabilities contribution of each partner and determination of whether there are any complementarities, gaps and redundancies
- *Cultural fit analysis*
  - Examines the similarities and differences in corporate, industrial and national cultures and devises suitable countermeasures to avoid potential conflicts
- *Organisational fit analysis*
  - Entails examination of partners' organisational structure systems to ensure smooth collaboration between partners. Elements to be examined include:

      (a) Degree of decentralisation and formalisation of decision-making

      (b) Extent of documentation of policies and rules

      (c) Accounting and reporting methods and systems and nature of incentives used in management.

7. In negotiation and design:

- *Operational scope*
  There are four types of alliance design, depending on the type of:
  - Partnerships (learning alliances or coalitions/co-specialisation alliance)
  - Operational capabilities
- *Interface and governance*:
  The following six aspects needs to be considered:
  - Legal structure and decision-making mechanism (the issue of 'control')
  - Degree of task integration (how activities carried out by the alliance and partners are to be co-ordinated and integrated)
  - Appointment of executives (including the alliance manager and various functional/line managers)

- Distribution of value (profit-sharing versus revenue-sharing)
- Reporting and communication processes (both vertical and horizontal communication between and within partners)
- Conflict resolution mechanism (the creation of an internal mechanism for resolving conflicts).

8. At the implementation stage, there are two important aspects to consider:

- *Integration and co-ordination*
  Particularly to avoid the 'death valley' issue, when a vicious cycle develops in which communications are shut off, which puts the viability of the alliance in question
- *Learning* (learning from the alliance and/or partner):
  - Strong learning capabilities include:
    - (a) Organised intelligence
    - (b) Networked internal information exchange
    - (c) 'Why' attitude – curiosity, searching for benchmarking and outside best practices
    - (d) Planned approach to skill acquisition
    - (e) Internal training
    - (f) Allocation of time and budgets to 'learn'
    - (g) Recruitment of people based on 'social' as well as professional skills.

Learning assignments

1 The text distinguishes between alliances – coalitions, co-specialisation and learning. To which category do you think the One World Alliance in which American Airlines, British Airways and Cathay Pacific participate belongs? What do such partners look for?
2 What are the sources of value creation in an alliance?
3 What are the criteria to be assessed in order to determine the strategic fit between partners?
4 What is an extractive agenda in an alliance?
5 What impact may cultural differences between partners have on global alliances?
6 What are the six domains that need to be negotiated about the interface and governance of an alliance?
7 What are the criteria for successful alliances?

Key words

- Alliance
- Capabilities fit
- Coalition alliance
- Constellations
- Co-specialisations
- Cultural fit
- 'Death valley'

- ▫ Extractive agenda
- ▫ Joint ventures
- ▫ Learning alliances
- ▫ Options agenda
- ▫ Organisational fit
- ▫ Sharing agenda
- ▫ Strategic fit
- ▫ Venturing agenda

Web resources

<http://www.bah.com/viewpoints/alliances_series.html>
Booz Allen & Hamilton web site which describes various issues in alliances.

<http://www.mckinseyquarterly.com/ca tegory_editor.asp?tk=86032::25&L2=25>
McKinsey Quarterly – Alliances.

Notes

1. It is interesting to observe that in May 2002, General Motors was finalising an acquisition of Daewoo Motors.
2. Gomez-Casseres (1995, chapter 1).
3. This example is drawn from 'General Electric and SNECMA' (A, B and C), written by Krishna and Gee under the supervision of Yves L. Doz (1994, 1997).
4. *Ibid.*, p. 66.
5. Kogut (1991, pp. 19–33); Williamson (1999, pp. 117–26).
6. 'Alza Ciba Geigy Advanced Drug Delivery Systems', written by Mark Cunningham under the supervision of R. Angelmar and Yves L. Doz (1994).
7. Geringer and Hebert (1989, pp. 235–54).
8. Bleeke and Ernst (1991, pp. 127–35).
9. Yoshino and Rangan (1995, chapter 8).
10. See, for instance, Harrigan (1986) and also Dent (1999).
11. See p. 122 below.
12. This section is largely based on Doz and Hamel (1998, chapter 7).
13. This section is largely based on Doz and Hamel (1998, chapter 8). See also Gomez-Casseres (1995).
14. Gomez-Casseres (1995, chapter 9)
15. Africa, de la Torre and Smith Ring (2001, pp. 109–31).

References and further reading

Ariño, Africa, José de la Torre and Peter Smith Ring, 'Relational Quality: Managing Trust in Corporate Alliances', *California Management Review*, 44(1), 2001, pp. 109–31.

Bleeke, J.A. and David Ernst, 'The Way to Win in Cross Borders Alliances', *Harvard Business Review*, November–December 1991, pp. 127–35.

Cunningham, Mark, 'Alza Ciba Geigy Advanced Drug Delivery Systems', INSEAD Case Study 2/94-4243, 1994.

Dent, Stephen M., *Partnering Intelligence: Creating Value for your Business by Building Smart Alliances*. Palo Alto, CA: Davies-Black Publishing, 1999.

Doz, Yves L. and Gary Hamel, *Alliance Advantage*. Boston, MA: Harvard Business School Press, 1998.

Ernst, David and Tammy Halevy, 'When to Think Alliance', *McKinsey Quarterly*, 4, 2000, pp. 47–55.

Friedheim, Cyrus F., 'The Battle of the Alliances', *Management Review*, September 1999, pp. 46–51.

Geringer. J.M. and Louis Hebert, 'Control and Performance of International Joint Ventures', *Journal of International Business Studies*, Summer 1989, pp. 235–54.

Gomez-Casseres, Benjamin, *The Alliance Revolution: An Entrepreneurial Approach to Globalization.* Cambridge, MA: Harvard University Press, 1995.

Hamel, Gary, C.K. Prahalad and Yves L. Doz, 'Collaborate with your Competitors, and Win', *Harvard Business Review*, January–February 1989, pp. 133–9.

Harrigan, Kathryn, *Managing for Joint Venture Success.* Lanham, MD: Lexington Books, 1986.

Inkpen, Andrew C., 'Learning and Knowledge Acquisition through Strategic Alliances', *The Academy of Management Executive*, November 1998, pp. 69–80.

Inkpen, Andrew and Jerry Ross, 'Why Do Some Strategic Alliances Persist Beyond Their Useful Life?', *California Management Review*, 44(1), 2001, pp. 132–54.

Kogut, Bruce, 'Joint Ventures and the Option to Expand and Acquire', *Management Science*, 137(1), 1991, pp. 19–33.

Krishna, L.N. and Francesca Gee, 'General Electric and SNECMA', INSEAD Case Study 04/94-3450, 1994.

Krishna, L.N. and Francesca Gee, 'General Electric and SNECMA', INSEAD Case Study 11/98-3450, 1998.

Lorenzoni, G. and C. Baden-Fuller, 'Creating a Strategic Centre to Manage a Web of Alliances', *California Management Review*, 37(3), 1997, pp. 1–18.

Moss Kantor, Rosabeth, 'Collaborative Advantage', *Harvard Business Review*, July–August 1994, pp. 96–108.

Reich, R.D. and E. Mankin, 'Joint Ventures with Japan Give Away Our Future', *Harvard Business Review*, March–April 1986, pp. 78–86.

Spekeman, Robert E. and Lynn A. Isabella, *Alliance Competence: Maximising the Value of Your Partnerships.* New York: John Wiley, 2000.

Williamson, Peter, 'Strategy as Options for the Future', *Sloan Management Review*, Spring 1999, pp. 117–26.

Yoshino, M.Y. and U. Rangan, *Strategic Alliances: An Entrepreneurial Approach to Globalization.* Boston, MA: Harvard Business School Press, 1995.

5

Global mergers and acquisitions

This chapter focuses on the strategic and managerial issues involved with global mergers and acquisitions (M&As). Global M&As have grown at an accelerated pace since 1990. M&As are instruments used by companies to increase their global reach and competitiveness. Even in the Asia Pacific region, traditionally allergic to M&As, the financial crisis that struck the region in 1997 opened the door.

In this chapter we will look at the two phases of M&As: the *pre-acquisition* phase and the *post-acquisition* phase. The pre-acquisition phase deals with the decision-making process: how companies decide, give a value and negotiate the deal. The post-acquisition phase refers to the managerial processes involved in the integration of the merged companies. This phase is considered by consultants and academics to be the most important source of success or failure.

The critical elements of the pre-acquisition phase are to determine the *strategic and financial value* of the proposed merger or acquisition. The strategic value relates to the increased competitive advantage that firms gain in these deals: whether it increases their global market presence or improves their costs or quality. A merger or an acquisition is justified if, and only if, the value of the new merged or combined entity is bigger than the sum of the value of the independent entities prior to the merger. The financial value of the deal is calculated on the basis of a detailed evaluation of the *future cash flow*. The data needed to calculate cash flow and to identify potential future problems are collected through a due diligence process and, several valuation models are examined in the chapter.

The post-acquisition phase consists of two main sequential steps: the *transition management* and the *strategic-consolidation* leading to the integration of the merged companies. The transition phase is often critical since it sets the *emotional and organisational context* of the integration. It involves a series of actions aiming at establishing confidence and credibility and focusing people's attention on the achievement of practical results.

The consolidation phase aims at establishing an ongoing working relationship between the two entities. We shall discuss three integration modes related to the operational interdependencies required between the two companies in order to achieve synergies, and the organisational autonomy that the acquired company requires owing to differences in market and environmental conditions. The three modes examined are: preservation, absorption and symbiosis.

At the end of this chapter one should be able:

- To identify the critical elements of value creation in an acquisition
- To plan and implement integration
- To understand the various phases of integration
- To understand the different modes of integration

THE RATIONALE FOR CROSS-BORDER M&As

Cross-border M&As grew in prominence during the 1990s: mostly fuelled by the globalisation of markets and competition (see Figure 5.1). In the oil and gas, telecommunication, pharmaceutical and banking industries,[1] there was the emergence of 'megamergers' (Table 5.1). Three particular events accelerated the movement: the Single European Market (SEM), followed by the advent of the Euro, the 1997 Asian crisis and the use of the shareholder value model of corporate governance. The SEM and the Euro created the economic conditions for consolidation of European companies, the Asian crisis gave an opportunity to Western corporations to buy Asian assets and finally the shareholder value model forced companies to de-diversify but also to concentrate on *core activities*. The example of Aventis illustrates this last point. Aventis was the result of the merger of the life-sciences activities of Rhône Poulenc Rorer (France and United States) and Hoechst (Germany). Before merging, Hoechst and Rhône Poulenc spun off their chemical businesses. The strategic rationale for M&As is not that different than those we described in Chapter 4 for global alliances.

There are three main value-creation objectives behind cross-border M&As.

- *Consolidation*: search for scale economies – BP/Amoco/Arco, Aventis
- *Global reach*: extension of international markets – Daimler Benz/Chrysler, Whirlpool/Philips, Vodaphone/Mannesman
- *Competencies acquisitions or options in related or new technologies* – Sony/Columbia, Vivendi/Universal Studios. This will include vertical integration and diversification.

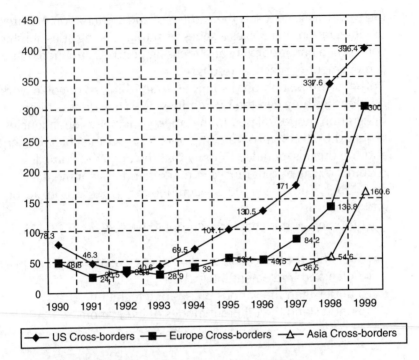

Figure 5.1 Trends in cross-border M&As, 1990–9 ($billion)

Notes: US includes US acquisitions abroad and foreign acquisitions in the United States.
Europe includes only intra-European cross-border M&As.
Asia includes intra-Asia Pacific plus European cross-border M&As in Asia.
Source: Mergers & Acquisitions (February 2000); *Mergers & Acquisitions Asia* (January 2000).

Table 5.1 Cross-border megamergers, 1990s and 2000

Acquirer	Target or merged company	Countries' acquirer/target	Industry	Price/deal value (US$ billion)
Vodafone	Airtouch	UK/USA	Telecom	60.3
British Petroleum	Amoco	UK/USA	Oil and Gas	48.2
Daimler Benz	Chrysler	Germany/USA	Automotive	40.4
Zeneca	Astra	UK/Sweden	Pharmaceutical	34.6
Rhône Poulenc	Hoechst	France/Germany	Pharmaceutical	21.9

Source: Mergers & Acquisitions (February 2000).

CASE EXAMPLES

Before engaging in a discussion about global M&As, we need to consider some case examples.

SONY/Columbia Studios[2]

In 1989, SONY put up $3.4 billion for the purchase of Columbia Pictures in the United States. Akio Morita, SONY's Chairman, spelled out the strategic logic of the deal when he declared that since SONY was the largest video hardware company, he wanted to have a video software company. The synergies were to be found in the complementarity of VCR manufacturing and film-making. Besides the political and somewhat anti-Japanese feelings that this deal generated, the integration of Columbia studio into SONY's empire was plagued with many problems. SONY was confronted with big cultural clashes due not only to US–Japanese differences, but also and above all by the huge gap between running a hardware manufacturing company and a film studio. In 1994, SONY took a $2.7 billion write-off attributed to loss of goodwill in the Columbia studio. Although today Columbia is still part of SONY's empire, it took the company at least a decade and substantial cash outflows to digest this acquisition.

SmithKline and Beecham[3]

In 1989, Bob Bauman, CEO of Beecham in the United Kingdom and Henry Wendt, CEO of SmithKline Beckman Corp. in the United States, announced an equal merger between the two companies to create SmithKlineBeecham with turnover of $10 billion.

It was agreed that the new entity would be led by Bob Bauman and that the two companies would create a new culture based on the motto 'Now we are one' and 'The simply better way' management philosophy and practice. An integration plan was immediately put in place. Supervised by a seven-member Merger Management Committee (four from Beecham and three from SmithKline), nine planning groups were created to produce a practical integration plan for all the main functional and business activities of the combined group; 200 'project teams' formed of six–eight members from both companies were given the task of producing detailed recommendations within five months. Eighteen months after the announcement the integration was nearly complete, and a new chairman, Jan Leshly, was appointed to lead the new group for the next decade.

Electrolux and Zanussi[4]

The acquisition of the Italian company Zanussi by the Swedish group Electrolux took place in the late 1980s. It remains a classic case of a well-planned and executed integration. The logic of the deal was simple. In the appliance industry, competition was becoming increasingly regional and global in certain market segments. With the advent of the SEM, it was obvious that two main industry features would emerge. First, market segmentation in Europe was no longer based on national characteristics but more on life style. Producers of white goods needed to implement a product and brand policy cutting across national barriers. Second, pressure on costs would make concentration of production for standard components such as motors or compressors necessary. Electrolux had gradually grown through 200 acquisitions with the ambition of becoming a European, and later global, leader in white goods. Zanussi was a well-established family-owned firm, well entrenched in washers in southern Europe but suffering a leadership vacuum owing to the loss of its top management team in a plane crash. The company was in disarray, but for Electrolux it represented a good strategic fit. Electrolux used a methodology developed in-house to conduct due diligence. Talks with trade unions preceded the decision to go ahead. When the deal was signed, Electrolux appointed as the leader of the acquired company an Italian manager who had worked previously for a Swedish multinational. He and his management team, made up of managers from Zanussi and Electrolux, immediately implemented a process of integration based on the work of integration teams who were assigned clear objectives to propose rapid and practical solutions to operational problems. Communications with employees, suppliers, distributors and government helped the re-establishment of confidence with those stakeholders. Through a well-planned execution of the integration process, Zanussi became one of the leading regional centres for washers in the Electrolux group.

Toyo Ink and Francolor[5]

In 1992, Toyo Ink, a Japanese printing ink company, acquired Francolor, a French company specialised in organic pigments. This was one of the first Japanese acquisitions made in Europe. The rationale for the acquisition was essentially to expand the geographic base of Toyo Ink as well as to complement its product lines and to benefit from the technological capabilities available at Francolor. Instead of trying to impose its way of doing things, Toyo management was very careful first to preserve Francolor's autonomy: they kept the existing management team; they progressively discovered and then put in place jointly with the French team adequate mechanisms of implementing synergies. Today, Francolor is the European hub of Toyo operations.

CROSS-BORDER ACQUISITIONS PERFORMANCE

The four examples quoted above show how difficult it is in the evaluation of M&As to disentangle what is due to international aspects and what is due to good or bad management practices. Several studies have tried to assess the value created by M&As; some have analysed M&A deals and their results without differentiating between domestic acquisitions and international ones. Overall, those studies have shown that between 45–75 per cent of acquisitions failed to deliver the value that was expected by their initiators.[6] John Kitching[7], looking at cross-border acquisitions in Europe, found that overall 25 per cent were straight failures and 25 per cent not worth doing, giving a success score of 50 per cent, while a McKinsey team found a 57 per cent rate of success in their own study of cross-border M&As.[8] The conclusion one can derive is that international M&As are no worse than domestic ones. One of the reasons for this is that most cross-border acquisitions are *horizontal* (i.e., in core business) and all the studies found that horizontal acquisitions tended to be more successful than others. The McKinsey studies found that in their sample cross-border acquisitions were essentially done in core businesses, while this was less the case in domestic ones. Since no research has tried to compare performances of horizontal international and horizontal domestic M&As, it is difficult to disentangle what are the specific success/failure factors of international acquisitions. The intuitive conclusion that can be drawn is that, on top of all other management factors, *cultural differences* can be a specific challenge in cross-border deals, as the SONY case demonstrates.

Academics and consultants who have analysed M&As generally come to the same conclusions.[9] Success or failure comes from two key issues:

- The quality of the *pre-acquisition process*: how companies make the M&A decision, give it a value and negotiate the deal
- The quality of the *post-acquisition process*: how the integration is managed. This process is considered the most important source of success or failure

In the remainder of this chapter we will concentrate on the process through which cross-border acquisitions are planned, decided (pre-acquisition) and implemented (post-acquisition), as illustrated in Figure 5.2.

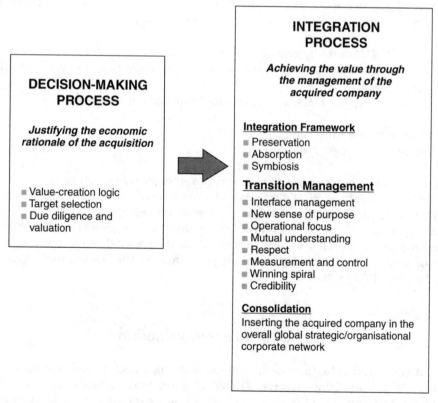

Figure 5.2   The pre-acquisition and post-acquisition processes in global M&As

Source: Adapted from Haspeslagh and Jemison (1991).

DECIDING ON THE M&A

Value creation

Theoretically M&As contribute to enhancing the economic value of the companies involved. The economics of M&As is simple: a merger or an acquisition is justified if, and only if, the value of the new merged or combined entity is bigger than the *sum of the value of the independent entities prior to the merger*.

From a strategic point of view M&As can create the following types of value:

- *Consolidation* of companies operating in the same business area – horizontal M&A: SmithKline/Beecham or Electrolux/Zanussi belong to this category
- *Global reach* – extension to international markets: Vodaphone/Mannesmann
- *Vertical integration* – merging of businesses which are suppliers or buyers of each other's products: Francolor/Toyo Ink possibly belongs to this category
- *Diversification* – companies operating in different business domains – the SONY/Columbia deal
- *Options* or the acquisition of a firm in a *new technology or market* to monitor its evolution: for instance the acquisition by the Swiss pharmaceutical group Ciba-Geigy in early 1980s of the Californian company Alza in order to get access to advanced drug delivery systems technologies.

International M&As usually belong to the first or second type, but the rush toward the 'new economy' (see Chapter 14) has triggered the development of diversification and options M&As.

Whatever the type of M&A, value is created through two modalities:

- Short-term one-off value
- Long-term strategic value.

Short-term value comes from the one-off post-merger realisation of cash benefits coming from a tax shield, asset disposals and immediate cost savings or debts leverage.

Long-term value comes from the competitive advantage gained from the merger: either it provides enhanced differentiation capabilities, a larger market, new growth opportunities, enhanced competencies or cost advantages through economies of scale or scope. These advantages are often referred as the 'synergistic' effects of a merger. (see Table 5.2).

Due diligence and valuation

Due diligence and **valuation** are among the main handicaps to global acquisitions, particularly in emerging markets. There are three main reasons for this. First, marketing and strategic information are often less accurate and reliable, or at least less accessible, than in the home country of the buyer. Second, political or nationalistic attitudes may hamper fair assessment. Third, accounting standards are not

Table 5.2   Value creation in M&As

Types of value creation	Benefits
Short-term value creation	
▪ Tax shield	▪ Diminution of tax bill (cost benefits)
▪ Asset disposals	▪ Lower capital invested (higher return, lower cost):
▪ Financial engineering:	– Lower cost of capital (assuming cost of debts lower than
– Debt leverage	cost of equity)
– Price/earnings (P/E) ratio leverage	– Total market value increased after the merger (assuming a P/E
	differential between buyer and seller and a positive market
	reaction)
Long-term value creation	
▪ Pooling and sharing resources	▪ Economies of scale and scope (cost benefits)
and assets	
– Joint purchasing	
– Manufacturing rationalisation	
– Joint distribution and logistics	
– Common IT and central services	
– Common Treasury	
▪ Enlarged market	▪ Growth potential enhanced
– Geography	▪ Richer value proposition (higher reach and possibly higher
– Products	differentiation)
▪ Transfer of competencies	▪ Higher differentiation
– Technology	▪ Processes more effective
– Best practices	▪ Innovation (higher differentiation and lower costs)

necessarily in line with international standards. In Korea, for instance, *chaebols* do not usually consolidate their accounts, and do not eliminate inter-company transactions within the same group: this can lead to inflated revenues. In South East Asia accounting ledgers are kept for tax purposes and the figures have very little relevance for asset valuation. Major adjustments have to be made:

▪ *Inventories* may be overvalued
▪ *Employees' retirement benefits* may not appear or may be underfunded and provisions have to be made for future liabilities
▪ In certain cases *accruals* are ignored and have to be restated
▪ *Real estate* has to be valued at market prices, and necessary tax adjustments have to be made
▪ *Hidden liabilities* such as legal actions may be uncovered.

Those adjustments are the most frequent. In the event of the acquisition of a company that is part of a conglomerate, adjustments for any cross-subsidiaries transfers which may have distorted announced profitability may have to be made, and checks made as to whether any licences, distributors, or contractual arrangements are still in place after the acquisition. If such contractual assets had originally been granted to the mother company, adequate transfers have to be included in the acquisition agreement. More time and effort is required to validate data than normal: detailed interviews with customers, suppliers and bankers all have to be part of due diligence.

Economic **valuation** is necessary in order for a potential buyer to decide at what price it is willing to conclude the deal – or, in the case of a merger, the relative proportions of shares to be exchanged.

Three main methods are used for such valuations[10]:

Asset-based valuation

This method determines the *actual value of assets minus liabilities*, using a replacement price for physical assets and adjusting for inventories or debtors book value. Intangible assets and goodwill are estimated using comparable value for similar businesses or using formulas such as dollars per customer. If the company's assets are predominantly physical, this approach may give a fair estimation of its value. When, on the other hand, the company's profitability relies on intangible resources and capabilities such as employees' commitment, knowledge and competencies, this method fail to give a good economic price.

Market-based valuation

This approach relies on *direct market valuation* if the company is listed on a stock exchange or otherwise on market equivalent valuation. When using stock exchange market value, the transaction will require that the bidder puts a premium on the deal. Premiums are based on an anticipation of value added from the merger, either short- or long-term through *synergies*. Research has found that 30–100 per cent premiums over market value are not unusual in cross-border acquisitions.[11] In order to calculate how much premium the company is ready to accept, one is forced to turn to a kind cash flow method of valuation since the future profit coming from the merger will accrue over the years and no other method is available to calculate a premium. Stock market prices may not always reflect the economic reality of a firm in countries where stock exchanges are not efficient owing to lack of liquidity, partial listing, lack of proper regulations or insider trading.

When the target company is not listed on the stock market, one can use market equivalent measurements such as P/E ratio, price/cash flow ratio or price/revenues ratio calculated from similar deals or comparable companies listed on the stock exchange. Such a measurement is crude, and should be used only as a reference since no deal and no company, even in the same industry, is exactly the same. In addition, particular deals may have been done on the basis of unsound calculations and there is no reason to replicate them.

Cash flow-based valuation

Economic theory would say that this is the only valid method, apart from the actual market price put on the stock market when the market is efficient.[12]

With this method, the value of a firm's equity is equal to the *net present value of future cash flows discounted with the weighted average cost of capital (WACC) minus debts*. In practice, this method implies:

- A calculation of *future cash flows*: revenues – cash costs – increase in required working capital – future investments – taxes

- A determination of the *WACC*, taking into account the risks of the deal; the WACC is the weighted average of the cost of equity and cost of debts.

In order to calculate future cash flows, one is forced to forecast revenues based on demand, price and market share assumptions as well as costs over a period that reflects a sound strategic horizon. As mentioned earlier, this can represent a big challenge in cross-border acquisitions in emerging countries or emerging industries where forecasting is more a matter of guesswork than hard computation. Another issue that can arise is the estimation of the WACC: WACC could be risk adjusted to take into consideration different risk profiles in different countries.[13] Another method is to adjust the cash flows for potential risks (see Chapter 13 for more details).

Two kinds of future cash flows needs to be valued in M&As:

- The *future cash flow* of the merging or of the acquired company calculated as if the company continued its activities without the merger. This is the **stand-alone value**. Normally, if the company is listed on the stock market its market capitalisation should reflect its stand-alone value, otherwise forecasting and discounting are needed.
- The *future value of the added value brought* in short-term and long-term by the merger of the two companies (see Table 5.2). This is the **synergies value**.

Those two streams of cash flow give a present value that reflects the **bargaining range** of the price negotiation. Below the stand-alone value no seller would sell (unless as a finesale or because of extreme non-economic pressure) since she/he could achieve this value without being acquired. Above the stand-alone plus synergies value the buyer should not buy since, if the calculation is correct, she/he transfers the value to the seller and does not get anything for her/himself (Figure 5.3).

INTEGRATING THE COMPANIES: THE INTEGRATION PHASE

The *integration* phase starts once deals have been negotiated and the acquisition or the merger decided. All researchers consider this phase of M&A as the most important, and the major source of failure when not handled properly. Table 5.3 summarises the main sources of failures and their effects. Ultimately, factors enumerated in

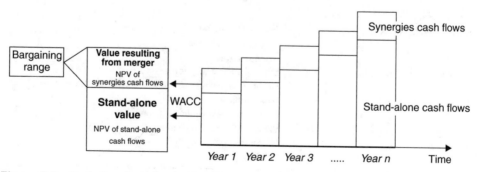

Figure 5.3 Cash flow-based valuation for M&As

Table 5.3 lead to *value destruction* instead of value creation. This is the reason why a proper integration process needs to be put in place.

The integration process is structured in three phases:

(a) The integration framework leading to an *integration plan*
(b) The *transition* management
(c) The strategic *consolidation*.

Integration framework

An integration *framework* is needed as road map for implementing a merger. Since the post-merger phase is a period of intense anxiety and uncertainty for the employees, suppliers and distributors of the companies involved, it is important that a framework guides the management of the process. Various frameworks have been offered by academics and consultants and they belong to two broad categories:

Table 5.3 Failures in the integration process

Source of failure in integration process	Effects
Lack of strategic direction	Actions and decisions not understood
	Resistance to change
	Unco-ordinated decisions
Lack of integration plan	Improvisation
	Time lost
	Anxiety not reduced
	Lack of quick response to events
Leadership vacuum	Anxiety not reduced
	Bureaucratic hassles
	Politic fights
Determinism (stubborn implementation of the integration plan)	Trying to impose 'pre-fabricated' solutions
	Arrogant behaviour from acquirers' employees
	Discouragement of front-line staff
Lack of communication	Anxiety not reduced
	Fears and rumours
Cultural mishandling	Stereotyped clashes, 'Them and us' syndrome
	Politicking
	Retreat
Lack of operational focus	Too much talk, no action
	Lack of concrete results
	No 'quick wins'
Loss of key management talent	Less productive workforce
	Negative signalling to internal and external stakeholders
Wrong synergies	Loss of efficiency
	Dysfunctional operations
	Waste of financial resources
Lack of buy-in	No motivation, passivity
	Politicking

Sources: Haspeslagh and Jemison (1991); Mitchell and Holmes (1996); Viscio *et al.* (1999); Habeck, Kröger and Träm (2000).

Table 5.4 An example of a linear framework for integration

Post-merger integration element	Guiding principles/best practices
Vision	▪ Agree on strategic intent and let it guide vision for merger integration
	▪ Work to get both sides of the deal to buy into vision and intent
	▪ Explicitly identify critical sources of expected value
Architecture for change	▪ Begin planning early and create detailed plans
	▪ Set the right pace; work with a sense of urgency
	▪ First attack opportunities that combine the lowest risk with the highest reward
Architecture for the new company	▪ Focus on relentless identification of sources of value (revenues, cost, etc.)
	▪ Incorporate strengths of both companies
	▪ Restructure the organisation to maximise value
	▪ Handle personnel issues swiftly
Leadership	▪ Choose new leadership quickly
	▪ Pick the right people and dedicated resources for the integration process
	▪ Show fairness and objectivity by using data to make decisions and by including people from both companies in the decision-making process
	▪ Set credible milestones and maintain pressure for progress by providing incentives to reach targets
	▪ Keep focus of the integration team on economic value-creation
	▪ Address cultural issues directly with an explicit plan
	▪ Communicate clearly, early, honestly and often; use a decisive tone; do not forget those outside the two companies

Source: Booz Allen in Viscio et al. (1999).

- *Linear frameworks* that are step-by-step or checklist approaches to integration that apply to all M&As. Table 5.4 illustrates one such framework.
- *Contingent frameworks* that differentiate integration processes according to environmental and strategic factors. This type of framework does not assume a unique approach to integration. We present here the contingent framework developed by Philippe Haspeslagh and William Jemison (1991).

In their contingent framework, Haspeslagh and Jemison identified three modes of integration, depending on:

(a) The degree of *required operational interdependencies* between the two companies that are needed to achieve synergies. For instance, the rationalisation of manufacturing or the transfer of competencies between companies.

(b) The degree of *required organisational autonomy* that the acquired company would need because of the difference in market and environment conditions with the acquirer; for instance, an acquisition in a different business or country.

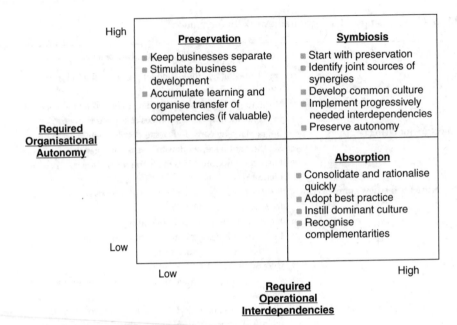

Figure 5.4 Contingent integration modes

Source: Adapted from Haspeslagh and Jemison (1991).

The three integration modes that Haspeslagh and Jemison identified are (Figure 5.4):

1. The *preservation* mode of integration
2. The *absorption* mode of integration
3. The *symbiotic* mode of integration.

The **preservation mode** fits with situations in which very few operational synergies can be gained and the business context calls for a large autonomy of decision-making, as in the case of diversification or option acquisitions. Since no benefits for interdependencies are to be expected and no major value can be brought in by forcing integration of processes, assets and decision-making, the key objective is first to 'preserve' the identity and autonomy of the acquired company, keeping in place, as far as possible, the existing management and learning progressively the 'rules of the game' of the business. The source of value here essentially comes from an *enlargement of markets and products* as well from the *transfer of resources or new competencies*. In this mode, one should not try to expedite the transfer of new competencies until one has understood their logic and their impact on the organisation and culture of the recipient company. Transfer of resources comes essentially from the injection of capital or stimulation of business development by giving access to logistical, IT or distribution facilities to the acquired company. Transfer of people has to be done more for learning than for controlling purposes in such cases. The danger of this mode of integration is that of being confronted by a 'weak' management team in the acquired company that behaves opportunistically in siphoning off the resources of the acquirer. This was the case in the mid-1980s when the UK Midland Bank acquired a Californian financial company.[14]

The **absorption** mode of acquisitions takes place when value is to be expected from the realisation of operational synergies in companies operating in similar business contexts. The objective here is to achieve the necessary *consolidation and rationalisation* as rapidly as possible. Since the businesses are very similar, the top management of the acquirer or the top management of the merging firms are competent rapidly to find sources of savings and to understand which best practices have to be adopted. As mentioned earlier, this rationalisation may raise some practical difficulties in the case of 'equal mergers' when duplicated functions have to be eliminated. The ultimate objective, as in the case of SmithKline Beecham, illustrates that the 'Now we are one' motto is rapidly to create a common culture.

Finally the **symbiotic** mode of acquisitions tries to achieve a balance between *interdependencies and autonomy*. This is often the case in cross-border horizontal acquisitions where a lot of value is gained from the achievement of synergies but the differences in contexts require a high degree of autonomy. In this mode, the starting point is to use a preservation mode and to find jointly the *real sources of synergies and their practicalities*. The approach was used by Toyo Ink with Francolor or Electrolux with Zanussi.

INTEGRATING THE COMPANIES: THE TRANSITION PHASE

Whatever the mode of integration is, there is a critical phase in any merger and acquisition, the *transition phase*. Just after a merger or an acquisition, the various stakeholders of the acquired or the merged firms are in a state of shock, or at least of anxiety, and the operations may suffer from the uncertainties surrounding the pre-acquisition phase. In Asia Pacific, for instance, during the late 1990s, Western firms made a lot of acquisitions of financially strapped companies: the situation required a fast turnaround. The transition period is the one during which the acquirer or the merging partners establish their *credibility* and demonstrate their ability to *manage the new concern*.

Eight main issues need to be solved at this stage:

(a)　The appointment of an executive team capable of *leading the integration process* and *managing the interface* between the two companies

(b)　The expression of a new *sense of purpose*, demonstrating to stakeholders that the acquisition or the merger was well planned

(c)　The focus on *concrete operational results* that motivate employees and distract them from sterile rumours.

(d)　The development of a *mutual understanding*, bridging or palliating the cultural gap

(e)　The showing of *respect for the acquired company personnel*, avoiding arrogant behaviour and preventing the 'brain drain' of valuable employees

(f)　The installation of *measurement tools* to measure and control progress

(g)　The creation of a '*winning spiral*' that reinforce a sense of success and achievement

(h)　The demonstration of *credibility* that reassures stakeholders and reduces anxiety.

Appointment of an executive team and interface management

In the case of a merger, the critical issue is to install a management team that is capable of understanding the cultures of the two parties and *transforming* them *into a new culture*. Most of the time this change will be demonstrated by a new logo that may or may not combine the two names of the founding companies: Aventis in the case of Rhône Poulenc-Hoechst, or SmithKlineBeecham. People problems (who is in charge?) need to be sorted out before the beginning of the transition phase, at least for the key roles, to avoid confusion. The projected merger between SKB and Glaxo Wellcome could not be carried through because of disagreements over the designation of the CEO of the new entity. This problem did not arise when Smith-Kline and Beecham merged.

In acquisitions, the critical issue is to trade off the need to *control* and the need to *preserve the key contacts and knowledge* of the previous management team. There is also the need to make sure that the appointed management team will be an efficient interface between the acquired company and the foreign acquirer. The best way to achieve an efficient interface is to appoint, as managing director, an executive or a team of executives having the capabilities to understand the cultures of both the seller and the buyer organisation, and to serve as a bridge between the newly acquired entity and the new owners.

New sense of purpose

Anxiety and resistance reduction can best be achieved if new management communicates credible goals, demonstrating to stakeholders that the merger or the acquisition was well planned, thus reassuring them of a determination to lead the company to success. *Systematic and structured communication campaigns* need to be organised. Through meeting with managers, and employees, publications or social events, the new management can disseminate the main messages: what are the objectives, what main direction is the company going to take?

Operational focus

Focusing the attention on *concrete operational details* and *performance targets* has two major advantages. First, it is likely to erase the uncertainty created by the takeover by demonstrating that the company is back in business. As in the case of alliances discussed in Chapter 4, one of the most powerful methods is to create *integration teams*. Task forces are appointed made up of personnel from the acquirer and acquired companies for each of the key operational activities (accounting, purchasing, quality, etc.) and ask the working party to discuss and propose concrete solutions to operational aspects: what kind of software to use for inventory controls, what method to adopt in order to recover ongoing receivables, how to deal with distributors, what the possibilities are of cost reduction in logistics, etc. The advantage of such an approach is that it gives people a tangible sense of participation in the integration process. It also helps to develop mutual under-standing among the employees of both the buyer and seller organisations.

Such teams can also rapidly correct any intrinsic weaknesses of the acquired organisation. One has to go for a rapid turnaround, and this is a means of establish-ing confidence and of demonstrating the visible benefits of the acquisition. Effect-iveness is more important than optimised efficiency: a quick minor gain is more important at this stage than a slow major one. This is the reason why the use of integration teams to put in place practical solutions to practical problems is so useful. The involvement of technical and administrative or commercial middle management is critical here, because their technical expertise, if properly combined, can bring quick results.

Mutual understanding and respect

Cross-cultural issues are likely to arise, and especially in cross-border mergers. The ability of the two entities to understand each other is critical for the success of any integration. The objective at the transition phase is not so much to merge the two cultures as to create a climate of *mutual understanding*. The kind of culture that will surface from the merger is contingent upon the mode of acquisition. A preservation mode will not attempt to blend the two cultures but on the contrary will keep them separate, while absorption would seek to create a common culture.[15] Mutual under-standing is enhanced when the acquiring company staff and executives show respect for the employees of the acquired company and adopt a attitude sensitive to cultural differences and avoid behaving like the 'conquerors' of a besieged city. The risks are high if the acquirers come and impose their viewpoints, their method-ologies and work processes, as if the merged company's practices were not worth considering. Acquirers should instill a climate of mutual understanding by studying carefully the existing practices of the acquired company, and seeking opinions from the employees before introducing change.

Measurement and control

Talking with facts and figures helps communication, allows a measure of improvement and reduces the risk of 'cultural excuses'. The cultural excuses are used in the event of difficulties or disagreements, and are based on impressionistic or ste-reotypical judgements. The collection of marketing, operational and financial hard facts and figures is a necessary condition for an efficient and productive dialogue. In the case of the merger between SmithKline and Beecham, a specific methodology was introduced in the integration team to guide the process and to measure its progress.

Winning spiral

The search for tangible immediate performance improvement should also be on the agenda of the transition-period management. 'Quick wins' usually derive from the joint efforts of the integration teams, as illustrated in the cases of SmithKline Beecham and Electrolux. Rapid performance improvements in quality, costs and market success give people a sense of achievement and enhance their confidence in the whole acquisition process.

Credibility

Confidence is not likely to be established if the various stakeholders do not perceive that what the new owners say, and do, is credible. Credibility relies essentially on the *quality of the people* who are put in place to run the company, and the perception of their real power within the mother organisation. It is essential that managers appointed to run the acquired company work closely with the back-up of central headquarters to make sure that the acquisition is well supported by the centre, and that sufficient resources are devoted to making it work.

INTEGRATING THE COMPANIES: THE CONSOLIDATION PHASE

The consolidation phase is the one that sees the final integration of the two companies and the definition of the respective strategic roles of the *merged company*. In the case of a merger, it consists in creating and finalising a new organisational structure in which the ex-merging firms dissolve themselves into the new design. SmithKline and Beecham, with the programme of a 'Simply better way' and a strategic definition of the vision of the new company under the umbrella of 'Global health care', achieved this phase after one year.

In the case of a cross-border acquisition, the consolidation phase consists of providing the acquired company with a *strategic identity* and making sure that it has a specific role in the overall regional or global strategy of the acquirer. Employees, governments and the local community may see the acquisition generally as a foreign intrusion, reminiscent of the old colonial days. During the transition phase described earlier, the purpose was to give confidence to the various stakeholders about the will and capabilities of the acquirer to contribute to the development of the firm. At the consolidation phase, there is a need to confirm that the acquisition is not only a trading of assets or a good bargain, but also a real *strategic move* in which the acquired firm has a role to play. This gives employees a sense of direction and self-esteem. The acquired firm's employees must not feel that they are pawns, but strategic partners, that they are part of a strategic vision and that their contribution is essential in achieving it. One of the best methods is to give the firm some responsibilities in leading strategic initiatives in terms of business or product developments. In the case of Electrolux's acquisition in Italy, Zanussi was given the strategic leadership for washers in Europe while in the case of the Toyo Ink acquisition, Francolor was given the responsibility for European co-ordination.

The second challenging task is to be able to make the acquired company part of the family by plugging it into the existing network of *knowledge* and *competencies*. This is achieved through secondment of personnel to other subsidiaries, in participation in conferences and seminars, and by teamwork in various operational areas where transfer of competencies can produce value added results. Control has to be exercised without stifling entrepreneurial benefits. The ideal situation is to rely on most of the existing senior and middle-management talent already existing in the acquired company and to support it with adequate training and reward. An important consideration is the practice of '**fair process**' that gains the loyalty and commitment of managers.[16] Fair process is a management practice based on combining those integration principles advantageous to achieving both efficiency and local entrepreneurship. This has also the tremendous benefit of buying in the loyalty of the employees, and the goodwill of governments and local communities. In this way the acquirer is neither an intruder nor an invader, but an *insider*.

SUMMARY AND KEY POINTS

1. Cross-border M&As:
    - Are motivated by three factors:
        - *Consolidation* (achieving economies of scale)
        - *Global reach* and competencies acquisition
        - Options in *technologies*
    - Value creation is short-term and long-term:
        - *Short-term*
            - (a) Tax shield benefits
            - (b) Asset disposals
            - (c) Financial engineering
        - *Long-term*
            - (a) Pooling and sharing resources and assets
            - (b) Enlarged markets (in terms of geography or products)
            - (c) Transfer of competencies (including technologies and best practices)
    - Types of economic valuations for mergers and acquisitions include:
        - *Asset-based valuation:*   uses replacement price
        - *Market-based valuation:*   uses direct market information
        - *Cash flow-based valuation:* discounted cash flows method
    - In the cash flow analysis:
        - *Stand-alone value*: is the future cash flow of the merged or acquired firm if the company continued its activities without the merger
        - *Synergies value*: is the future value of the added value brought in short-term and long-term by the merger of the two companies
        - *Premium*: the premium amount is less than or equal to the synergies value
    - The success of an M&A depends on the quality of:
        - *Pre-acquisition* processes
        - *Post-acquisition* processes.
2. The pre-acquisition process consists of three steps:
    - Determination of *value creation*
    - *Target* selection

█ *Due diligence* and *valuation*:
   (a) Due diligence and valuation are difficult in international M&As owing to the problem of institutional context
   (b) For global acquisitions in emerging markets, due diligence and valuation are more difficult:
      (i) Emerging markets are fraught with unreliable marketing and strategic information
      (ii) Local accounting standards may not be compatible with international standards
      (iii) Political/nationalistic attitudes may hamper unbiased assessment.

3. The post-acquisition process (i.e. the integration phase) can have six sources of failure:

   █ Leadership vacuum
   █ Determinism (stubborn implementation of integration plan)
   █ Cultural mishandling
   █ Loss of key management talent
   █ Wrong synergies
   █ Lack of:
      – Strategic direction
      – Integration plan
      – Communication
      – Operational focus
      – Buy-in
   █ There are three phases in the integration process:
      – The *integration framework* leading to an integration plan
      – The *transition management*
      – The *strategic consolidation*.

4. The three modes of integration within the contingent framework are:

   █ *Preservation* mode
      – Used when there is high need for organisational autonomy but low need for operational interdependencies
      – The integration process involves keeping the businesses separate, stimulating business development and accumulating learning
   █ *Absorption* mode
      – Used when there is a low need for organisational autonomy but a high need for operational interdependencies
      – The integration process involves consolidating and rationalising quickly, recognising complementarities, adopting best practices and instilling a dominant culture
   █ *Symbiotic* mode
      – Used when there is high need for organisational autonomy but low need for operational interdependencies
      – The integration process commences with a preservation mode but subsequently develops a common culture and implements progressively the necessary interdependencies while preserving autonomy.

5. The transition management is concerned with seven issues:

    - Appointment of an executive team and interface management
    - Instilling a new sense of purpose
    - Focusing on concrete operational results
    - Development of mutual understanding and respect
    - Introduction of measurement tools to measure and control progress
    - Creation of a winning spiral
    - Demonstration of credibility.

6. The strategic consolidation process:

    - For *mergers:* Involves creating and finalising a new organisational structure
    - For *acquisitions:* Is concerned with providing the acquired company with a strategic identity and ensuring that it has a specific role in the overall regional or global strategy of the acquirer
    A practice of 'fair process' is important in order to gain loyalty and commitment of managers of the acquired company.

Learning assignments

1 The chapter describes four examples of cross-border mergers: can you identify the source of value creation in each case?
2 What are the problems in conducting due diligence in a global context?
3 What determines the bargaining range of a negotiation?
4 What are the critical issues in the post-acquisition transition phase?
5 In what circumstances is the symbiotic mode of integration appropriate?
6 What are the most frequent sources of failure in M&As?

Key words

- Absorption mode of integration
- Due diligence
- 'Fair process'
- Integration process
- Interface management
- Post-acquisition process
- Pre-acquisition process
- Preservation mode of integration
- Stand-alone value
- Symbiotic mode of integration
- Synergies value
- Valuation

Web resources

<http://www.bain.com/bainweb/about/insights/pract_insights.asp?status=1&sort=capability&capability_id=34>
Bain – Merger and Acquisition.

<http://www.mckinseyquarterly.com /category_archive.asp?tk=86032::&L3 =4>
McKinsey Quarterly – Merger and Acquisition.

Notes

1. Purshe (1996, pp. 110–19); Ernst and Steinhubl (1999, pp. 49–57).
2. Kou and Spar (1994).
3. Hyde and Haspeslagh (1994).
4. Ghoshal and Haspeslagh (1990).
5. Probert and De Meyer (1998).
6. A series of studies by consulting firms Mercer, McKinsey and Bain & Co. show a rate of unsuccessful acquisitions ranging from 50 per cent to 75 per cent. These aggregate figures do not differentiate between domestic and international acquisitions.
7. Kitching (1973).
8. Bleeke *et al.* (1990, pp. 46–55).
9. The following literature covers both domestic and cross-border acquisition processes: Haspeslagh and Jemison (1991); Von Krogh, Sinatra and Singh (1994); Mitchell and Holmes (1996); Habeck, Kröger and Träm (2000).
10. Eccles, Lanes and Wilson (1999, pp. 136–46); Hawawini and Viallet (1999, chapter 12).
11. Eccles, Lanes and Wilson (1999).
12. Financial theory would argue that markets implicitly use the cash flow method by discounting the flow of future dividends to determine a price: this is the efficient markets theory.
13. Lessard (1996).
14. Davidson and de la Torre (1989, pp. 296–318).
15. Smith (2000, pp. 45–50).
16. Chan and Mauborgne (1997, pp. 65–75).

References and further reading

Books and articles

Ashkenas, Ronald, Lawrence DeMonaco and Suzanne C. Francis, 'Making the Deal Real: How GE Capital Integrates Acquisitions', *Harvard Business Review*, January–February 1998, pp. 165–78.
Bleeke, Joel, James Isono, David Ernst and Douglas Weinberg, 'Succeeding at Cross-Border M&A', *McKinsey Quarterly*, 3, 1990, pp. 46–55.
Capron, Laurence, 'The Long-Term Performance of Horizontal Acquisitions', *Strategic Management Journal*, 20(11), 1999, pp. 987–1018.
Chan, Kim and Renée Mauborgne, 'Fair Process: Managing in the Knowledge Economy', *Harvard Business Review*, July–August 1997, pp. 65–75.
Davidson, William H. and José de la Torre, *Managing the Global Corporation: Case Studies in Strategy and Management*. New York: McGraw-Hill, 1989, pp. 296–318.
Eccles, Robert G., Kersten L. Lanes and Thomas C. Wilson, 'Are You Paying Too Much For That Acquisition?', *Harvard Business Review*, July–August 1999, pp. 136–46.
Ghemewat, Pankaj and Fariboz Ghadar, 'The Dubious Logic of Global Megamergers', *Harvard Business Review*, July–August 2000, pp. 64–72.
Ghoshal, Sumantra and Philippe Haspeslagh, 'Electrolux: The Acquisition and Integration of Zanussi', INSEAD Case Study 09/90-123, 1991.
Habeck, Max, Fritz Kröger and Michael Träm, *After the Merger: Seven Rules for Successful Post Merger Integration*. London and Englewood Cliffs, NJ: Financial Times/Prentice-Hall.
Haspeslagh, Philippe and William Jemison, *Managing Acquisitions: Creating Value Through Corporate Renewal*. New York: Free Press, 1991.
Hawawini, Gabriel and Claude Viallet, *Finance for Executives*. Cincinnati, OH: South-Western Publishing, 1999, chapter 12, pp. 379–428.
Hyde, Dana and Philippe Haspeslagh, 'The Making of the Simply Better Healthcare Company: SmithKline and Beecham: The Simply Better Way', INSEAD Case Study 03/95-4449, 1994.

Khou, Julia and Deborah Spar, 'SONY Corporation and Columbia Pictures', Harvard Business School Case 9/795/025, 1994.

Kitching, John, 'Acquisitions in Europe', *Business International*, Research Report 73-3, Geneva, 1973.

Lessard, Donald, 'Incorporating Country Risks in the Valuation of Offshore Projects', *Journal of Applied Corporate Finance*, 9(3), 1996.

Mitchell, David and Gary Holmes, *Making Acquisitions Work: Learning from Companies' Successes and Failures*. London: Economic Intelligence Unit, 1996.

Probert, Joselyn and Arnoud De Meyer, 'Francolor Pigments: A Toyo Ink Acquisition', INSEAD Case Study 05/98-4756, 1998.

Purshe, William, 'Pharmaceuticals: The Consolidation is Not Over', *McKinsey Quarterly*, 2, 1996, pp. 110–19.

Smith, Kenneth, 'A Brand New Culture for the Merged Firm', *Mergers & Acquisitions*, June 2000, pp. 45–50.

Von Krogh, George, Alessandro Sinatra and Harbir Singh (eds), *The Management of Corporate Acquisitions: International Perspectives*. London: Macmillan, 1994.

Viscio, Albert, John Harbison, Amy Asin and Richard Vitaro, 'Post-Merger Integration: What Makes Mergers Works?', Strategy+Business, Fourth Quarter, 17, 1999, pp. 26–33. Also available at http://www.strategy-business.com.

Journal

Mergers & Acquisitions, Thomson Financial Securities Data, USA, monthly.

6

Assessing countries' attractiveness

Within the overall framework of their global strategy firms have to choose the geographical locations where they will set up operational assets. This kind of decision, known as the 'entry' decision, demands that firms take into consideration several factors:

- First, there is the need to assess the *attractiveness* of the country, either in absolute terms or relatively to other country. This is generally known as '**country attractiveness analysis**'.
- Second, there is the need to decide on a *form* of entry. This is generally known as '**entry strategy**'.

In Chapter 6, we will concentrate on country attractiveness assessment, while in Chapter 7 we will discuss entry strategies.
Country attractiveness is a function of the *market prospects*, the *competitive context* and the *risks of operating* in a country. The chapter presents a framework of assessing market attractiveness as well as country risks.
At the end of the chapter one should be able:

- To organise a complete assessment of market opportunities and industry structure in a country
- To understand and value various types of risks involved in operating in a country
- To compare different countries as investment opportunities.

'WHY IS A COUNTRY ATTRACTIVE?'

Theoretically a country will be attractive for a foreign investor if, in investing in that country, she/he gets a return that is equal to or higher than her/his *risk adjusted weighted cost of capital*. In fact, the foreign investment decision is fundamentally the same as any investment decision. If we apply the concept to a business investment (as opposed to a financial portfolio investment of securities), the logic of the decision is embodied in two key questions:

(a) Are the market prospects and the competitive conditions in a particular country such that given a set of competitive advantages, the business is likely to generate a return *equal to or higher than the cost of capital?*
(b) Are the risks of operating in this country *acceptable for the shareholders and employees?*

The fundamental question of a foreign investment thus falls into the general framework of opportunities and risks analysis, as shown in Figure 6.1.

Although foreign investments fall into the general category of an opportunities/risks trade-off, the assessment of the international context raises some challenging issues. Many scholars, consultants and practitioners have proposed methodologies for country assessments. Table 6.1 summarises the various approaches, giving relative rankings or scores of countries according to different economic, political and social dimensions. What we propose here is an analysis of the various dimensions that contribute to country attractiveness. These can be grouped into two broad categories:

- Market and industry opportunities
- Country risks.

One has to bear in mind first that market and competitive opportunities vary according to the *type of industry,* and risks affect them differently. Generalisations are thus difficult to make. Secondly, the merit of a country is first evaluated in *absolute terms* to check whether it presents minimum characteristics of opportunities and risks, and then it is generally compared with other countries having *similar features*. For instance, a company may evaluate investing in Chile and then compare

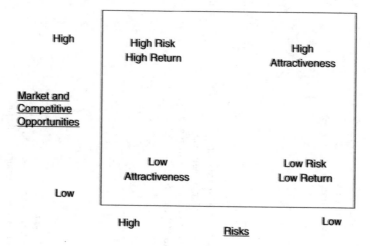

Figure 6.1 General investment framework

Table 6.1 Models and sources of countries' assessment

Organisation/publication	Type of rating	Methodology
IMD *The World Competitiveness Yearbook*[1] Published annually <http://www.imd.ch/wcy.html>	Ranking of 47 countries on a world competitiveness scoreboard Assesses competitiveness as well as location attractiveness	Uses statistical and survey data to score 288 criteria grouped into eight categories: ▪ Domestic economy ▪ Internationalisation ▪ Government ▪ Finance ▪ Infrastructure ▪ Management ▪ Science and technology ▪ People
Economic Intelligence Unit Business ranking published in *Country Forecast Quarterly* report <http://EIU.com>	Ranking of 60 countries on the quality of the attractiveness of the investment environment	Uses subjective and objective indicators grouped into 10 categories of 70 criteria: ▪ Political environment (11 criteria) ▪ Macroeconomic environment (5) ▪ Market opportunities (8) ▪ Policy toward private enterprises and competition (8) ▪ Policy toward foreign investment (4) ▪ Foreign trade and exchange control (4) ▪ Taxes (6) ▪ Financing (6) ▪ Labour market (8) ▪ Infrastructure (10)
ICON Group Publishes market analysis and forecasts <http://www.icongroupedition.com>	Measures latent demand and market accessibility, by industries	Latent demand is measured by economic, demographic, urbanisation, geographical and cultural factors; accessibility is measured by eight factors: ▪ Openness to trade ▪ Openness to direct investment ▪ Marketing and entry alternatives available ▪ Local human resources

- Local risks
- Political stability
- Cultural homogeneity
- Demand concentration

Euromonitor
Global market information data base
<http://www.euromonitor.com>

Provides market sizing and forecasts for 330 consumer products across 49 countries plus marketing parameters (1,000 types of data) for 209 countries over 20 years

Gives:
- Market size
- Country data
- Forecasts
- Company and brand profiles
- Information sources
- Special industry reports

BERI SA
Business Risk Service (BRS)

Monitors 50 countries three times per year to assess quantitatively and qualitatively political, operational and financial risks

Computes three indices and composite score
The indices are:
- *Political Risk Index* that measures socio-political change with eight external and internal causes as well as two symptoms of risk.
- *Operational Risk Index* that measures with 15 criteria the degree to which complex operational conditions affect production as well as end-profits
- *R factor* that measures the financial risks
- An overall index, the *Composite Score* position of the country on a risks scale.

World Economic Forum
Global Competitiveness Report

Ranks 59 countries according to their competitiveness and the growth of their competitiveness
Ranking is based on Porter's 'Competitive Diamond'[2]

Uses two categories of factors:
- A ranking of company operation and strategy based on 15 measures of competitiveness of domestic firms
- A ranking of the quality of national business environment (48 measures of infrastructure quality, demand quality, supporting industries and competitive rivalry)

Professor Steve Guisinger[3]
(University of Texas, Dallas) ECLIPTER Model

Defines an exhaustive list of attributes called 'geovalent components' that define the international businesses environment that differentiates countries

Components are grouped into eight categories:
Econography (climate, proximity to major markets, physical size, infrastructure)

Table 6.1 (Continued)

Organisation/publication	Type of rating	Methodology
		■ Culture (values, beliefs, attitudes)
		■ Legal system (common, civil, religious)
		■ Income profile (GNP per capita, growth, income inequality)
		■ Political risks (government instability, corruption, bureaucratic instability, quality of government)
		■ Tax system (effective rate)
		■ Exchange rates (exchange rate variability, over-valuation/under-valuation)
		■ Government restrictions (tariffs, quotas, investment controls)
Political Risk Services (PRS)[4]		
■ ICRG risk rating system	■ Rates political, economic and financial risks	■ Evaluates 24 risk components:
■ The Coplin-O'Leary System	■ Rates risks related to regime stability, internal turmoil, financial transfer, direct investment and export	– Political (13 criteria)
		– Financial (5 criteria)
		– Economic (6 criteria)
		■ Mixes subjective and objective measures
		■ Gives points from 0 to 100
		■ Classifies countries into five categories from Very High Risk to Very Low Risk
		■ Classifies countries into A, B, C, D types according to the level of risk
Institutional Investor		
Country creditworthiness	Information provided by 75,100 leading banks	Grades from 0 to 100
Euromoney		
Country credit rating	Assessment based on markets, credit, political, economic indicators	Grading system
Economic Freedom Ratings		
■ Heritage Foundation	Publish ratings based on assessment of political and economic freedom; the assessments are not immune from ideological positions	
■ Fraser Institute		

Chile with Argentina. Thailand may be compared with the Philippines, Malaysia or even Indonesia, Vietnam with Cambodia, France with the United Kingdom or Germany and India with China.

MARKET AND INDUSTRY OPPORTUNITIES (SEE FIGURE 6.2)

Market opportunities assessment measures the *potential demand* in the country for the products or services of the firm:

- Market *size*
- Market *growth*
- Quality of *demand*.

Industry Opportunities assessment measures how easy it is to *compete* in the country:

- The quality of the *competitive* climate
- The quality of the *industry competitive structure*
- The *investment incentives* granted by governments.

Appendix 6.1 (p. 183) gives a short summary of the differences between China and India for household expenditures.

Figure 6.2 Framework for country market and industry attractiveness assessment

Assessing market opportunities

The classical tools of market forecasting and analysis are used here, in a logical sequence.

Broad assessment of the overall demand, given macroeconomic data

In many instances, this broad assessment uses some sort of correlation between macroeconomic social or institutional indicators such GDP *per capita* with some measure of consumption of certain products. Table 6.2 gives some of the most frequently used **macroeconomic indicators**. Applying forecast GDP growth figures given by International Financial Organisations (IFOs) such as the World Bank, IMF or OECD gives a crude estimate of the anticipated size of the market

Figure 6.3 gives a graphical representation of household appliances consumption as a function of GDP *per capita*. The correlation between the two indicators is partial. The R^2 of the regression is only 46 per cent, indicating that other factors than the overall economic standard 'drives' expenditure on appliances. For instance, the difference between Hong Kong and Singapore is striking. Those two markets (Hong Kong is not a 'country') have a lot in common in terms of economic indicators, but the value of the appliances purchases *per capita* is almost 9 times higher in Hong Kong than in Singapore ($548 against $65). This may be explained by differences in lifestyle, climatic conditions and social behaviour.

Plotting trends

As a first cut, the macroeconomic correlation approach may give some interesting insights into the potential size of a market. When it is used in combination with other factors such as the degree of urbanisation, climatic conditions, income

Table 6.2 Macro indicators correlates used in international market assessments

Economic	Sociological	Demographical	Institutional
▪ GDP size ($)	▪ Urbanisation	▪ Population	▪ Government spending
▪ GDP size (PPP)*	▪ Socio-economic distribution	▪ Population growth	▪ Infrastructure: –Power –Telecom –Roads
▪ GDP*per capita ($) ▪ GDP*per capita (PPP) ▪ Disposable income ▪ Income distribution ▪ Export/imports ▪ Saving rate ▪ Investment rates		▪ Age distribution	

Note: *PPP (Purchasing Power Parity) calculations take into account differences in prices and cost of living. Generally developing countries can buy many more goods and services with one US$ than in the United States and therefore have a much higher GDP calculated with PPP than with market exchange rates.

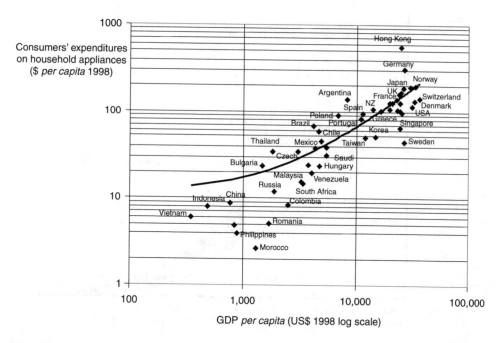

Figure 6.3 Relationship between GDP *per capita* and household appliances' market *per capita*, 1998 figures in US$

Source: Euromonitor.

distribution, lifestyles and saving rates, it may give a more precise prediction. Plotting trends for comparable countries (in terms of economic conditions, economic factors, etc.) also gives a view about the potential future of demand on a *per capita* basis as well as in absolute value (see Figure 6.4).

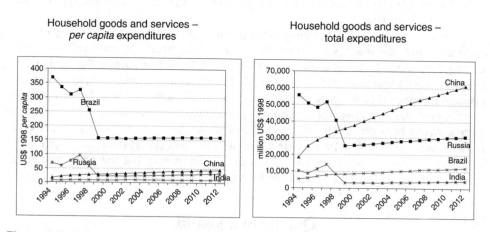

Figure 6.4 Demand for household goods and services in China, India, Brazil and Russia, 1994–2012

Source: Euromonitor.

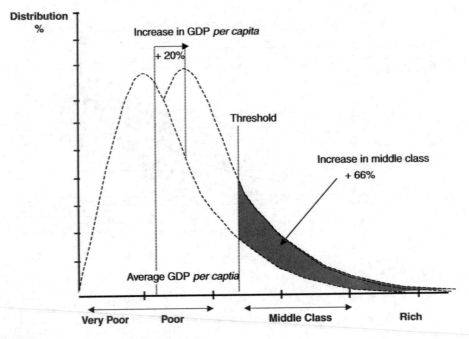

Figure 6.5 The 'middle-class effect'

Note: With an increase of 20% of GDP, the middle class increases by 66%.

The middle-class effect

The demand for most of the mass consumer goods and their related inputs is often triggered by the presence of an affluent middle class. Emerging markets particularly experience what is known as the 'middle-class effect,' illustrated in Figures 6.5 and 6.6. The middle-class effect is due to the skewed nature of the income distribution in emerging countries.

As illustrated in Figure 6.5, demand for modern branded products emerges when disposable income reaches a certain threshold. This threshold varies according to the kind of goods but it is around 1,500–2000 US$ per household. People beyond the threshold are considered middle-class. Their number increases faster than the average income; this triggers a rapid increase in demand for branded goods and consumer durables. This phenomenon is illustrated in Figure 6.6 in the case of China, where between 1990 and 1995 the GNP *per capita* increased by 36 per cent but the demand for VCRs increased by 158 per cent and refrigerators by 79 per cent. This effect is more visible in urban centres like Shanghai, Beijing or Guangzhou, hence the huge inflow of foreign investments in those cities.

Quality of demand

The quality of demand describes the nature and diversity of **market segmentation** prevailing in a country, and the profile of the customers value curve in each

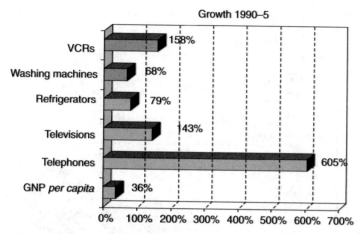

Figure 6.6 'The middle-class effect' in China

Note: An increase of 36% in Gross National Product (GNP) *per capita* is correlated with an increase of 68–605 % in consumer durables.

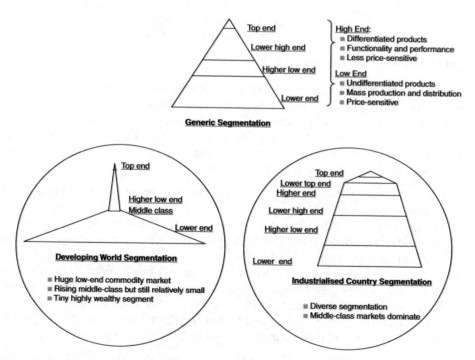

Figure 6.7   Market segmentations

segment. Marketers and strategists generally distinguish two generic segments, 'low-end' and 'high-end' (Figure 6.7).

In developing countries, the main bulk of the market is a large undifferentiated, price-sensitive segment co-existing with a growing more differentiated middle-class segment. In mature advanced economies, segmentation is more diverse in societies

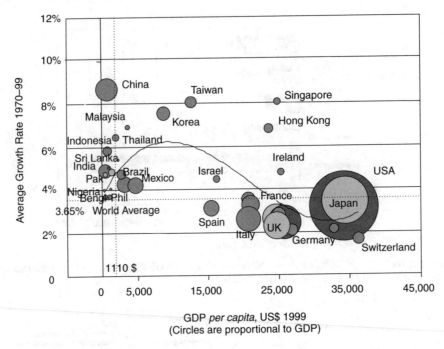

GDP *per capita*, US$ 1999
(Circles are proportional to GDP)

Figure 6.8 Country life cycles

that are essentially middle-class. However, in practice with economic development markets become more sophisticated than this simple dual segmentation implies.

Countries follow a pattern known as the '**country life cycle**', illustrated in Figure 6.8. On the horizontal axis is plotted the wealth of the country measured by GDP *per capita*, while on the vertical axis is plotted the long-term growth rate. One can distinguish four different country clusters:

(a) On the extreme left of the chart are the *developing countries*, characterised by low income *per capita* and low growth: India, Pakistan, Nigeria, and Bangladesh.
(b) On the upper left-hand part of the chart are the countries with high growth rate and low income. These are the *emerging countries* such as China, Indonesia, Thailand and Malaysia.
(c) In the upper middle part of the chart are the *Newly Industrialised Economies* (NIEs), characterised by high growth and moderate–high wealth: Korea, Taiwan, Hong Kong, Singapore and to a certain extent Ireland and Israel.
(d) The final cluster (bottom right-hand part of the chart) consists of the low-growth/ high-wealth industrialised countries of North America, Europe and Japan.

The market characteristics of those clusters are described in Table 6.3.

ASSESSING INDUSTRY OPPORTUNITIES

The objective of this section is to determine the profitability potential of a presence in a country given its industry competitive context, its resource endowment and the incentives provided by government to encourage foreign investments.

Table 6.3 Characteristics of demand according to country life cycle clusters

Demand characteristics	Developing countries	Emerging countries	Newly industrialised economies	Industrialised countries
Growth	Low	High	High	Low
Size	Small	Small to high	Small to high	High
Segmentation	▪ Dominant subsistence sector	▪ Fast growing middle-class	▪ Established middle-class	▪ Established middle-class
	▪ Large low-end segment	▪ Large low-end segment	▪ Increased diversity of segments	▪ Diverse and sophisticated segmentation
Customer value curve	▪ Price	▪ Price	▪ Product functionality	▪ Product functionality
	▪ Availability	▪ Distribution	▪ Performance	▪ Performance
		▪ Emerging advertising	▪ Services	▪ Services
				▪ Diversity
Distribution	▪ Push logistics	▪ Push logistics	▪ Pull	▪ Mass retail important
		▪ Beginning of pull	▪ Beginning of mass retailing	
Competition	▪ Regulated	▪ Beginning of de-regulation	▪ De-regulated	▪ De-regulated
		▪ New entrants	▪ Active	▪ Active
			▪ Diverse	▪ Diverse

Industry and competitive structure

Professor Michael Porter has proposed the concepts and techniques of **industry analysis** for strategic decision-making in his seminal book *Competitive Strategy* (1980). Figure 6.9 reproduces the five-forces framework that, according to Porter, determines the *long-term profitability potential* of an industry. For international business investment purposes we have added a *sixth force* under the heading of government intervention; it is beyond the scope of this chapter to describe in detail the various forces that are presented in Porter's original work as well as in all classic textbooks on business strategy. In an international context, the following five parameters may affect the competitive context:

- *Entry barriers* can be increased by the licensing policy or government auctions. Distribution networks, locational space, incumbent competitive positions as well as cultural specificities are likely to affect entry costs.
- *Suppliers' bargaining power* is somewhat bigger in protected economies where raw materials are in the hands of state monopolies or when there is a scarcity

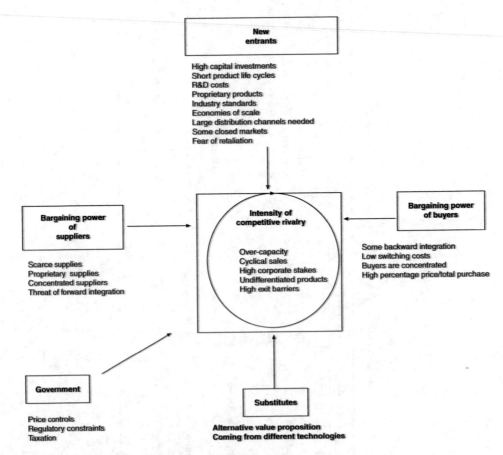

Figure 6.9 Adapted industry analysis framework

Source: Porter (1980).

of skilled labour or of intermediate suppliers of goods and services. Suppliers' bargaining power is greater when governments adopt a 'local content' policy.

■ *Buyers' bargaining power* may also be bigger when distribution networks are tightly controlled, as in the case in Japan.

■ Government may introduce *artificial entry barriers* by putting special constraints on foreign investors. Alternatively, governments may lower entry barriers by deregulating or subsidising factors costs.

■ Government policies may influence profitability and competitiveness though *preferential treatment, price control, taxation* and the like.

Resource endowment

The resources that attract foreign investors fall into three broad categories:

1. *Natural* resources
2. *Human* resources
3. *Infrastructure and support industries* resources.

Natural resources

Table 6.4 gives an overview of the main resource endowment for minerals, mining, palm oil and forestry. Countries that do not use their production for national consumption are prone to export raw materials, to promote processing by domestic companies or to invite foreign firms to invest in processing and export. Governments are very sensitive about the protection of their natural resources and more than often require controls on foreign activities in this domain by negotiating production-sharing agreements as well as joint ventures. Oil and gas is probably the most globally sensitive industry, given the highly strategic nature of the commodity, the inherent risks of exploration, the capital intensity of the investments and the geographical location of the reserves. It is not by chance that the most sophisticated country-risks methodologies have been developed in this industry.[5]

A particular type of natural resource is *geographical location* which, combined with good infrastructure and support services and industry, may give to certain countries or regions within country the role of a '**hub**' or a regional centre. Singapore, located at the end of the Strait of Malacca, Hong Kong, located at the doors of continental China, Brussels for the EU or Miami for Latin America, have developed as hubs based on their geographical location.

Human resources

The quality and cost of labour is the cause of the migration of international investments that took place in the 1950s and 1960s. Offshore factories in South East Asia and Latin America have set up in Export-Processing Zones (EPZs) for the production and assembly of labour-intensive products. International sourcing under the form of Original Equipment Manufacturing (OEM) or straight procurement gave an opportunity for local companies in Japan in the 1950s, in Korea, Taiwan and Brazil in the 1960s, Singapore, Hong Kong and Tunisia in the 1970s, and China, Vietnam and India in the 1980s to develop manufacturing volume and competencies and establish their international presence.

Table 6.4   Reserves of natural resources

Bauxite	Million tons	Copper	Million tons	Iron ore	Million tons
Guinea	5,900	Chile	120	Russia	59,944
Australia	4,600	USA	90	Australia	33,528
Brazil	2,250	Russia	54	Canada	25,502
Jamaica	2,000	Australia	41	USA	25,197
India	1,200	Peru	32	Brazil	17,577
Cameroon	640	Zambia	34	India	12,090
World	23,200	World	570	World	125,000

Lead	Thousand tons	Manganese	Million tons	Nickel	Thousand tons
Australia	28,000	South Africa	2,631	Cuba	22,680
USA	22,000	Russia	454	N. Caledonia	15,422
Canada	15,000	Gabon	172	Brazil	13,427
South Africa	6,000	Australia	152	Canada	13,427
Mexico	4,000			Indonesia	5,262
Peru	3,000			Philippines	4,627
World	125,000	World	3,538	World	100,690

Tin	Thousand tons	Uranium	Tons	Oil	Million tons
Malaysia	1,100	Australia	526,000	Saudi Arabia	23,000
Indonesia	680	USA	298,100	Kuwait	10,000
Brazil	650	South Africa	313,000	Russia	8,600
China	400	Canada	214,000	Mexico	8,032
Russia	300	Niger	170,400	Iran	6,600
Thailand	270	Brazil	163,000	Iraq	6,000
World	4280	World	2,214,000	World	94,000

Natural gas	Billion m³	Forests	Thousand ha	Palm oil	Thousand tons
Russia	35,000	Russia	929,000	Malaysia	8,850
Iran	11,000	Brazil	514,000	Indonesia	5,360
USA	5,835	Canada	436,000		
Algeria	3,150	USA	298,000		
Qatar	3,150	Zaire	177,000		
Saudi Arabia	2,050	Indonesia	117,000		
World	85,500	World	4,121,000	World	17,587

Note: For Palm oil, the statistics report production and not reserves.

Source: *World Resources 1998–1999* and Palm Oil Research Institute (Malaysia).

In practice, two human resource elements are attractive: *cost* and *quality*. Figure 6.10 shows that there is a correlation between those two attributes (R=0.66), but one can see that countries in the upper left-hand quadrant have received the highest foreign investment *per capita*, indicating that the countries that have been able to combine low cost and quality have been seen as attractive for foreign investors despite the fact that most of them have a relative low market size (average GDP is $200 billion/country in this quadrant as opposed to $2,000 billion/country in the high-cost/high-skills quadrant and $340 billion/country in the low-cost/low-skills one).

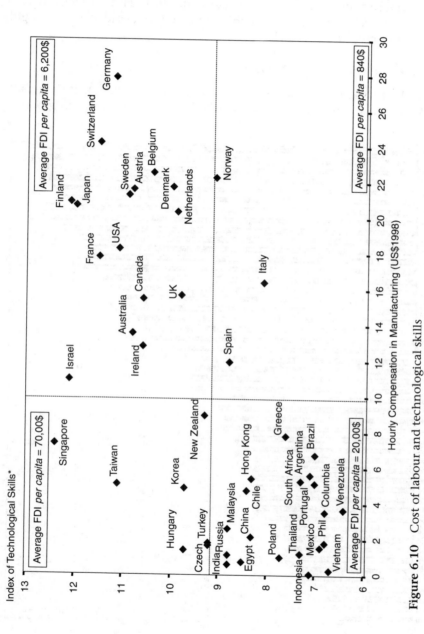

Figure 6.10 Cost of labour and technological skills

Note: *Indices of technological sophistication plus maths and science education.

Source: The Global Competitiveness Report, (2000), World Economic Forum.

Low labour-cost countries tend to attract labour-intensive low-value added production. Since the mid-1980s India, the Philippines and to a certain extent China have tried successfully to strengthen the production of computer software, particularly in the data capture segments. India, for instance, has focused its attractiveness on offering international companies a combination of low-labour cost but highly skilled computer software personnel.

Infrastructure and support industry resources

The third type of resource that can be of interest to foreign investors is the quality of *communication and logistics infrastructures*, as well as the availability of supporting

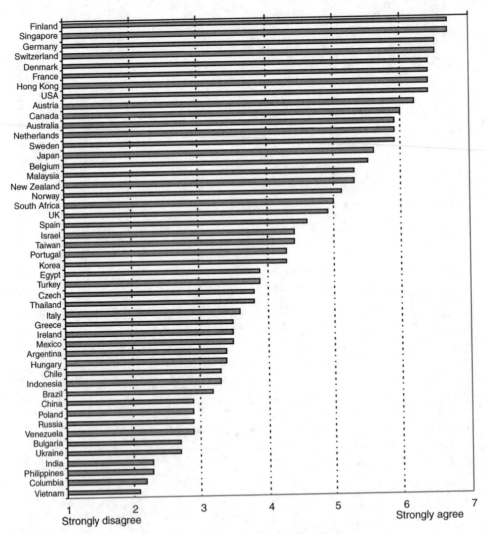

'The quality of the infrastructure is among the best in the world.'

Figure 6.11 Overall quality of infrastructure

Source: Global Competitiveness Report (2000), World Economic Forum.

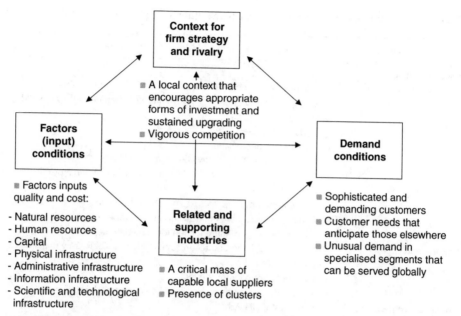

Figure 6.12   Porter's 'country diamond'

Source: Porter (1998).

industries and services. Figure 6.11 gives an overall ranking of countries, established by the *World Economic Forum*, based on the quality of their infrastructure.

The country 'diamond'

Professor Michael Porter (1998) has argued that countries or regions within countries (what he calls **'clusters'**) can build competitive advantages that make them attractive for business development in certain industries. He distinguishes four major drivers of national competitive advantage. These four drivers constitute the country or regional 'diamond' (see Figure 6.12):

(1) The *natural resource* endowment
(2) The quality of the *demand*
(3) Vigorous *competition*
(4) The presence of *supporting industries*.

Examples given by Porter of successful clusters are the German printing press industry, the US patient monitoring industry, the Italian ceramic tile industry and the Japanese robotics industry.

Government incentives

In order to attract foreign investors, governments have designed and implemented a series of *incentives*: fiscal, financial, and competitive operational.[6] These incentives are summarised in Table 6.5.

Table 6.5 Major types of incentives for foreign investments

Type of incentive	Nature of incentive
Fiscal incentives:	
Tax reduction	▪ Tax holiday for a certain period
	▪ Ability to write off losses against profits after the end of the tax holiday period
	▪ Reduced tax rate
	▪ Accelerated depreciation
	▪ Reduction in social security contributions
	▪ Special deductions of taxable incomes based on certain types of activities (social, R&D, etc.)
	▪ Exemption from property taxes or others special taxes
	▪ Reduction of tax base on local content or employment levels
	▪ Income tax exemption/reduction for expatriate personnel
Imports and exports	▪ Exemption of import duties and value added taxes for raw material, capital equipments and parts
	▪ Exemption from export duties
	▪ Tax credits on domestic sales based on export performance
Financial incentives	▪ Subsidies of all kinds
	▪ 'Sweetener loans'
	▪ Guaranteed loans
	▪ Export credits
	▪ Equity participation
	▪ Risks insurance (exports, exchange rates)
Competitive incentives	▪ Protection against imports
	▪ Capacity regulation
	▪ Monopolistic position
	▪ Preferential purchases
Operational incentives	▪ Preferential rates – rents, land, power, telecoms, etc.
	▪ Assistance for market studies
	▪ Utilisation of public services or government agencies for company operations
	▪ Secondment of personnel

Source: UNCTAD (1996).

Impact of incentives on foreign investor behaviour

A series of research studies on the role of incentives in foreign investment decisions has shown that their role is limited.[7] Market attractiveness, competitive conditions, resource endowments are more important than incentives, but if those conditions are comparable in several locations, incentives may play a positive role in the decision to invest in one country in particular.

COUNTRY RISK ANALYSIS

The purpose of country risk analysis is to assess the probability that adverse circumstances owing to political, economic or social actions will negatively affect

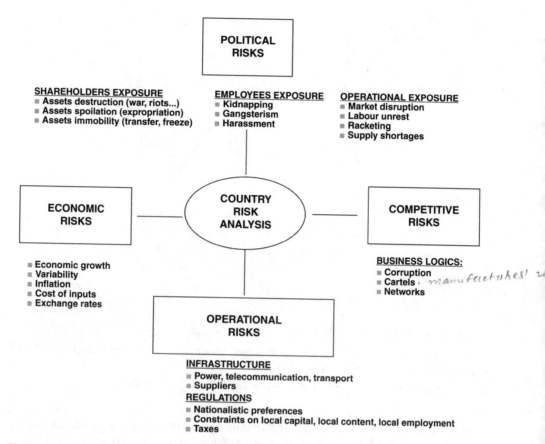

Figure 6.13 Framework for country risk analysis

business performance.[8] Country risks can be grouped into four categories (see Figure 6.13):

1. *Political* risks
2. *Economic* risks
3. *Competitive* risks
4. *Operational* risks.

Political risks are probable disruptions owing to internal or external events or regulations resulting from political action of governments or societal crisis and unrest. Political risks may expose business performance in various ways.

■ A first type of risk exposes *shareholder's value*, in terms of loss of capital or loss through the inability to repatriate dividends. This type of risk is associated with asset destruction linked to external or civil wars or riots, asset spoliation owing to expropriation or asset lock-in through funds freezing or interdiction on capital transfer. The regions of the world that score high on this type of risk are the Middle East and Africa (see Figure 6.14).

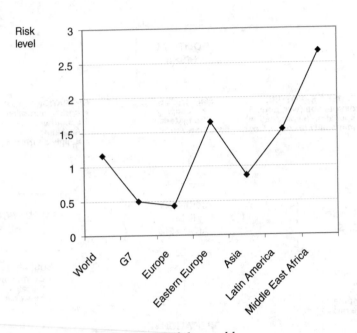

Figure 6.14 Shareholder risks in regions of the world

Note: The score is an average of risks of armed conflict, risk of social unrest and risk of expropriation, from 0 = No risk to 5 = High risk).

Source: Economic Intelligence Unit, *Global Outlook* (August 2000).

- Another type of political risk lies in *employees' exposure* linked to gangsterism, crime and kidnapping as well as *operational exposure* linked to labour unrest, racketeering or market disruptions or supplies shortages linked to criminal activities.
- *Economic risks* expose business performance to the extent that the economic business drivers can vary and therefore put profitability at stake. As an example, Figure 6.15 shows the growth rate of Brazil as compared to India from 1970 to 2000. While the two countries have a similar annual growth rate (4.52 per cent against 4.25), Brazil has more variability than India (coefficient of variation of 1.06 against 0.55) and therefore *ceteris paribus* presents a higher economic risk.
- *Competitive risks* are related to non-economic distortion of the competitive context owing to cartels and networks as well as corrupt practices. The competitive battlefield is not even and investors who base their competitive advantage on product quality and economics are at disadvantage.
- *Operational risks* are those that directly affect the bottom line, either because government regulations and bureaucracies add costly taxation or constraints to foreign investors or because the infrastructure is not reliable.

A comparative picture of the score of India and China country risks is reported in Figure 6.16. It shows that in the EIU assessment overall China is perceived as more risky than India except for economic risk.

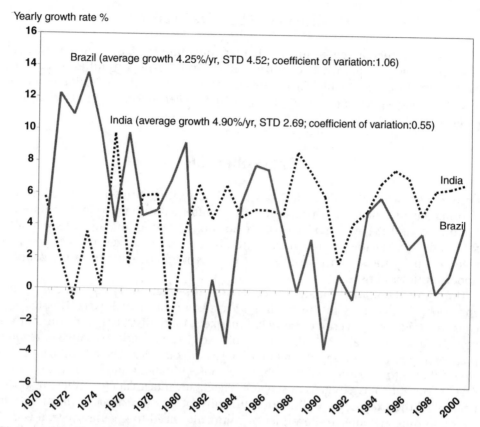

Figure 6.15 Variability of economic growth, India versus Brazil, 1970–2000

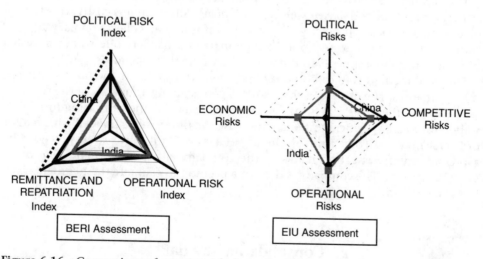

Figure 6.16 Comparison of country risks between China and India

Sources: Economic Intelligence Unit, *Global Outlook* (August 2000); BERI Business Risk Services (2000).

PUTTING IT ALL TOGETHER

The various factors presented in this chapter constitute the basic raw materials for assessing whether a particular country is likely to offer opportunities to conduct business safely and profitably. Such assessments first require the collection of a large amount of *information* and second, the capacity to *collate* information in a meaningful fashion.

Data collection

Despite the fact that various data-bases and consulting firms propose statistical information and analyses, managers are often confronted with problems in relevance, the quality and the accessibility of strategic and marketing intelligence specific to their industry. Macroeconomic data are too broad, and managers need to complement them by their own investigation. Various methods exist to assess country opportunities and risks.

The most traditional mode of collecting information is the *'Grand Tour'* approach. This consists in the sending of a mission of several executives to visit countries and meet government officials, bankers, journalists, academics and other opinion makers or analysts. At the end of this exercise, managers exchange notes and prepare a report comparing the relative merits of countries. The advantage of the *Grand Tour* is to give a real feel of what the context is about and to focus on issues that are specific to its products or services. The disadvantages are the inherent superficiality of the exercise as well as the difficulty of *cross-validation* of information owing to time pressure. To be valuable, companies need to organise several *Grand Tours* and to complement them with other forms of data collection and analysis. The exercise becomes quite costly, and for that reason many SMEs cannot afford it.

The second method is to rely on *diplomatic sources, commercial attachés, professional organisations* and *foreign banking institutions*. Although less costly, this type of data-gathering lacks specificity and depth. Information collected this way may suffer from lack of objectivity since diplomats and bankers often have a vested interest to push investments in the territories where they operate.

The third method is to call on *consulting firms* who specialise in country risk and market analysis. The quality of the results depends upon the quality of the relationship between the *client* (the firm) and the *service provider* (the consulting firm). It is important to ask specific questions, otherwise the firm may be flooded with masses of irrelevant data. To be fruitful, the use of a consultant needs to be preceded by a preliminary investigation made by the company either via a *Grand Tour* or by desktop research. The company is then in a position to calibrate the mandate given to the consultant.

Consolidating the data

As the previous paragraphs have illustrated, several parameters shape opportunities and risks. The combination of these parameters generates various *country profiles*

Table 6.6   Cluster characteristics, Asia Pacific

	Hubs	Emerging giants	Newly industrialised economies	Resource-rich developing* countries	Advanced countries
Population	L	H	M	M/H	M/ H
GDP	L	M	M	L	H
GDP *per capita*	H	L	M	L	H
Infrastructure	H	L	H	L	H
Skills	H	L	H	L	H
Labour costs	M	L	M	L	H
Risks	L	M	L/M	H	L
Natural resources	L	M	L	H	Japan = L Australia = H

Notes: L = Low, M = Medium, H = High.

* These countries share many common characteristics with the emerging giants.

that distinguish types of countries according to the attractiveness factors of interest to foreign investors. To take the example of the Asia Pacific region, and to refer to our earlier discussion of country clusters, one can classify countries into five main groups:

- *Hubs*: Singapore and Hong Kong
- *Emerging giants*: India and China
- *Newly industrialised economies*: Taiwan, Korea, Malaysia
- *Resource-rich developing countries*: Indonesia, the Philippines, Thailand
- *Advanced countries*: Australia and Japan. Table 6.6 gives the key characteristics of those clusters. The choice of countries between clusters and within a cluster will ultimately depend on the *strategic ambition* of the global firm and the relative importance it attaches to the various factors.

SUMMARY AND KEY POINTS

1. Entry decisions take into account:
   - *Country attractiveness* analysis
   - *Entry strategy* (to be discussed further in Chapter 7).
2. A country attractiveness *assessment* is based on two dimensions:
   - *Market* and *industry opportunities*
   - *Country risks* (many organisations publish country assessment results based on various economic/political/social factors).
3. Market opportunities assessment measures the *potential demand* in the country for a firm's products or services based on:
   - Market size
   - Growth
   - Quality of demand.

4. Demand:

■ overall demand is assessed based on a combination of:
   - *Macroeconomic correlation* approach (estimating demand based on correlation with given macroeconomic indicators)
   - Consideration of *other factors*:
     (a) Degree of urbanisation
     (b) Climatic conditions
     (c) Income distribution
     (d) Lifestyles
     (e) Savings rates
   - *Trend analysis* with comparable countries:
     (a) On a *per capita* basis
     (b) On absolute value

■ Demand for most mass consumer goods in emerging markets is often triggered by the 'middle-class effect':
   - The increased number of people who become middle-class (i.e. reach a certain *disposable income threshold*) causes an increased demand for modern branded products

■ Quality of demand:
   - *Nature and diversity* of market segmentation prevailing in a country and the profile of customers *value curve* in each segment
   - There are two *generic segments*:
     (a) Low-end segment:
       (i) Undifferentiated products
       (ii) Mass production and distribution
       (iii) Price-sensitive
     (b) High-end segment:
       (i) Differentiated products
       (ii) Functionalities and performances
       (iii) Less price-sensitive
   - Developing world segmentation
       (i) Huge low-end commodity market
       (ii) Rising middle-class but still relatively small segment
       (iii) Tiny highly wealthy segment
   - Industrialised country segmentation:
       (i) Diverse segmentation
       (ii) Middle-class market dominates

■ Demand characteristics of a country:
   - Market growth, market size, segmentation, customer value curve, distribution and competition
   - Depends on country *life cycle cluster* country belongs to
   - country life cycles clusters:
     (a) Defined based on a country's wealth and its growth rate – a country goes through a 'country life cycle' depicting the relationship between the country's wealth and its long-term growth rate

    (b) Types of country life cycle cluster include:

        (i)   Developing countries

        (ii)   Emerging countries

        (iii) Newly industrialised economies

        (iv) Industrialised countries.

5. Industry opportunities assessment determines *profitability potential* of a company's presence in a country given the following factors:

- Quality of *industry competitive structure* (including Porter's five-force Industry Analysis Framework):

  - Intensity of rivalry
  - New entrants and entry barriers:

    (a) High capital investments
    (b) Short product life cycles
    (c) R&D costs
    (d) Proprietary products
    (e) Industry standards
    (f) Economies of scale
    (g) Large distribution channels
    (h) Some closed markets
    (i) Fear of retaliation
    (j) Regulatory requirements, e.g. licences

  - Bargaining power of:

    (a) Suppliers

        (i)   Scarcity or proprietary nature of supplies
        (ii)   Concentrated suppliers
        (iii) Threat of forward integration

    (b) Buyers:

        (i)   Low switching costs
        (ii)   Concentrated buyers
        (iii) Threat of backward integration

  - Threat of substitutes: alternative value proposition
  - Profitability:

    (a) Short-term
    (b) Long-term

- Resource availability:

  - Natural resources:

    (a) Examples include raw materials and geographical location
    (b) Governments are protective of country's natural resources

  - Human resources: examples include low-cost labour, skilled personnel (e.g. technological skills)
  - Infrastructure and support industries resources:

    (a) Examples include power, telecoms, roads
    (b) When combined with good geographical location, provide a competitive advantage to a country to become a regional centre

- Government:
    - Investment incentives granted by governments:
        (a) Types of incentives
            (i)   Fiscal incentives – tax reduction, exemption of import or export duties
            (ii) Financial incentives – subsidies
            (iii) Competitive incentives – preferential purchases
            (iv) Operational incentives – preferential rates for rents, land, power and telecoms
        (b) Incentives play only a limited role in inducing foreign investment
    - Government intervention:
        (a) Price controls
        (b) Regulatory constraints
        (c) Taxation.

6. There are four categories of country risk:

- *Economic* risks:
    - Economic growth
    - Variability of economic factors
    - Inflation
    - Cost of inputs
    - Exchange rates
- *Competitive* risks (non-economic distortion of competitive context):
    - Corruption
    - Cartels
- *Operational risks*:
    - Infrastructure:
        (a) Power, telecoms and transport
        (b) Suppliers
    - Regulations:
        (a) National preferences
        (b) Constraints on local capital, local content or local employment
        (c) Taxes
- *Political* risks:
    - Employees' exposure:
        (a) Gangsterism
        (b) Kidnapping
    - Operational exposure:
        (a) Market disruption
        (b) Labour unrest
        (c) Racketeering
        (d) Supplies shortage
- Shareholders' exposure (loss of capital or loss through inability to repatriate dividends):
        (a) Asset destruction (e.g. war or riots)
        (b) Asset spoliation
        (c) Asset immobility (e.g. freeze).

Appendix 6.1 Comparison of China and India, household expenditures

Table 6A.1 and Figure 6A.1 give statistical and risk-profile assessment data.

Table 6A.1 China and India, statistical data, 2000 and 2005

	2000		2005	
	China	India	China	India
Population (million)	1,276	1,006	1,321	1,082
GDP (US$ billion)	1,090	432	1,600	569
GDP (PPP$ billion)	5,450	1,895	8,048	2,500
GDP per capita (US$)	850	429	1,210	525
GDP per capita (PPP$)	4,275	1,880	6,055	2,310
GDP real growth rate since 1980	9.50	5.66	7.4	5.7
Coefficient of variability (1980–2000)	0.350	0.313	0.052	0.049
Urban population (million)	440	293	512	335
Urban population (%)	34.5	29.1	38.8	31.0
Number of households	344	200	404	211
Household size	3.7	5	3.3	5.1
Consumer expenditure on household goods and services ($billion)	37.7	7	49.5	8
Monthly earning, industry	102	81	115	85
Monthly earning, agriculture	52	24	72	29
Electricity production (million KWh)	1,107	493	1,520	644
Possession of (% of household):				
Air conditioning	18.2	6.2	6.4	19
Microwave	15	0.6	17.5	1.1

Table 6A.1   (Continued)

| | 2000 | | 2005 | |
	China	India	China	India
Refrigerator	79.4	7.5	82.2	7.8
Washer	92.4	1.4	94.3	3.7
Average growth of household expenditures %	15	7	6	3
Risk profile	2.18	2.37	1.98	2.17
Size of household expenditures	37.7	7	49.5	8

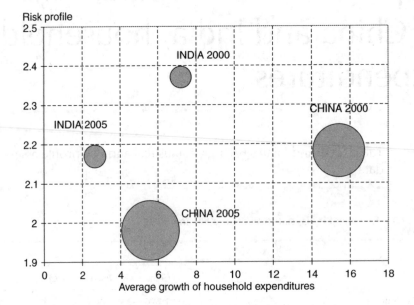

Figure 6A.1   China and India, risk-profile data, 2000 and 2005

Learning assignments

1 Take two countries of your choice and compare their country risk profile.
2 What is the 'middle-class effect'?
3 What determines the quality of demand?
4 What are the tools of governments to promote foreign investments?
5 Can you give examples of a hub in Africa, an emerging giant in Latin America and a resource-rich country in Eastern Europe?

Key words

■ Clusters
■ 'Country diamond'

- Country life cycle
- Country risk analysis
- 'Grand Tour'
- Hub
- Incentives
- Industry analysis
- Macroeconomic indicators
- Market opportunities
- Market segmentation
- 'Middle-class effect'

Web resources

<http://surveys.ft.com/>
Financial Times country survey.

<http://dsbb.imf.org/>
IMF site for country statistics.

<http://www.mckinseyquarterly.com/category_archive.asp?tk = 86032::& L3 = 8>
McKinsey Quarterly – Country Reports.

<http://www.mckinseyquarterly.com/category_archive.asp?tk = 86032::& L3 = 10>
McKinsey Quarterly – Productivity and Performance.

<http://www.neatideas.com/inflationwatch/annual/ globalreview.htm>
Global *Annual Economic Review*, which contains comparative table on various definitions of money, real GDP, GDP deflator, Consumer Price Index (CPI), current account balance, government surplus/deficit, short-term interest rates and exchange rates.

<http://www.timeinc.net/fortune/sections/>
A book on global management with various CEOs' views and management philosophies.

<http://www.zambeasy.com/country-intelligence/>
Business opportunities in the emerging economies in Europe.

<http://www.cpss.org>
Web site of the Center for Political and Strategic Studies (CPSS).

<http://www.crg.com>
Consulting specialist in business risks.

<http://www.grai.com>
Global network headed by Jerry Rogers, a former US Air Force intelligence officer.

<http://www.prsgroup.com>
Country reports online.

Notes

1. *The World Competitiveness Yearbook*, IMD, 23 Ch. de Bellerive, PO Box 915, Lausanne <http:/swww.imd.ch//wct.html>.
2. Porter (1998).
3. Guisinger (unpublished paper).
4. PRS Group <http://www.polrisk.com>.
5. See country Petroleum Risk Environment <http://www.riskworld.com>.
6. UNCTAD (1996).
7. Guisinger (1985, 1992).
8. Literature is abundant on country risk: Brewer (1985); Howell and Chaddick (1994, pp. 70–90); Rogers (1997).

References and further reading

Austin, James E., *Managing in Developing Countries: Strategic Analysis and Operating Techniques*. New York: Free Press, 1990.

Brewer, Thomas L. (ed.), *Political Risks in International Business: New Directions for Research, Management and Public Policis*. New York: Praeger, 1985.

Guisinger, Stephen, 'Environment and Structural Complexity in International Business Theory', unpublished paper.

Guisinger, Stephen, *Investment Incentives and Performance Requirements*. New York: Praeger, 1985.

Guisinger, Stephen, 'Rhetoric and Reality in International business: As Note on the Effectiveness of Incentives', *Transnational Corporations*, 1, 1992, pp. 111–23.

Guisinger, Stephen, 'From OLI to OLMA: Incorporating Higher Levels of Environmental and Structural Complexity into the Eclectic Paradigm,' *International Journal of the Economics of Business*, 8(2), 2001, pp. 257–72.

Howell, Llewellyn D. and Brad Chaddick, 'Models of Political Risk for Foreign Investment and Trade: An Assessment of Three Approaches'. *Columbia Journal of World Business*, Fall 1994, pp. 70–90.

James, Mini and T.M. Koller, 'Valuation in Emerging Markets', *McKinsey Quarterly*, 4, 2000.

Lasserre, Philippe and Hellmut Schütte, *Strategies for Asia Pacific: Beyond the Crisis*. London: Macmillan Palgrave, 1999.

Porter, Michael, *Competitive Strategy: Techniques for Analysing Industries and Competitors*. New York: Free Press, 1980.

Porter, Michael, *The Competitive Advantage of Nations*. New York: Free Press, 1998.

Rogers, Jerry (ed.), *Global Risk Assessments: Issues, Concepts and Applications*. Riverside, CA: Global Risk Assessment, Inc., 1997.

UNCTAD, *Incentives and Foreign Direct Investment: United Nations Conference on Trade and Development*. Geneva: United Nations Publications, 1996.

7

Entry strategies

Having performed the analysis of country attractiveness and decided positively to enter, a company has to work out an *entry strategy* that consists in setting up three types of choices:

(a) *Entry objectives* (what the company is looking for in this country)
(b) *Timing* of entry (when to enter)
(c) *Mode* of entry (what kind of operations and under which legal form).

There may be four categories of objectives: to develop the market, to access critical resources, to capture knowledge available in the country and to set up a regional or global centre for co-ordinating various activities.

The *timing* of entry can be critical for building sustainable competitive advantage. First-movers can capture initial advantages over competitors but run a variety of risks.

The choice of a *legal structure* is contingent upon many external and internal factors. There are six legal forms of entry: wholly-owned operations built from scratch, acquisitions, joint ventures, licensing or franchising, distributors' agreements, or a representative office. The advantages and disadvantages of each of those forms are discussed. The chapter ends by looking at entry strategy as a 'real option', and a numerical example is examined.

At the end of the chapter one should be able:

▪ To complete a full analysis of various entry alternatives
▪ To assess the advantages and disadvantages of alternative entry strategies in a concrete situation
▪ To conduct a financial pro-format analysis of alternatives.

'CARREFOUR'S ENTRY STRATEGY'

When Carrefour, the French mass retailer, decided in the late 1980s to enter the Asia Pacific region, it analysed the countries in the region to see whether their economic and social characteristics were favourable to the hypermarket concept. To be a sustainable retailing concept, a hypermarket requires a growing urban concentration of middle-class populations benefiting from an income per household above $1000 per annum and an infrastructure capable of handling the heavy logistics demanded by continuous supplies. Finally, the country should have institutional and political stability. Having eliminated Japan, because of its retailing structure and its astronomic real estate cost, Carrefour considered four countries that, at that time, corresponded to their business concept criteria: Singapore, Korea, Hong Kong and Taiwan. Taiwan was chosen because, unlike Hong Kong and Singapore, mass retailing was not yet developed and Korea was not open to foreign companies in the retailing sector. Carrefour's motivations were to capture the opportunities offered by an increasing wealthy middle class in Taiwan. It also could 'learn' how to operate in a Chinese-speaking environment and to understand Chinese consumer behaviour. Such learning would be highly valuable for a further expansion in China and in South East Asia where a large middle class of overseas Chinese resided. Taiwan required foreign retailers to tie up with a local firm in joint venture agreements. Carrefour was not against a local partner because it needed to acquire contacts with government officials and suppliers as well as to learn about this new environment, but the company wanted to run the operation by itself. It was fortunate to find a strong local partner, the President Group, who was willing to help but did not interfere in operations.

After a few years, Carrefour expanded to other Asian countries: Malaysia, Thailand, China, Indonesia (under the form of joint ventures) and Hong Kong, Singapore and Japan (with a wholly-owned subsidiary). In all these countries Carrefour adopted different entries strategies. This short example illustrates the topic of this chapter, the multifarious aspects of entry strategies.

A company's entry strategy involves answering three questions:

1. Why does the company *want to enter* the country?
2. When is it *appropriate* to enter?
3. *How* can it enter?

WHY ENTER? DEFINING STRATEGIC OBJECTIVES FOR A COUNTRY PRESENCE

One can distinguish four major types of strategic objectives, not necessarily independent of each other:

1. *Market development* objectives
2. *Resources access* objectives
3. *Learning* objectives
4. *Co-ordination* objectives.

Market development objectives apply to those countries offering size and growth opportunities. To a certain extent, all countries in the world offer some kind of market opportunity as a function of their population and income. Some countries, however, are more critical than others owing to their size or the quality of their customer base. Those countries are often referred as *key countries*; i.e. countries in which a presence is needed for global long-term competitiveness. China, the United States, Japan, Germany, France, and the United Kingdom are often considered as key countries for that reason. Market development objectives constitute the most common entry objectives.

Resources access objectives are based on the presence of a key resource – mineral, agricultural or human – that contributes to competitive advantage. An investment in a resource-rich country will essentially be made to extract the resource by setting up the appropriate operational asset – a mine, an exploration field, a plantation, an assembly plant or a software centre.

Learning objectives are the basis of investments in countries where the industry is state of the art and in which a foreign investor gains knowledge and competencies by being present, even if the long-term market prospect is not favourable. Automobile companies set up operations in Japan in the 1980s to be close to the network of car manufacturers and component suppliers and to learn about their mode of relationships. California, Washington State or Texas may similarly be considered as learning ground for the 'new economy' (see Chapter 14), while companies dealing with fashion and perfume may consider Paris or Milan as an investment site.

Co-ordination objectives apply to hub countries where a presence is justified for the regional co-ordination of activities thanks to their location and infrastructure advantages.

Table 7.1 gives a summary of the four types of objectives and the expectations of foreign investors in each category.

When to enter? First-mover, follower or acquirer?

The timing of entry is contingent upon the *window of opportunity* as well as the type of risk the company is willing to take.

For market-based objectives, a window of opportunity is open when the demand starts to become significant and the competitive context is not yet well established. For resource-based objectives, it is opened when rights of access are available and closed when competitors have established a strong market presence or pre-empted available resources. In such cases, only acquisitions or innovation can allow entrants to open the window. The concept of a window of opportunity is not unique to international entry. It applies also to new product or service development. In the entry context, one can distinguish four phases:

1. The *'premature phase'*, during which a significant investment in the country would not generate enough long-term revenues because of a lack of purchasing power or the absence of a demand for the product or service. This phase is characteristic of developing countries at an early stage or of a product that does not fit the demand in a particular country. Although in the United States credit card business is very active, smart card manufacturers have found it difficult

Table 7.1 Entry strategy objectives

	Market	*Resources*	*Learning*	*Co-ordination*
Expectations	▪ Market penetration and development. ▪ Capture a share of market	▪ Access to natural resources ▪ Access to skilled low-cost labour ▪ Access to suppliers	▪ Understand state-of-the art technology ▪ Close to best practices ▪ Learn to compete in difficult and sophisticated markets	▪ Set up base for global or regional development ▪ Establish logistic centres ▪ Close to financing institutions
Key Performance Indicators (KPIs)	▪ Growth ▪ Market share ▪ Gross margin	▪ Costs ▪ Quality ▪ Supply access	▪ Know-how ▪ Process improvement	▪ Speed ▪ Control ▪ Synergies

Timing	▪ Window of opportunity
	 ▪ First-mover versus follower
		▪ First mover in order to pre-empt resources	▪ As soon as country is recognised as 'competence' centre	▪ Three stages:
				  Initiation
				  Growth
				  Co-ordination

Type of countries	▪ All types prioritised as a function of market potential, quality and competitive context	▪ Resources-rich countries	▪ Countries with strong technological and know-how infrastructure	▪ Hubs
Mode of entry	▪ Depending upon risks, opportunities, timing and skills. ▪ All modes of entry may apply	▪ Wholly-owned (if allowed and if low risk) ▪ Joint venture (if requested) ▪ Long-term sourcing contracts	▪ Joint venture ▪ R & D centre ▪ Observatory	▪ Representative office ▪ Global HQ ▪ Regional HQ ▪ Logistic centre ▪ Training centre ▪ Financial HQ

to penetrate the market because of the lack of support from the banking industry. A significant investment in smart cards in the 1980s or 1990s would not have been appropriate until the window of opportunity was open. It is not suggested that no investment is required at this stage, but it should be limited to representative offices, listening posts or distribution agreements.

2. The *'window phase'*, during which the market takes off but the competitive landscape is not yet well established. At this stage, the choice is to take a *first-mover view* or a *follower view*. The advantages and disadvantages of being first movers have been widely discussed[1] and there is empirical evidence that to be the first to enter in a country can lead to a strong competitive advantage[2] in emerging markets. Table 7.2 lists the arguments for and against being a first mover.

Table 7.2 Advantages and disadvantages of being a first mover

Advantages	Disadvantages

■ Pre-empt resources:
  – Distribution
  – Location
  – People
  – Contacts
  – Suppliers
■ Establish brands
■ Establish standards
■ Learn about customers
	■ Take risks:
	  – Market immature
	  – Product unfitted
	  – Lack of infrastructure
	■ Struggle for the benefit of others (do the ground work)

3. The *'competitive growth phase'*, when various competitors have taken advantage of the window of opportunity and are jockeying for market share in a high-growth situation. New entry at this stage is hazardous and requires either massive resources or a highly differentiated competitive strategy. One way to circumvent the handicap of being a late-comer is by an acquisition or joint venture.
4. The *'mature phase'*. At this stage, the competition is well established and acquisition or direct investment with an innovative product is generally the only way to enter.

ENTRY MODES: HOW TO ENTER?[3]

From the point of view of a foreign investor, the typical choice on entering a country is based on a combination of two major dimensions:

1. The *ownership* dimension: going it alone with wholly-owned operations in which the foreigner has full control and ownership or entering into partnerships
2. The *investment* intensity dimension: investing in assets and competencies for value adding activities or limiting operations to commercial, development and administrative activities.

This leads to the various types of entry mode represented in Figure 7.1. Those choices should generally be determined by the following factors:

1. The *overall attractiveness* of the market, as discussed in Chapter 6
2. The *political and operational risks* involved
3. The *government* requirements
4. The *time pressures*
5. The *internal capabilities* of the firm to enter and develop local resources, assets and competencies in order to gain and sustain competitive advantage
6. The *costs/benefits analysis* and the expected *return on investment*.

Ownership

		None or limited control	Full or absolute control
Intensity of Investment	High	■ Joint venture with minority, equal or non-absolute position ■ Consortium partner	■ Wholly-owned subsidiary by greenfield investment ■ Full or dominant acquisition Joint venture with absolute majority (*above 66 %*)
	Low	Arm's-length agreements ■ Distributor ■ Licensing ■ Agent ■ Representative ■ Franchisee ■ Correspondent	■ Regional headquarters ■ Marketing subsidiary ■ Procurement office ■ Representative office ■ Technical observatory

Figure 7.1 Entry modes

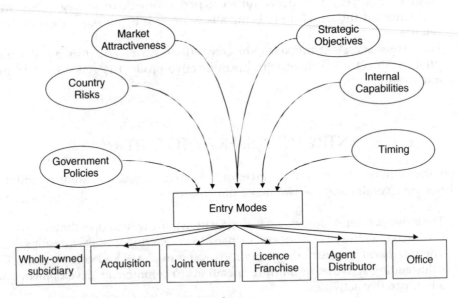

Figure 7.2 Factors influencing entry modes

The next part of the chapter is devoted to analysing the main forms of entry along these dimensions. Particular attention will be devoted to the *joint venture mode*, as it is in most cases the typical entry mode in emerging countries. As far as the acquisition mode is concerned, the factors examined in Chapter 5 will apply here, and so this particular mode of entry will be discussed in less detail here. The analysis is summarised in Table 7.3 and Appendix 7.1, where an example of various alternative entry modes is developed using a practical example.

Table 7.3 Types of local partners for country-based joint ventures

Image (arrow); *Vertical integration (VI)*; *Downstream VI*; *Upstream VI*

	Suppliers	Customers/distributors	Competitors	Diversifiers	Investors	Government
Prime motive of local partner	▪ Secure sales of raw material ▪ Learn about downstream technology ▪ Pre-empt competitors ▪ 'Control' price	▪ Access to product/process 'technology' ▪ Pre-empt competitors ▪ Control price of raw material or components	▪ Collusion ▪ Technology ▪ Product complementation ▪ Upgrading ▪ Market control ▪ Best practices	▪ Additional source of profit ▪ Capture new opportunities ▪ 'Risk' spreading	▪ Return ▪ Shareholder values	▪ National development ▪ Technology ▪ Employment ▪ Political payoff
Prime motive of foreign partner	▪ Secure raw material resources	▪ Market access ▪ Learn about market	▪ Market access ▪ Learn about market ▪ Resources ▪ Assets ▪ Competencies ▪ Market control ▪ Market power	▪ Power/contacts ▪ Flexibility ▪ Potential target for acquisition	▪ Contacts ▪ Satisfy legal requirements ▪ Capital	▪ Satisfy legal requirement ▪ Favourable preferences
Advantages	▪ Resources	▪ Distribution		▪ Contacts ▪ No or little interference ▪ Some operational support	▪ Contacts ▪ No or little interference	
Disadvantages	▪ Technology change ▪ Quality ▪ Flexibility ▪ Pressure for vertical acquisition by partner	▪ Lack of overall industrial competencies ▪ Short-term mindset of partner ▪ Dependancy ▪ Pressure for vertical acquisition by partner	▪ Technology leakage ▪ Conflicts with other products	▪ Thin resources from partner ▪ Little 'learning' ▪ Opportunism	▪ No 'learning' ▪ No operational support	▪ Bureaucracy ▪ Politics

ENTERING A COUNTRY THROUGH WHOLLY-OWNED SUBSIDIARIES

This entry mode is the one that gives the most control over operations, but also involves the highest mobilisation of resources and competencies and bears the highest risks. Creating a subsidiary in a country calls for the following requirements:

- Assuming that a proper country attractiveness and risk analysis has been done prior to the investment, one needs first to familiarise oneself with the *legal, institutional, commercial* and *relational* environment. It is one thing to have analysed the market and competition for decision-making, it is another thing to master the nitty-gritty of a full greenfield investment or an acquisition. This is the role of the *feasibility study* that analyses the various aspects of an investment dealing with real estate, construction, project management, sourcing, recruitment, incorporation, registrations, financing, fiscal and legal matters. Feasibility studies should be supported by a full financial plan projecting future cash flow calculations and financial needs. Feasibility studies as well as project management can be contracted out to locally-based consultants or engineering firms, but the overall control and responsibility falls upon the foreign investor.
- Managing a construction project in a foreign country involves a series of practical and sometimes difficult impediments, such as the norms and standards of construction, the professionalism of local contractors and their commercial practices, the availability of supplies, customs clearance of imported materials and components, the behaviour and attitude of project workforces and the local bureaucratic hassles. When an investor is investing in a greenfield operation for the first time in a country, it is advisable that they should rely on a *locally-based project manager*.
- A further impediment of a greenfield operation is the need for *recruitment, training* and *management* of a local workforce and the capacity of expatriate personnel to get quickly culturally acquainted and able to *transfer technology*. This determines the timing and the cost of the investment that will ultimately affect the overall profitability and cash flow of the project.
- On the positive side, a greenfield wholly-owned investment gives the investor full control over operations and access to the *full profitability* of the investment. Sometimes the feeling of 'full control' may be illusory if the company has sent expatriates with a superficial knowledge of the country and a lack of cultural understanding. In such case, expatriate top managers will be isolated in an ivory tower and local personnel manages the operations their own way, hiding themselves behind apparent obedience and respect.
- On the financial front, a wholly-owned investment demands that foreign investors bear the full risk of *equity and debt financing*, sometimes facilitated by export credit insurance granted by the home country government or insurance community.

ENTERING A COUNTRY THROUGH ACQUISITIONS

Chapter 5 has dealt with international acquisitions and there is no need to repeat here what was examined there. Overall, the advantage of acquisitions as an entry mode is the immediate availability of resources, assets and competencies that saves time for the foreign investor. Another advantage is the access provided to a market of resources when the competitive arena is already well occupied and the window of opportunity is closed. On the less positive side, acquisitions in foreign environments demand *cross-cultural integration skills* that may not be the prime talent of investors. Acquisitions of local firms by foreigners can also be seen in certain case as an intrusion that bruises national pride. Finally, acquisitions are often made with high acquisition premiums that make this mode of entry more costly than other alternatives.

ENTERING A COUNTRY THROUGH JOINT VENTURES[4]

A **joint venture** is an ambiguous concept, since it embraces several forms of partnership. In this chapter, we shall consider joint ventures as *equity participations in separate legal entities* in which two or more partners invest tangible and intangible capital. Some countries, like China, have set up the concept of 'contractual joint ventures' that are a hybrid form of equity and project partnership agreement, but these are relatively limited and in practice the implications of their management are very similar to equity joint ventures. In emerging markets, joint ventures have been the main form of foreign direct investment (FDI). In 1996, in Korea, joint ventures represented around 77 per cent of all FDI, 72 per cent in China, 52 per cent in Latin America and 54 per cent in Eastern Europe.[5]

Three major forces seem to drive foreign investors to enter joint ventures.

Administrative requirements

Some governments want their own people to benefit from industrialisation; they often push foreign investors to ally with local firms before granting access to markets or resources. This concern is strongest in countries with import-substitution policies: governments in Indonesia, Malaysia, China, India and Russia, and in the past Japan or Korea, have been most successful in imposing partnerships on foreign investors. Countries like China, which endorsed wholly-owned foreign ventures in March 1992, still encourage Western companies to choose joint ventures. However, since the early 1990s governments have been more flexible and have accepted, in some cases, 100 per cent foreign ownership. In strategically sensitive sectors like media, telecoms, defence or legal professions (including in industrialised countries), foreign investment is banned or the foreign investor is obliged to share ownership with local firms. Foreign equity participation has sometimes also to be shared in order to encourage some ethnic citizens to participate in industrial development. Such was the case in Malaysia with the New Economic Policy (NEP) that forced local Malay (*Bumiputra*) equity participation in foreign projects.

Finally some foreign firms choose to enter into joint ventures to win contracts for important government infrastructure projects. In countries like Singapore, which has no protectionist regulations, the government has a policy of positive discrimination towards foreign contractors with local joint ventures.

Capabilities requirements

The need for a foreign company to access critical resources, assets and competencies has also favoured joint ventures. In most cases, foreign partners look for a local firm with capabilities in distribution, sales, local market know-how, local production expertise or, more importantly, contacts with decision-makers and business networks. Managerial and human resources are often the most critical resources provided by a local joint venture partner.

Successful multinational companies with experience and resources will be less inclined to tie up with a local partner for that reason: they assume that the market will adjust to them, so they do not need to adjust to the local market. Companies with strong international brands entering newly developing markets may need less local support than late entrants with unknown brands.

Risk hedging

Foreign firms may seek to reduce risk, especially when financial investment is high, or the return on investment (ROI) uncertain. They usually have one of three motivations:

- *Complexity* of a project
- *Uncertain market acceptance* of a product or service
- Country risk in terms of *macroeconomic* and *political stability*.

PARTNER SELECTION

The type of partner to be selected is a function of the strategic dimensions mentioned earlier. As illustrated in Figure 7.3, there are various partner-choice combinations; Table 7.3 shows the various types of partner available.

When there is no legal obligation to partnership and the foreign investor has the resource and capabilities to operate alone, the best choice is not enter into a joint venture unless risks and low opportunities push the company to search for a partner. When there is a legal obligation and the company possesses the resources and capabilities, the choice would be to search for a 'non-active' or 'sleeping partner', such as an investment company or some firms who are willing to let the foreign firm take command of the venture. If there is no legal pressure for joint venture and the company needs a partner because it lacks capabilities, it would look for a potential acquisition. If the government requires joint ventures, the choice would be more delicate. Since the foreign party will look for an active partner who can bring the needed capabilities, the assessment of strategic capabilities and cultural fit is critical.

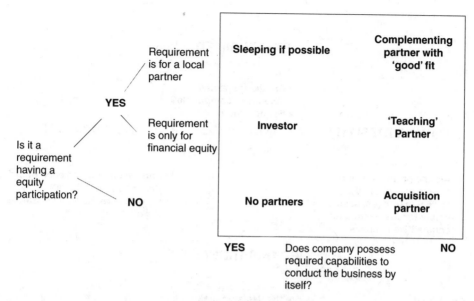

Figure 7.3 Partner choices in country-based joint ventures

In any case the selection of a potential partner has crucial, long-term consequences. It is important to find a partner with *compatible objectives*, and with whom it is possible to communicate and build a stable, lasting partnership; the foreign firm's success will depend on the partner's capabilities and willingness to cooperate, and the climate of mutual trust. Often, firms conduct far too little *advance planning*. In Asia Pacific, for instance, where joint venture had been a predominant entry mode, Western foreign firms conducted little or no screening and, in many cases, ended up choosing a long-time local agent or distributor without searching for alternatives.

To investigate potential partners thoroughly, foreign firms should:

- Require *information*
- Interview in depth the *owner*, top *managers, operating staff* in manufacturing and sales
- Ask for *financial data* (although these may be of limited value)
- Interview the local firm's *other joint venture partners, bankers, suppliers, customers* and *competitors*, as well as diplomats and established foreign investors.

Selection criteria

As already described in Chapter 4, the assessment of **fit** is an important selection criterion (see Figure 7.4).

1. A **strategic fit** exists when the two partners have *compatible long-term objectives*. They will pool some of their resources to reach goals that they cannot attain alone. Assessing strategic fit involves analysing the partners' implicit or explicit

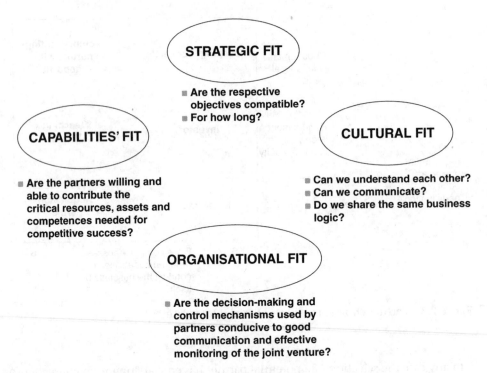

Figure 7.4 Partner fit analysis

motives for joining forces, as well as the benefits they expect to gain. In joint ventures for market entry, one typically finds three main types of strategic agenda:

- The *venturing agenda*, in which the two partners want to develop the potential of a given market by creating a new business activity. In this case, the primary intention is to join forces rather than to take advantage of the other partner.
- The *extractive agenda*, in which one partner wants to acquire a key resource, asset or competence from the other. Local partners typically seek product or process technology, hardware and software from foreign joint ventures; they may also want to gain access to international markets. Foreign partners often use joint ventures to build relationships and win market access, or to make up-front profits through high transfer pricing on equipment, components or management services; sometimes they are interested in access to raw materials or low-cost labour rather than in promoting the business of the joint venture itself.
- The *opportunistic agenda*, in which the local partner may want to capitalise on *citizenship* and *political contacts*, or seek a *financial return*. The foreign partner may be complying with regulations, or want to enter into a short-term 'deal'.

A classic example of conflicting goals would be a foreign partner who wants to acquire marketing expertise and a local partner looking for technological expertise.

The degree of commitment to the joint venture is particularly important: the moment of truth comes when unexpected problems arise in day-to-day operations. Even if individual managers assigned to a joint venture are committed, the two parents may give it relatively low priority. When a co-operative agreement is purely opportunistic, commitment is problematic; this is why many opportunistic partnerships end in failure.

2. A good **capabilities fit** means that both partners must be able to contribute to the resources and competencies needed; they must *identify and solve potential gaps* in contribution.

   A classic mistake is to overestimate one's partner's contribution to the joint venture. Problems also arise when initial resources, assets and competencies become insufficient to sustain competitiveness over time. New funding will be needed; profits will have to be reinvested into the business. A short-term orientation, opportunism or simply inconsistency of one or both partners may aggravate a potential resource gap.

   Valuing contributions that do not have a market price, because they are either not traded or intangible, can cause conflict. Intangibles and technology are often the most valuable contributions brought to a joint venture, and can become a key element in the negotiation.

3. **Cultural dissimilarity** emanating from corporate, industry or national and ethnic differences are always present in international joint ventures, and can create many problems and conflicts when it comes to the practical operations of the venture. As already indicated in Chapter 4, cultural differences often lead to a difficult period of adaptation called the '**death valley**', that requires patience and flexibility on the part of managers. It is therefore important that prior to engaging in an agreement a *cultural fit assessment* be made by trying to answer questions such as: Can we understand each other? Do we speak the same business language? Do we share a common logic? Can we communicate with each other?

4. Finally **organisational fit** analysis looks at the way differences in *management systems and procedures* are likely to shape the functioning of the joint venture and communication between the two partners. A local entrepreneurial firm with no procedures may have trouble co-operating with a big, bureaucratic multinational corporation. Organisational fit is hard to achieve when it comes to integrating the local joint venture into the parent companies' network of subsidiaries.

Staffing joint ventures

Joint ventures require managers with *political* and *cultural skills* as well as technical competencies. Foreign managers unprepared for cultural complexity will not handle critical situations properly and will jeopardise their parent company's ability to learn. The most important task of managers assigned to joint ventures, particularly when the strategic intent is to extract knowledge from the local environment, is to synthesise and transmit *learning experiences* to each relevant department in their parent company. It would be a mistake to assign managers lacking clout or prestige to a foreign joint venture; the local partner may interpret this as a lack of commitment to the partnership. The worst attitude is to consider such postings as a form of exile for undesirable personnel.

When recruiting local employees, identity and loyalty are critical. Do they feel that they belong to their parent company, or to the joint venture? Most of the time, the local partner will recruit local staff; foreign partners should monitor hiring carefully to ensure that the new employees are loyal to the joint venture, not just to the local partner.

Control

Joint ventures are controlled by a Board of Directors consisting largely of executives, as well as a few non-executive directors; these are usually local personalities who can play a useful role as go-betweens in cases of conflict with the local partners. Western companies tend to prefer having a majority stake in a joint venture, although there is no evidence that this allows them to exert real control. When a firm controls more than 70 per cent of capital, the joint venture can be considered a 'quasi-acquisition', in which case the majority partner is in command. Below 70 per cent, it is not necessarily the case. Several studies have failed to demonstrate significant correlation between shareholding and control: some companies who are in charge of key operational functions can be in control even with a minority stake.

JOINT VENTURE DECAY AND FAILURE

It is common for joint ventures to experience a rapid deterioration immediately after start-up as the partners find out more about each other and make efforts to adapt. After this 'death valley' period, relative stability follows, which can last three–six years; after that, mutual interest suddenly drops. The resulting crisis can lead to a split, and this phenomenon, known as **joint venture decay**, happens when both partners feel that they have acquired whatever advantage they sought from their association; at this moment the impetus for further collaboration can vanish. If both partners want to avert a divorce, they must revitalise their association by *increasing the range* or *broadening the scope* of its activities (Figure 7.5).

The experience of foreign companies in joint ventures has not always been a happy one. Empirical evidence on international joint ventures indicates that at most 40 per cent–50 per cent end up producing the expected return.[6] Most companies have become disillusioned because of unforeseen problems in setting up and operating their partnerships. There are five main causes of failure or difficulty:

- The *absence of strategic vision*. When a joint venture is launched hastily, or for purely defensive or opportunistic reasons, the foreign firm often fails to evaluate the intentions and capabilities of the local partner. A classic error in an industrial partnership is to choose a distributor whose corporate culture is likely to

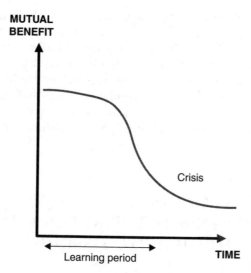

Figure 7.5   Joint venture decay

be inappropriate to a slow cash flow cycle, and who will probably privilege a few rapid cash flow deals instead of investing for the long term.

■ *Believing without seeing*. The art of appearances can be highly refined in some countries and many a foreign investor has been led into mistaking elaborate ceremony for a real commitment.

■ Failing to understand the local partner's *strategic logic*. In most cases, a thorough investigation would reveal the real intent – for example, to achieve vertical integration to appropriate technology, or simply to enter into an opportunistic deal.

■ *Haste in negotiation*. The desire to conclude a deal rapidly often leads the negotiators to concentrate on financial or legal clauses and neglect *technological* or *operational* issues. In Asian countries, for instance, the contractual stage must be preceded by an *overall planning session* for the project, during which the partners will agree on objectives and strategies. This implies a minimum investment in understanding the partner's logic. It is a good idea to advance step by step: a licensing contract, for example, can be a good way of testing the capacities of the other party before making a longer-term commitment.

■ *Insufficiently prepared staff and lack of organisational support*. Unprepared expatriate managers who fail to understand their partner's and employees' logic can exacerbate tensions, and damage the reputation of both the joint venture and the foreign parent. Local partners in emerging countries are often highly respected businessmen, and when they suffer what they see as inappropriate treatment at the hands of unsophisticated foreign staff, they quickly become disillusioned. Besides, the joint venture is often poorly served by headquarters (delays in technical assistance, delivery of poorly adapted products, exorbitant transfer pricing, exaggerated administrative rules or constraints that ignore local conditions).

These five causes of failure are often inter-related, contributing to a *vicious circle of misunderstanding* which can degenerate into open conflict and end in frustration, loss of market share and sometimes legal action. Studies on joint ventures have shown that good cultural and strategic fit leading to trust between partners are the crucial factors for success. Foreign enterprises that seriously consider setting up through joint ventures should devote enough resources and effort to carefully preparing and monitoring the selection of a partner and management of the venture as well as management of the continuous flow of communication with their local partners.

ENTERING A COUNTRY THROUGH ARM'S-LENGTH AGREEMENTS: LICENSING, FRANCHISING, AGENTS AND DISTRIBUTORS

When a direct investment is not justified, foreign companies can still be present in a particular country by contracting an agreement in the form of a licence, a franchise, an agency or a distribution contract.

Those contractual arrangements are made when one or more of the following characteristics is present:

- The market is *too small* for the company to justify a full investment
- The country is perceived as *too risky*
- There is already a direct investment in a nearby country and an additional one would be *redundant*
- The government does not allow *any other form of presence*
- The company wants to *test the market*.

Licensing agreements[7] are contractual arrangements by which a company (the *licensor*) transfers to another company (the *licensee*) its product and/or process technology with the right to exploit it commercially. The brand name of the licensor may or may not be part of the licensing agreement. The licensor receives financial compensation in the form of royalties and an up-front lump sum payment. Royalties can be calculated as a percentage of sales or as a fixed amount per unit sold. In addition to the transfer of technology, the licensor may send its engineers to help in technology transfer and functioning. It may also receive some form of technological fees. Finally, within a licensing agreement, a licensor can contractually force the licensee to buy intermediate products or components. In that case, the licensor gets the benefits and profits associated with those sales.

The benefits of licences are the low commitment in term of personnel and capital involved. It is an economic way to enter a market. However, the disadvantages are manifold. First, there is a risk of *technological appropriation* by the licensee, who may become a future competitor. This has been the case in the past with Framatome of France, who licensed in the technology of high-pressure nuclear reactors from Westinghouse and which progressively became more advanced and more competitive than the licensor. Another risk involves *quality control*. Particularly when the licence includes the brand name of the licensor, if the licensee is not quality conscious it may ruin the name of the licensee. The main strategic disadvantage of licensing is that the licensors are very distant from the market and have no control over the company's destiny in the licensee country.

Franchises[8] are another form of indirect contractual arrangement through which the *franchiser* grants the *franchisee* the right to use its name and receive a financial compensation similar to the licensing agreement (fixed plus royalties). The franchiser generally forces the franchisee to adopt a certain number of operating policies so that it can maintain a standard level of quality associated with its brand name. Examples of international franchises can be found in the hospitality industry (Hilton, Accor), beverages (Coca-Cola bottling), fast food (McDonald's) and distribution (Benetton, Gap).

The advantages and disadvantages of franchises are very similar to those of licensing.

ENTERING A COUNTRY THROUGH LOCAL AGENTS AND DISTRIBUTORS

The appointment of a local agent or distributor is probably the most frequent mode of entry for the thousands of SMEs who want to reach international markets. For the most established large multinational enterprises, this is also a means to reach countries that are either risky, or whose size does not justify a major investment. It can also be an economic way to test markets without committing too many resources up front. The distinction between an *agent* and a *distributor* is that the latter carries out the logistical tasks of stocking, transporting and billing, while the former is simply a salesperson and an order-taker. In emerging markets one can often find three categories of agents and distributors: domestic companies (most often medium-sized firms or large multi-business family conglomerates), government monopolies in planned economies or large international trading companies like Jardine Matheson, the East Asiatic Company, Diethelm or Swire in the Asia Pacific region.

The main advantage of distribution agreements is that they require a limited amount of resources from the global firm; the main disadvantages are the lack of contact with the market and the conflict of interest that can emerge when sales reach a certain level.[9] The economic reason for this conflict is caused by the fact that distributors are generally remunerated by a commission as a percentage of sales. When sales grow, the total commission may reach a point where it is bigger than the fixed costs required to set up a wholly-owned marketing subsidiary. The multinational firms then try to get rid of the local distributor, as it has seen in Europe with the Japanese car-makers who have progressively replaced their distributors by their own organisation in major countries. Knowing this, the local distributor may be tempted to fail to push sales when it is obvious that a substitution point is approaching. Instead of fighting a lost cause, international distributors have often adopted a strategy of becoming 'partners' rather that pure distributors and raising the value added of their services to both customers and principals in order to raise 'switching costs'. However, when the country becomes a significant portion of the turnover and becomes 'key', the global firm will generally turn to another, more direct mode of entry.

ENTERING A COUNTRY THROUGH REPRESENTATIVES, PROCUREMENT OR A TECHNICAL OFFICE

The *representative office* is another very frequent entry mode, considered as a stepping-stone or a 'beachhead'. In China, Russia, Vietnam and newly-opened countries this type of entry consists of sending an expatriate manager (sometime using a locally recruited person) to collect information, establish contacts, organise direct sales, lobby for licences, negotiate distribution or joint venture agreements and recruit local personnel. This entry mode is frugal in resource consumption and beneficial in competencies-building, but it reaches its limit when it comes to actually running a business. It fits corporations that are selling big projects (railways systems, airport, defence contracts, turnkey plants) at the pre-bidding phase. In these cases, representative offices complement and control the local agents who are lobbying for information and access to decision-makers.

Technical or procurement offices are another form of entry. Technical offices are most relevant when the country is considered to be a source of technological innovation and a presence can give access to useful contacts and information.

Procurement or purchasing offices are most appropriate for large retailers or big commodity buyers who set up an office in order to be close to suppliers, to negotiate contracts and to control their execution. Some companies specialise in buying for third parties and are used by firms which do not want to commit resources to establishing their own office.

ENTRY MODES SEEN AS 'REAL OPTIONS'

The concept of the **'real option'** has been proposed in recent business strategy literature to explain some investment decisions, including foreign investment decisions.[10] The theory of the real option is directly derived from the financial theory of options. According to the real option proponents, some investments can be assimilated to a 'call option', that is to say a preliminary investment to observe the future development of the business, and at the end of a period of 'trial', the company has the possibility to expand or retreat. The cost of making the preliminary investment is equivalent to the price of an option. If the company sees that the foreign investment is creating future value then it can exercise its option and expand – i.e. increase its stake in a joint venture, transform a licence into an acquisition or replace a distributor by a full investment. If the business does not seem to be developing, it stops the investment, sells its share in the joint venture and continues under licence or as a distributor or sells the business.

COMPARING ENTRY MODES

Each mode of entry described earlier has its advantages and disadvantages. Table 7.4 summarises the pluses and minuses of each of them on various criteria, while Figure 7.6 illustrates the cash flow profile for the parent foreign company of different forms of foreign investments based on the example given in Appendix 7.1 (p. 211).

Table 7.4   Comparing various entry modes

	Wholly-owned	Acquisition	Joint venture	Licensing	Representative office	Agent/distributor
Up-front investment, financial and managerial	HIGH	HIGH	MEDIUM	LOW	LOW/MED	LOW
Speed of entry	SLOW	QUICK	QUICK	MEDIUM	LOW	POSSIBLY QUICK
Market penetration	MEDIUM	HIGH	MED/HIGH	MED/LOW	LOW	MED/LOW
Control of market (customer knowledge)	HIGH	HIGH	MEDIUM	NIL	LOW	LOW/NIL
Political risk exposure	HIGH	HIGH	MEDIUM	LOW	LOW	LOW
Technological leakage	LOW	LOW	HIGH/MED	HIGH	LOW	LOW
Managerial complexity	HIGH	HIGH	HIGH	LOW	MEDIUM	LOW
Potential financial return	HIGH RISK HIGH/ MEDIUM RETURN HIGH PAYOUT	HIGH RISK HIGH/ MEDIUM RETURN HIGH PAYOUT	MEDIUM/ HIGH RISK HIGH/ MEDIUM RETURN MEDIUM PAYOUT	LOW RISK HIGH RETURN LOW PAYOUT	LOW RISK RETURN?	LOW RISK RETURN?

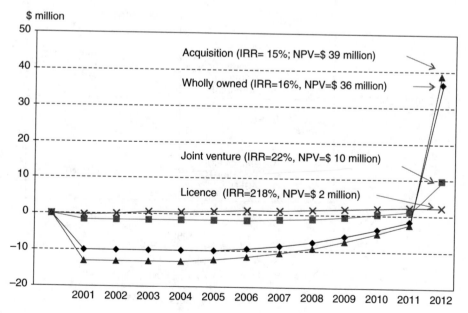

Figure 7.6   Cumulative cash profiles for a foreign investor, 2001–12

Table 7.4 shows that *wholly-owned approaches* and acquisitions have the most significant market impact and subsequent present value of the investment. The return on investment is high to moderate and, in our example, is close to the cost of capital. The reason is that in the case of a wholly-owned investment, it takes time to build a market presence and in the case of an acquisition, the original investment requires an up-front premium. The residual value in those two cases explains most of the return, indicating that those two kinds of investments are valid from a long-term perspective and should be used only when country risks are limited. Licensing is highly profitable from a return viewpoint. This is owing to a minimal up-front investment and a constant flow of royalties, but the absolute value is small. This fits a situation of high risks and low commitment. The long-term impact of a licensing agreement is weak. Joint ventures are middle of the road and the numerical example Appendix 7.1 gives that strategy a higher return than both the wholly-owned or acquisition modes. However, joint ventures, as mentioned earlier, do not have a brilliant performance record, showing that the theoretical value of this mode of entry is often hampered by poor implementation.

(See Appendix 7.1 for details. The cash flows are the cumulative flow of investments paid by the foreign firm and the dividends or royalties received plus the terminal value at the end of the period. NPV assumes a cost of capital of 15 per cent.)

CHOOSING AN ENTRY MODE

The choice of one mode is a function of the factors described at the beginning of the chapter and illustrated in Figure 7.2 (p. 192). There is no ideal solution and the

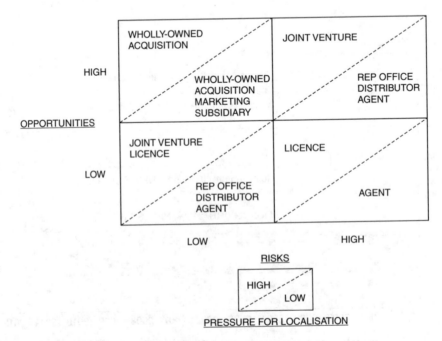

Figure 7.7 Mapping of entry modes choices

choice is up to each company, according to the weighting given to corporate global strategy, country risks and opportunities, capabilities, timing and government constraints. Figure 7.7 gives a mapping of possible choice as a function of some of these factors, but in the end, the final decision is a multidimensional one that resists a simplistic 2 × 2 representation.

Over time, with economic growth and increased internal capabilities, foreign investors may shift from one mode to another. In China, for instance, wholly-owned foreign enterprises overtook equity joint ventures in 1997.[11]

SUMMARY AND KEY POINTS

1. Entry strategy concerns three aspects:
   - Entry *objectives* (*why*)
   - *Timing* of entry (*when*)
   - *Mode* of entry (*how*).

2. Entry objectives:
   - *Market development* objectives are to enter a market because of:
     - Size and growth opportunity – depends on income and population of a country
     - Criticality of countries – there are key countries in which a presence is needed for global long-term competitiveness owing to size or quality of customer base
   - *Resource access* objectives – extracting key resource such as natural or human resources which contribute to competitive advantage
   - *Learning* objectives – gains in knowledge/competence in countries where industry is state-of-the-art
   - *Co-ordination* objectives – regional co-ordination of activities owing to favourable location and infrastructure advantages.

3. Timing of international entry – there are four phases:
   - *Premature* phase:
     - Absence of demand
     - Common in developing countries at an early stage or for a product that does not fit demand in a particular country
     - Appropriate investment at this stage is the establishment of any of:
       (a) Representative offices
       (b) Listening posts
       (c) Distribution agreements
   - *Window* phase ('Window of opportunity'):
     - Take-off of the market with relatively less competition
     - Potential strategies include:
       (a) Follower
       (b) First mover:
          (i) Advantages – pre-empt resources; establish brands; establish standards; learning about customers
          (ii) Disadvantages – take risks; others can 'free ride' your ground work

- *Competitive growth* phase:
  - High market growth but competitors have received first-mover advantages
  - Potential strategies:
    - (a) Hazardous entry but with massive resources or a highly differentiated strategy
    - (b) Acquisition or joint venture arrangement
- *Mature* phase:
  - Well-established market
  - Potential strategies:
    - (a) Acquisition
    - (b) Direct investment with innovative product.

4. Mode of entry:
   - Factors influencing entry mode:
     - Corporate global strategy
     - Country risks (political and operational risks)
     - Opportunities
     - Company's internal capabilities
     - Time pressure
     - Government requirements
   - *Types* of entry mode:
     - *Wholly-owned subsidiaries*:
       - (a) Advantages – gives most control over operations; low technological leakage
       - (b) Disadvantages – requires the highest mobilisation of resources and competencies; highest risk; high up-front investment; slow entry
     - *Acquisition*:
       - (a) Advantages – immediate availability of resources, assets and competencies; enables access to market when window of opportunity is closed; high market penetration; high control of market; low technological leakage
       - (b) Disadvantages – requires cross-cultural integration skills which acquiring company may not possess; some nationalities may view acquisition by foreigners unfavourably; costly, as often associated with high acquisition premiums; high political risk exposure
     - *Joint venture*
       - (a) Advantages – quick entry; medium to high market penetration
       - (b) Disadvantages – medium to high technological leakage; high managerial complexity
       - (c) Partner selection – depends on a combination of legal requirements and internal capabilities the firm possesses
       - (d) Partners categories:
         - (i) Sleeping
         - (ii) Complementing
         - (iii) Investor

        (iv) 'Teaching'
        (v)   Acquisition
   (e) Partners types – each has their own advantages and disadvantages:
        (i)   Supplier
        (ii)   Customer/distributor
        (iii) Competitor
        (iv) Diversifier
        (v)   Investor
        (vi) Government
   (f)   Partner evaluation – uses the same criteria used in assessing alliance partner: strategic fit, capability fit, cultural fit and organisational fit
   (g) Management:
        (i)   Staffing – foreign managers should possess political and cultural skills; local staff should ideally be loyal to the joint venture, not to the local partner
        (ii)   Control – can be obtained through shareholding ownership or responsibility over operational functions
   (h) Termination renewal:
        (i)   Termination – potential problems are the *'death valley' issue* (development of a vicious cycle in which partners' communications are shut off) and *joint venture decay* (drop of mutual interest and loss of impetus for further collaboration)
        (ii)   Failures/problems – absence of strategic vision; 'believing without seeing'; failure to understand local partner's strategic logic; haste in negotiation; insufficiently prepared staff or lack of organisational support
        (iii) Renewal – revitalise the joint venture by increasing range or broadening scope of its activities
- *Licence or franchise*
   (a) Advantages – economic (low commitment of personnel and capital); low political risk exposure
   (b) Disadvantages – risk of technological appropriation by licensee who may become future competitor; damage to brand name if licensee is not quality conscious; licensor's lack of control over licence destiny in the licensee country
- *Agent or distributor*
   (a) Frequently used by SMEs for reaching international markets
   (b) Entry mode for reaching countries that are either risky or whose size does not justify a major investment
   (c) There are three categories of agent or distributor in emerging countries:
        (i)   Multi-business family conglomerates
        (ii)   Government monopolies
        (iii) Large international trading companies
   (d) Advantages:
        (i)   Economic (low resource commitment)
        (ii)   Possible quick entry
        (iii) Low political risk exposure
        (iv) Low technological leakage

        (e) Disadvantages:
-      (i)   Lack of contact with market
-      (ii)   Conflict of interest when the sales reach certain level
- *Office* (representative office/procurement office/technical office)
  - (a) Representative office
    - (i)   Advantages – Frugal in resource consumption; beneficial in competence building; appropriate when corporations are selling big projects at the pre-bidding phase; low political risk exposure; low technological leakage
    - (ii)   Disadvantages – Slow entry; low market penetration; low control of market
  - (b) Technical or procurement offices:
    - (i)   Useful when country is source of technological innovation and company presence give access to useful contacts and information
    - (ii)   Procurement offices most appropriate for large retailers or big commodity buyers who want to be close to suppliers and control contract execution
- ▪ *Choice* of entry mode – dependent on weighting a company assigned to various factors influencing entry modes
- ▪ As a 'real option' (a call option)
  - Price of option is the cost of making the preliminary investment
  - Choices from real option are:
    - (a) Expand investment if foreign investment is creating future value
    - (b) Terminate investment if foreign investment does not seem to develop.

Appendix 7.1 Examples of entry modes financial profiles

Toronto Auto Chemicals Ltd is a Canadian company specialising in various auto parts and speciality chemicals used in car manufacturing and maintenance. In late 1999, the company sent a mission to Korea to analyse the market and prepare an analysis of various investment alternatives. Korea was only slightly affected by the Asian crisis and was on the way to recovery. The Korean car industry was completely restructured: Hyundai, the largest *chaebol* had acquired Kia, Samsung's car division was sold to Renault and Daewoo was on the verge of bankruptcy and being considered for sale to an international consortium. However, the market was recovering and had positive prospects. The study team had concentrated on one particular type of product: liquid brake additive. It estimated that the current domestic market of 4,000 tons a year would grow at a rate of 7 per cent a year over the decade from 2001 to 2010. The competition was made up of one domestic firm which controlled 70 per cent of the market and one Japanese joint venture which controlled 30 per cent. The study team concluded that there were four major alternatives for market entry:

(1) *Set up a greenfield operation and operate as a 100 per cent Korean subsidiary.* The minimum economic capacity was 6,000 tons for a total investment of US$ 10 million. The financing of the investment would be done entirely by the mother company and it could expect to repatriate a dividend of 50 per cent of net profit when this became positive. The subsidiary could not expect to capture more than 20 per cent the first year, growing progressively to 50 per cent after the sixth year of operations. Export output would be a maximum of 3,000 tons/year. Other factors to consider were:

- *Exchange rate*: US$ 1 = 1,200 Korean Won (the study considered this rate would remain unchanged)
- *Prices/costs*:

Selling price (domestic)	= 2400 Wons/kg
Selling price (export)	= 1.9 $US/kg
Working capital requirement	= 33 per cent of Turnover
Tax rate on profit	= 30 per cent
Production costs	= Declining function with cumulated volume
	$= 2,000 - 0.025 * 10^{\log \text{cum volume}}$
Administrative/marketing costs	= 1,200 million Won, increasing to 1,600 million Won

Weighted Average Cost of Capital (WACC) = 15 per cent

Table 7A.1 Analysis of entry alternatives, 2001–2012

First alternative: greenfield 100% operation

	2001	2002	2003	2004	2005	2006	2007	2008	2009	2010	2011	2012
Subsidiary cash flow	-12000	-1557	-941	676	1227	1647	1747	2586	3130	3537	3946	46612
Subsidiary cumulative cash flow	-12000	-13557	-14498	-13822	-12595	-10948	-9201	-6615	-3484	52	3999	50611
Subsidiary NPV at WACC	2 304											
Subsidiary IRR	17%											
Shareholder cash flow	-10.00	0.00	0.00	0.00	0.00	0.46	0.92	1.28	1.62	1.95	2.30	37.85
Shareholder cumulative cash	-10.00	-10.00	-10.00	-10.00	-10.00	-9.54	-8.61	-7.33	-5.71	-3.76	-1.46	36.39
Shareholder NPV WACC	0.78											
Shareholder IRR	16%											

Second alternative: acquisition

	2001	2002	2003	2004	2005	2006	2007	2008	2009	2010	2011	2012
Subsidiary cash flow	-15600	-1862	-41	510	2133	2537	2944	3354	3767	4184	4603	51403
Subsidiary cumulative cash flow	-15600	-17462	-17503	-16993	-14860	-12324	-9380	-6026	-2259	1925	6527	57931
Subsidiary NPV at WACC	2 354											
Subsidiary IRR	17%											
Shareholder cash flow	-13.00	0.00	0.00	0.00	0.48	0.82	1.16	1.50	1.85	2.20	2.55	41.55
Shareholder cumulative cash flow	-13.00	-13.00	-13.00	-13.00	-12.52	-11.69	-10.53	-9.03	-7.18	-4.98	-2.44	39.11
Shareholder NPV WACC	-0.40											
Shareholder IRR	15%											

Third alternative: joint venture

	2001	2002	2003	2004	2005	2006	2007	2008	2009	2010	2011	2012
Subsidiary cash flow	-12000	-2128	-1319	34	868.7	1453.3	1581.7	1925.6	2302.7	2717.9	3177	39551
Subsidiary cumulative cash flow	-12000	-14128	-15446	-15412	-14543	-13090	-11508	-9582.7	-7280.0	-4562.1	-1385	38165
Subsidiary NPV at WACC	-1 205											
Subsidiary IRR	14%											
Shareholder cash flow	-1.50	0.00	0.00	0.00	0.00	0.00	0.22	0.37	0.53	0.71	0.90	8.59
Shareholder cumulative cash flow	-1.50	-1.50	-1.50	-1.50	-1.50	-1.50	-1.28	-0.91	-0.38	0.32	1.23	9.82
Shareholder NPV WACC	1.02											
Shareholder IRR	22%											

Fourth alternative: licensing

Shareholder cash flow	2001	2002	2003	2004	2005	2006	2007	2008	2009	2010	2011	2012
Investment	-200.0	-200.0	-200.0	0.0	0.0	0.0	0.0	0.0	0.0	0.0	0.0	0.0
Royalties	0.0	660.0	671.2	183.2	196.0	209.7	224.4	240.1	256.9	274.9	294.2	314.7
Total million Won	-200.0	460.0	471.2	183.2	196.0	209.7	224.4	240.1	256.9	274.9	294.2	314.7
Total $ million	-0.2	0.4	0.4	0.2	0.2	0.2	0.2	0.2	0.2	0.2	0.2	0.3
$ Cumul	-0.2	0.2	0.6	0.8	0.9	1.1	1.3	1.5	1.7	1.9	2.2	2.4
Shareholder WACC	15%											
Shareholder NPV	1.00											
Shareholder IRR	218%											

Notes: IRR = Internal rate of return.
NPV = Net present value.
WACC = Weighted average cost of capital.

■ *Domestic loans* interest rate: 10 per cent

■ *Debt servicing*: 7 years

(2) The second alternative was to *buy the domestic competitors*. The acquisition price would be US$ 15,600 million but one could expect to capture the 70 per cent market share right away. The other hypothesis, as compared with the first alternative, would be the same.

(3) A third option would be to *replace the Japanese company as a joint venture partner with an existing Korean firm*. The immediate market share would be 30 per cent, rising to 50 per cent in the third year owing to the improved technology of the Canadian firm. The financing of the joint venture would be 30 per cent equity to be shared 50/50 with the local partner and 70 per cent debts to be serviced over seven years. The maximum exports in that case would only be 2,000 tons/year. All other hypotheses would remain the same.

(4) Finally, it was possible to conclude a *licensing agreement with a local firm* who, at best, could use and transform its existing facilities and obtain 20 per cent market share. In such case, Toronto Auto Chemicals Ltd would have to invest US$ 600,000 over the next three years to transfer its technology and receive a royalty of 200 Won/kg.

The financial analysis gives the results in Table 7A.1.

Learning assignments

1 What are the relative advantages/disadvantages of setting up a wholly-owned subsidiary instead of a joint venture?
2 What is a 'window of opportunity'?
3 Under which conditions does being a first mover give sustainable competitive advantage?
4 What are the major problems associated with licensing?
5 What potential problems does a foreign investor experience in an industrial joint venture with an ex-local agent or distributor?
6 Why do joint ventures often fail?

Key words

■ 'Death valley'
■ Entry modes
■ Extractive agenda
■ First mover
■ Fit analysis
✓ Franchise
✓ Joint venture
■ Joint venture decay
✓ Licensing
■ Opportunistic agenda
■ Partner selection
■ Real option
■ Representative offices
■ Sleeping partner

- Venturing agenda
- Wholly-owned operations
- Window of opportunity

Web resources

<http://www.strategicdirectinvestor.co.uk/>
Strategic Direct Investor is a magazine on cross-border direct investment which has editorials, breaking news stories, in-depth features, location studies and big-name corporate interviews.

<http://www.wto.org/english/tratop_e /tratop_e.htm>
WTO's trade topics including anti-dumping rules, GATT rules, technical barriers to trade, subsidies, import licensing issues and intellectual property rights.

Notes

1. Lieberman and Montgomery (1988, pp. 41–58).
2. Luo and Peng (1998, pp. 141–63).
3. On entry mode, see: Anderson and Gatigon (1986, pp. 1–26); Kim and Hwang (1992, pp. 29–53).
4. Beamish and Bank (1987, pp. 1–16).
5. Adakar, Adil, Ernst and Vaish (1997, pp. 120–37).
6. Kogut (1989, pp. 183–98).
7. See Contractor (1981); Beamish (1996).
8. Gompers and Connely (1997).
9. Arnold (2000, pp. 131–7).
10. Kogut and Kulatilaka (1994, pp. 52–71); Luermann (1997, pp. 51–67); Williamson (1999, pp. 117–26).
11. Vanhonacker, Wilfried, 'Entering China: An Unconventional Approach; *Harvard Business Review*, March–April 1997, pp. 130–41.

References and further reading

Adarkar, Ashwin, Asif Adil, David Ernst and Paresh Vaish, 'Emerging Market Alliances: Must They Be Win–Lose?', *McKinsey Quarterly*, 4, 1997, pp. 120–37.

Anderson, Erin and Hubert Gatignon, 'Modes of Foreign Entry: A Transaction Costs Analysis and Propositions', *Journal of International Business Studies*, 17(3), 1986, pp. 1–26.

Arnold, David, 'Seven Rules of International Distribution', *Harvard Business Review*, November–December 2000, pp. 131–7.

Beamish, Paul, 'Note on International Licensing', Richard Ivey School of Business, University of Western Ontario, Note 9A96G008, 1996.

Beamish, Paul and John Bank, 'Equity Joint Ventures and the Theory of the Multinational Enterprise', *Journal of International Business Studies*, 18(3), 1987, pp. 1–16.

Cavusgil, S. Tamer and Pervez N. Ghauri, *Doing Business in Developing Countries: Entry and Negotiation Strategies*. London: Routledge, 1991.

Contractor, Farok, *International Technology Licensing: Compensation, Costs and Negotiation*. Lexington, MA: D.C. Heath, 1981.

Gompers, Paul and Catherine Connely, 'A Note on Franchising', Harvard Business School, Note 9-297-108, 1997.

Kim, Chan and Peter Hwang, 'Global Strategies and Multinational Entry Mode Choice', *Journal of International Business Studies*, 23(1), 1992, pp. 29–53.

Kogut, Bruce, 'The Stability of Joint Ventures: Reciprocity and Competitive Rivalry', *Journal of Industrial Economics,* 38(2), 1989, pp. 183–98.

Kogut, Bruce and Nalin Kulatilaka, 'Options Thinking and Platform Investments: Investing in Opportunity', *California Management Review,* Winter 1994, pp. 52–71.

Lieberman, Marvin and David Montgomery, 'First Mover Advantages', *Strategic Management Journal,* 9, 1988, pp. 41–58.

Luermann, Timothy, 'Investment Opportunities as Real Options: Getting Started on the Numbers', *Harvard Business Review,* July–August 1997, pp. 51–67.

Luo, Yadong and Mike Peng, 'First Mover Advantages in Investing in Transitional Economies', *Thunderbird International Business Review,* 40, 1998, pp. 141–63.

Miller, Robert, Jack D. Glen, Frederick Jasperen and Yannis Karmokolias, *International Joint Ventures in Developing Countries: Happy Marriages?,* International Finance Corporation, Discussion Paper, 29, 1996.

Rigman, Tom, 'Window of Opportunity: Timing and Entry Strategies', *Industrial Management and Data Systems,* 96(5), 1996.

Root, Franklin, *Entry Strategies for International Markets.* San Francisco: Jossey-Bass, 1994.

Williamson, Peter J., 'Strategy as Options on the Future', *Sloan Management Review,* Spring 1999, pp. 117–26.

Williamson, Peter J. and Hu Qionghua, *Managing the Global Frontier: Strategies for Developing Markets.* London: Pitman. 1994.

Part II

Managing globally

Part II, Managing Globally, considers the various *managerial issues* in the various business functions.

Chapter 8   Global marketing

Chapter 8 starts by discussing the theory of customers' convergence and then analyses the practical approach to global marketing in the various elements of the marketing mix: branding, pricing, global account management, global solution selling and global distribution.

Chapter 9   Global operations

Chapter 9 deals with the localisation of operational facilities, the various roles of manufacturing plants in a global network, global procurement and the management of the supply chain. It then discusses the various phases of project management.

Chapter 10   Global innovation

Chapter 10 deals with the management of research and development (R&D) in global companies as well as knowledge management, transfer of best practices and the issues of technology transfer and protection of intellectual property rights (IPR).

Chapter 11   Cross-cultural management

Chapter 11 discusses the impact of cultural differences on the management of cross-cultural teams, on international negotiations and on business practices. It begins with a presentation of different streams of research showing international differences in business cultures and economic organisations.

Chapter 12   Global human resources management

Chapter 12 addresses the practical managerial aspects of human resources in global firms. Besides the classic problems of expatriation, it looks at the means of developing local talent in the various countries in which the firms operate and creating a real global organisational culture.

Chapter 13   Global financial management

Chapter 13 addresses some of the most current issues that global corporations face in managing their financial resources. The first section deals with the risks associated with foreign exchange fluctuations and the hedging techniques used to cover those risks. The second part looks at project financing. The third part discusses the source of global financing both equity and debts. Finally trade financing is described in a fourth part. The chapter ends by giving an expanded example.

---

convergence - to come towards each other at a point.
(अभिसरण करना)

divergence -

8

Global marketing

In 1989, Theodore Levitt, in a far-sighted article (1983), predicted the 'globalisation of markets'. His arguments were based on the *convergence of consumer needs and behaviours* that would erase national differences and would lead to the standardisation of marketing policies.

In Chapter 1 it was shown that since 1980, globalisation had definitely gained ground and that many companies had designed, launched, promoted, priced and sometime distributed products and services globally. Brands such as Coca-Cola, Sony, Intel, Kodak or Windows are known in nearly all cities on the planet. In early 2000 Unilever, one of the oldest and multinational corporations, announced that it would reduce the number of its brands from 1,600 to 400. The TV cable CNN maintains that it reaches viewers all over the globe. The *International Herald Tribune*, a joint publication of the *New York Times* and of the *Washington Herald Tribune*, based in Paris, is simultaneously printed in 11 cities and distributed in 164 countries. This chapter discusses the practical implications of globalisation for marketing, as well as its limitations. It starts by examining the validity of the theory of customer convergence and then looks at the practical approach to global marketing in the various elements of the marketing mix.

At the end of the chapter one should be able:

- To understand customer behaviour divergence and convergence across countries
- To understand differences in segmentation
- To design a product policy, towards standardisation or adaptation
- To decide whether the company will push global or local brands
- To decide whether the company should have a global pricing policy

- To design an appropriate global distribution system
- To develop a global account and global solution selling policy.

CUSTOMER BEHAVIOUR, CONVERGENCE AND GLOBAL SEGMENTATION

The prime task of any marketing manager is to understand customers' needs, embodied in customer value curves. Customer needs are driven by a series of factors, as summarised in Table 8.1.

It can be seen from Table 8.1 that several factors shaping needs are linked to *culture and geography*. For instance, Schütte (1998) has argued that Asian customers have a different hierarchy of needs and consequently exhibit value curves that differ from Western ones[2] (Figure 8.1) and Parker (2000) shows that bioclimatic conditions change customer preferences.

Beside Levitt, Ohmae (1985) and Yip (1994) are the defenders of global **convergence**, arguing that an increasing percentage of the population, at least in the market-led economies, share the same tastes and needs for larger quantities of products and services. Ohmae has proposed the term '*Californisation*' to describe this convergence.

There is no conclusive evidence of full convergence for consumer goods except in the case of few products or services that are highly publicised (portable computers,

Table 8.1 Customer needs and value curves

Factors shaping customer needs	
Consumer markets	*Business-to-business markets*
- Income	- Industry type
- Psychology	- Usage
- Social habits	- Cost/benefit
- Social status	- Technological requirements
- Climatic conditions	- Time availability
- Time availability	
Typical customer value curve elements	
- Product/service functionalities (comfort, design, appeal, etc.)	- Product/service functionalities
	- Product/service performances
- Product/service quality	- Reputation
- Image	- Relationships
- Price	- Price and associated costs
- Availability	- Associated services
- Convenience	- Financing
- Associated services	- Network effects
- Financing	
- Network effect	

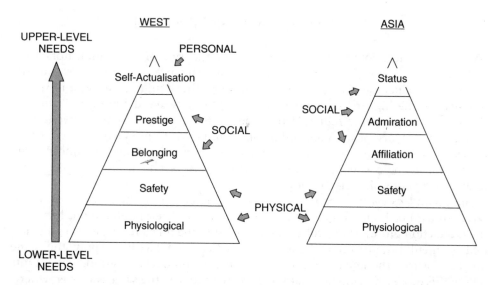

Figure 8.1 Western versus Asian hierarchy of needs

Source: Schütte (1998).

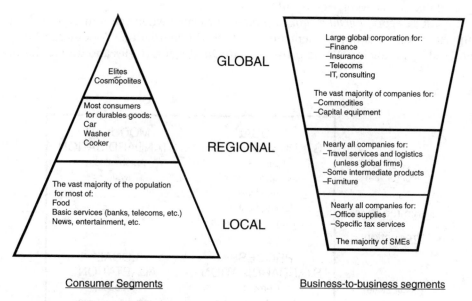

Figure 8.2 Customer segmentation

mobile phones, luxury goods). However, in business-to-business sectors convergence is gaining ground, since purchasing motives are essentially technical and economic. Each industry market can be divided into different broad segments, as illustrated in Figure 8.2.

PRODUCT STANDARDISATION

The standardisation of products and services is a function of two main factors. First, *customer value curves:* the more similar are customer needs across the world, the more the product can be standardised. Second, the minimum economic size of production: the higher the volume required, the more standardisation. Figure 8.3 shows four categories of product, depending on the importance of those two factors.

The first category, *global standardisation,* corresponds to products or services that target global customer segments and require a high volume of concentrated production to be cost-competitive. This is the case of chemicals, aircraft, micro-processors or consumer electronics.

The second category, *process standardisation,* refers to products or services that serve similar needs but do not require a high volume. Their production is localised, the production process standardised and, as a result, the final product is also standard-ised. Cement production is local in production and factories apply the same processes across the globe for delivering standard products. Fast-food restaurants follow this model: McDonald's hamburgers are produced the same way everywhere. Over the years, McDonald's has adapted its products offering to cater for national differences (no beef in India, wine in France), but the process follows very strict global rules.

The third category, *local adaptation,* is products or services that are fully tailored to local needs, like foods or consulting services.

The last category, *modular standardisation,* is needed when economies of scale are important but customers demand product differentiation. Modularisation is achieved by producing standard components in global factories and differentiating

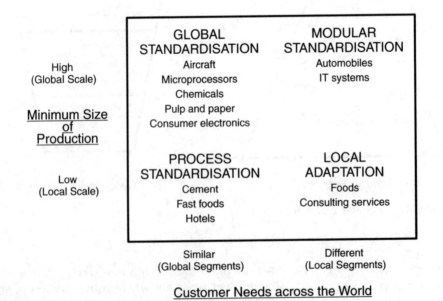

Figure 8.3   Global product standardisation types

the product at the assembly stage. This is the case of automobiles or computers, such as Dell or ACER.

GLOBAL BRANDING[1]

A brand is *global* when the product or service it represents is marketed across the world under its name. The most famous global brands are listed in Table 8.2.

Global brands may be the name of individual products or services (Pampers) or the name of the corporation that produces them (SONY, Visa, Coca-Cola). In the latter case, the brand is the symbol of *corporate identity* and it is encapsulated into a logo that is present in all documents of the firm, and associated with individual products or services even if those have an individual trademark. Global branding is a combination of both types: global firms develop a corporate name that will apply to all subsidiaries in the world and they also try to limit the individual product names and market products under a global name. For instance, Intel is the corporate brand and Pentium is the trademark of a family of microprocessors; Nestlé is the corporate name and Nescafé or Perrier are global names of individual products. The same would apply to Microsoft and Windows, Explorer or Office. It does not mean that all products of a global firm will make use of the same name, either corporate or product. Coca-Cola, Heineken or Electrolux use the corporate name for some of their products (global products or services) and market products locally under a local or regional name (Table 8.3).

According to Professor John Quelch the common features of global brands are:

- Strong in their home market
- Consistent in product positioning
- Present geographically in a balanced way across regions
- Address similar consumer needs worldwide

Table 8.2   Global brands

Brand	Country of origin
Coca-Cola	United States
Lewis	United States
IBM	United States
McDonald's	United States
SONY	Japan
Intel	United States
Kodak	United States
Nike	United States
Mercedes	Germany
Macintosh	United States
Nescafé	Switzerland
Swatch	Switzerland
Nokia	Finland

Table 8.3   Examples of corporations using global and local brands

Global Corporate Name	Global Brand	Local/Regional Brand
Coca-Cola	Coke	Beverly (herbal soft drink, Italy)
		Lilt (citrus soft drink, Ireland)
		Mezzo (mineral water, Germany)
		Splash (citrus soft drink, Germany, Spain)
Electrolux	Electrolux	Husquvarna (Sweden)
		Electro Helios (Greece)
		Eureka (United States)
		Arthur Martin (France)
		Zappas (Belgium, Italy, Norway, France)
		Zanussi (Italy)
		AEG (Germany)
		Volta (Sweden)
		Faure (France)
		Rex (Italy)
		Flymo (United Kingdom)
		McCulloch (United States)
Heineken	Heineken	80 local brands among which are:
	Amstel	Tiger (Asia Pacific)
	Murphy	Bintang (Indonesia)
		33 Export (France)
		Moretti (Austria)
		Cruzcampo (Spain)
		Zywieck (Poland)

- Easy to pronounce
- Similar to corporate name
- Associated with a product category.

The two last attributes are no longer valid, and as mentioned earlier many global brands are dissociated from the corporate name (Nestlé and Nescafé, Unilever and Lipton Tea) and many global names are used in many product categories (SONY, ABB).

For Hankinson and Cowing (1996), global brands can be categorised in a 2 × 2 matrix according to the degree of consistency in brand positioning (whether they convey the same message to the same segments across the world) and according to the standardisation of the products or services they represent. (See Figure 8.4.) Volvo is an example of a brand representing a standardised product with different country segmentation, Nescafé has the same brand positioning with products adapted to customer tastes. McDonald's started initially with a standardised product and the same positioning across the world but has been obliged to adapt products to local conditions.

This classification shows that the meaning of global branding can be quite diverse and obliges companies to define a 'global branding' strategy by which they articulate what they striving at in implementing it.

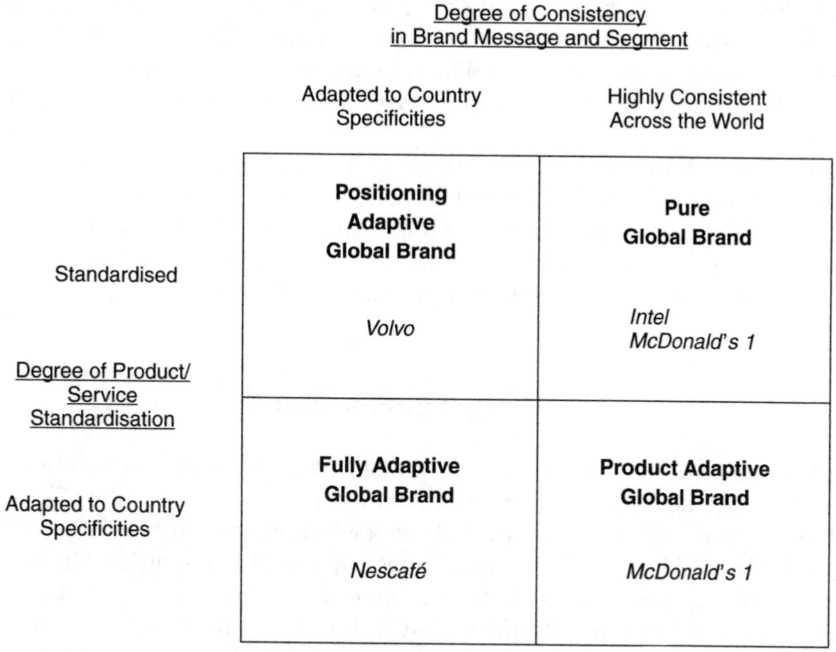

Degree of Consistency
in Brand Message and Segment

	Adapted to Country Specificities	Highly Consistent Across the World
Standardised	**Positioning Adaptive Global Brand** *Volvo*	**Pure Global Brand** *Intel* *McDonald's 1*
Adapted to Country Specificities	**Fully Adaptive Global Brand** *Nescafé*	**Product Adaptive Global Brand** *McDonald's 1*

Degree of Product/ Service Standardisation

Figure 8.4   Global brand positioning

Source: Hankinson and Cowing (1996).

Advantages of global branding

There are three main advantages of global branding – strategic, economic and organisational.

From a *strategic* point of view, it is likely to reinforce market power thanks to a concentration of marketing effort on a single name, as well as the ability to benefit from a spillover effect from country to country. It also saves time in launching new products first because if the product is under the umbrella of a global name, it facilitates customer awareness and benefits from a more efficient promotion roll-out.

From an *economic* point of view, global branding brings savings in external communication with customers (advertising, promotion, direct selling), as well as internal costs since it reduces inventories, product administration and accounting, as well as training and internal communication costs.

Finally, from an *organisational* point of view, it reinforces corporate identity, and facilitates transfer of personnel and best practices across the organisation.

Disadvantages of global branding

The detractors of global brands argue that they ignore national differences in terms of culture, customer behaviour and stages of economic development, and lead to over-standardisation and heavy corporate headquarter centralisation, stifling entrepreneurship. There are abundant anecdotes of so-called global names that had negative or aggressive connotations in certain cultures. The whole argument boils down to opportunity costs, the global brand skims the markets and forgos the main sources of growth that lie in the masses of customers who are still culturally centred.

The arguments have proven to be true on many occasions. In the case of the beer industry in China, for instance, global marketers are still suffering from relying too much on their global brand to conquer the second largest (and soon to be the first) market in the world. Foster, Asahi and Budweiser accumulated losses for not pushing local brands as South African Brewery has done successfully.[3]

Building a global brand

Riesenbeck and Freeling (1991) have identified two approaches to building global brands: the waterfall model and the sprinkler model.

In the **waterfall model** the brand is developed in one country at a time, while in the sprinkler model it is developed simultaneously in all key countries. The **sprinkler model** is currently favoured by global marketers, as seen in the launch of new computers (iMac) and software (Windows 2000). However, one of the main issues that major global companies are facing is the need to 'globalise' under a single name a large variety of existing local subsidiaries' names and acquisitions. Allianz, the German insurance company, was confronted with multiple subsidiaries' names after their acquisitions of the French Assurances Générales de France, the US Fireman's Fund or the UK Cornhill[4], and had to cope with the difficulties of adopting Allianz as a global corporate brand.

ADVERTISING

The issue of *conveying the brand's image to the public* is related to global branding. This is the task of advertising:

- Should the company use a *single* advertising agency for the world or *local* agencies?
- Should the *advertising content* be the same or differentiated?

The trend today for global companies is to deal with a single agency across the world. This trend leads the industry to consolidate and globalise (Table 8.4).

There are four main advantages of single agency[5]:

- *Simplicity* in relationships
- Easy *control*
- *Buying power* over global media and global supports (brochures, promotion material)
- *Economies of scale* in production.

Table 8.4 Major global advertising agencies, 2001

Agency	Country of origin and global presence	Development
Omnicom Group <http://www.omnicomgroup.com/>	United States 300 offices 74 countries	Includes three global global agencies: ■ BBDO ■ DDB ■ TBWA Billing 1999 = $30 billion
McCann–Erikson <http://www.mccann.com/>	United States 130 countries	– McCann–Erikson Worldwide – Universal McCann Weber Shandwickann – Momentum Worldwide – Zentropy Partners – Future Brand – Torre Lazur McCann Healthcare Billing 1999 = $18.5 billion
WPP Group /Young & Rubicam (YR) (merger announced in 2000) http://www.wpp.com/ <http://www.yr.com/>	United States WPP has 1,300 offices in 92 countries YR has 339 offices in 73 countries	WPP = 52 companies YR = 9 unique partners Consolidated billing 1999 = $28 billion
HAVAS Group <http://www.havas-advertising.com/>	France 300 agencies 75 countries	– Euro RSCG Worldwide – Arnold Worldwide Partners – Media Planning Group – 50 diversified independent agencies Billing 1999 = $12 billion

Source: *Industry Week Global Manufacturing Resource Guide* <http://industryweek.com/> (24 January 2001).

Concerning content, global firms are careful not to offend local cultures and adapt their advertisements while retaining the same message. In 2000, the advertisement of a French perfume in Europe represented a naked young lady. In the United States the same lady was dressed. Benetton and Swatch are the 'avant-garde' of global advertising, using the same content and message everywhere, sometimes with unfortunate results.[6]

Global pricing

Global pricing consists of setting a *consistent pricing policy* across borders. The only differences in prices are due to taxation or regulatory reasons. Swatch watches are sold at a price that varies little around the equivalents of US$40.

There are three main advantages of global pricing:

■ It avoids *arbitrage.* When countries are not isolated geographically and when there are no barriers to trade, consumers can shop at the lowest-priced place. In the 1980s, French car dealers were buying French cars in Belgium, where

Mini Examiple 8.1   Sub-optimisation

Suppose that for a particular product the customer's utility curve generates a *demand function*:

In country A: volume sold $(V_A) = 204 - 6 * $ Price (P_A)
In country B: volume sold $(V_B) = 160 - 4 * $ Price (P_B)

The *cost function* of the product is

Total cost $(C) = 600 + 10V$ (10 is the variable cost of the product)
The *total revenue* function is: total sales $(S) = P * V$

Then the profit is: profit $(R) = R - C = P * V - C$

In the case of country A

Profit is $R_A = -6P_A{}^2 + 264P_A - 2,640$
Profit is maximum when $264 - 12P_A = 0$ or $P_A = 264/12 = 22$

In the case of country B

Profit is $R_B = -4P_B{}^2 + 200P_B - 2,200$
Profit is maximum when $200 - 8 P_B = 0$ or $P_B = 200/8 = 25$

It can be seen that profit is maximised when prices are differentiated and not global.

The maximum profit is 564 when prices are set at 22 in Country A and 25 in Country B

If one adopts a global pricing the profit will be lower:

- ▪ If price is 22, profit is 548
- ▪ If price is 23, profit is 542
- ▪ If price is 24, profit is 536
- ▪ If price is 25, profit is 510
- ▪ If price is 23, profit is 542
- ▪ If price is 24, profit is 536
- ▪ If price is 25, profit is 510

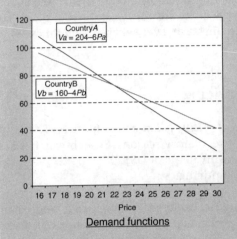

Demand functions

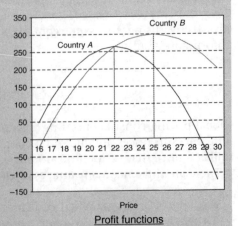

Profit functions

prices were lower, to resell them. The price differences were due in part to differences in taxes (VAT) but also to policies of car manufacturers who priced differently depending upon the country's competitive climate. With the development of the EU and the arrival of the Euro, prices tend to converge.

- It protects the *brand integrity*. Customers who discover that the same product they buy in one country is sold at a discount in another may question the reason why it is so and may attribute it to an overall lower quality.
- It facilitates the servicing of *global customers*.

The disadvantages are that global pricing does not account for differences in customer utility curves and leads to *sub-optimisation*. (See Mini-Example 8.1)

In practice, global pricing can be implemented in one or several of the following cases:

- When the product or service is targeted at customers that have *similar profiles* and share the same or similar *value curve*, the so-called 'global segments'. In the case of consumer goods one find luxury goods (Dom Perignon, Louis Vuitton, Gucci, etc.), fashion items (Swatch, Benneton, Esprit, etc.), personal computers and software (iMac, IBM, Microsoft Office, etc.). In the case of B2B marketing it applies to products or services sold to subsidiaries of multinational companies (global accounts).
- When the product or service is sold under a strong '*global brand*'.
- When there are strong possibilities of *arbitrage*.
- When the company deploys a *multi-brand policy* of global and local products and wants to differentiate clearly the global brand from the rest.
- When the product or service has *standardised* functionalities, qualities and features.

Global account management

Global accounts are customers that have a presence in many countries and require products or services delivered according to the terms of a centrally co-ordinated buying agreement. Global account management is the organisational process by which global accounts are served. Global accounts are primarily used in the following industries:

- *Financial services*: catering for the varied financial needs of the subsidiaries of multinational companies. Citibank, for instance, created the World Corporate Group in 1974 in order to serve the cross-border financial needs of 450 major companies (see Mini-Example 8.2 (p. 228) for a description of Citibank's global account management[7]).
- *Advertising*: developing and implementing campaigns worldwide. Saatchi and Saatchi initiated the concept of global supermarkets in the late 1970s.
- *Telecoms equipment manufacturers*: catering for the equipment and associated services needs of globalising telecom operators. Ericsson set up a global account management organisation in 1994 serving 30 clients located in 10 home countries such as ATT, Cable and Wireless, Vodafone, Telstra, Nynex and BT[8].

Mini-Example 8.2   Citibank Global Account Management

Citibank installed a World Corporate Group (WCG) within the corporate finance division in 1974 with a portfolio of 450 global accounts. The WCG had its own staff of several hundred Parent Account Managers (PAMs) and Subsidiaries' Account Managers (SAMs). Each year the PAMs negotiated with the client a Global Account Plan to be implemented locally. Revenues were calculated per account and a complex system of reallocation to the local branches was put in place. Citibank increased its market share in global finances thanks to this system. However, the WCG was dismantled in 1981 because it was creating a 'dual' structure in the local subsidiaries. It was re-instituted in 1985, but then WCG had only a co-ordinating role in a matrix format, with the PAMs and SAMs reporting both to the branches and to WCG. The number of global accounts was around 300 by the end of the 1990s. WCG customers were US, European, and Asian firms, with 6,000 subsidiaries.

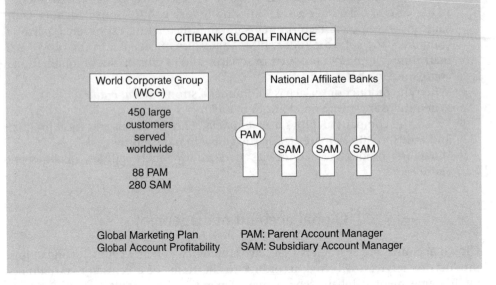

- *Telecoms services operators*: providing seamless communication data and voice services; Global One, BT, Cable and Wireless, ATT all had organised global accounts in the 1990s.
- *Computer equipment manufacturers or software companies*: providing IT equipment and services. Hewlett Packard (HP) led the way, followed by IBM for global IT delivery. Cap Gemini, EDS and Oracle in the service sectors have set up account management.
- *Accounting firms*: PriceWaterhouseCoopers, etc.
- *Aerospace manufacturers*: to support airlines operations.

The principle of global account management is illustrated in Figure 8.5 and Mini-Example 8.2, with a fictitious example in banking. The corporate headquarters is in London, but the client is a big chemical firm in Munich. The bank parent account

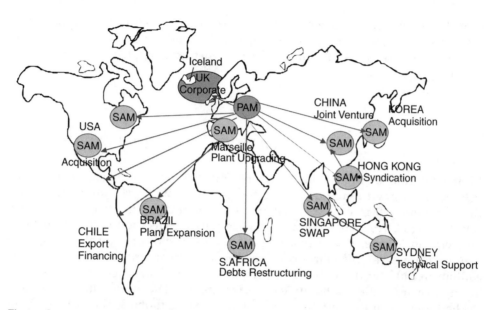

Figure 8.5 A financial global account management network servicing a leading European manufacturer

Source: Adapted from Malnight (1995).

manager (PAM), located at the branch close to the client's corporate headquarters, negotiates with the client's financial CFO a global financing plan for financial deals or services in various parts of the world. The subsidiaries' account managers (SAM), located in the bank's international branches deliver the services under terms negotiated centrally. In such a system, trade-off and arbitrages are done centrally: it may well happen that a 'good discount' is granted in the Brazilian investment but, as a counterpart, the bank will get a profitable deal in a Hong Kong syndication. The four main advantages of global account management are:

- The ability to provide *full and consistent services* to customers, reducing the hassle to negotiate deal after deal
- A *lower overall cost* for the customer, partly owing to volume purchases
- The ability for customers to *optimise their procurement strategy* (in the case of banking, their financing strategy)
- For the product and service provider, it *enlarges the overall sales and optimises profitability.*

In the implementation of a global account management system, three main issues arise:

- Customer subsidiaries may be reluctant to accept global procurement. Local operations may find that it is cheaper or better to source locally.
- Supplier subsidiaries may be reluctant to abandon potential sources of local income for the benefit of the global account.
- A complex internal accounting system may be required for reallocating income among subsidiaries.

Global account systems have proven to be beneficial to companies that have been the first to implement it in their industries, setting the standards for others. In the sectors mentioned earlier the question is not whether to implement it, but how to do it properly.[9]

GLOBAL SOLUTION SELLING

Global solution selling is a mirror image of global account management. It consists of mobilising the resources and competencies of several subsidiaries across the world in order to offer a valuable solution to a client located in a particular country (Figure 8.6). The company, a large power generation corporation headquartered in Europe, has to make an international bid for a turnkey project in Tianjin, China. The offer has to be complete and requires not only the sale of equipment but also the training of personnel and the management of the plant during five years under a Build Operate Transfer (BOT) contract. In order to give the best solution at the best price, the company has to mobilise the expertise of its US, French, German and Australian subsidiaries. The lead officer, who is in charge of preparing the bid, is located in Hong Kong; he is also in charge of negotiating the financing of the deal with a global consortium of banks with branches in Hong Kong.

This type of global solution selling is frequent in industries such as:

- *Banking*: to mount a complex financing package (all major global banks)
- *Consulting:* to offer a complete business solution including strategy, IT, organisation and change management (Accenture, McKinsey,BCG, etc.)

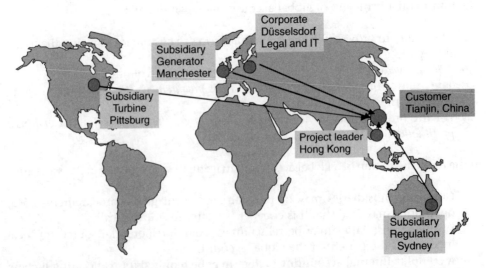

Figure 8.6 Global solution selling: an international bid for a power plant in China

- *Information technology:* to offer a complete seamless IT solution (IBM, HP, EDS, Cap Gemini, SAP, etc.)
- *Telecom operators:* to bid for a UMTS (Universal Mobile Telecommunications System) licence, or a complete mobile infrastructure and operational network (all major operators)
- *Engineering:* turnkey projects or BOT contracts (ABB, Enron, Alstom, GE, all major international engineering firms).

The issues are quite similar to those in global account management. Global solution selling draws on resources, experience and expertise of the international business units. What matters is the speed and the coherence of the solution package, as well as the leadership of the solution selling team. It requires the co-operation of local subsidiaries and an appropriate mechanism to divide the revenues among them. There is a temptation for the local business units to 'charge' for their respective contributions; if this happens, the overall proposal will be uncompetitive and there-fore needs a central global leader who decides on the overall price/content of the solution. Another issue is the allocation of resources to global projects when those resources may be more fruitfully allocated to domestic projects for which the local subsidiary would obtain full credit. Figure 8.7 describes graphically the capabilities needed to implement a global solution selling system.

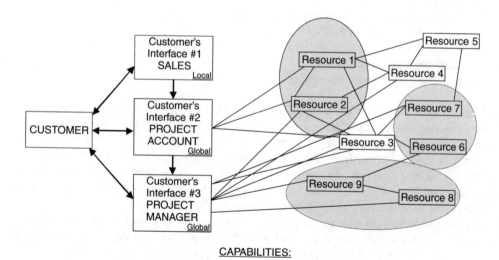

CAPABILITIES:

- Ability to understand customers' problems
- Ability to interpret customers' problems and to design 'solutions'
- Ability to formulate solution package
- Ability to cultivate relationships and support
- Ability to transfer solutions to customers' subsidiaries across the world
- Ability to provide consistent services across the world

- Ability to identify internal and external resources and competencies
- Ability to mobilise resources
- Ability to co-ordinate the use of resources
- Ability to maintain cost and price at competitive levels

Figure 8.7 Capabilities required for global solution selling

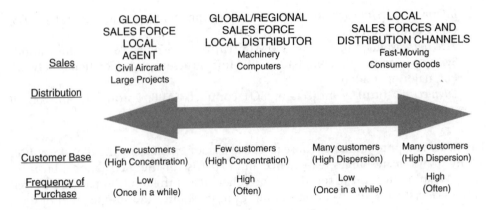

Figure 8.8 Sales and distribution

Global sales and distribution

Sales and distribution are probably the marketing mix elements that are the most difficult to standardise globally. There are many reasons:

- Languages
- Social codes in supplier/buyer relationships
- Negotiation cultures
- Spatial dispersion of customers
- Local regulations
- Existing distribution structures.

However, the ability to sell and distribute globally, as against the need to localise the sales forces and the distribution channels, will depend upon the frequency of purchase and the dispersion of customers (Figure 8.8). The more a product or service is sold to a limited number of customers and sales are infrequent, as for instance selling aircrafts to airlines, the less the need for a local sales force. Salespersons located at corporate or regional headquarters can handle negotiations with the help of a local agent or representative.

At the other extreme, frequent purchases to a numerous widely-spread customer base calls for a local sales force and distribution either through a subsidiary or through a local or international distribution company.

GLOBAL MARKETING POSITIONING

Global marketing can take several forms. For each element of the marketing mix a trade-off has to be made between a fully-fledged standard global approach and a complete local adaptation. The combination of choices leads to a variety of marketing strategies and policies, as illustrated in Figure 8.9. The final choice, as seen in this chapter, is a function of many parameters:

● = Standardized element	Bacardi	Adidas Torsion	Gervais Danone	American Express	Henkel Pritt	Levi 501s	Gillette	Samsonite	Johnnie Walker	Parker Pen	Benetton	Swatch
Product												
- Positioning	-	-	●	●	-	●	●	●	●	●	●	●
- Brand name	●	●	●	●	●	●	●	●	●	●	●	●
- Core product	●	●	●	●	●	●	●	●	●	●	●	●
- Ingredients	-	●	-	-	-	●	●	●	●	-	●	●
Advertising TV spots												
- Concept	-	-	-	-	●	●	●	●	●	●	●	●
- Execution	-	-	-	-	●	●	●	●	●	●	●	●
Print												
- Concept	-	-	-	-	●	-	-	●	●	●	●	●
- Execution	-	-	-	-	-	-	-	-	●	●	●	-
Packaging												
- Design	●	-	-	-	●	-	-	-	-	●	-	●
- Size	-	-	-	-	-	-	-	-	-	●	-	●
Pricing	-	-	-	-	-	-	-	-	-	-	●	●
Sales promotion	-	-	-	-	-	-	-	-	-	-	-	-
PR	-	-	-	-	-	-	-	-	-	-	-	-
Sales concept (distribution)	-	-	-	-	-	-	-	-	-	-	●	●

Hajo Riesenburg and Anthony Freeling, from McKinsey, reported the result of a survey on global brands. Concerning the issue of standardization they concluded:

> 'Creating an effective global brand does not mean rote standardization. Nor does it mean simply using a single brand name in a variety of countries. The task, instead, is to review separately each element of the marketing mix and then, from the menu of available options, to select the best approach for each. Our survey asked managers to assess the degree of standardization for each element of the marketing mix for their international brands. We found no completely standardized global product (see exhibit). Indeed most successful brands had made some local adaptation to local situations, usually more in terms of distribution and trade infrastructure than overall positioning or product features.'[10]

Figure 8.9   Various global marketing positioning

Source: Riesenbeck and Freeling (1991).

- Customers' needs and value curve
- Customers' dispersion
- Frequency of purchase
- Importance of solution selling and account for globally dispersed customers
- Economies of scale.

The ultimate choice will have to be made with regard to the global strategic positioning issues discussed in Chapter 2.

SUMMARY AND KEY POINTS

1. Convergence of customer needs:
   - No conclusive evidence of convergence of all consumer goods but gaining ground in B2B sector
   - Different global product standardisation types available for various types of customer needs:
     - *Similar* customer needs (global segment):
       - (a) Global standardisation, if high minimum size of production
       - (b) Process standardisation, if low minimum size of production
     - *Different* customer needs (local segment):
       - (a) Modular standardisation, if high minimum size of production
       - (b) Local adaptation, if low minimum size of production
   - Customer value curves:
     - Embody *customer needs*
     - Potential *elements* include:
       - (i) Price
       - (ii) Product/service functionalities
       - (iii) Product/service quality
       - (iv) Image
       - (v) Availability
       - (vi) Convenience
       - (vii) Associated services
       - (viii) Network effect.

2. Global branding:
   - *Definition:* a global firm develops a corporate name that will apply to all subsidiaries while trying to limit individual product names and market products under a global name
   - *Advantages:*
     - Reinforce market power through high concentration of marketing effort on a single name
     - Cost savings in external communication with customers – advertising, promotion, direct selling
     - Reinforces corporate identity
   - *Disadvantages:*
     - ignores national differences and hence major sources of growth
   - *Global brand:*
     - Definition: when the product or service it represents is marketed across the world under its name
     - Includes the following features:
       - (a) Strong in home market
       - (b) Consistent in product positioning
       - (c) Present geographically in balanced way across regions
       - (d) Addresses similar consumer needs worldwide
       - (e) Easy to pronounce
     - Positioning of global brand depends on:
       - (a) Degree of consistency in brand message and segment
       - (b) Degree of product/service standardisation

   - Building of global brand:
     (a) *Waterfall model*: develops brand one country at a time
     (b) *Sprinkler model*: develops brand simultaneously in all key countries.

3. Advertising:

   - A single advertising agency is commonly used; advantages include:
     - *Simplicity* in relationships
     - Easy *control*
     - *Economies of scale* in production
     - *Buyer power* over global media and global support.

4. Global pricing:

   - Involves setting *consistent pricing policy* across borders
   - *Useful*:
     - When product/service is targeted at 'global segments' (customers with similar value curve)
     - When product/service is sold under strong 'global brand'
     - When there are strong possibilities of arbitrage
     - When company implements a multi-brand policy of global and local products
     - When product/service is standardised
   - *Advantages*:
     - Avoids arbitrage (when customers shop in the lowest-priced country)
     - Protects brand integrity
     - Facilitates servicing of global customers
   - *Disadvantages* are sub-optimisation owing to lack of consideration for differences in customers utility curve.

5. Global account management:

   - The organisational process which serves global accounts (customers present in many countries and requiring products/services as specified in a *central buying agreement*)
   - *Advantages*:
     - For the customer.
       (a) Low overall cost partly owing to volume purchase
       (b) Ability to optimise procurement strategy
     - For the seller:
       (a) Enlarges overall sales and optimises profitability
       (b) Reduces transaction cost (deal negotiation cost) and enhances ability to provide full and consistent services to customers
   - *Disadvantages*:
     (a) Customers' subsidiaries reluctant to accept global procurement
     (b) Suppliers' subsidiaries reluctant to abandon potential source of local income
     (c) Complex internal accounting system required to reallocate income among subsidiaries.

6. Global solution selling:

   - Involves mobilising resources and competencies of several *worldwide subsidiaries* to offer a valuable solution to a client in a specific country

- *Key issues*:
  - Speed of solution delivery
  - Leadership of solution selling team
  - Revenue distribution among parties involved
  - Optimisation of resource allocation.

7. Global sales and distribution:
  - Very *difficult to standardise*:
    - Languages
    - Social codes in supplier/buyers relationships
    - Negotiation cultures
    - Spatial dispersion of customers
    - Local regulations
    - Existing distribution structures
  - Determinants of need for *local sales force* are:
    - Frequency of purchase
    - Extent of customer dispersion.

8. Global marketing positioning:
  - Choice of *marketing mix* depends on:
    - Company's global strategic positioning
    - Customers' needs and value curve
    - Customers' dispersion
    - Frequency of purchase
    - Importance of solution selling and account for globally dispersed customers
    - Economies of scale.

Learning assignments

1 What are the benefits of global standardisation?
2 Can you identify 10 'global' products?
3 In Table 8.2, (p. 223) most of the top global brands are from the United States. Why do you think this is?
4 Why has Unilever announced that it is reducing its brands from 1,600 to 400? What are the risks of so doing?
5 What potential problems will a marketer encounter in having a 'global' advertising campaign?
6 What are the benefits of using a single advertising agency?
7 Why can global pricing lead to sub-optimisation?
8 What is the difference between global account management and global solution selling?
9 What are the typical problems associated with global account management?

Key words

- Advertising agency
- Arbitrage

- 'Californisation'
- Convergence
- Customer value curve
- Global accounts
- Global solution selling
- Hierarchy of needs
- Marketing positioning
- Modularisation
- Segmentation
- Sprinkler model
- Sub-optimisation
- Waterfall model

Web resources

<http://www.acrweb.org/>
Link to Association for Consumer Research.

<http://www.mckinseyquarterly.com/category_editor.asp?tk=86032::16&L2 =16>
McKinsey Quarterly – Marketing.

Notes

1. This section is partly based on Riesenbeck and Freeling (1991, pp. 3–17) and Quelsh (1999, pp. 1–14).
2. Quelsh (1999, p. 3).
3. Williamson (1999).
4. Tribewalla (2001).
5. Quelsh (1999, p. 11).
6. Pinson and Tribewalla (1999).
7. Malnight (1995).
8. Dragonetti and Noda (1999).
9. David, Birkinshaw and Toulan (2001, pp. 8–20).
10. Riesenbeck and Freeling (1991) p. 15.

References and further reading

Books and articles

Aaker, David A. and Erich Joachimsthaler, 'The Lure of Global Branding', *Harvard Business Review*, November–December 1999, pp. 137–44.
Arnold, David, 'Seven Rules of International Distribution', *Harvard Business Review*, November–December 2000, pp. 131–7.
Barth, Karen, Nancy J. Karch, Kathleen McLaughlin and Christiana Smith Shi, 'Global Retailing: Tempting trouble?', *The McKinsey Quarterly*, Number 1, 1996, pp. 117–25.
David, Arnold, Julian Birkinshaw and Omar Toulan, 'Can Selling be Globalized?: The Pitfalls of Global Account Management', *California Management Review*, 44(1), 2001, pp. 8–20
Dragonetti, Nicolas and Tomo Noda, 'Building A Customer Oriented Networked Organisation: Ericsson's Global Account Management Programme', *INSEAD*, Case Study 11, 1999-4857, 1999.

Hankinson, Graham and Philippa Cowing, *The Reality of Global Brands*. London: McGrawHill, 1996.

Levitt, Theodore, 'The Globalisation of Markets', *Harvard Business Review*, May–June, 1983, pp. 92–101.

Malnight, Thomas, 'Citibank: Global Customer Management', Harvard Business School and Wharton School Case Study 9-395-142, 1995.

Narayandas, Das, John Quelch and Gordon Schwartz, 'Prepare Your Company for Global Pricing', *Sloan Management Review*, Fall 2000, pp. 61–70.

Ohmae, Kenichi, *Triad Power*. New York: Free Press.

Parker, Philip, *Physioeconomics*. Cambridge, MA: MIT Press.

Pinson, Christian and Vikas Tribewalla, 'Benetton', *INSEAD* Case Study, 2001.

Quelsh, John, 'Global Branding: Taking Stock', *Business Strategy Review*, 10(1)1999, pp. 1–14.

Riesenbeck, Hajo and Anthony Freeling, 'How Global are Global Brands?', *McKinsey Quarterly*, 4, 1991, pp. 3–17.

Schütte, Hellmut, *Asian Consumer Behavior*. London, Macmillan, 1998.

Schütte, Hellmut and Diane Ciarlante, *Consumer Behaviour in Asia*. Paris/London: INSEAD/Macmillan, 1998.

Tibrewalla, Vikas, 'Allianz: The Power on Your Side', *INSEAD* Case Study, 2001.

Williamson, Peter J., 'China's Beer War', *INSEAD Euro Asia Centre* Case Study, 05/98-4755, 1999.

Yip, George, *Total Global Strategy*, Englewood Cliffs, NJ: Prentice-Hall, 1994.

Journals

International Journal of Advertising (Quarterly), NTC Publications, United Kingdom
<http://www.warc.com>.

Journal of Global Marketing (quarterly), Haworth, United States.
<http://www.haworthpress.com>.

Journal of International Consumer Marketing (Quarterly), Haworth, United States.
<http://www.haworthpress.com>.

International Marketing Review (Quarterly), MCB University, United Kingdom.
<http://www.emeraldinsight.com>.

Journal of International Marketing (Quarterly), American Marketing Association, United States
<http://ciber.bus.msu.edu /jim/>.

9

Global operations

Global operation management is concerned first with the issues of deciding where to set up the operational productive and logistical facilities such as factories and distribution centres. This kind of decision is known as the *location decision*: it requires a multiple-criteria analysis taking into account regional resources and risk characteristics as well as customer proximity. Second, an *integrated network of production and operational facilities* has to be managed. This chapter presents different categorisations of global manufacturing networks. Third, the *procurement function*, including the recent development of electronic purchasing through Electronic Data Interchanges (EDIs) or through the Internet, is considered. The fourth domain, of operational management, is concerned with the managerial issues associated with the physical flow of goods known as 'logistics'. The chapter ends with the analysis of the managerial issues associated with the handling of large-scale international infrastructure projects.

At the end of the chapter one should be able:

- To understand the various factors contributing to the location decision
- To understand the different roles of international factories, and their evolution
- To evaluate the advantages and disadvantages of centralised versus decentralised purchasing
- To understand the roles played by the Web-based E-procurement marketplaces
- To understand the functions of a global logistics system
- To understand the various phases in international infrastructure projects, and their management design.

In 1970, Hewlett Packard chose Singapore to build a factory to produce components – four years later it made a complete product – a hand-held calculator. In the following years more and more products were transferred there, still designed in the USA, but gradually by the mid-80s it started to redesign products and introduce new products and in the mid-90s it developed a new product: the Deskjet 505.

Hewlett Packard exemplifies the topic of this chapter dealing with Global Operations defined as an integrated network of world-wide facilities procuring, producing, distributing and servicing products or offering services to customers. Global operations include four major decision dimensions (Figure 9.1):

1. *Location*: where to put facilities?
2. *Production*: what to produce, where?
3. *Sourcing*: from whom to buy, what and how?
4. *Logistics*: how to manage the flow of goods and information?

These decisions come together in the global operations network (Figure 9.1).

The first type of decision consists of selecting countries and regions to set up *operational facilities*. Table 9.1 presents the various criteria usually utilised to choose a location for facilities such as a plant, a back office, a distribution facility, or a service centre.

Such choice is contingent upon the kind of facilities and their role in the network. Procurement offices will be located in places where resources and suppliers are available, while distribution centres will be located close to dense markets. Rotterdam in Europe, Singapore or Hong Kong in Asia play a major role as distribution and logistics centres in their respective regions because of their nodal geographical position and their world-class infrastructure. Bangalore or Manila will be chosen in the field of computer software because of their skilled and low-cost programmers, while Shenzhen in China or Batam in Indonesia are locations for labour-intensive processing.

A global operational production network is a set of *integrated production centres* deployed across the world. One can broadly define two kinds of global production networks: manufacturing networks and services networks.

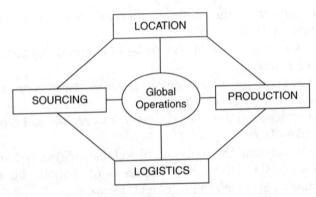

Figure 9.1   The global operations network

Table 9.1   Criteria for facilities' location

Costs	Labour costs	Compensation level
		Skill level
		Skill availability
		Productivity
		Social regulations
		Flexibility
		Unionisation
	Operational costs	Raw material costs
		Telecoms
		Energy, water transport,
		Property, rental
		Logistics
		Services
		Financial costs
		Environmental costs
		Expatriate cost of living
	Taxation	Tariffs
		Indirect taxes
		Income taxes
	Incentives	Subsidies
		Tax relief
Proximity	Customer proximity	Fast delivery
		Fast servicing
	Supplier proximity	Ability to customise
		Availability of raw materials
		Quality of raw materials
		Reliability of supplies
	Logistics	Import/export facilities
	Professional	Financial institutions
Environment		Legal/consultancy services
		Training services
	Intellectual	Libraries
		Information
		Universities
	Quality of life	Government regulation
		Freedom of movement
		Climate
		Housing
		Presence of international schools
		Crime
Learning	Learning from suppliers	Quality of international and domestic suppliers
		Suppliers' innovativeness
	Learning from customers	Variety of segmentation
		Variety of customer demand
		Customer sophistication
	Learning from competitors	Variety of competitors
	Learning from institutions	Innovation context owing to universities, technical and design centres

Sources: Haigh, Ernst & Young (1992), De Meyer and Vereecke (1994); Ferdows (1997).

Global manufacturing networks

Ferdows's strategic roles model

Based on an extensive longitudinal research, Kasra Ferdows (1997) has proposed a model of classification of manufacturing centres in a global network leading to the definition of various **strategic roles**. This classification is based on two main variables:

- The *primary strategic reason* for setting up a plant in a particular country. Ferdows identifies three main reasons:
  - To access low-cost production
  - To access skills and know-how
  - To access markets.
- The *competencies of the plant,* in terms of the various tasks that a given site is capable of doing:
  - The ability to *assume responsibility* for production
  - The ability to *maintain technical processes* (maintenance responsibility)
  - The ability to *purchase locally* (sourcing/logistic responsibility)
  - The ability to *make process improvements*
  - The ability to *develop suppliers*
  - The ability to *develop processes*
  - The ability to *make product improvement recommendations*
  - The ability to *develop products* (product development responsibility)
  - The ability to *supply global markets*
  - The ability to *become a global hub* for product and process knowledge.

Based on those two main dimensions, Ferdows identifies six types of global plants in a network (Figure 9.2):

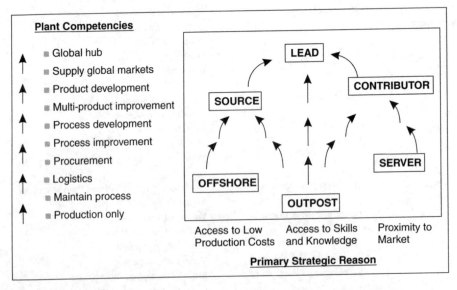

Figure 9.2 Strategic roles of international factories and their evolution

Source: Ferdows (1997).

Table 9.2 Strategic roles of global factories

Type	Role	Example
Offshore factory	Role is to produce low-cost items to be re-exported either for sale or to be re-worked/integrated with other components	Located in low-cost factor countries with limited skills and infrastructures:
	Factory works on design coming from other locations	Special Economic Zones (SEZs) in China;
	Tasks are limited to production of goods according to imported planning and control methods and maintenance of the process	Offshore factories in Vietnam
	Raw materials and components are shipped to the factory; the logistics are handled outside factory	
Source factory	Role is mainly to produce low-cost items, but factory has larger responsibilities for procurement, production planning, process modifications, re-design and logistics	Countries with low-cost factors but skilled labour and infrastructures: Malaysia, Singapore in the 1980s
Server factory	Primary role is to produce products or components for local or regional markets Relatively autonomous in the network for production planning and modification, but dependent on technology and critical components inputs	Countries with high-import-substitution policies: India
Contributor factory	Role is to produce for local or regional markets but with a wider range of responsibilities in term of local sourcing, product re-design and process modification	Areas with big markets and good infrastructures and technical skills: Brazil; Shanghai
Outpost factory	Primary role is to be close to competition and key suppliers and to learn about technological development	Areas with dominant players: Japan; Silicon Valley (for non-US firms)
Lead factory	Designs and produces products for the entire global network Responsible for the whole value chain of a product category	Countries with technological resources, good infrastructure and skills: Singapore in the 1990s

Source: Ferdows, (1997).

- The offshore factory
- The source factory
- The server factory
- The contributor factory
- The outpost factory
- The lead factory.

Each of those has a precise role, defined in Table 9.2

According to Ferdows, the role of international factories may evolve as shown in Figure 9.2; the possible evolution paths are illustrated with arrows. Overall, the combination of the various types of factories constitutes a *global manufacturing network* in which all production centres are to some extent interrelated. The architecture of the network and the shifting roles of factories evolves according to new opportunities and competitive pressures. Ferdows advocates the design of what he calls a 'robust' network that evolves without resorting to drastic measures, such as plant closures or abrupt shifts of production from one country to another.

De Meyer and Vereecke's network architecture model

De Meyer and Vereecke (1995), in addition to the traditional roles of foreign factories as supply bases, emphasise the role of plants as *information and knowledge creators*. They define four main categories of plants in a network:

- *Isolated plants*, concentrating on the production of products for specific geographical markets and which do not communicate greatly with others. Those plants are installed in import-substitution countries that require local production for their domestic markets.
- *Blueprint plants*, receiving a lot of innovation but not creating any. They produce goods according to blueprint received from elsewhere. Those plants could be located in low-cost countries or Export Processing Zones (EPZs) that manufacture components or goods based on designs developed in other centres.
- *Host plant*, network players here are the well-established factories serving large markets that have developed a high degree of competencies in state-of-the-art manufacturing technology but are not at the forefront of innovation.
- *Innovator plant*, network players here play a central role in product and process adaptation and innovation and are the source of inspiration for other factories.

Global services networks

One of the key distinctions in respect of services, as opposed to manufacturing, is the relative importance of the *front-office* compared to *back-office* activities.[4]

In **front-office** activities, *consumption and production are concomitant*: in an airplane the traveller consumes the travel at the same time as its production, in a retail store the consumer consumes the act of buying at the same time that the act of selling is performed. In back offices, goods or support to services (software, insurance policies, bank transfer processing) can be performed separately from their consumption; goods or services support can be stockpiled. In global services, **back-office** activities can be classified in a similar way to manufacturing plants.

- Offshore centres perform *isolated acts* of *production*: computer entry performed in Guandong, for instance
- Source centres produce with a certain degree of *autonomy* for supporting local markets: catering facilities, distribution centres
- Contributor centres may have a *regional* role: maintenance centres, regional warehousing, dispatch centres
- Outpost centres: *market intelligence*
- Lead centres: *Design function*.

Front-office operations are those that are in immediate contact with the customer and need to be close to the market. There are two main types of front office:

- The *physical* front office: banking branch, retail store, restaurant, repair centre, hotel
- The *remote* front office: call centre, reservation office, E-commerce centre.

Front-office activities, because of their high degree of interaction with customers, demand a particular attention to language, customs and social codes adaptation.

GLOBAL SOURCING

Global sourcing is the organisation of a *co-ordinated approach* to the selection of suppliers located across the world and the **procurement** of goods and services for the global supply chain. Global sourcing can take several forms, depending on the degree of centralisation and integration of the procurement function, as illustrated in Figure 9.3.

The outsourced global procurement model

In this model, the global firm delegates the procurement to an *international buying* or *purchasing agent* who is in charge of the whole procurement function. Li & Fung,

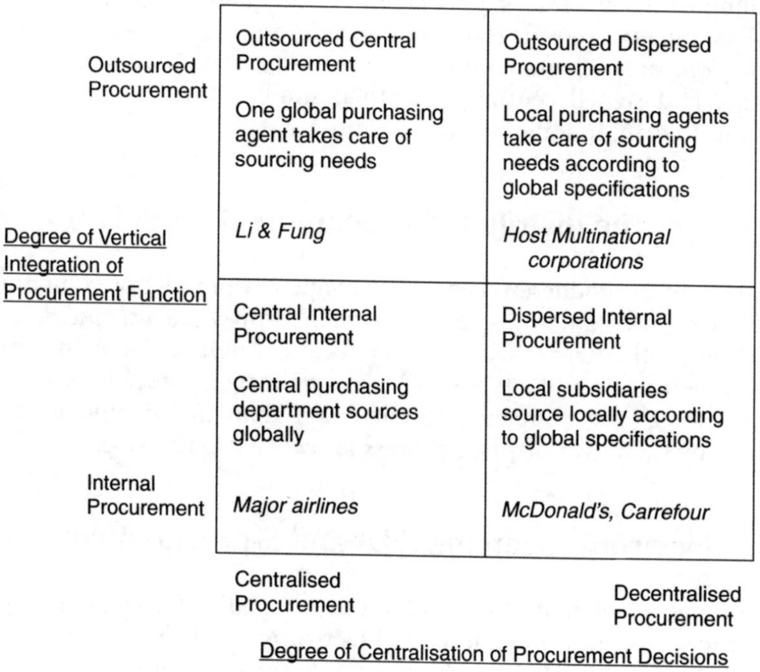

		Centralised Procurement	Decentralised Procurement
Degree of Vertical Integration of Procurement Function	Outsourced Procurement	**Outsourced Central Procurement** One global purchasing agent takes care of sourcing needs *Li & Fung*	**Outsourced Dispersed Procurement** Local purchasing agents take care of sourcing needs according to global specifications *Host Multinational corporations*
	Internal Procurement	**Central Internal Procurement** Central purchasing department sources globally *Major airlines*	**Dispersed Internal Procurement** Local subsidiaries source locally according to global specifications *McDonald's, Carrefour*

Degree of Centralisation of Procurement Decisions

Figure 9.3 Different global sourcing designs

who set up the concept of a 'virtual factory'[2], provide a good example of this model. Mini-Example 9.1 provides a description of Li & Fung's global sourcing.

Mini-Example 9.1   Li & Fung's 'virtual factory' concept

Founded in Guangzhou, Li & Fung began as a traditional exporter of Chinese porcelain. Today, this family-owned group has 42 offices in 20 countries, employing 2,500 employees in Asia, Europe and Africa. It deals with a network of more than 3,000 manufacturers for textiles, toys, sporting goods and furniture. Its main customers are major retail chains in the United States and Europe. The company participates in the design and engineering of products with its customer, selects suppliers, deals with quality control, final assembly and testing as well as logistics issues. A product like a parka, for instance, will be made of various components manufactured in different international locations: Korea (the shell), Taiwan (the lining), Japan (the zip), Hong Kong (the elastic, studs, toggles and string) and China (the filler and final assembly).

The internal central purchasing model

In this model, a central department with its own offices located in the major sourcing countries centralises the purchase of key components, raw materials or products. The purchasing division will act exactly the same way as an *independent purchasing agent*, dealing with the whole supply chain from request for quotations, to negotiation, orders, quality control, reception, expedition, logistics and payment. Nike, for instance, operates a central 'virtual' enterprise from its headquarters in Oregon. The product is designed centrally and then sourced from different factories in Korea, Japan, Taiwan, Indonesia and the United States.

The distributed procurement model

In this model, each production centre in charge of a product or component takes care of its own procurement, based on *centrally defined product specifications*. This model applies particularly when there is a local content requirement imposed by a country or when a subsidiary has the complete responsibility for a product. It is not unusual for global companies to encourage their major suppliers to localise factories nearby their own plants, a process known as *piggybacking*.

Electronic sourcing (EDI and E-procurement)

The development of digital IT has enhanced the ability for companies to source globally. Proprietary software, known as **Electronic Data Interchange (EDI)** links corporations to their suppliers, making possible the exchange of information and the automatic ordering/tracking of orders. The Internet, thanks to its connectivity and language compatibility, has given birth to **electronic marketplaces** (e-market-places) that complement and to some extent replace traditional EDI. We can distinguish three main types of procurement marketplaces and various forms of contracting methods:

- The *horizontal marketplaces* (aggregators), that specialise in one category of product or service for all types of industries. An example is SciQuest <http://www.sciquest.com> that is a marketplace for scientific products used mainly by pharmaceutical, chemical, biotechnology and educational organisations as well as R&D laboratories across several industries.
- The *vertical marketplaces*, that specialise in one type of industry offering a one-stop shop for a large variety of products and services for a particular industry sector. There are numerous examples of E-procurement sites ranging from food, energy to chemicals. VerticalNet <http://www.verticalnet.com> organises marketplaces for 58 industries.
- The *exchanges*, that organise spot markets among a large number of suppliers and buyers for certain types of commodities like steel <http://www.e-steel.com> or pulp and paper <http://www.paperexchange.com>.

Transactions can be one-to-one transactions or made in the form of reverse auctions. Mini-Example 9.2 gives an example of an auction organised by Free-markets Online <http://www.freemarkets.com>, a reverse auction market-maker for more than 100 buyers and 11,100 suppliers from 64 countries.

In theory, electronic procurement enhances the capability to organise global procurement because it gives the opportunity to reach a larger number of suppliers than in more traditional methods. It allows the company also to maintain valuable interaction between suppliers and buyers. These reach capabilities are at the roots of B2B marketplaces where global sourcing can develop. However, companies need to invest in integrated software called Enterprises Resources Planning (ERP) that is offered by companies such as SAP <http://www.sap.com> or Oracle <http://www. oracle.com>.

Mini-Example 9.2   Freemarkets Online[3]

Founded in Pittsburg, Freemarkets Online organises E-procurement for industrial companies using a proprietary competitive bidding software. Freemarkets Online works in the way shown in the following diagram:

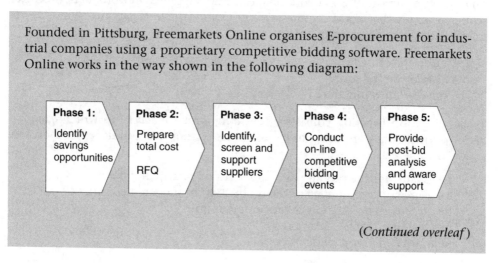

Phase 1:	Phase 2:	Phase 3:	Phase 4:	Phase 5:
Identify savings opportunities	Prepare total cost RFQ	Identify, screen and support suppliers	Conduct on-line competitive bidding events	Provide post-bid analysis and aware support

(Continued overleaf)

The actual auction takes place in real time and can achieve 30–40 per cent savings, as illustrated in the following bidding example.

(x) RFQ = Request For Qualification

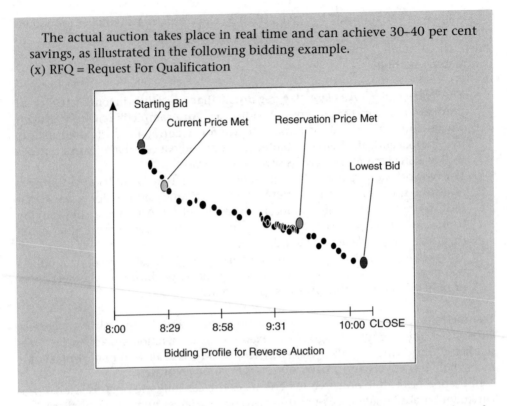

Bidding Profile for Reverse Auction

E-procurement does not eliminate the need for the physical movement of goods, that requires good logistics as well as attention to all the vagaries of international trade such as import barriers, quotas or duties.

GLOBAL LOGISTICS

The interconnection of a network of specialised suppliers and production centres scattered across the world requires *timely, secure and 'lean' logistics*. Logistics are made up of three major functions:

- An *allocation* function
- A *distribution* function
- A *transportation* function.

The allocation function consists of deciding which *products*, in which *quantity*, and *when/where* they are going to be sent. This type of decision depends upon five majors parameters:

(a) The *demand* for the product or component in a particular place
(b) The degree of *specialisation* of the production or procurement unit
(c) The *capacity* of production or procurement unit
(d) The level of *acceptable inventories*
(e) The estimated *transportation time*.

Michelin, in 1995, controlled a global network of 67 factories worldwide (22 in France, 20 in other European countries, 19 in North America, four in Asia and two in South America)[4]. Figure 9.4 gives a representation of the European flow of products. The production planning is done at the central level and each factory is specialised in the production of certain categories of goods in order to benefit from economies of scale. The logistic function is in charge of dispatching around 2,000 different product categories to several thousand dealers for the replacement tyres (RT) market and several dozen car assembly factories across Europe for the original equipment market (OEM).

The central element of the system is the *forecasting function* performed at the level of countries; a central allocation demand function then uses algorithms to specify which products go where and when. The specialisation of factories is such that no country is self-sufficient. Goods are sent either directly to vehicle assemblers for OEMs or to distribution centres that organise the grouping/separation of goods to be allocated either directly to large-volume dealers or indirectly to independent distributors for low-volume dealers.

The distribution function consists of selecting the various *channels* to be used in the chain. Michelin uses three major types of centre:

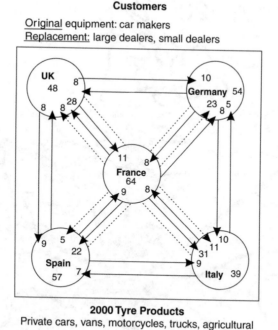

Customers

Original equipment: car makers
Replacement: large dealers, small dealers

2000 Tyre Products
Private cars, vans, motorcycles, trucks, agricultural

Figure 9.4 Michelin's European flow of products

Note: Figure 9.4 shows the percentage of local consumption coming from different countries. Spain produces 57 per cent of its consumption and gets 9 per cent from the United Kingdom, 5 per cent from Germany, 22 per cent from France and 7 per cent from Italy.

Source: Dornier (1997).

- The factory warehouse – organises grouping and supply of distribution centres and handling of large orders
- The distribution centre – in charge of proximity storage and supply to dealers
- The advanced inventory – is dedicated to the OEMs and can be located in a factory or on a carrier site located near the customer's sites.

The transportation function, handles the *physical flow*. Michelin uses three modes of transport:

(a) Its *own fleet*
(b) *Rented* trucking services
(c) *Messenger* services.

It distinguishes two delivery modes: the proximity zone that handles two deliveries a day and a shipment zone that handles delivery once a day.

Another example of a cross-border logistic network is given in Figure 9.5, showing how Airbus Industrie organises the flow of aircraft components leading to final assembly in either Hamburg or Toulouse.

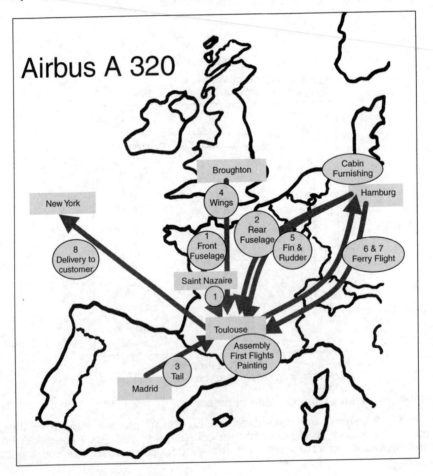

Figure 9.5 Airbus logistics

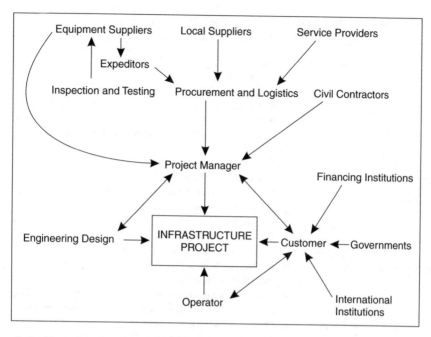

Figure 9.6   Players in an international infrastructure project

THE GLOBAL MANAGEMENT OF INFRASTRUCTURE PROJECTS

Large infrastructure projects such as airports, power plants, petrochemical plants, pulp and paper mills, railways systems, bridges, toll roads, real estate developments etc. are a particular category of global operation. Those projects involve various players, as described in Figure 9.6.

The various phases of international project management are described in Table 9.3.

There are many configurations of project management, but they can be grouped into three main categories:

1. The *direct project management* configuration, in which the customer fulfils the role of project manager. For instance, when the Republic of Singapore decided to build a mass-transportation system, it created a special organisation, the Mass Railways Transit (MRT), in charge of managing the project up to completion. The customer could call upon engineering firms to supervise the work and actually manage the project, but the engineering project team acts on behalf of the customer and is financially responsible only for the amount of its fees.
2. The *turnkey project* configuration, in which the customer contracts out the whole project to a specialised engineering firm or to a consortium of equipment suppliers. The project manager takes care of completion at a fixed price and delivery time and hands over the project to the customer after the start-up phase. The project manager is financially responsible for the whole amount of the contract.
3. The *Build, Operate and Transfer (BOT)* configuration and its derivatives, where the project manager is not only in charge of the construction, but also of the

Table 9.3 Phases in international infrastructure projects

Phases	Content
Pre-feasibility	■ Project concept
	■ Need/market assessment
	■ Strategic plan
	■ Approach IFIs
	■ Approach engineering consultants and major industrial specialists
	■ Get overall financial envelope
Feasibility	■ Assign consultant for feasibility study
	■ Get broad project characteristics, leading to cash flows and computation of financial returns
	■ Get financing
	■ Choose project organisation
	■ Select engineering firm
Basic engineering	■ Define basic technical parameters
	■ Infrastructure blueprints
	■ Project decomposition in various technical areas (civil engineering, electrical, chemical, power generation, IT, regulation, etc.)
Detailed engineering/tendering	■ Prepare documents for tendering
	■ Tenders, negotiation/selection of equipment and contracting suppliers
	■ All detailed parameters in each project part defined
Expediting/site construction	■ Preparation of construction site
	■ Civil engineering and construction (piling, infrastructure – roads, ports, pipelines, transmission, power, building contractors)
	■ Reception of equipment
	■ Erection/assembly of machinery
	■ Layout of pipes, electrical cables, water, etc.
	■ Final assembly
Training	■ Recruitment of personnel
	■ On-the-job training at suppliers' sites
	■ Mock-up training
Start-up	■ First operations
	■ Verification of technical parameters
	■ Reception by client
Operation	■ Managing the operation

operation. At the end of a given period, the infrastructure is handed over to the customer. The project manager is responsible for the output and is paid on the basis of a predetermined price per unit of output ($ per kilowatt/hour, $ per toll fee, $ per cubic meter of water, etc.). There are three main derivatives:

- BOO (Build, Operate and Own), the project manager keeps ownership
- BOOT (Build, Own, Operate and Transfer), the project manager has full ownership of the infrastructure during the period of operation
- ROT (Refurbish, Operate and Transfer), similar to BOT but involving refurbishment of old installations.

More and more infrastructure projects are now made on the basis of BOT contracts in emerging countries. BOT projects have an intrinsic risk, that can be analysed as a 'hostage risk'. Before the completion of the project, the customer is willing to accept favourable conditions because she/he needs the infrastructure. Once the infrastructure is set up, the supplier has no more bargaining power and its investment is sunk in the project. Customers may argue that contracted fees for the supply of the final output are too high. This *hostage* problem has been described by Wells and Gleason (1995) and is well illustrated by the Enron Power plant at Dabhol in the state of Maharashtra in India, (see Mini-Example 9.3).

Mini-Example 9.3 Enron in India: the Dabhol Power Plant[5]

The Dabhol Power Company (DPC) is a consortium of Enron Power, Bechtel Enterprises and General Electric, led by Enron. In 1995, DPC signed a contract with the Maharashtra State Electricity Board for the construction and operation of a 625 megawatt power plant costing US$ 922 million. According to the contract, the state committed to buy the output at a level of tariff structure that would provide DPC with a 25.22 per cent return on investment. During the same year, general elections brought to power a different state government who cancelled the project, invoking a lack of transparency and too high a tariff. After negotiations, the project, was re-designed and finally accepted with different terms. The first phase of the project was completed and the financing of a second phase was closed in 1999. However, by April 2001 Enron was threatening to withdraw from India because the local utility was not complying with its obligations. Following Enron's financial debacle, the Dabhol Power Plant was for sale in early 2002.

SUMMARY AND KEY POINTS

1. Global operations:
   - Defined as an integrated network of facilities located across the world performing the functions of procurement, production, distribution and servicing of products for customers.
   - Four major decision dimensions:
     - Location
     - Production
     - Sourcing
     - Logistics.

2. Choice of location:
   - *Criteria for location* include:
     - Costs:
       - (a) Labour
       - (b) Operational
       - (c) Taxation
       - (d) Incentives

- Proximity:
  - (a) Customers
  - (b) Suppliers
  - (c) Logistics
- Environment
  - (a) Professional
  - (b) Intellectual
  - (c) Quality of life
- Learning:
  - (a) From customers
  - (b) From suppliers
  - (c) From competitors
  - (d) From institutions
- ■ *Ultimate choice* depends on:
  - Kind of facilities
  - Role of facilities in the network.

3. Global production networks:
   - ■ Set of integrated production centres deployed across the world
   - ■ Two kinds of global production networks:
     - Global manufacturing networks
     - Global service networks.

4. Global manufacturing networks:
   - ■ *Classifications*:
     - 'Network architecture model' based on the role of plants as information and knowledge creators
       - (a) Four main types of plants:
         - (i) Isolated – concentrate on production of products for specific geographical markets; do not communicate much with others; installed in import-substitution countries that require local production for their domestic markets
         - (ii) Blueprint – receive (but not create) a lot of innovation; produce goods according to blueprint received from elsewhere; located in low-cost countries or EPZs
         - (iii) Host plant network player – well-established factories serving large markets that have developed a high degree of competence in state-of-the-art manufacturing technology; not at the forefront of innovation
         - (iv) Innovator plant network player – play central role in product and process adaptation and innovation; source of inspiration for other factories
     - 'Strategic roles model' classified according to strategic role based on two main variables:
       - (a) Primary strategic reason for setting up plant in a particular country, including accessing:
         - (i) Low-cost production
         - (ii) Skills and know-how
         - (iii) Markets

    (b) Competencies of plant – tasks a given site is capable of doing:
- (i)   Assume responsibility for production
- (ii)   Maintain technical processes
- (iii)   Purchase locally
- (iv)   Make process improvements
- (v)   Develop suppliers
- (vi)   Develop processes
- (vii)   Make product improvement recommendations
- (viii) Develop products
- (ix)   Supply global markets and become global hub for product and process knowledge

▪ Types of *global plants in a network*:

– *Offshore* factory	Produce low-cost items to be re-exported either for sales or to be reworked and integrated with other components
– *Source* factory	Produce low-cost items but factory has larger responsibilities for procurement, production, planning, process modifications, re-design and logistics
– *Server* factory	Produce products or components for local or regional markets, relatively autonomous in the network for production, planning and modification, but dependent on technology and critical components' input
– *Contributor* factory	Produce for local or regional market but with wider range of responsibilities in local sourcing, product re-design and process modification
– *Outpost* factory	Close to competition and key suppliers to learn about technological development
– *Lead* factory	Factory design and producing products for the entire global network, responsible for the whole value chain of a product category

▪ Evolutionary path of a global plant:
- An outpost factory evolves to become a lead factory either directly or indirectly through becoming first a source factory or contributor factory
- An offshore factory evolves to a source factory and possibly becomes a lead factory in the long term
- A server factory evolves to a contributor factory and possibly becomes a lead factory in the long term
- involves change of plant competencies:
  - (a) Production only
  - (b) Maintain process
  - (c) Logistics
  - (d) Procurement and local
  - (e) Process improvement
  - (f) Process development
  - (g) Multi-product improvement
  - (h) Product development

       (i) Supply global markets

       (j) Global hub.

5. Global services network:

- In the *back offices*, goods or support to services can be performed separately from their consumption – goods or services can be stocked.
- Global services can be *classified* as:

– Offshore centres	Perform isolated act of production
– Source centres	Produce with certain degree of autonomy for supporting local markets – catering facility, distribution centres
– Contributor centres	May have regional role
– Outpost centres	Market intelligence
– Lead centre	Design centre

- *Front-office* operations:
  - In immediate contact with customers and need to be closed to the market.
  - Physical front office and remote front office
  - Require special attention to language, customs and social code adaptation

6. Global sourcing:

- A *co-ordinated approach* to the selection of suppliers located across the world and the procurement of goods and services to be filled in the global supply chain
- Various forms depending upon the degree of *centralisation* and degree of *vertical integration* of the procurement function:
  - *Outsourced global procurement model*
    The firm delegates the procurement to an international buying or purchasing agent responsible for the whole procurement function.
  - *Internal central purchasing model*
    A central department with its own offices located in the major sourcing countries centralises the purchase; the purchasing division acts like an independent purchasing agent
  - *Distributed procurement model*
    Each production centre in charge of a product or component takes care of its own procurement based on centrally defined product specifications; applicable when there is local content requirement or when a subsidiary has the complete responsibility for a product

- *Electronic sourcing*
  - *EDI* (proprietary software which links corporations to their suppliers and permits exchange of information, automatic ordering and tracking of orders)
  - *E-procurement* (procurement on the Internet):

    (a) Types of e-procurement sites:

        (i) *Horizontal marketplace (aggregators)* specialises in one category of product/service for all types of industries

        (ii) *Vertical marketplace* specialises in one type of industry offering a one-stop shop for a large variety of products/services.

       (iii) *Exchanges* which organise spot markets between a large quantity of suppliers and a large number of buyers for certain types of commodities.

    (b) Transactions can be one-to-one or made through reverse auctions

    (c) Provides reach and rich capabilities, opportunity to reach a larger number of suppliers than more traditional methods

    (d) Does not eliminate the need for the physical movement of goods.

7. Global logistics:

- *Allocation* function:
  - Which products, what quantity, when and where
  - Five major parameters.
    - (a) Demand for the product
    - (b) Degree of specialisation
    - (c) Capacity of production
    - (d) Level of acceptable inventories
    - (e) Estimated transportation time

- *Distribution* function:
  - Selection of channels to be used in the chain
  - Three major types of centres:
    - (a) Factory warehouse — Organises grouping and supply of distribution centres and handling of large orders
    - (b) Distribution centres — Responsible for proximity storage/supply to dealers
    - (c) Advanced inventory — Dedicated to OEM that can be located in a factory

- *Transportation* function:
  - Handles physical flow
  - Three modes of transport:
    - (a) Own fleet
    - (b) Rented trucking services
    - (c) Messenger services
  - Two delivery modes:
    - (a) Proximity zone (two deliveries a day)
    - (b) Shipment zone (one delivery a day).

8. International infrastructure projects:

- Various players – project managers, civil contractors, service providers, local suppliers, customers, government, financing institutions, operator and international institutions
- Phases:
  - Pre-feasibility
  - Feasibility
  - Basic engineering
  - Detailed engineering/tendering
  - Expediting/site construction
  - Training
  - Start-up
  - Operation

- Configuration of project management:
  - Direct project management:
    - (a) Customer fulfils role of project manager
    - (b) If engineering firm supervises and manages the work, engineering project team is financially responsible for the amount of its fees
  - Turnkey project:
    - (a) Customer contracts whole project to specialised engineering firm or to consortium of equipment suppliers
    - (b) Project manager:
      - (i) Is responsible for completion at fixed price and delivery time
      - (ii) Hands over project to customer after the start-up phase
  - BOT (build, operate and transfer):
    - (a) Has 'hostage risk', i.e. once infrastructure is set up, supplier has no bargaining power
    - (b) Project manager:
      - (i) Is in charge of construction and operation
      - (ii) Is responsible for output
      - (iii) Is paid on basis of a pre-determined price per unit of output
    - (c) BOT variants include:
      - (i) *BOO* (build, operate and own): project manager keeps ownership
      - (ii) *ROT* (refurbish, operate and transfer): similar to BOT but refurbishing old installations.

Learning assignments

1 Compare Singapore and Malaysia as a possible location for: (i) a PC assembly plant, (ii) a wafer factory, (iii) a regional maintenance centre, (iv) a customer training centre for international customers, (v) a chemical processing plant.
2 According to Ferdows (1997), what are the differences between a 'contributor' factory and an 'outpost' factory?
3 What are the new roles that De Meyer and Vereecke (1995) assign to 'foreign' factories?
4 What differentiates global manufacturing of goods from global production of services?
5 What is a vertical electronic marketplace?
6 Surf the Internet and find: one horizontal E-procurement site, one vertical E-procurement site, and one exchange (different from the examples given in the text).
7 What are the three major functions of global logistics?
8 For the point of view of an infrastructure, client compare the relative advantages and disadvantages of turnkey projects, direct project management and BOT.
9 What is the 'hostage' problem in BOT contracts?

Key words

- Back office
- BOT
- Competencies of plant
- Distribution function
- Electronic Data Interchange (EDI)

- Electronic marketplaces
- Front office
- Location
- Logistics
- Network architecture
- Plant competencies
- Procurement
- Strategic role
- Turnkey project

Web resources

<http://knowledge.insead.fr/category.cfm?catid =15>
Link to the data-base of INSEAD Knowledge under the category of Producing, Operating and Supplying.

<http://www.bain.com/bainweb/about/insights/pract_insights.asp?status=1&sort=capability& capability_id =60>
Bain & Co. – Supply Chain Management.

<http://www.bain.com/bainweb/about/insights/pract_insights.asp?status=1&sort=capability &capability_id =38>
Bain & Co. – Operations Excellence.

<http://www.mckinseyquarterly.com/category_editor.asp?tk=86032::1&L2=1>
McKinsey Quarterly – Operations.

Notes

1. Teboul (1991).
2. St George and Knoop (1998).
3. Rangan (1998).
4. This example is from Dornier (1997), reproduced in Ernst, Kawelis, Dornier and Fender (1998, Chapter 2)
5. Wells *et al.* (1996); *Financial Times* (2001).

References and further reading

Books and articles

Bartmess, Andrew and Keith Cerny, 'Seeding Plants for a Global Harvest', *The McKinsey Quarterly*, 2, 1993, pp. 107–32
De Meyer, Arnoud and A. Vereecke, 'Strategies for International Manufacturing', INSEAD Working Paper, 94/25, 1994.
Dornier, Philippe Pierre, 'Michelin', ESSEC Case Study, 1997.
Ernst, Ricardo, Pavos Kawelis, Philippe-Pierre Dornier and Michel Fender, *Global Operations and Logistics: Text and Cases*. New York, NY: John Wiley, 1998.
Ernst & Young, 'Region of the New Europe: A Comparative Assessment of Key Factors in Choosing Location', *Report*, 1992.
Ferdows, Kasra, 'Making the Most of Foreign Factories', *Harvard Business Review*, March–April 1997, pp. 73–88.
Haigh, Ronald, 'Selecting a US Plant Location: The Management Decision Process in Foreign Companies', *Columbia Journal of World Business*, 3, Fall 1990.

Kotabe, Masaaki, 'Efficiency vs Effectiveness Orientation of Global Sourcing Strategy: A Comparison of US and Japanese Multinational Companies', *The Academy of Management Executive*, November 1998, pp. 107–19.

Rangan, Kasturi, 'FreeMarketsOnline', Harvard Business School Case Study 9-598-109, 1998.

St George, Anthony and Carin-Isabel Knoop, 'Li & Fung: Beyond Filling in the Mosaic, 1995–1998', Harvard Business School Case Study 9-398-092, 1998.

Teboul, James, *Managing Quality Dynamics*. Englewood Cliffs, NJ: Prentice-Hall, 1991.

Wells, Louis T. and Eric S. Gleason, 'Is Foreign Infrastructure Investment Still Risky?', *Harvard Business Review*, September–October 1995, pp.44–55.

Wells, Louis T., Anu Bhasin, Mihir Desai and Sarayu Srinivasan, 'Enron Development Corporation: The Dabhol Power Project in Maharashtra, India' (A), (B) and (C), Harvard Business School Case Studies 9-797-085, 9-595-101, 1996.

Journals

International Journal of Operations & Production Management, MCB University, United Kingdom <http://www. emeraldinsight.com/ijopm.htm>.

International Journal of Physical Distribution and Logistics Management, MCB University, United Kingdom <http://www.napm.org/Pubs/journal scm/>.

Journal of Supply Chain Management (quarterly), *Institute for Supply Management*, United States <http://www.napm.org/Pubs/journal scm/>.

10

Global innovation

The ability to create and quickly diffuse new products and processes is one of the main benefits of global management, as noted in Chapters 1 and 3. This chapter will look at the evolution of the management of innovation within multinational and global companies. It starts with a presentation and criticism of the classic model known as the *international product life cycle*, then examines the classic trade-off between centralised and distributed R&D using the case of Nestlé as an example. The issues involved in international transfer of technology will then be discussed and the chapter will end by presenting a recent model of knowledge management and transfer of best practices within global firms and examining the problems of intellectual property rights.
   At the end of the chapter one should be able:

- To understand logic and the limitations of the international product life cycle
- To understand different design of global R&D networks
- To understand the different management issues in the global management of R&D
- To understand the issues of international transfer of technology
- To understand knowledge management
- To understand the recent development towards 'metanational' management of global knowledge creation
- To understand the issues in the international protection of intellectual property.

THE INTERNATIONAL PRODUCT LIFE CYCLE MODEL

In the early 1960s, Raymond Vernon proposed the theory of the *International Product Life Cycle* (1966) to explain how product innovation and production could migrate

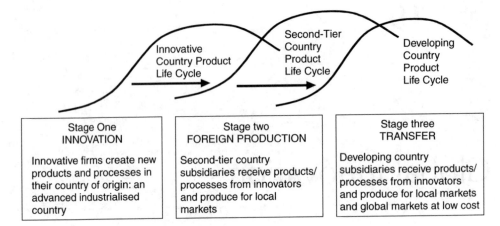

Figure 10.1 The international product life cycle

Source: Adapted from Vernon (1966).

from the country of origin of the innovative firms to other country subsidiaries (Figure 10.1).

The international product life cycle theory was built on observation of the TV set industry in the 1950s and 1960s. As shown in Figure 10.1, the theory identifies three stages in the international development of products and processes. In stage 1, *new products and processes* are designed in the laboratories of firms located in the innovative country. In the 1950s in the TV set industry, the innovative country was the United States. RCA, Zenith, General Electric and Motorola were the innovators and, at this stage, the products were designed in the United States for the US market. Some production was exported, mainly to Europe. In stage two, (1960s) some production was moved to industrialised countries such as Europe and Japan, either under the form of *local subsidiaries* of the innovative firms or through *technology transfer* to local firms (Matsushita, Sony, Thomson, etc.). Some adaptations to fit local needs were made to the products. Finally, in stage three, *emerging developing countries* (Korea, China) took the lead in the production of TV sets, because of cost advantages and market potential.

Criticism of the international product life cycle

In spite of its simplicity and appeal, the theory failed to explain the globalisation of innovation that took place after the 1960s. Despite the fact that R&D resources are predominantly concentrated in developed, industrialised countries, there is no longer a major difference between the United States, Japan and Europe (see Table 10.1).

Today, a large variety of products are developed globally for world markets and launched at almost same time in the key countries of America, Europe and Asia Pacific. The migration of R&D and production centres does not necessarily follow the sequential evolution predicted by the theory. Many research centres are set up where scientific and marketing resources are available, and global companies use global R&D networks to develop world products, as the following example illustrates.

Table 10.1 R&D capabilities

Country type	Expenditures on R&D per cent of GNP	Scientists and Engineers in R&D (per million people)	High-technology exports $ million	Patent applications 'Residents'
Low-income countries	0.57	257	24,475	23,772
Upper-middle income countries	1.08	607	92,114	99,111
United States	2.63	3,676	170,681	125,808
Europe	2.16	2,162	225,832	101,097
Japan	2.80	4,909	94,777	351,487
World	**2.18**	NA	820,617	798,003

Source: World Bank World Development Indicators (2000).

Global R&D networks: the case of Nestlé[1]

Nestlé is the second largest food company in the world. Its portfolio encompasses a large array of products including leading brands such as Nescafé. A Swiss multinational, Nestlé was one of the first to expand its operations worldwide. At the end of 2000 it had 479 operating units in 81 countries and 90 brands grouped into 17 product categories. Food processing technologies call for competencies in multiple scientific domains such as nutrition, plant sciences, food preservation and biosciences. Since its origin, Nestlé has been a leader in R&D, with laboratories at first located in Vevey, near Geneva and in France. Over the years, Nestlé had acquired companies around the world and through those acquisitions inherited research laboratories. On the top of these, international expansion led the company to create some research centres in countries where nutritional habits were quite different from those in Western Europe. At the end of the 1980s, Nestlé had 13 Technical Development Centres located in 13 countries. In 2000, the Nestlé R&D network comprised the Nestlé Research Centre in Lausanne, eight Product Technologies Centres, two regional adaptation centres, and around 480 application groups located in Nestlé factories worldwide.

The way Nestlé manages its R&D centres across the world is based on two main principles:

- Research programmes and efforts need to be *co-ordinated centrally*. For that purpose, a small organisation, NESTEC (Nestlé Technological Centre) has been created to co-ordinate R&D activities.
- R&D activities are *decentralised in the local centres*, the Research Companies (RECOS) that are responsible for carrying the programmes and are organised as profit centres. Local RECOS are located closed to a manufacturing centre so that research is not done in a vacuum but close to actual reality. Those local organisations carry development work on products, processes and systems. Typically, they employ 60–200 people. Research planning and budgeting is organised by NESTEC with the participation of local RECOS. The objective is to avoid duplication of effort and to develop an *overall corporate research strategy*.

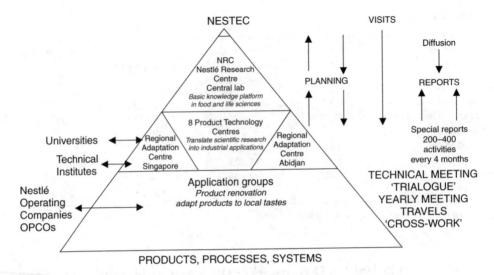

Figure 10.2   The Nestlé global R&D architecture

Source: De Meyer (1993).

Progress reports are send by RECOS to NESTEC, which organises their diffusion. NESTEC also organises technical conferences and transfer of personnel. Each RECO establishes links with local universities and technical institutes. Regular 'trialogue' meetings between researchers, marketers and manufacturers are organised to enhance the symbiosis between these functions.

This system is shown in Figure 10.2, and it illustrates various facets of managing innovation in a global corporation. We shall now discuss the benefits and constraints of global R&D, before explaining the different organisational design for the management of the R&D network.

GLOBALISATION OF R&D: BENEFITS AND CONSTRAINTS

As illustrated in the Nestle example, a global R&D network involves a decentralised distributed approach to the management of innovation.

Benefits

There are four main potential benefits of decentralised as opposed to centrally managed R&D:[2]

- *Proximity to market* – the ability of a global firm to adapt or to create products fitting local customers' specificities.
- *Access to geographical clusters of knowledge creation and development* – universities, suppliers, researchers, start-up firms, venture capitalists; Michael Porter

(1998) has illustrated the concept of technological centres clusters of excellence such as Insulin in Denmark

- *Learning* – the ability of a global firm to leverage local knowledge across subsidiaries and to cross-fertilise this knowledge within a global network; De Meyer (1992) pinpointed the importance of 'learning' in international R&D:

  'Learning about different markets, different problem-solving methods, different sources of technological progress, different cultures, different competitors, and rapid diffusion of that learning throughout the organisation, is definitely enhanced by creating an international network of laboratories'.

- *Access to low-cost and good-quality scientists and engineers* – some empirical evidence for this motivation is apparent when one looks at the development of Bangalore as a centre for computer software or the science parks of Singapore, or Taiwan (Hinshu), which were developed originally on that basis. However, except for routine activities, this motivation is not sufficient to justify a decentralised R&D network.

Constraints

However, there are also two major constraints in implementing a global distributed R&D network, the loss of critical mass and of face-to-face communication:

- *Critical mass constraints* exist when one activity, in order to be performed efficiently and effectively, needs to mobilise a minimum amount of resources. Research activities belong to this category – scientists and technologists are not lonely inventors; they need to benefit from the complementarities of colleagues in their field as well as in related domains. They also need assistance from technical staff, and they use more and more expensive laboratory instruments. Below a certain threshold of such resources, research projects have difficulties in taking off, hence the need for centralisation and concentration of R&D activities. Having too many laboratories dilutes resources and hampers research performance. The solution to the problem is to be found in the creation of '**centres of excellence**', specialising in one type of technological development where scientific resources are concentrated for that particular type of research. Paradoxically, centres of excellence may solve the critical-mass problem, but do not particularly favour internationalisation of research activities concentrated in one location.
- *Communication constraints* are due to the overwhelming evidence that innovative activities require face-to-face informal communication.[3] **Innovation** is based on a combination of well-defined methodological procedures as well as ill-defined, tacit, intuitive intellectual processes, personal encounters and conversations among researchers. Geographical distance, despite all information and communication technologies such as videoconferencing, is less conducive to inductive, intuitive and ill-defined discoveries. These communication constraints militate in favour of *co-located research*, where research projects are self-contained

within a single geographical location in order to minimise communication between units and maximise it within units.

In total, the benefits of a distributed network of innovative centres outweigh the costs as more and more global companies develop a decentralisation of R&D networks.

DESIGN OF GLOBAL R&D NETWORKS

Research centres in a global network belong to four main types[4]:

1. *Research laboratories*, in charge of long projects dealing with new technologies or scientific discoveries that are not necessarily related to a particular product. Those laboratories are global by nature, and are most often, but not always, located near the corporate centre.
2. *Development laboratories*, in charge of projects whose objective is to lead to a product or process innovation
3. *Supporting/adaptive units*, that provide product or process adaptation according to local contexts
4. *Scanning units*, whose mandate is to monitor technological development and contribute to the knowledge platform of the company.

The way these units are set up and organised depends upon the global evolution of the firm over time, that usually follows the pattern shown in Figure 10.3.

When the company is past the stage of central R&D activities, local laboratories are set up in order to provide local products or processes adaptation. In the third stage, centres of excellence that can specialise in basic research or certain products or process applications are established in innovative resource-rich countries. A **networked organisation** is established to organise the exchange of ideas, technologies, people and information. Nestlé, as described earlier, has reached this stage.

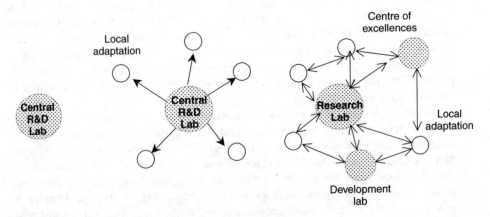

Figure 10.3   Evolution over time of global R&D activities

Management of global R&D networks

The management of a global R&D or innovative networks requires adaptation in structure, systems, and people/culture.

Structure

The structural aspects of R&D management relate to size, specialisation, project organisation and performance evaluation:

- *Size*: Research demands *communication* and *flexibility*. Large-size organisations are unfitted to provide a proper innovative environment. In their research, Pearce and Singh (1992) found that 50 per cent of international laboratories employed fewer than 50 people and 80 per cent fewer than 200 people. In the case of Nestlé, the size of laboratories was between 20 and 200 employees. When a research site employs a bigger number of scientists and technicians, it is usually divided into smaller self-contained specialised units.
- *Specialisation*: Specialisation can be *discipline-centred* or *product/process-centred*. The first case applies more to upstream research, while the second fits more with development work where multi-disciplinary teams work on the many facets of product design, utilisation, marketability and production.
- *Project organisation*: The most common arrangement for R&D is the project management structure, in which a *project leader* is responsible for the planning, budgeting, control and completion of a particular development. Projects can be managed purely locally and then transferred to other units in the global network (projects are *co-located*), or can be organised by interdependent tasks distributed across units (*multiple-location projects*). As mentioned already, co-located projects are likely to be more effective because of the communication constraints examined earlier, but co-location does not take advantage of the richness of a global network
- *Performance evaluation*: Performance evaluation mechanisms may take various forms, depending upon the kind of performance that it is wished to enhance. Table 10.2 gives some indication of the various methods according to the performance enhancement objective.

Table 10.2 Performance evaluation criteria

Performance	Measurement
Scientific innovation	Number of patents
	Number of publications in research journals
Commercialisation	Time to market
Profitability	Research unit as profit centre
Cost	Budgeting targets
Collaboration	Organisation of conferences and internal seminars
	Internal presentation of papers
	Number of publications listed on the intranet

Project management design within a global network can be categorised into:

1. *Self-contained co-located independent projects*, in which one research unit in the network is responsible for the complete design and development of a product/process. In this case, the communication flow between engineers, technicians, marketers and manufacturers is entirely limited to the research unit located on one site in the network. On completion of the project, the product or process is transferred to other units. In the case of an engine manufacture, for example, a particular unit would be responsible for the whole design of a certain type of engine.

2. *Integrated distributed projects*, in which several research centres take responsibility for one different inter-related element in the design and creation of the product/process. One centre will take care of the combustion chamber of an engine, while another will design the regulation. In such a case, inter-unit communication is maximised since researchers will have to exchange a lot of information to make the different parts fit together.

3. *Parallel distributed projects*, in which a project is still divided between several units but in such a way that inter-unit communication is limited to only a few parameters. In the case of the engine, one unit would be responsible for the combustion chamber including the regulation, while another would take charge of the compressor system. There would still be some interdependencies to manage, but fewer than in the previous case.

- An example of the distinction between the various project types is provided by the case of Hewlett Packard's development of a portable printer in Vancouver and Singapore.[5] HP wanted to develop a new printer (code name Alex) based on inkjet technology by splitting the work between Vancouver and Singapore. Vancouver was responsible for the product design and marketing while Singapore was in charge of the electronics parts design, sourcing, manufacturing design, tooling and testing. The project was designed as an integrated distributed one, demanding a large number of interactions between the two units. The project could not be completed in time and was dropped. The Singapore unit later obtained permission from headquarters to develop a printer for the Japanese market, adopting a self-contained co-located approach. This attempt was not successful either, because the unit did not benefit from the experience gained in inkjet printer design and marketing in Vancouver. Several years later, similar product developments were divided differently. Singapore was put in charge of printer engines (a self-contained key component) while Vancouver of the ergonomic and functional design, a parallel-distributed project. The results were successful because each team could work separately with a minimum of interactions and at the same time maximise their respective skills. The overall project organisation was based on the co-location principle, as illustrated in Figure 10.4.

- *Performance evaluation*: Performance evaluation mechanisms may take various forms, depending upon the kind of performance that it is wished to enhance. Table 10.2 gives some indication of the various methods according to the performance enhancement objective.

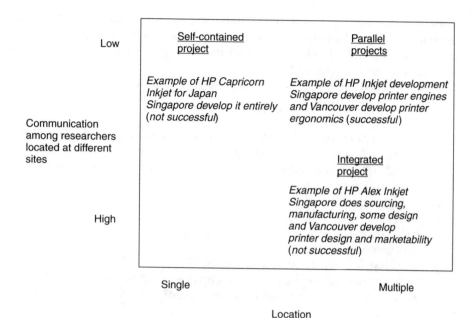

Figure 10.4   Global R&D projects

Systems

The effective management of a global R&D network calls for the implementation of systems and processes for *planning and control* and *knowledge documentation and dissemination*:

▪ *Planning and control systems* consist of the orderly definition of research projects and their distribution across units, the allocation of resources to the projects and the control of resources utilisation alongside the monitoring of project achievements. Project definition and attribution is generally done by a global central unit like that described for Nestlé above (NESTEC), on the basis of the overall project management philosophy described earlier. Project proposals are initiated either by the research units within the framework of their mandate or decided centrally and then delegated by the central co-ordination unit. Global product managers can initiate projects based on the assessment of market needs. An important consideration in the budgeting of research projects is to give research centres some 'free budgets', consisting of unallocated resources that can be used at the discretion of the unit head for contingencies or the exploration of new unplanned investigations.

The degree of *standardisation* of the planning system is a function of the nature of the research project. More fundamentally, advanced research programmes are given a 'budgeting envelope' without asking for too detailed justification, while more applied, business-specific projects may require cash flow forecasts similar to any strategic investment.

Planning processes are not only useful for resource allocation but also as a *communication* mechanism. Planning can be linked with scientific conferences, during which various laboratories present their projects before the actual planning and budgeting exercise begins.[6]

Controls are exercised through *internal reporting*, measuring progress against technical and commercial milestones.

█ *Knowledge diffusion and documentation*   Knowledge management is not limited to R&D, and next section of the chapter considers it in more detail. For global R&D, knowledge diffusion and documentation are based on seven main mechanisms:
  – People rotation
  – Conferencing
  – Data bases
  – Publications
  – Personal networking
  – Electronic knowledge management platforms
  – Research has shown that global companies tend to use a *portfolio of mechanisms* usually co-ordinated by a central staff office.[7]

People and culture

There are four people-related practices particularly conducive to global R&D:[8]

█ *Temporary assignments* as a way for researchers to be familiar with the work of other laboratories and sometimes to be assigned to a marketing team. Training programmes, constant travel and conferences allow inter-personal exchanges and the inculcation of socialisation and an 'open' culture of sharing.
█ *Creation of 'gatekeepers' roles* in each laboratory, where the task is to translate the work from other laboratories into the language of his/her own laboratory.
█ *Creation of a small central staff* whose role is to ensure a proper diffusion of information and research results.
█ *Promoting openness and sharing* as an important corporate values.

INTERNATIONAL TRANSFER OF TECHNOLOGY

Every process of globalisation implies some process of **technology transfer**. During the 1960s and 1970s, international technology transfer was considered a critical issue because of the emergence of newly independent countries who aspired to industrialise[9] and demanded an appropriate and complete transfer of technologies from multinational corporations. With the increased liberalisation of economies, this topic has lost its geopolitical connotations but still remains a managerial issue when dealing with the developing or emerging world.

Table 10.3 gives a classification of the various forms of technology that can be transferred.

Technology transfer takes place under five main *organisational and contractual* forms:

Table 10.3 Classification of technology

	Physical	*Informational*
Product Technology	Blueprints	Product development methodologies
	Formulation	Research heuristics
	Pictures, design	Creative methods
	Models	Testing methods
	Samples	Data mining
	Research protocols	
	Lab equipment	
	Data bases	
Process technology	Plant layouts	Process control
	Equipment	Quality insurance
	Process charts	Maintenance processes
	Process handbooks	Logistics and supply chain
Management technology	Handbooks	Marketing management
	Flow charts	Financial management
	Manuals	Strategic planning
	IT equipment	Human Resources Management
	Accounting documents	(HRM)
	Planning templates	Project management

- Licensing agreements
- Projects (turnkey projects, BOT, etc.)
- Technical agreements with joint venture companies or local subsidiaries
- Joint projects
- Sales of equipment.

The typical issues in technology transfer are *appropriateness and completeness*.

Technology transfer is *appropriate* if it fits with the local context. The classic trade-off is between modern, state-of-the-art technology that requires a solid infrastructure of human capital as well as support industries and a more modest, less advanced technology that can be assimilated locally. Global companies have often been blamed for transferring old and obsolete technology in order to protect their competitive advantage, but on the other hand many cases of expensive, advanced technology, the 'white elephants', have also been criticised as resource-wasting. When Volkswagen set up the first Western factory of modern cars (the Santana) in China in the early 1980s, it would have been difficult to transfer the new models manufactured and sold in Europe at the time. The state of the roads, the network of available suppliers, the volume involved and the skill level could not have permitted the assimilation of such complex advanced manufacturing systems. But, over time, the progressive improvement of local conditions made the transfer of modern technology feasible. SHAIC, the Chinese partner of Volkswagen, later entered a joint venture with General Motors to produce a more advanced model than the Santana with a more sophisticated production technology.

A technology transfer is *complete* when the recipient of technology is able to perform by itself the product of the transfer. This raises the issue of the transfer of *informational technology.* The knowledge embodied in those elements is often non-explicit and calls for a 'coaching approach' to the transfer, instead of just shipping equipment or organising a standard lecture.[10] Developing countries often regret that global companies restrict their transfer to physical content and limit information transfer to a strict minimum in order to maintain their future bargaining power. Although this interpretation is often too extreme, it is frequently true that engineers in global firms are not fully prepared to cope with the considerations of education and patience that a proper transfer implies.

GLOBAL KNOWLEDGE MANAGEMENT

Knowledge is the ability to understand and give a meaning to facts and information. In the corporate world, knowledge applies not only to techniques and physical sciences, but all aspects of corporate behaviour. **Knowledge management** then consists of the ability for a firm to create, combine and share knowledge among its members. Global R&D management is only one sub-set of knowledge-based strategies. Beyond the strict management of R&D, the strengths of global companies is their capability to create, combine and share knowledge across borders. According to the Japanese social scientists Nonaka and Takeuchi (1995), knowledge can be created and shared at the individual, group and organisational level. They distinguish between **explicit knowledge** (i.e. knowledge that can be codified and explained verbally, in writing or with symbolic language) and **tacit knowledge** (that cannot be codified and that can be transferred only by imitation or observation, by 'teaching'). They distinguish four types of knowledge conversion:

1. *Socialisation,* the process of sharing tacit knowledge through social interaction, apprenticeship and observation
2. *Externalisation,* the process of articulating tacit knowledge into explicit concepts through metaphors, pictures and theoretical formulations
3. *Combination,* the process of combining different elements of explicit knowledge into written, codified formats
4. *Internalisation,* the process of transforming explicit knowledge into tacit knowledge; when knowledge is internalised it becomes part of the way of doing things and its explicitness may be lost.

According to Nonaka and Takeuchi, those four processes form a *knowledge spiral* of organisational knowledge-creation from individuals to groups and then to whole organisations.

For global companies, knowledge management creates both opportunities and constraints (Table 10.4).

Transfer of best practices

Global companies build management processes in order to overcome the constraints and take advantage of the opportunities of knowledge management. One

Table 10.4 Opportunities and constraints for knowledge management in global companies

Opportunities	Constraints
Diversity of contexts	Languages
Variety of experiences	Differences of cultures and mindsets
Economies of scope in knowledge-creation	'Not invented here' reactions
Economies of 'speed' by not 'reinventing the wheel'	Unwillingness and lack of motivation to share knowledge
	Incentive systems reinforcing local performance and not rewarding 'global' citizenship
	'Siloed,' nationalistic perspectives
	Lack of trust between units

such process is the 'Transfer of best practices', that has been documented by Szulanski (1996). Transfer of best practices consists in the *systematisation of exchange of internal practices* developed in one unit and considered as 'superior' to other units. 'Practices' are the use of knowledge applied to all kinds of managerial activities – the running of a customer service centre, the management of a product launch, the training of salespersons or the control of accounts receivable. Szulanski found that three major factors can hamper transferring practices, what he calls *internal stickiness*:

- *Causal ambiguity* between the various elements of the practices that make it difficult to model precisely causes and effects relationships. Causal ambiguity exists when tacit knowledge is at the core of the functioning of the practice.
- *Lack of absorptive capacity* by the recipient unit which is not capable of interpreting the knowledge transfer and applying it. Here again, tacitness may constitute a barrier to knowledge transfer when the recipient unit has not got the internal resources to 'crack' the implicit, non-verbal elements of the practices.
- *Arduous relationships* that exist when tacit knowledge requires multiple interactions between individuals, particularly when geographical and cultural distance are present.

Szulanski's work challenges the classic views about knowledge transfer, as indicated in Table 10.5, and focuses the attention on the predominant sources of stickiness, which are closely related to the amount of tacitness involved in knowledge.

The metanational corporation

Doz, dos Santos and Williamson (2001) have developed the concept of the 'Metanational Corporation' that puts knowledge transfer at the centre of a mode of managing global companies, beyond the classical organisational models described in Chapter 3. The metanational corporation is capable of forgetting the concept of knowledge transfer and substituting the capability of knowledge 'melding' (a neologism comprising *melting* and *welding*). Melding knowledge implies that the tacit elements of knowledge are effectively *assimilated* and *put into practice*.

The metanational model is built on the interaction of two factors: the *location* factor (the place where knowledge is created shared and *melded*) and the *context* factor (the intellectual foundations underlying knowledge creation such as language, mental mapping, codes, implicit rules, etc.). The basic argument is that useful knowledge is frequently tacit and that tacitness is embedded in a particular context. Tacit knowledge-creation, sharing and melding requires *co-location*: the ability for people involved to benefit from frequent interactions, random encounters ('corridor' or the 'coffee shop' interactions). This is precisely the reason why co-location is so important in the case of R&D projects. In global companies, locations between units can be distant and contexts very diverse (multiplicity of language, education, social codes, etc.). The key problem of a global company is then to take advantage of the *diversity* and at the same time resolve the *co-location* imperative. The various forms of knowledge-creation, sharing and melding are represented in Figure 10.5.

■ In the *C&C* (Co-location and Co-setting) model, knowledge is entirely co-located with people sharing the same intellectual context transferred to other business units. This is the classic use of *centres of excellence*, in which one particular business unit is the creator of knowledge that becomes the 'best practice' to be transferred. This eliminates the problem of tacitness at the level of knowledge-creation but not at the level of transfer. The issue of stickiness is still present.

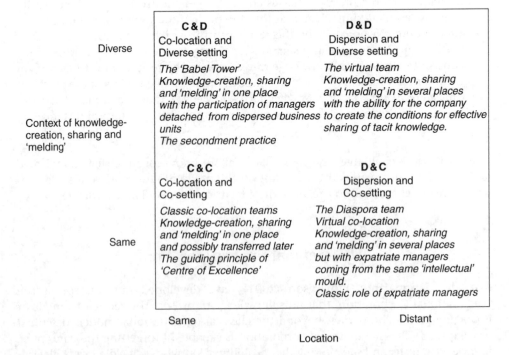

Figure 10.5   Knowledge-creation, sharing and 'melding' in global firms

Source: Doz, dos Santos and Williamson (2001).

Table 10.5 Tools and approaches used for knowledge management in the metanational corporation

---

- Business units and team leaders trained and experienced in *D&D practices*
- *Socialisation* before teamwork implying 'non-productive' social interfaces
- *Transitional encounters* (conferences, seminar, workshops, etc.) with loose agenda to allow tacit knowledge to be shared
- Teams made aware of *contexts* through visits, education
- Strong, accessible open user-friendly knowledge management platforms (electronic libraries, case studies, chat rooms, etc.)
- Deadlines for project completion
- Yellow pages (who is who for what?).

- In the *D&C* (Dispersion and Co-setting) model, knowledge is created at different locations under the leadership of 'expatriates' who share the same intellectual and contextual background. They understand one another across cultures and they are able at the same time to adapt knowledge to local conditions and to share it, since the stickiness is reduced thanks to the common cultural background. This was the classic practice of multinational firms relying on a talented and mobile expatriate group. The problem of this approach is the difficulty of taking advantage of the contextual diversity of country units and may lead either to an inflexible application of 'central' recipes or a complete acculturation of the expatriate managers – the 'going native' syndrome.

- The *C&D* (Co-location and Diverse settings) model tries to take advantage of a *physical co-location* of managers coming from various parts of the world and working on a common project. This is the idea behind 'impatriation' practices. This can lead to 'Babel Towers' consequences because of a lack of common contextual background of participants and the lack of explicit management of the cultural differences.

- Finally the *D&D* (Disperse and Diverse) model, the model of the 'metanational' corporation, is the one in which the creation, sharing and melding of knowledge in a dispersed and diverse world is explicitly managed. Table 10.5 lists the major organisational tools used for managing a D&D environment.

Global knowledge and the protection of intellectual property rights

The protection of **intellectual property rights** (IPR) is a source of concern and sometimes an impediment to practicing true global knowledge management. Global firms are often confronted with imitation, reverse engineering and trademark copies. Table 10.6 gives a list of the various forms of intellectual properties and their infringement.

Protection against infringement of IPR can involve the measures summarised in Table 10.7.

Table 10.6 Intellectual property rights and their infringement

IPR	Infringement
Patents	Reverse engineering Straight copy ■ Drugs, chemicals, mechanical and electronics products, auto parts
Trademarks	Straight copy Imitation (with minor change) ■ All branded products
Copyrights	Rights of creators ■ Texts, software, video, movies, training packages
Industrial designs	Original concept and design ■ Fashion, auto parts, electronics, appliances
Trade secrets	Employee poaching, espionage ■ List of clients, marketing and strategic plans, financial information, industrial and management processes
Genetic codes	Copy, employee poaching, ■ Bio-engineering

Source: UN, *Intellectual Property Right and Direct Foreign Investment*, (1993), Shengliang *et al.* (1996).

Table 10.7 Protection of intellectual property rights

Parties involved	Protection methods
Employees	Restrict disclosure of IP to selected employees Require key employees to sign individual secrecy agreements Establish a strict catalogue of level of confidentiality Keep IP in secure location Educate employees on the rationale and the consequences of infringement Regularly interview employees Prepare handbook listing items to be protected, and what to do in case of leakage suspicion; give recommendations about best practices
Suppliers	Non-disclosure agreements Establish rules about what can and cannot be disclosed
Joint venture partners	Be specific in the joint venture contract Use 'black box' approach when technically feasible Screen partners' employees
Legal issues	Lobby governments Use diplomatic channels to support actions Engage in legal action as soon as possible, even if legal context is unfavourable

SUMMARY AND KEY POINTS

1. International product life cycle:
   ■ How product innovations and production *migrated* from country of origin of innovative firms to other country subsidiaries

- *Stages*:
    - Stage 1: innovation – *innovative country product life cycle*:
      Innovative firms create new products and processes in their country of origin
    - Stage 2: foreign production – *second-tier country product life cycle*
      Second-tier country subsidiaries receive products/process from innovators and produce for local markets
    - Stage 3: transfer – *developing country product life cycle*
      Developing countries subsidiaries receive products/processes from innovators and produce for local markets and global markets at low cost
- *Criticisms*
    - Cannot explain the globalisation of innovation that occurred after the 1960s
    - Migration of R&D and production centres does not necessarily follow sequential evolution described by the International Product Life Cycle.

2. Global R&D network:

- *Management* of global R&D network needs to adapt structure, systems and people/culture:
    - *Structure*
        (a) Large-size organisation not conducive to communication and flexibility required in research
        (b) Specialisation
            (i) *Discipline-centred* (applies more to upstream research) or
            (ii) *Product/process-centred* (applies more to development work requiring multi-disciplinary teams)
        (c) Project organisation:
            (i) Can be managed locally (co-location project)
            (ii) Loses benefits arising from richness of a global network
            (iii) Organised by interdependent tasks distributed across units (multiple-location projects)
            (iv) There are three forms of project management design: self-contained co-located independent projects; one research unit in the network responsible for complete design and manufacture of a product/process; communication flow within the research unit at one site
            (v) Integrated distributed projects: different research centres take responsibility for one different inter-related element in design and creation of the product/process; maximum inter-unit communication
            (vi) Parallel distributed projects: project divided between several units, as in integrated distributed projects; inter-unit communication is limited to only a few parameters; fewer interdependencies among units
            (vii) Performance evaluation: scientific innovation; commercialisation; profitability; cost; collaboration
    - *Systems*
        (a) Planning and control
            (i) Allocation of resources (including budgeting)
            (ii) Control of resource utilisation
            (iii) Monitoring of project achievements

     (b) Knowledge diffusion and documentation:
        (i)   People rotation
        (ii)   Conferencing
        (iii)   Data bases
        (iv)   Publications
        (v)   Personal networking
        (vi)   Electronic knowledge management platforms

- *People and culture* – favourable factors:
  (a) Temporary assignments
  (b) 'Gatekeepers' in each laboratory
  (c) Small central staff
  (d) Openness

■ *Nestlé*:
- Central co-ordination (not management) of research programmes and efforts including:
  (a) Central planning of technical conferences and personnel transfer
  (b) Regular 'trialogues' between researchers, marketers and manufacturers to enhance the symbiosis
  (c) Visits to local research centres
- Central monitoring of progress reports sent by local research companies
- Decentralised R&D activities in local centres (local research companies):
  (a) Run as profit centre
  (b) Located near manufacturing centre
  (c) Performing development work on products, processes and systems
  (d) Involved in research planning and budgeting
  (e) Linked with local universities and technical institutes
- Corporate research strategy to prevent duplication of efforts

■ *Benefits*:
- Proximity to market (adapt or create products fitting local requirements)
- Access to geographical clusters of knowledge creation and development
- Learning

■ *Constraints*:
- Critical-mass constraint where a minimum amount of resources is required for an activity to be performed efficiently and effectively
- Communication constraint is partly based on ill-defined, tacit, intuitive intellectual processes, personal encounters and conversations among researchers

■ Types of *research centres*:
- *Research laboratories*: long projects and new technologies/scientific discoveries
- *Development laboratories*: product/process innovation
- *Supporting/adaptive units*: providing product/process adaptation according to local contexts
- *Scanning units*: monitoring technological development and contributing to the knowledge platform of the company

■ *Evolution*:
- First stage is central R&D lab
- Second stage is the set-up of local laboratories to provide local products or processes adaptation

- Third stage is the establishment of Centres of Excellence specialising in basic research or process applications in innovative resource-rich countries.

3. International technology transfer:
   - Types of *technology*
     - Product
     - Process
     - Management
   - Forms of *technology transfer*
     - Physical
     - Informational
   - *Key issues*
     - Appropriateness
       (a) Appropriate if fits with local context
       (b) Trade-off between state-of-the-art technology requiring a solid infrastructure of human capital against less advanced technology that can be assimilated locally
     - Completeness
       (a) Complete if recipient of technology is able to perform by itself the product of the transfer
       (b) Non-explicit knowledge often requires a 'coaching' approach for technology which is informational.

4. Global knowledge management system:
   - *Definition*:
     - Knowledge is the ability to decipher and give a meaning to facts and information
     - Knowledge management is the ability of a company to create, combine and share knowledge among its members
   - Conversion of knowledge forms a *knowledge spiral* of organisational knowledge-creation:
     - *Socialisation*: process of sharing tacit knowledge through social interactions/apprenticeship
     - *Externalisation*: process of articulating tacit knowledge into explicit concepts
     - *Combination*: process of combining different elements of explicit knowledge into codified formats
     - *Internalisation*: process of transforming explicit knowledge into tacit knowledge – when knowledge is internalised, it becomes part of the way of doing things
   - *Opportunities* for knowledge management:
     - Diversity of contexts
     - Variety of experiences
     - Economies of scope in knowledge-creation
     - Economies of 'speed' by not reinventing the wheel
   - *Constraints*:
     - Languages
     - Differences of cultures and mindsets
     - 'Not invented here' reactions
     - Unwillingness and lack of motivation to share knowledge

- – Incentive system reinforcing local performances and not rewarding 'global' citizenship
- – Nationalistic perspectives
- – Lack of trust between units
- ▪ *Transfer* of best practices made less effective by:
  - – Casual ambiguity (difficult to have a precise model of cause and effect relationship, especially for tacit knowledge)
  - – Lack of capacity for absorption
  - – Arduous relationships (tacit knowledge transfer requires multiple inter-actions between individuals)
- ▪ Useful *tools/approaches*:
  - – Trained business units/team leaders
  - – Socialisation
  - – Transitional encounters
  - – Teams trained on contexts
  - – Strong, accessible open user-friendly knowledge management platforms
  - – Deadlines
  - – Yellow pages
- ▪ *Knowledge-creation, sharing* and *'melding'*:
  - – Dependent on location and context
  - – Models
    - (a) C&C model (Co-location and Co-setting)
      - (i) Centre of excellence in which one particular business unit creates knowledge and becomes a 'best practice' to be transferred
      - (ii) Benefits include elimination of the tacitness problem
      - (iii) Problem of stickiness still persists
    - (b) D&C model (Dispersion and Co-setting)
      - (i) Expatriate managers who share intellectual and contextual background adapt knowledge to local conditions
      - (ii) Benefit of reducing stickiness
      - (iii) Problem of contextual diversity of the country causing 'going native' syndrome or 'central recipes'
    - (c) C&D model (Co-location and Diverse setting)
      - (i) Benefits of 'impatriation' practices
      - (ii) Problem of 'Towers of Babel' owing to lack of common context-ual background of participants and lack of explicit manage-ment of cultural differences
    - (d) D&D model (Dispersion and Diverse setting) – major organisational tools:
      - (i) Trained and experienced management and staff
      - (ii) Socialisation
      - (iii) Transitional encounters
      - (iv) Increased awareness of contexts through education
      - (v) Strong open user-friendly knowledge management platforms
      - (vi) Deadlines for project
      - (vii) Yellow pages.
5. Intellectual property rights (IPR):
   - ▪ *Types*:
     - – Patents

- Trademarks
- Copyrights
- Industrial design
- Trade secrets
- Genetic codes
- *Infringement* – common for all types of intellectual property rights
- *Protection*: methods can involve any of the following:
  - Employees
  - Suppliers
  - Joint venture partners
  - Legal sanctions.

Learning assignments

1 Why is the international product life cycle model no longer appropriate to explain global innovation?
2 What are the constraints on implementing a distributed R&D network?
3 What are the appropriate HRM practices conducive to global R&D?
4 When is technology transfer complete?
5 Give two examples of 'explicit' knowledge and 'tacit' knowledge in a business context of your choice.
6 What are the major challenges that the 'metanational' model of knowledge-creation, sharing and 'melding' tries to address?
7 How can one measure performances of research?
8 How can one protect intellectual property rights (IPR) in a global firm?

Key words

- Best practices
- Centre of excellence
- Co-location
- Combination
- Explicit knowledge
- Externalisation
- Innovation
- Intellectual property
- Internal stickiness
- Knowledge management
- Metanational
- Networked organisation
- Socialisation
- Tacit knowledge
- Technology transfer

Web resources

<http://www.hbsp.harvard.edu/hbsp/topics/browse/view.asp?path=>Knowledge+management&search_type =>
Harvard Business Review – Knowledge Management.

<http://knowledge.insead.fr/category.cfm?catid =11>
Link to the data-base of INSEAD Knowledge – Knowledge Management.

<http://www.mckinseyquarterly.com/category_arch ive.asp?tk=86032::& L3=35>
McKinsey Quarterly – Innovation.

Notes

1. This example is based on De Meyer (1993).
2. These categories are based on De Meyer (1982) and Wortmann (1990, pp. 175–84).
3. Allen (1997).
4. This taxonomy is inspired by Pearce and Singh (1992) and Chiesa (2000, pp. 341–59).
5. Thill and Leonard-Barton (1994).
6. De Meyer (1991, pp. 49–58).
7. De Meyer (1991).
8. De Meyer (1991).
9. Silvèse (1979); Amsalem (1983).
10. Lasserre (1995).

References and further reading

Books and articles

Allen, T.J., *Managing the Flow of Technology*. Cambridge, MA: MIT Press, 1977.
Amsalem, Michel, *Technology Choice in Developing Countries*. Cambridge, MA: MIT Press, 1983.
Chiesa, Vittorio, 'Human Resource Management Issues in Global R&D Organizations: A Case Study', *Journal of Engineering and Technology Management*, 13, 1996 pp. 189–202.
Chiesa, Vittorio, 'Global R&D Project Management and Organization: A Taxonomy', *Journal of Product Innovation Management*, 17, 2000, pp. 341–59.
De Meyer, Arnoud, 'Tech Talk: How Managers are Stimulating Global R&D Communication', *Sloan Management Review*, 49, 1991, pp. 49–58.
De Meyer, Arnoud, 'Nestlé SA', INSEAD Case Study 07/91-093, 1993.
De Meyer, Arnoud, 'Management of International R&D Operations', Chapter 8 in O. Granstrand, S. Spölander and L. Håkanson (eds), *Technology Management and International Business*. New York: John Wiley, 1992.
Doz, Yves, José dos Santos and Peter J. Williamson, *The Metanational Corporation*. Boston, MA: Harvard Business School Press, 2001.
Kuemmerle, Walter, 'Building Effective R&D Capabilities Abroad', *Harvard Business Review*, March–April 1997, pp. 61–70.
Lasserre, Philippe, 'Training: Key to Technology Transfer', *Long Range Planning*, 15(4), 1995.
Nonaka, Ikujiro and Hirotaka Takeuchi, *The Knowledge Creating Country: How Japanese Companies Create the Dynamics of Innovation*. Oxford University Press, 1995.
Pearce, Robert D. and Satwinder Singh, *Globalizing Research and Development*. London: Macmillan Palgrave, 1992.
Porter, Michael, *The Competitive Advantage of Nations*. New York: Free Press, 1998.
Senrat, Silvèse, *Technology Transfer: A Realistic Approach*. Houston, TX: Gutt Publishing Co., 1979.
Shengliang, Robert. *et al.*, 'A Guide to Intellectual Property Rights in South East Asia and China', *Business Horizon*, 39(6) November–December 1996.
Szulanski, Gabriel, 'Exploring Internal Stickiness: Impediments to the Transfer of Best Practices Within the Firm', *Strategic Management Journal*, 17, Special Issue, 1996, pp. 27–43.
Thill, George and Dorothy Leonard-Barton, 'Hewlett-Packard: Singapore', Harvard Business School Case, 9-694-035, 1994.
United Nations, *Intellectual Property Right and Direct Foreign Investment*. New York: United Nations, 1993.

Vernon, Raymond, 'International Investment and International Trade in the Product Life Cycle', *Quarterly Journal of Economics*, 29(2), 1966, pp. 190–207.

Wortmann, M., 'Multinationals and the Internationalisation of R&D', *Research Policy*, 19(2), 1990, pp. 175–84.

Journal

Research and Development (monthly), Cahners, United States.

11

Cross-cultural management

Chapters 8–10 have studied the managerial issues of designing and running the three key operational functions of innovation, production and marketing in a global context. In Chapters 11–13 we will look at how globalisation affects the management of the two key resources of corporations: *human resources and financial resources*. Before addressing the global human resource management (HRM) problems, we need to explore the underlying complexity that arises in human relations as a result of international cultural differences.

This chapter presents the results of academic research that has studied cultural differences. We will then look at the impact of cultural differences on the management of *cross-cultural teams*, on *international negotiations* and on *business practices*.

At the end of the chapter one should be able:

- To understand the meaning of culture and the various layers of culture
- To identify the key characteristics of international cultural differences
- To understand the different management issues associated with cultural differences
- To understand the managerial issues associated with cross-cultural teams
- To understand how cultural differences affect international negotiations
- To identify the key characteristics of an economic culture
- To be aware of differences in ways of conducting business across cultures.

FAILURES IN CROSS-CULTURAL INTERACTION

Global corporations are by nature organisations that *interact* with customers, employees, partners and suppliers from different national cultures, giving rise to the anecdotal gaffes well documented by David Ricks in his book, *Blunders in International Business* (1993). Beneath the surface of these 'travellers' tales' lies one of the main challenges that global firms have to confront. Do the various players in the global ecosystem give the same meaning to the same concepts, behaviours or attitudes? Do employees around the world get the same message when policies are enacted, memos exchanged or rewards distributed? Do customers of the same age, urbanisation and wealth value similar product or service attributes? Do employees in multinational teams share similar assumptions and causal relationships about decision parameters? When a contract, a business venture or a loan is being negotiated, do the parties understand each other's 'silent language'? These are the questions that all global companies have to address in their cross-cultural management competencies.

THE DIFFERENT FACETS OF CULTURE

There is no universal definition of culture. Schneider and Barsoux (1997) identify 164 different definitions made by anthropologists. More relevant broad definitions of culture include 'a shared pattern of behaviour' (Margaret Mead, 1953), 'system of shared meaning or understanding' (Claude Levi-Strauss, 1971; Clifford Geertz, 1973) or 'a set of basic assumptions, shared solutions to universal problems...handed down from one generation to another' (Edward Schein, 1985). All these definitions have in common the concept that culture is '*shared*', and imply an implicit decoding of an underlying pattern of *cause and effect relationships*, whether cognitive (meaning, assumptions), attitudinal/emotional (behaviour) or decisional (solutions). Schein adds the dimension of *generational transmission*, which implies a certain degree of stickiness of culture over time.

Instead of a definition, some scholars have attempted to describe the *content* of culture. Figure 11.1 shows three major layers of culture: Basic assumptions and meaning; values, beliefs and preferences; and behaviour. In ascending order, basic assumptions are the least visible and probably the most entrenched, since they deal

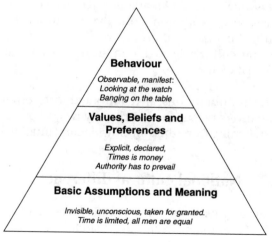

Figure 11.1 The three layers of culture

Source: André Laurent (1986).

with ingrained models of understanding, meanings and causal relationships that have been shaped by history and transmitted through the educational process to children, pupils and students. Religious faith and assumptions about human nature belong to this category. Basic assumptions are difficult to change in adults. Values, beliefs and preferences are the explicit expression of assumptions incorporated into a set of *codes* or, *norms* that provide some sort of ethical and normative governance mechanisms for social groups. Values can be changed to some extent by new information and confrontation with new situations. A manager whose assumption about human nature is that men or women are fundamentally greedy, for example, will probably believe that only materialistic rewards will motivate employees. She/he may change this belief when exposed to situations where people sacrifice financial reward for others' benefit.

Behaviour is the most visible part of the iceberg. It is manifested in action and can be modified through education as well as through some forms of 'conditioning'. Behavioural change does not imply a modification of beliefs or assumptions. An autocratic leader may be told to change her/his style of leading a meeting although she/he still believes that employees 'have to be told' (belief) based on the assumption that human beings are fundamentally divided into 'born leaders' and 'passive followers'. In such a case, behavioural change will be superficial.

In the management field that, by nature, is concerned with economic achievement of social groups (companies), culture will be manifest in four key dimensions:

- **Corporate culture**: the accumulated assumptions, values, beliefs and behavioural norms resulting from the history of the company (good and bad experiences), its existing and past leadership imprint (the legacy of charismatic CEOs) its ownership structure (family-owned, publicly listed, private, government-owned) and its size (big or small).
- **Industry culture**: any rules derived from the professional norms of a particular industry: heavy manufacturing, services, oil and gas, etc.
- **Professional culture**: derived from the training and professional norms/constraints of different functions within corporations: accountants, researchers, production personnel, sales and marketing people, etc. As Lawrence and Lorsh (1969) have described, professional orientation introduces a large amount of differentiation within organisations.
- **National or ethnic culture**: derived from the national, religious or ethnic origin of citizens or social groups.

Global companies, as any other firms, are confronted with corporate, industrial and professional cultural diversity, but this complexity is compounded by national and ethnic differences stemming from their worldwide implantation.

National cultural differences

The systematic analysis of national cultural differences in a business management context is the result of four main streams of research:

1. *Ethnological research*: 'silent language' differences (Edward and Mildred Reed Hall, 1990)

2. *Managerial values and assumptions*: work-related values differences (Geert Hofstede, 1980); values orientations differences (Fons Trompenaars, 1993; Hampden-Turner and Trompenaars, 2000); management assumptions differences (André Laurent, 1986)
3. *Countries clusters*: the grouping of nations according to similarities of cultural traits (Ronen and Shenkar, 1985; Huntington, 1997)
4. *Economic cultures differences*: how business systems are organised and business interactions are governed (Albert, 1991; Berger and Dore, 1996; Whitley, 1999; Redding, 2001).

'Silent language' differences

According to Hall (1960), cultures differ in the way they communicate through non-verbal means or **'silent language'**. They identify six 'silent languages': *time, space, material goods, friendships, agreements* and *context*.

- Cultures differ according to their perception of **time**. Time can be seen as *sequential and scarce*, as in the case of Germanic culture, leading to the quest for preciseness, punctuality and deadline-keeping. Some cultures, see time as *fluid, circular and abundant*, as in Arabic countries, where people will be less punctual and not really disturbed by delays and postponements.
- Differences in the perception of **space** relates to the concept of *social distance* that measures not only the length of physical proximity in social interaction but also of emotional intimacy. In high-social distance cultures, people will tend to avoid physical and emotional proximity – a typical British trait–while in low-social distance cultures – the Latin countries – people will see no objection to physical contact and the sharing of emotions.
- The language of **material goods** is linked to the importance attached to financial wealth as a sign of status – a materialistic trait of Americans – as opposed other status signifiers such as family, education or seniority.
- **Friendship** is built and maintained quite differently. In some societies, one can make friends rapidly but at the expense of superficiality and the friendship may not last long. The 'silent language' of this sort of friendship may shock people coming from societies where friendships are not so quickly built but last longer.
- The 'silent language' of **agreement** quite often opposes Western cultures to Eastern ones. In Western societies, most agreements or disagreements are explicitly stated and documented in writing. In Eastern cultures, verbal and sometime ambiguous agreements are accepted. In Indonesia, for instance, it is often difficult for a business partner to say a straight 'no', but a 'maybe' may in fact have the same negative connotation.
- The 'silent language' of **context** attaches to the importance given to the person rather than the content in a communication. In high-context societies – mostly Asian, South American or Latin – the important part of an interaction is the person (with *whom*) and the emphasis given to the setting, the ambiance and ceremonials. In low-context societies – Anglo-Saxon, Nordic or Germanic – the *what* dominates the communication, hence the importance attached to written documents and technical specifications.

Hofstede's work-related values differences

Hofstede's research is probably some of the most frequently quoted in the international management literature, related to the vast amount of data collected by the author. Hofstede's original (1980) survey was made with 116,000 employees at IBM worldwide. He asked questions related to their preferences in management styles and work values and related the answers to national origin; he found that national cultures differed according to four main dimensions: *power distance, individualism, uncertainty avoidance* and *masculinity*:

- **Power distance** is the extent to which people in certain societies accept *inequality in power distribution* or, on the contrary, have a somewhat *egalitarian view* of power distribution. High-power distance societies will accept hierarchical control and respect authority – as, for instance, in Malaysia – while egalitarian societies will have a more democratic view of social control with no particular reverence for high-ranking functions – as, for instance, in Denmark.
- **Individualism** characterises a culture in which individuals look after their own or immediate relative interests. This is the case in most Western cultures. This will translate into individual *assertiveness and initiative* in business contexts. Collectivist cultures, on the other hand, will put group interests above individuals: *consensus and harmony* will be preferred to assertiveness. East Asian cultures commonly put society ahead of the individual.
- **Uncertainty avoidance** is typical of societies where ambiguity and unpredictability is not accepted, and there is a continual search to codify, plan and regulate the environment (Japan, Spain). At the opposite end of the scale, one will find social groups where tolerance and risk-taking is accepted and rewarded (United States, Sweden).
- **Masculinity** refers to the high value given to assertive, competitive behaviour. Feminity, on the other hand, refers to societies where quality of life, non-aggressive behaviour, interpersonal relations and concern for the weak are dominant values.

The 40 countries of Hofstede's original study were clustered around those four dimensions. The scores on these dimensions for a sample of countries are reported in Table 11.1.

Figure 11.2 shows the mapping of some countries along the power-distance/individualism dimensions.

Trompenaars' value orientation differences

The cultural differentiation proposed by Trompenaars (1993), also based on survey data, identifies six value orientations that differentiate cultures and impact on the way countries conceive organisations (see Table 11.2). Trompenaars found significant differences in national groups; most Asian cultures, for instance, differ from Western cultures in all dimensions (Table 11.2).

291

Table 11.1 Hofstede's country scores on cultural dimensions

	Power distance	Individualism	Masculinity	Uncertainty avoidance
USA	40	91	62	46
UK	35	67	66	65
Germany	35	67	66	65
Australia	36	90	61	51
Canada	39	80	52	48
Sweden	31	71	5	29
Denmark	18	74	16	23
France	68	71	66	65
Italy	50	76	70	75
Spain	57	51	42	86
Japan	54	46	95	92
Indonesia	78	14	46	48
India	77	48	56	40
Thailand	64	20	34	64
Hong Kong	68	25	57	29
Taiwan	58	17	45	69
Singapore	74	20	48	8
Malaysia	104	26	50	86
Brazil	69	38	49	76
Mexico	81	30	69	82
Arab Countries	80	38	53	68

Note: Scores are obtained from statistical factors.
Source: Hofstede (1980).

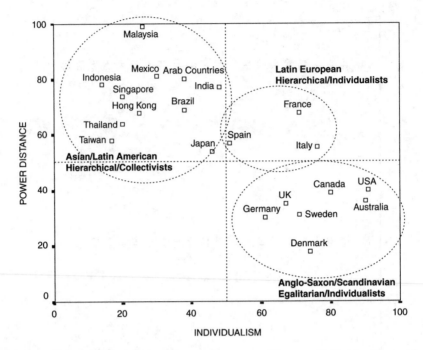

Figure 11.2 The mapping of countries on the power-distance/individualism scales
Source: Hofstede (1980).

Table 11.2 Trompenaars' six value orientations

Value orientation	Description	Examples
Universalism vs Particularism	Rule-based behaviour; general application	Nordic countries
	Circumstance, relation-based behaviour; specific application	South East Asia, China, African countries
Individualism vs Communitarism	Individual rights are supreme; Individual performances are valued	Western countries
	Group's rights are supreme; Harmony and cohesion are valued	Asian countries
Specificity vs Diffusion	Objective, analytical, reductionist reasoning	Germany, France
	Holistic, synthetic reasoning	Middle East, Asia
Achieved status vs Ascribed status	Status and respect achieved by 'doing'	United States
	Status and respect achieved by 'being'	Malaysia, China
Inner direction vs Outer direction	Knowledge of 'right' and 'wrong' lies inside the individual ('guilt culture')	Protestant countries
	Knowledge of 'right' and 'wrong' comes from society ('shame' culture)	Confucian societies
Sequential time vs Synchronous time	Time is an arrow, is consumed in one direction	Western
	Time is a circle	Arabic, African, Asian countries

Sources: Trompenaars (1993); Hampden-Turner and Trompenaars (2000).

Laurent's management-assumption differences

André Laurent (1986) asked precise questions related to organisational and managerial issues of international managers of various nationalities attending executive seminars over 25 years. He found a systematic pattern of national differences:

- Most managers seems to be more motivated by *obtaining power than by achieving objectives* (Latin European countries nationals – Italian, French, Spaniards – agree with this statement, while Danes, Swedes or Norwegians disagree)
- It is important for managers to have at hand *precise answers to most of the questions that a subordinate may raise about their work* (Asian and Latin nationals strongly support this statement, while Anglo-Saxon and Nordic cultures do not)
- In order to have efficient working relationships, it is often necessary to *bypass the hierarchical lines* (Nordics and Anglo-Saxons agree while Chinese, Italian, Spaniards or Indonesians strongly disagree)
- An organisation structure in which subordinates have *two direct bosses should be avoided at all costs* (Chinese, Italians, French and Indonesians reject this organisational mode, while Americans or Swedes accept the idea of working for two bosses)
- The main reason for having a hierarchical structure is so that everybody knows *who has authority over whom* (Chinese, French, Japanese or Indonesians agree while American, Swedes or British disagree).

Laurent's results consistently show that basic managerial and organisational assumptions concerning power, structure, clarity of roles and hierarchy are still deeply embedded in national cultures. These differences in assumptions pose a challenge to global firms that need to organise, lead and motivate people of diverse cultural heritage. Laurent (1986) even found that 'cultural differences in managerial assumptions were not reduced as a result of working for the same multinational companies', thus rejecting the idea that national cultures converge thanks to corporate cultures.

COUNTRY CLUSTERS

The clustering approach consists of grouping countries according to their degree of geographical, linguistic, religious, historical and social proximity. One example of country clusters is given in Figure 11.3.

Another type of clustering was developed by Huntington (1997), who grouped countries in what he call **'civilisations'** based on language, religion, values, beliefs, and institutional and social structures. He identified eight modern 'civilisations':

- **Sinic**: the societies of China and Chinese communities as well as Vietnam and Korea; confucianism is a major cultural trait of this 'civilisation'
- **Japanese**: a distinctive civilisation identified with one country

Figure 11.3 Country clusters

Source: Ronen and Shenkar (1985).

- **Hindu**: essentially India, Bangladesh and Sri Lanka
- **Islamic**: encompasses most of the Middle East and North Africa as well as Indonesia and part of Malaysia
- **Orthodox**: centred in Russia and Central Europe
- **Latin American**: Central and South America
- **African**: from Central to South Africa
- **Western**: North America, Western Europe and Australia.

Huntington's grouping has more to do with *geopolitics* than with management – he asserts that more and more conflicts in the world will be due to clashes of 'civilisations'.

ECONOMIC CULTURES

Cultures have a pervasive effect on social, economic and political institutions and on competitive behaviour. In the early nineteenth century, Max Weber, a German sociologist, explained differences in competitive and business behaviour between Latin European countries and Northern and Anglo countries as caused by the influence of religions. In Northern Europe, Protestantism encouraged *individual achievement* leading to free enterprises and favouring the emergence of modern 'capitalism', while Catholicism in Spain, and to a certain extent in France, induced *state control*. Several scholars have identified various forms of *business systems*[2], *economic cultures*[3] or *forms of capitalism*[4] that explain international variations in institutional governance and competitive behaviours. Gordon Redding (2001) explains these differences according to the interaction of three sets of parameters (Table 11.3).

(a) The *culture set* that constitutes the foundation of social values, composed of three components:

- *Rationale*, which describes the way societies set objectives and the importance they attach to formal systems and processes in setting objectives
- *Authority*, which describes how societies set rules for vertical order (where the legitimate source of power is)
- *Identity*, which describes the rules of horizontal order (what makes citizens stick together)

(b) The *institutional fabric* that represents the organisation, development and allocation of resources, made up of three components:

- The *financial capital*, its formation and allocation
- The *human capital*, how human skills are developed
- The *social capital*, the way trust is created among economic agents

(c) The *business system* that presides over the way economic activities are governed, made up of:

- The *ownership system*, who are the primary owners of enterprises?
- The *networking system*, how do companies and business agents relate to each other?
- The *management system*, how are employees induced to co-operate?

Table 11.3 summarises some differences in economic cultures.

THE IMPACT OF CULTURES ON GLOBAL MANAGEMENT

The effects of cultural differences on the management of global companies are pervasive: there is no aspect of corporate life that is not impacted by culture. Six aspects of corporate life are particularly strongly influenced by cultural differences:

- Marketing and customer communications (see Chapter 8)
- Human resources (see Chapter 12)

Table 11.3 Differences in economic cultures

	Anglo/American	German and Nordic European	French and Latin European	Japan	Korea	Overseas Chinese
Rationale The societal ends are agreed as well as the means of pursuing them	Material success Democratic process Rational system Rules-led competition	Community Democratic Consensus-led co-operation	Democratic Negotiation-led conflict resolution	Employ people Democratic Consensus-led national	Autocratic National Militaristic	Autocratic Familistic
Authority The ground rules for vertical order Origin of power	Constitution Law decentralisation	Law decentralisation	State Law centralisation	State Corporations Decentralisation	State Corporations Centralisation	Family centralisation
Identity The ground rules for horizontal order (What makes society stick together)	Individual rights contracts Heterogeneity (microcultures)	Social welfare Homogeneity	Social welfare Cultural identity Heterogeneity (microcultures)	National belonging Cultural identity Homogeneity	Nationalism Cultural identity Homogeneity	Clans Ethnic bonding
Capital How financial capital is found and channelled	Financial markets Low gearing	Banks Medium gearing	State and market Medium gearing	Banks High gearing	State High gearing	Family High gearing
Human capital How human skills are developed	Academic performance-led	Academic and apprenticeship	Academic elitist	Academic plus on-the-job elitist	Academic elitist	Academic plus on-the-job elitist
Social capital How trust is created	High-trust contracts Legal institutions	High-trust contracts	Low-trust Negotiation	High trust within groups	High trust within groups, low outside	High trust within family, low outside

Ownership Who owns enterprises	Shareholders	Banks, employees Shareholders	State, shareholders	Banks Cross-shareholding	Business groups Cross-shareholdings	Family groups
Networking How economic agents relate to each other (The rules of business transactions)	Contracts	Contracts Some elitist relationships	Elitist relationships State interventionism	Elitist relationships	Personal relationships State intervention	Personal Relationships
Managing How employees are induced to co-operate in the firm	System-led Motivation Performance measures	Hierarchical Technical competence Performance measures	Hierarchical bureaucracy Negotiation	Corporate identity Corporate loyalty	Hierarchical Corporate loyalty	Hierarchical Family Loyalty

Sources: Albert (1991); Berger and Dore (1996); Whitley (1999); Trompenaars (2000); Hampden-Turner and Redding (2001).

- Partnerships, M&As (see Chapters 4 and 5)
- Multicultural teams
- Negotiations
- Business practices.

Marketing and partnership/acquisition have already been dealt with and Chapter 12 will consider human resources. This chapter focuses on teamwork, negotiations and business contexts.

Cross-cultural teams

In most activities, global firms make use of teamwork – committees, task forces, cross-functional teams, etc. Many departments at corporate, regional or subsidiary levels are staffed by managers of different nationalities and cultures (see Table 11.4).

Given the variety of cultural heritage, communication and decision-making processes can be blunted by *cultural noise*: multi-cultural teams can perform either significantly worse or better than mono-cultural firms. The performance of multi-cultural groups is a function of three factors[5]:

(1) Multiplicity of perspectives, experiences and viewpoints increases the *richness of information*
(2) Possible *loss of cohesion* owing to miscommunication, misunderstanding and stereotyping
(3) The ability of team leaders to combine the variety of perspectives and achieve group *synergy*.

The relative impact of those three factors can lead to polarised performance. In an interesting study made with German and American staffed work teams, two

Table 11.4 Types of multi-cultural teams

Business development	Members of different nationalities working on development/launch of new products
Regional headquarters	Different functions occupied by different nationals for regional co-ordination
Corporate headquarters	Permanent or temporary assignment of executives and staffs of different nationalities having global responsibilities
Joint ventures and alliances	Managers and employees assigned from different partners, or an employees' pool
Task forces	Multi-function, multi-country teams in charge of a particular project

Source: Schneider and Barsoux (1997).

researchers found that German rational, analytical approaches to problem-solving combined with the action oriented, free-wheeling, innovative approaches of American members contributed to high performance. However, performances were poor when the team leader was not able to introduce team-building procedures that facilitated information-sharing and group reflection of cultural assumptions.[6]

Negotiation

Negotiations generally follow a sequential six-stage chronology that can be assimilated to a 'ritual'[7]:

1. **Pre-negotiation**: each party prepares its negotiation strategy
2. **Climate-setting**: introduction of negotiators, greetings, physical context
3. **Presenting**: agenda-setting, opening statements
4. **Mid-point bargaining**: substantive debate, request for clarification, search for common ground, trial 'concessions'
5. **Closure**: Binding concessions offered, search for agreements, final drafting/ signing
6. **Post-negotiation**: ratification of agreements by corporate headquarters, or government bodies.

There can be a large variety of cultural diversity in approaches and behaviours during these stages. Table 11.5 summarise the key differences between American and Japanese negotiation approaches.

Negotiation styles have different impacts on outcomes, and managers engaged in international negotiations should be aware that a certain number of precautions and recommendations must be made in order to minimise failure owing to cultural hang-ups. The following checklist is a useful list of prescriptions.[8]

1. Understand one's own cultural 'lens', using a list of negotiation parameters as in Table 11.5.
2. Understand the other party's cultural 'lens', using a similar checklist. An example of typical attitudes of Chinese negotiators is provided in Table 11.6.
3. List negotiation items likely to be affected by cultural differences and anticipate counterparts' responses.
4. Assess potential responses and list those that are likely to fit and those that are likely to conflict.
5. Try to disentangle 'cultural' divergences from 'business' divergences in order to be ready to adjust behaviour and avoid being trapped in 'cultural' clashes.

Table 11.5 Impact of culture on negotiating behaviour: a comparison of US and Japanese responses

Negotiation parameters	Typical American response	Typical Japanese response
Basic approach to business in general	Transactional; profit oriented; detail-conscious; legalistic	Structured; strategic; starting from trust
Central purpose of negotiation	Reaching agreement on a contract	Launching a long-term relationship
Selection criteria for negotiator(s)	Verbally articulate generalists; technical competence; 'rational abilities'	Rank; position; 'social competence'
Appropriate **number of negotiators**	Few	Many: in order to demonstrate seriousness and for functional coverage, including learning.
Appropriate **role(s) of lawyers(s)**	Key participant: leader, contract advisor, and/or draftsperson	None: seen as adversarial trouble-makers.
Attitude toward **decision-making process**, and appropriate degree of delegation of authority to negotiators	Top-down decision-making; very high degree of delegation of authority	Consensual, middle-up decision-making (*ringi seido*); little or no authority delegated to negotiators
Appropriate **tone** for negotiation and communication	Direct; informal; familiar; egalitarian; candid	Highly indirect; highly formal; hierarchical; reserved
Negotiators' interest in **personal feelings** and values of counterparts	Little or none; irrelevant or improper; logic more important than emotions; issues more important than personalities	Acute; personal rapport essential to establish trust (*ningen kankei*)
Appropriateness of **socialising** with counterparts	Inappropriate; unacceptable; risks conflict of interest and loss of personal control	Highly appropriate; and traditional behaviour; also, ritualised gift-giving
Attitude toward **time** during negotiations	Acutely time-conscious; 'time is money'; impatient	Patience is the key
Attitude toward **silence** during negotiations	Strongly averse; uncomfortable; 'fill the void'	Essential: for decorum and for non-verbal communication and empathy (*haragei*)
Reaction to **cross-cultural** signals	Unaware; or consider it unimportant	Aware indifference
Attitude toward **sequential bargaining** and negotiating progress	Strongly attracted to both	Unimportant
Attitude toward **sharing information**	Open; willing	Collect it avidly, but do not give it out
Attitude toward **closure**	Essential for a successful negotiation; results oriented, not process oriented	Not necessary or even important; take the long view
Form of the contract	Long; detailed; covering all foreseeable contingencies	Prefer very short; and limited to general principles and affirmations
Commitment to the contract	Totally binding	Weak; the relationship is what counts, not the document; and inevitable changing conditions will necessitate later amendments

Source: Sunshine (1990).

Table 11.6   Chinese business negotiating styles

- Large team, vague authority, presence of technical people, often with incompetent interpreter
- Exploit 'agreed principles'
- Play 'home court'
- Buy best technology but show no appreciation for monetary value of knowledge
- Masking interests
- Price-sensitive
- Stalling, delay and indecision
- Hierarchical
- Non-legalistic approach (rely on 'relationships')
- Play competitors off against each other
- 'Sweet and sour' approach
- Attritional negotiation
- 'Shaming' technique (point out mistakes by the other party)
- Exploiting vulnerabilities
- Taking surprise actions
- Showing anger
- 'Friendship means obligation'
- Double standards
- 'The richer partner bears the heavier burden'
- Mixed feelings toward foreigners
- Re-negotiate issue thought concluded.

Source: Fang, (1997).

Business practices

Business practices refers to the day-to-day interactions that managers experience in their dealings with customers, suppliers, partners and government officials. Beside the negotiation styles described earlier, three categories of practices are impacted by cultural differences – etiquette, relations and competition:

- **Business etiquette** represents the set of rituals that take place when people communicate in business dealings. It includes the way people address each others, speak, dress, eat, stand, sit, gesticulate, pose and deal with time
- **Relations** involve the way business transactions are established, whether personal relationships or legal/technical matters are the prime ingredient of transactions
- **Competition** indicates how competitive advantages are obtained. In some countries, competition will be perceived and practised as a fair game in which products, services and performances are compared and the winner ultimately decided on. In other countries, other criteria such as ethnic belonging, family connections or political considerations can determine the winner.

Table 11.7 shows examples of such practices.

Table 11.7 Business practice differences

Practices		Examples
Etiquette		
Addressing	How to name the other person	■ In Malaysia, nobility titles are the proper form of address (*Encik, Tan,* etc.)
		■ In France, people are addressed by their title (*Monsieur le Directeur*)
		■ In the United States, the first name is normal
		■ In Japan, the exchange of business cards is critical
Gesturing	How to position oneself and how to use body language	■ Showing the soles of the feet offends Arabs
		■ Left-hand shaking is not proper in Muslim countries
		■ Finger-pointing is considered as highly threatening and impolite in Asia
Dressing	Dress code	■ Malaysian businessmen use jacket and tie while in Singapore a long-sleeved shirt is normal business attire
Eating	Importance of meals in business dealing	■ French business transactions usually take place at a lunch or dinner table
	Behaviour at the table	■ Chinese banquets and sometimes drinking punctuate deals
Timing	How to control time	■ Signs of impatience are considered improper in many cultures
		■ Lengthy preliminaries are usual in the Middle East
Talking	Importance of verbal communication	■ Silent pauses are the norm in China or Japan
Relations		
Engaging	Importance given to establishing personal relationships in business transactions	■ Most Asian countries privilege the personalisation of contacts before engaging in business transactions
Contracting	Importance given to overall agreements on principles versus details	■ Legal contracting is the norm in the United States while broad-brush agreements are considered satisfactory in Japan
Competing		
Advantages	Product technology versus connections as a source of competitive advantage	■ In China, connections (*guanxi*) are still a very important factor in competitive advantage
Supplying	Preferences given to friends and families in supply contracts	■ In Asia the notion of 'extended families' implies that preferential treatment will be given to families/friends for supply contracts.

SUMMARY AND KEY POINTS

1. Cross-cultural management:
   - *Potential issues*:
     - Are concepts, behaviours or attitudes interpreted differently by different nationalities?
     - Do policies, memos and rewards convey the same message to employees all over the world?
     - Do worldwide employees share similar assumptions about decision parameters?
     - Do parties involved in the negotiation understand the counterparty's 'silent language'?
   - Culture can potentially *encompass*:
     - *Layers of culture*
       (a) Assumptions and meaning
       (b) Values, beliefs and preferences
       (c) Behaviour
     - *Dimensions of culture*
       (a) Corporate culture – assumptions, values, beliefs and behavioural norms resulting from company history, ownership structure and size
       (b) Industry culture – rules of trade of a particular industry
       (c) Professional culture – derived from training and professional norm/ constraints of different functions within corporations
       (d) National/ethnic culture – derived from belonging to certain national, religious or ethnic origins.

2. National culture:
   - Research on *national culture differences*:
     - *Ethnological research* ('silent language' differences):
       (a) Perception of time
       (b) Perception of space
       (c) Language of material goods
       (d) Friendship
       (e) Agreement
       (f) Context
     - *Managerial values and assumptions*:
       (a) Work-related values differences – four main dimensions of difference in national cultures:
         (i) *Power distance* (acceptance of hierarchical control and respect for authority)
         (ii) *Individualism*
         (iii) *Uncertainty avoidance* (tolerance towards ambiguity)
         (iv) *Masculinity* (value given to assertive and competitive behaviour)
       (b) Value orientations differences – six orientations can differentiate cultures:
         (i) *Rule-based* versus *relation-based* behaviour
         (ii) *Individualism* versus *Communitarism*
         (iii) *Objective/analytical reasoning* versus *Holistic/synthetic reasoning*

          (iv)   Status and respect achieved by *doing* versus *being*
          (v)   Knowledge of 'right' or 'wrong' arises from *within* versus from *society*
          (vi)   *Sequential* time versus *synchronous* time
     (c) Management assumptions differences – cultural heritage, i.e. national cultures have basic managerial and organisational assumptions on:
          (i)   Power
          (ii)   Structure
          (iii) Clarity of roles
          (iv) Hierarchy

- *Country clusters*
     (a) National grouping according to cultural traits proximity
     (b) 'Civilisations':
          (i)   Sinic (Chinese, Vietnamese, Korean)
          (ii)   Japanese
          (iii)   Hindu
          (iv)   Islamic
          (v)   Orthodox (Russia and Central Europe)
          (vi)   Latin America
          (vii)   African
          (viii) Western

- *Economic culture*
     (a) These are six main economic cultures:
          (i)   Anglo/American
          (ii)   German/Nordic European
          (iii)   French/Latin European
          (iv) Japanese
          (v)   Korean
          (vi) Overseas Chinese
     (b) Economic cultures vary according to three sets of parameters:
          (i)   Culture – rationality; authority; identity
          (ii)   Institutional fabric – financial capital; human capital; social capital
          (iii)   Business system: ownership system; networking system; management system.

3. Impact of culture on management:

   ■ *Multi-cultural teams*:

    - Types:
     (a) Business development
     (b) Regional headquarters
     (c) Corporate headquarters
     (d) Joint ventures and alliances
     (e) Task forces
    - Performance depends on:
     (a) 'Rich information' resulting from multiplicity of perspectives, experiences and viewpoints
     (b) Possible loss of cohesion
     (c) Ability for team leaders to achieve group synergy

- *Negotiations*:
- There are commonly six stages:

  (a) Pre-negotiation   Each party prepares negotiation
  (b) Climate-setting   Introduction, physical context
  (c) Presenting   Agenda-setting and opening statements
  (d) Mid-point bargaining
  (e) Closure   Search for agreements, final drafting/signing
  (f) Post-negotiation   Ramifications of agreements

- Impact of culture on negotiations:

  (a) Basic approach to business
  (b) Central purpose of negotiation
  (c) Selection criteria for negotiators
  (d) Appropriate number of negotiators
  (e) Appropriate role of lawyers
  (f) Attitude toward decision-making process
  (g) Appropriate degree of delegation of authority to negotiators
  (h) Appropriate tone for negotiation/communication
  (i) Negotiators' interest in personal feelings and counterparts' values
  (j) Appropriateness of socialising with counterparts
  (k) Attitude toward time
  (l) Reaction to cross-cultural signals
  (m) Attitude toward sequential bargaining/negotiation process
  (n) Attitude toward information-sharing
  (o) Attitude toward closure
  (p) Form of contract
  (q) Commitment to contract

- Checklist for negotiators:

  (a) Understand the 'cultural' lens of
      (i) Your own position
      (ii) Counterparty's position
  (b) List negotiation items which:
      (i) Risk being affected by cultural differences and anticipate counterparts' responses
      (ii) Are caused by mere 'business divergence' instead of 'cultural divergence'
      (iii) Are potential fits or conflicts with counterparty

■ *Business practices*:
- Negotiation style
- Business etiquette
- Relation practices:

  (a) Engaging   (emphasis on relationship establishment)
  (b) Contracting   (emphasis on overall agreement)

- Competition practices:

  (a) Advantages (product's technology versus connections)
  (b) Supply   (give preferences to friends/relatives).

Learning assignments

1 What types of cultural differences can business managers experience? Give examples.
2 What is the 'silent language' of negotiation?
3 A lower-level manager discovers that his boss is making a wrong decision that could affect the company negatively. Looking at Hofstede's cultural mapping shown in Figure 11.2, how would you expect this manager to behave if she/he was: – an Indonesian? – an Australian?
4 What consequences can you draw from Laurent's management assumptions differences for the organisation of a subsidiary in China?
5 What cultural issues can you anticipate when a partnership is planned between a UK listed E-company and a Korean family conglomerate?
6 How would you recommend an American manager to plan a negotiation with a Japanese counterpart?
7 What 'cultural misbehaviour' of misunderstanding have you experienced personally, or have you heard of? How could it have been avoided?

Key words

- Business etiquette
- Corporate culture
- Cultural heritage
- Economic cultures
- Individualism
- Industry culture
- National/ethnic culture
- Power distance
- Professional culture
- 'Silent language'
- Uncertainty avoidance

Web resource

<http://www.mckinseyquarterly.com/category_archive.asp?tk=86032::&L3=32>
McKinsey Quarterly – Teams.

Notes

1. Hall (1960, pp. 87–96).
2. Whitley (1992).
3. Berger (1986).
4. Berger and Dore (1996)
5. Adler (1997).
6. Stumpf and Zeutchel (2001, pp. 175–94).
7. Sunshine (1990).
8. This list is taken from Sunshine (1990, pp. 77–81).

References and further reading

Books and articles

Adler, Nancy, *International Dimension of Organizational Behavior*. Cincinnati, OH: South Western College Publishing, 1997.

Albert, Michel, *Capitalisme contre Capitalisme*. Paris: Seuil, 1991.

Berger, Peter, *The Capitalist Revolution*. New York: Basic Books, 1986.

Berger, Suzanne and Ronald Dore (eds), *National Diversity and Global Capitalism*. Ithaca, NY: Cornell University Press, 1996.

Brake, Terence, Danielle Medina and Thomas Walker, *Doing Business Internationally: Guide to Cross Cultural Success*. New York: McGraw-Hill, 1994.

Chu, Chi-Ning, *The Asian Mind Game: unlocking the Hidden agenda of the Asian Business Culture: A Westerner's Survival Manual*. New York, NY: Rawson Associates, 1991.

Fang, Tony, *Chinese Business Negotiation Style: A Socio-Cultural Approach*. Linköping University, 1997, p. 44.

Gahuri, Pervez and Jean Claude Usunier, *International Business Negotiations*. Oxford: Pergamon Press.

Geertz, Clifford, *The Interpretation of Culture*. New York: Basic Books, 1983.

Hall, Edward, 'The Silent Language in Overseas Business', *Harvard Business Review*, May–June 1960, pp. 87–96.

Hall, Edward and Mildred Reed Hall, *Understanding Cultural Differences*. Yarmouth, ME: Intercultural Press, 1990.

Hampton-Turner, Charles and Fons Trompenaars, *Building Cross-Cultural Competence*. Chichester: John Wiley, 2000.

Hofstede, Geert, *Culture's Consequences: International Differences in Work-related Values*. Beverley Hills, CA: Sage, 1980.

Huntington, Samuel P., *The Clash of Civilizations and the Remaking of World Order*. London: Simon & Schuster, 1997.

Inglehart, Ronald and Beth Rubin, 'Modernization. Cultural Change and the Persistence of Traditional Values', *American Sociological Review*, 65(1), 2000, pp. 19–51.

Jackson, Terence, *Cross Cultural Management*. London: Butterworth-Heinemann, 1995.

Kremenyuk, Victor, *International Negotiation Analysis: Approaches, Issues*. San Francisco: Jossey-Bass, 1996.

Laurent, André, 'The Cross-Cultural Puzzle of Global Human Resource Management', *Human Resources Management*, 25(1), 1986, pp. 91–102.

Lawrence, Paul R. and W. Jay Lorsch, *Organization and Environment*. New York: Irwin, 1969.

Levi-Strauss, Claude, *L'Homme Nu*. Paris: Plon, 1971.

Mead, Margaret, *Coming of Age in Samoa*. New York: Modern Library, 1953.

Redding, Gordon, *The Spirit of Chinese Capitalism*. Berlin: De Gruyter, 1990.

Redding, Gordon, (ed.) *International Cultural Differences*. Brookfield, VT: Dartmouth College, International Library of Management, 1995.

Redding, Gordon, 'Convergence or Divergence at the Millennium', INSEAD Euro Asia Centre, Working Paper, 70, 2001.

Ricks, David A., *Blunders in International Business*. Malden, MA: Blackwell Business, 1993.

Ronen, S. and O. Shenkar, 'Clustering Countries on Attitudinal Dimensions: A Review and Synthesis', *Academy of Management Review*, 10(3), 1985, pp. 435–54.

Schein, Edward, *Organizational Culture and Leadership*. San Francisco: Jossey-Bass, 1985.

Schneider, Susan C. and Jean-Louis Barsoux, *Managing Across Cultures*. London: Prentice-Hall, 1997; numerous references in this chapter are drawn from this book.

Stumpf, Siegfried and Ulrich Zeutchel, 'Synergy Effects in Multinational Work Groups: What We Know and What We Don't Know', in Mark Mendenhall, Torsten Kühlman and Günter Stahl (eds), *Developing Global Business Leaders*. Westport, CT: Quorum Books, 2001, pp. 175–94.

Sunshine, Russel B., *Negotiating for International Development*, International Development Law Institute. Dordrecht: Martinus Nijhoff, 1990.

Trompenaars, Fons, *Riding the Waves of Cultural Differences: Understanding Cultural Differences in Business*. London: Nicholas Brearley, 1993.

Whitley, Richard D., *Business Systems in East Asia: Firms, Markets and Societies*. London: Sage, 1992.
Whitley, Richard D., *Divergent Capitalisms*. Oxford: Oxford University Press, 1999.

Journals

Cross Cultural Research (Quarterly), United Kingdom Sage. <http://www.sagepub.co.uk/>.

Intercultural Management Quarterly, Washington <http://www.imquarterly.com>.

International Journal of Cross Cultural Management, United Kingdom, Sage.

Society for Intercultural Education and Research (bimonthly), United Kingdom, Elsevier. <http://www.sciencedirect.com/science/journal/01471767>.

12

Global human resource management

The success of global strategies relies on the *quality of the people* who are in charge of its implementation. Global management requires the deployment and development of personnel. This chapter addresses four kinds of managerial issues that a global strategy imposes on human resources:

- First, there is a need to adopt a worldwide policy of *international movement of personnel*, differentiating in the pool of managers those who will follow a 'global' career from those who will follow a 'local' career. This is the *assignment* issue.
- Second, there is a need to *manage the career* of the global managers. This is the *expatriates* management issue
- Third, there is a need to *recruit and motivate local personnel*. This is the *localisation* issue.
- Finally, there is the need to develop *skills* fitted with the requirement of global management. This is the *global skill development* issue.

These issues constitute the structure of this chapter (see Figure 12.1). At the end of the chapter one should be able:

- To understand the trade-offs in establishing a policy of reliance on expatriate global managers versus local ones
- To understand the sources of success and failure of an expatriate policy
- To contribute to the definition of an expatriate policy
- To contribute to plans for developing local management
- To participate in the design of global training programmes.

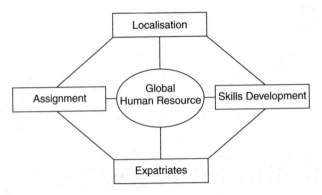

Figure 12.1   The global human resource issues

APPOINTING A DIVISION MANAGER IN FRANCE[1]

Helvetica Chemical was a Swiss-based multinational company engaged in pharma-ceuticals, agrochemicals, dyestuffs and industrial chemicals. It operated in more than 60 countries and was organised as a matrix of product and country divisions. The corporate headquarters in Basle was staffed with global central function services establishing and supervising policies in research, IT, legal, personnel and finance. In each country there was a Group Company Managing Director responsible for the total activities of local divisional units, and for the overall financial results of the country. Each Division General Manager had dual reporting: to the Group Company Managing Director (country head) and to the Global Division Director in Basle responsible for the worldwide performance of the product line. The case describes how a staffing decision can raise a general global strategic issue.

In France, the Group Company Managing Director, Lucien Boyer, was about to retire and the corporate headquarters designated Pierre Jourdan, General Manager of the French Pharmaceutical Division, to replace him. Jourdan's promotion opened the position of the Pharmaceutical Division in France, and the issue was to appoint a replacement for him. Two potential candidates had been identified.

1. *Philippe Dupont*, a French national, with a doctoral degree in pharmacy from Toulouse University, had been recruited two years previously from a competitor as Marketing Manager. He had had his entire career in France and had a deep experience of the French pharmaceutical industry. Since his recruitment at Helvetica, he had obtained excellent results. Dupont was Jourdan and Boyer's preferred choice.
2. *Michel Garnier*, a Canadian from Quebec, who had extensive international experience as a Marketing Manager in Canada, Brazil and the United States. He had spent two years in Basle at the corporate office in the Strategic Planning Department, and was at present managing the Pharmaceutical Division of Helvetica Chemical in Morocco, where he obtained excellent results. Garnier was the preferred choice of the Basle Global Pharmaceutical Division.

Whom to appoint?

Answers to the question provoked very emotional attitudes and heated debates. For some, it was obvious that Dupont was the best choice, given his knowledge of the French market, his experience and the support of the French management structure. For some others, Garnier should be appointed, because he would bring a global perspective that could enrich the French subsidiary and position Helvetica Chemical as a true global player capable of transcending national barriers. After the first instinctive reactions, it became obvious that the appointment decision was more than a pure personnel management issue, it was really a *global strategic issue*. In practice, both choices were valid, but each conveys a fundamentally different message to the employees, competitors and customers. If this kind of decision systematically obtains the same kind of answer, it will 'drive' the strategy of the company in a particular dimension.

Dupont was the perfect choice for a strategic orientation based on *local responsiveness*. His French education and experience with the market made him a perfect choice for the French subsidiary. No doubt, he would perform well and Jourdan would be happy to supervise a colleague with whom he could share the same 'culture'.

Garnier brought a 'global' perspective and his appointment would be an opening into the walled city of a national subsidiary. His international experience would give him the capability to transcend national cultures and to enhance a global corporate mindset. From an operational point of view, he would bring different methods and approaches to the French subsidiary.

The final choice depends upon the strategic orientation that Helvetica Chemicals wants to give to its global operation. If, from a competitive viewpoint, there is little advantage to be gained in adopting cross-border integration, and the prime objective is to let local subsidiaries focus on their own market, the choice of Dupont is the most effective. If, on the contrary, it becomes strategically important to adopt a worldwide co-ordinated strategy, then it is time to implement a global human resource management (HRM) approach that fits with this objective and Garnier would be the recruit of choice.

This example illustrates the four kinds of issues presented in Figure 12.1: assignment of personnel, expatriate management, localisation and skills development.

ASSIGNMENT OF PERSONNEL: THE GLOBAL HUMAN RESOURCE WHEEL

In term of personnel, a global company can be represented as a wheel, as in Figure 12.2.

At the centre is the corporate headquarters, where the Board of Directors and the key executives are located alongside the corporate staff. In many companies, the global business divisions are also located nearby the corporate headquarters, although this is not always the case.

The main wheel is constituted by the countries in which the company operates. Countries are staffed with three categories of personnel:

- **Local managers and staffs**, recruited at subsidiary level (the unshaded part of Figure 12.2). Their career is essentially within the local companies.
- **Global managers** (the middle circle in Figure 12.2). Their career is made up of successive appointments in different countries. Managers in this category are

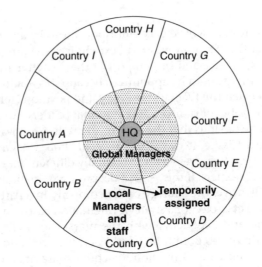

Figure 12.2 The global human resource wheel

considered as 'expatriates', although this terminology is progressively disappearing, to be replaced by the denomination of 'international' or 'global' managers.

■ **Temporary assignees** (the arrow in Figure 12.2). These are referred as 'detached' personnel.

The profile of the human resource wheel is not the same in a company that has adopted a global strategic posture as in a company that operates in a multi-domestic mode. Figure 12.3 shows the difference between the two models. In a multi-domestic

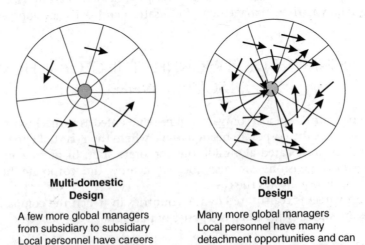

Multi-domestic Design

A few more global managers from subsidiary to subsidiary
Local personnel have careers in their own countries
Some temporary detachments
Example: Colgate-Palmolive

Global Design

Many more global managers
Local personnel have many detachment opportunities and can join the global manager group
Example: Shell

Figure 12.3 Human resource wheels

organisation global managers are relatively few and mostly from a dominant nationality. They move from place to place, generally in a top position. Local personnel progress in their own subsidiary, although they may be seconded occasionally to other subsidiaries for technical support or learning purposes. A global organisation will see a larger number of multi-cultural global managers moving around. Those global managers will integrate local personnel aspiring to a global career, and temporary assignments of local personnel to other subsidiaries and to headquarters will be more frequent. Cross-cultural teams generate frequent travel. Colgate-Palmolive is an example of the first model. The company in the mid-1990s had 170 managers that were part of the 'expatriate managers' group, 40 per cent of them being Americans out of a total employment of 35,000 people. By contrast, Shell employed 6,000 expatriates from some 70 different nationalities out of a total of 100,000 employees.

EXPATRIATE MANAGEMENT

Expatriate personnel ('expatriates' are people living and working in a non-native country) are often grouped into two categories: parent-country nationals (PCN), whose national origin is the same as that of the corporate headquarters and third-country nationals (TCN). An increased number of TCN over PCN indicates that firms are moving from a traditional international management mode toward a global one. American and European multinational firms employ a relatively larger number of TCN than Japanese or Korean corporations.

Success and failure of expatriation

Numerous studies have shown that expatriate personnel are confronted with a set of challenges, summarised in Figure 12.4. Rosalie Tung (1987, 1988) found that the main causes of failure among US expatriate managers were:

- Inability of the manager to adapt
- Inability of the manager's partner to adapt
- Family-related problems
- Manager's personality or emotional immaturity
- Manager's inability to cope with responsibility
- Manager's lack of technical competence
- Manager's lack of motivation

Other studies have shown that the recognition of cross-border assignments by colleagues at corporate headquarters and the support and understanding given to expatriate personnel by the corporate centre are crucial for the success of expatriation.[2] The research done on the topic all shows that extreme expatriate failure, as measured by the *recall rate* (i.e. the proportion of assigned personnel who fail to complete their predetermined contract) is relatively low (around 5 per cent). However, there are situations in which the assignments are less than satisfactory for both the firm and the individual manager.

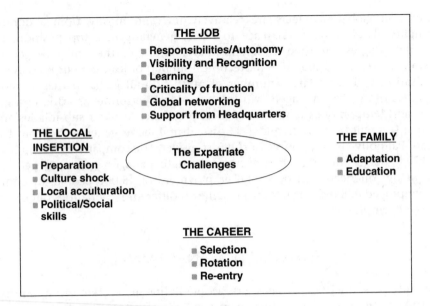

Figure 12.4   The expatriate challenge

Acculturation

Acculturation is the process by which group members from one culture adapt to the culture of a different group.[3] Acculturation can take four different attitudes – the 'four Fs' described in Figure 12.5.

- The **flight** attitude is adopted when a person wants to preserve their own cultural identity and, when confronted with a new environment, prefers to isolate him/her self.
- The **fight** attitude bears some similarity with the previous one except that instead of retreating and isolating oneself, the person criticises the host environment, a militant expatriate claiming the superiority of their own culture.

  Both the flyers and the fighters avoid socialising with the local community and prefer to live in 'expatriate ghettos'. For the global corporation, those types of personnel lack the flexibility to adapt to local conditions: they may be good at defending the global aspect of business strategies but poor at local responsiveness.
- The **fit** attitude describes persons who are capable of immersing themselves in the local culture and, at the same time, preserving their own culture. They look for contacts with locals, get interested in host-country customs, arts and culture. They have a balanced perspective between global and local competitive requirements: they are 'cosmopolitans'.
- The **follow** attitude indicates a willingness to embrace local culture and assimilate oneself to the host environment. The assimilated expatriate progressively loses

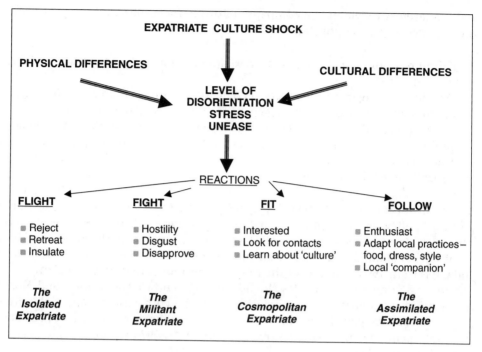

Figure 12.5 Expatriates' acculturation: the 'four Fs'

contact with the global headquarters and has difficulty in balancing global and local requirements.

The expatriate and the company

For the company, the cost of expatriate personnel kicks in at around two–three times the equivalent position in the 'home' country (see Mini-Example 12.1, p. 319 and Figure 12.7, p. 318 for cost elements). It is therefore necessary that global firms put in place a coherent set of policies and practices that optimises the benefits of expatriation to both the company and the individuals. Such policy has six major components:

1. Strategic vision
2. Selection and preparation
3. Compensation
4. Tenure
5. Support
6. Career follow-up.

Strategic vision

A **strategic vision** places expatriate assignments within the framework of the company's global strategy. Assignment policies vary according to the global positioning and management style of the company. Edstrom and Galbraith (1977) identified three modes of transfer policies:

1. **Filling position**, the classic policy of expatriation for key managers and technical support transfer.
2. **Develop manager**, a policy designed to utilise international postings as an instrument of developing management talents and skill developments.
3. **Develop organisation**, a policy that embraces the 'transnational' management philosophy by which people move around in order to develop products and lead marketing campaign with the view of developing the global strategic capabilities of the company.

A company of the 'multi-domestic' type in Figure 12.3 will focus more on the 'filling position' policy, while companies of the 'global' type will use the three policies conjointly. James Steward Blacke and Hal Gregersen researched the management of expatriates at about 750 US, European and Japanese companies in the 1990s (Blacke and Gregersen, 1999) and one of their key conclusions is that 'When making international assignments, companies should focus on knowledge creation and global leadership development.' This conclusion is in line with Edstrom and Galbraith's (1977) conclusions: global companies consider the worldwide movement of personnel as a tool to enhance their competitiveness through *knowledge transfer* and leverage of *cross-cultural richness*.

Selection and preparation

The **selection of expatriates** is a function of individual skills as well as the technical and competitive requirements of the company. Blacke and Gregersen conclude that: 'Successful companies assign overseas posts to people whose technical skills are matched or exceeded by their cross-cultural abilities.'[4]

Expatriates' skills are primarily *socio-cultural*. Figure 12.6 shows the ranking of skills that managers in Asia Pacific consider to be conducive to success.

Another study conducted by Günter Stahl with German managers (2001) revealed that seven factors were critical to success in international work assignments:

1. **Tolerance of ambiguity**: the ability to function effectively in a foreign environment where expatriates experience ambiguity, complexity and uncertainty
2. **Behavioural flexibility**: the capacity to vary one's behaviour according to the immediate requirements of the situation and the demands of the foreign culture
3. **Goal orientation**: the ability and desire to achieve one's task goals despite barriers, opposition and discouragement
4. **Sociability and interest in other people**: a willingness to establish and maintain meaningful social relationships, combined with a genuine interest in people
5. **Empathy**: the capacity to accurately sense other peoples' thoughts, feelings and motives, and to respond to them appropriately
6. **Non-judgementalness**: the willingness to critically re-examine one's own values and beliefs, and to avoid judging other people by one's own norms
7. **Meta-communication skills**: the capacity to clarify culturally different perceptions and to 'guide' the intercultural communication process.

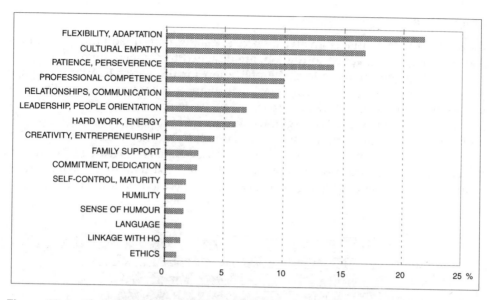

Figure 12.6 The primary ingredients of individual managerial behaviour required for success in expatriate assignments in Asia

Note: The percentage indicates a ranking of the frequencies of responses to the question: 'What do you consider to be the three most important factors for success?'.
Source: Lasserre *et al.* (1997).

The preparation of assignments involves several steps. First, and most importantly, international assignments must be part of a *career plan*, and the objectives of the assignment have to be clearly defined. If the assignment is only for 'filling a post', it is probably a one-shot event and the expatriate will be much more concerned about her/his future after the expatriation (a classic 're-entry problem') than by the intricacy of the foreign environment. She/he, and the family, needs to be informed about and prepared for the specific differences in living conditions and culture, but the primary concern is the 're-entry'. If the assignment is a step in an 'international' career, the person should have a 'mapping' of their future career development path. Specific learning about the foreign environment is necessary but, over the years and cumulated assignments, this aspect become relatively less important since the international manager 'learns to learn'.

The second and obvious step is the *cultural and logistical preparation* for the employee and the family. Numerous organisations provide cultural training[5], and most companies subscribe to them, and provide a pre-assignment trip for the expatriate and their family in order to obtain first-hand experience of living conditions. Some companies use short-term assignments or 'missions' of several weeks to immerse the future expatriate into the real working conditions.

Assessment centres are the third and probably the less used step in assignment preparation. This consists of measuring the future expatriate's skills alongside certain predetermined dimensions that are considered important for the job and the country, and according to the results, tailoring a certain number of specific programmes designed to repair any deficiencies. Daimler Chrysler Aerospace ran such a programme named QUICK.[6]

Compensation

Classic expatriate contracts involve a series of clauses that, in addition to the normal remuneration attached to the job, are designed to compensate for the difference in living conditions, prices, the obligation for the person/family to change accommodation, pension systems, health insurance, schooling, cost of living as well as any additional economic impacts of the assignment on the family. Generally, a 'hardship' allowance is also granted in the case of countries that have a significant deficit in security, infrastructure or social/political context. Mini-Example 12.1 shows the assignment policy for expatriates at Colgate-Palmolive. Figure 12.7 compares the cost of living in various cities of the world. An expatriate in Shanghai whose salary is based on Frankfurt living standards could expect to have the living-standard

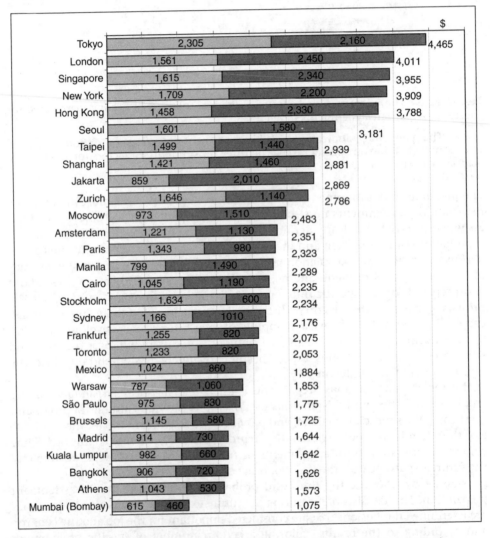

Figure 12.7 Cost of living in the world, US$ per month (general plus housing)

Source: Union des Banques Suisses: Prices and Earnings Around the Globe (2000).

component of their salary adjusted by +13 per cent (1421/1255) if the rent is paid by the company. In most cases, housing and childrens' education is paid for by the company.

Mini-Example 12.1   Colgate-Palmolive: international assignment policy

Colgate-Palmolive operates in more than 80 countries. Its businesses are in personal and household care. It started its international expansion in the early part of the twentieth century. In 1983, the company felt the need to set a policy for the management of its expatriate managers. In 1994, there were 170 expatriate managers, called 'Global management expatriates'; 40 per cent were American, they were between 35 and 50 and they had been selected on performance achieved in their initial position in their home country. The international assignment policy provided the following conditions:

Taxes

All expatriates had a US contract and were considered employees of the New York Headquarters. Expatriates were liable to taxation on their income based on hypothetical tax that determined what they should pay in New York. Any unfavourable difference from the amount of taxes due in the host country would be paid by the company.

Cost of living adjustment

If the cost of goods and services in the host country were higher than in New York, the expatriate would be eligible for an additional allowance. A goods and services index calculated by an external consultant served as a base for the compensation.

Housing

The company gave a housing allowance equal to the cost of rental and utilities in excess of a New York housing norm, representing what the expatriate would normally pay in New York given her/his family size and salary.

Relocation

Moving and relocation expenses such as storage, transport and insurances would be borne by the company. A lump sum would be provided to cover miscellaneous expenses up to US$10,000.

Sale or rental of principal residence

Should the expatriate choose to rent or sell his home in his home country, the company would pay for expenses associated with that transaction. The same would apply if the expatriate rented his house or apartment and was charged with fees for cancelling the lease.

Temporary living expenses

The company would reimburse all temporary living expenses such as hotels, car rentals, search for housing incurred five days prior to departure in the home country and 30 days after arrival in the host country.

- **Childrens' education**
  Full tuition fee, textbooks, transportation expenses related to education of pre-university children aged 4–19 would be borne by the company.

- **Vacation and leave**
  Expatriates were entitled to 30 days' annual vacation; transportation costs for the expatriate and his family were paid by the company.

- **Harsh country allowance**
  An additional allowance ranging from 10–20 per cent of base salary was given to expatriates living in a country where the facilities were considered 'considerably less desirable than in the US'.

- **Spouse assistance programme**
  Spouses were provided with assistance and counselling to facilitate the transfer to a foreign location. A sum of US$7,500 was provided to spouses for job searches in the host country. Language-training tuition and skill development courses for expatriate spouses were also borne by the company.

Source: Rosenweig (1994).

The left-hand bar in Figure 12.7 is the cost of a basket of goods and services and the right-hand bar is the rent of an average three-bedroomed unfurnished apartment.

Tenure

The length of expatriate assignments in a given country is a function of four key factors:

- The time needed to learn the *rules of business in the country* and to build the *relationships* with the various parties (customers, employees, government officials, partners, etc.) with whom the person needs to interact.
- The importance of personal relationships in the job and the required *continuity* of the task (the task of building a new business requires more time than, for instance, setting up a factory)
- The *contextual hardship* of the country (difficult living conditions)
- The company's policy with regard to *career development*.

Given that in most cases acculturation – that is, the process of getting acquainted with the other culture – takes between three and 12 months, and that a managerial job requires at least two years to show meaningful results, a 'normal' expatriate assignment should last at least three years for non-technical jobs. The classical trade-off for determining an optimal tenure is shown in Figure 12.8. The *local impact* of the expatriate, in terms of business results, is represented by curve *A*: it is a logistic function with a negative contribution during the learning period (acculturation). It progresses rapidly and then peaks when the person is in full control of the job.

Curve *B* in Figure 12.8 represents the *benefits of integration* – i.e. being in tune with the overall culture of the company, its core values and competencies that are shared

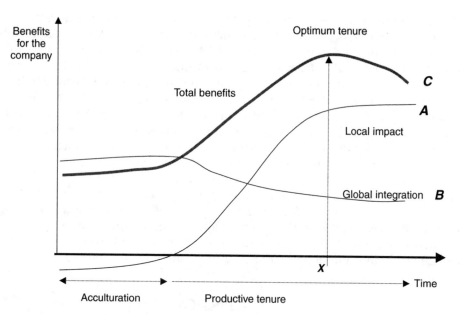

Figure 12.8   Expatriate tenure

across the world. Over time, if the expatriate becomes rooted in the local specificities, the risk is high that she/he will lose the *global spirit* and become *localised*. The combination of the *A* and *B* curves is given by curve *C*, showing an optimum benefit for the company at time *X* that would theoretically be when the assignment finishes. As indicated earlier, several factors affect the shape of the curves: if the acculturation is difficult and the relationships with customers are important, curve *A* moves to the right, making the optimum assignment period much longer.

Support

The overwhelming empirical evidence coming from the studies on expatriation shows that success is very closely correlated with the support and understanding coming from the mother company from which the person is detached. Support can take numerous forms, but is it the *psychological contact* – the feeling that one is not 'forgotten' or 'marginalised' – that matters the most. Some companies have put in place a process of **'mentoring'** by which a manager at 'Headquarters' is in charge of regular communication with an expatriate about personnel/career issues. Companies' internal newspapers should devote a large part of their editorial content to talking about events in world subsidiaries. Visits of key executives should not only include 'business' meetings but also internal dialogues with the detached personnel. In broad terms, an expatriate personnel should have the feeling that their assignment is important for the company.

Career follow-up

Traditionally, the career follow-up issue has been known as the *repatriation* problem. At the end of the assignment, the expatriate is concerned about finding a job at the mother company corresponding to his/her skills and performances. The repatriation problem assumes that the person was going to return to the 'home country'. This is the case for temporarily assigned personnel but is less and less true in the global management context described in Figure 12.3 as the 'global design', where international managers move from position to position in the worldwide corporate network. Further 'returning home' or 'going elsewhere', however, require from the company a *proactive international career management process*. In the research conducted by Steward Blacke and Gregersen (1999), it was found that 25 per cent of professionals returning from overseas assignments then left the company because of a lack of job opportunities. The accumulated experience lost by such attrition is considerable. Companies such as Monsanto prepare the return or the next assignment at least six months before the end of the current assignment: it involves the expatriate, the human resources (HR) management and the line manager to whom the person reports. The returnee indicates his/her preferences, the line managers and the HR department scan the potential job openings during the coming year as well as the returnee's skills and knowledge. They propose several alternatives, generally including additional training for preparation for the next job.

LOCALISATION

Although expatriate personnel serve as vital links of communication and knowledge transfer in the network of worldwide business units, the long-term competitiveness of global firms relies on the contribution and loyalty of *locally recruited personnel*:

- Localisation of managers and staff helps global companies to 'break the language barrier' and penetrate the intricate network of personal and business contacts needed to build and consolidate a presence in the various countries. In China, for instance, the building of relationships (*guanxi*) is still recognised as a major requirement for conducting a business venture.[7] While expatriate managers may be able to build good contacts at senior levels, local managers can gain access to critical relationships, particularly among the medium- and low-level echelons of government and company hierarchies.
- Modern business development also demands a large quantity of talent that the pool of international managers cannot satisfy. A fast-moving consumer good (fmcg) company found that, in order to maintain leadership in China, it had over a period of five years to recruit 2,500 sales people.[8]
- Localisation also reduces expatriate costs.
- Localisation is part of an overall global HR strategy, the aim of which is to attract talent everywhere in the world where the company operates, making the motto 'think globally, act locally' a reality.
- In some case, localisation is perceived by the authorities of emerging nations as a demonstration of the foreign enterprise's commitment to the country. Although in some cases government officials prefer to deal with high-ranking senior expatriates because of their greater decision-making power, they appreciate that below the very top jobs, foreign enterprises will progressively be managed by local nationals. Localisation is therefore an important way of developing beneficial goodwill for future expansion.

The main managerial issues in localisation are in recruitment, retention and career management and performance evaluation, reward practices and cultural differences.

Recruitment, retention and career management

In some countries, foreign firms are perceived favourably by the job market, but not in some others. Japan and Korea have traditionally been places where graduates from leading universities and institutions have had a marked preference for domestic firms. As a consequence, the market for foreign firms' employees has been narrow and foreign firms have suffered a competitive disadvantage in recruitment. In fast-growing emerging countries like China, the demand for skilled personnel far outpaced the supply, creating an unhealthy bidding process, and a high turnover rate.

The global companies' ability to enhance local recruitment depends on three main factors:

- The *image of the company*: firms with well-known branded products are more favourably placed than unknown ones. The latter have to promote themselves by making presentations at universities, giving scholarships, contributing to good causes and engaging in public relations, such as the sponsoring of sporting events or academic contests at schools and universities.
- The *career prospects and the training opportunities*. Firms that have a reputation of procuring good development opportunities will be in a better position to recruit.
- A good understanding of the *local qualifications and of the educational system*. Not all countries have the same technical and higher-education system. A simplistic projection of the US undergraduate/graduate system may miss opportunities to get the best graduates in Germany, France or Japan. In Germany or Japan, enterprises compensate for the highly theoretical academic orientation of the school system by organising some sort of on-the-job training. In France, the best graduate schools are not part of the university system at all.

Financial incentives have to be in line with normal practices – it is illusory to think that over-bidding on salaries will ultimately produce a higher retention rate.

The loyalty of local personnel to a global firm will be based more on career prospects and a subjective assessment of 'fair treatment' than on pure financial compensation. *Fair treatment* is the perception that local employees have an equal treatment with expatriates at a comparable level, and that their career prospects are not limited by a *glass ceiling*. 'Fair treatment' thus implies:

- The ability for local personnel to be able to join the group of 'global managers' if they have the competence and the desire
- Equal opportunities for development (training and career)
- Compensation based on the principle of 'equal job, equal pay' (expatriates' packages on housing/schooling being excluded from the comparison)
- Comparable involvement of local personnel and expatriates in information-sharing, meetings and decision-making sessions. Local personnel should not get the feeling that they are being excluded from important matters.

Performance evaluation, reward practices and cultural differences

The main difficulty in implementing global HRM practices is the need to align performance evaluation and reward processes with cultural differences. A global firm would prefer a standardised approach that fosters the diffusion of a common corporate culture and values as well as facilitating cross-border transfer of personnel. On the other hand, because of cultural differences, standard processes may not have the desired unifying impact and their implementation can be ineffective. In Asia, for instance, the most pronounced cultural divergences are found in four domains:

- *Giving and receiving feedback*. Most Western performance evaluation processes are based on the assumption that objective, open feedback between supervisors and employees is used. Oriental cultures have difficulty in accepting these assumptions. These are 'high-context' cultures (Hofstede), meaning that it is difficult to untangle what performance is due to the individual and what is due to the situation. In addition, feedback is considered as unidirectional: employees do not challenge their boss. Therefore, any 'unjust' judgement will be taken but not openly discussed, and may generate covert dissident behaviour, although the supervisor may think that the judgement has been 'accepted'.
- *Individual versus group performance*. As mentioned in previous chapters, most non-Western cultures place a higher importance on group belonging and assimilation than on individualism. Too great a focus on individual performance may encourage feelings of unfair favouritism, and ultimately induce group resistance or sabotage of management policies.
- *System-led versus personalised evaluation processes*. In the Asia Pacific region, loyalty is often to a person or a group (clan) rather than to an organisation. Neutral, mechanical systems based on numerical ranking and statistical distribution are not well understood. People prefer to be appreciated/evaluated by their supervisor through a holistic rather than an analytic approach.
- *Social impact of rewards or sanctions (importance of face saving)*. Reward and sanction not only affect individuals in their private life but also affect their standing in their community, hence the importance of face saving: ascribing blame in front of colleagues is considered unacceptable.

The dilemma is obvious: how can a company manage globally and still take into account the many cultural specificities of the countries in which it operates? There is no single answer to this, but the example of leading global firms such as Hewlett Packard, IBM, Unilever, ABB or Shell indicates that the progressive reinforcement of a strong corporate culture though education and career management gradually fosters a worldwide acceptance of common practices.

An example of localisation within an overall framework is given in Mini-Example 12.2, ABB in China.

Mini-Example 12.2   ABB's localisation programme in China, late 1990s

Asea Brown Boveri (ABB) had 15 joint ventures and eight representative offices in China in early 1997, and employed a total of 80 expatriate managers. The company reckoned that by the year 2000 it would have 25 joint ventures, and if nothing changed, its number of expatriate managers would then balloon to 250! If, on average, an expatriate manager cost an additional US$200,000–300,000 per year on top of his normal salary, 250 expatriate managers would increase the compensation bill by more than US$50 million per year.

The company set up a 'localisation of management committee' with the intention of locally staffing its middle-management positions within three years and its top management positions within five years. To show the company's commitment to the goal, its Vice-President of Human Resources for China sat on the committee as chairman. The committee, among other things, had the key task of identifying high-potential candidates among its China operations, and ensuring that these high-potential candidates possessed the necessary training and good communication with the operating units. More importantly, the company explicitly required its expatriate managers to set targets of localisation in their operations. Although ABB understood that expatriate managers were under pressure to meet short-term business goals, top management thought that the development of local managers was a long-term strategic concern and should be given priority. The expatriate managers were thus assessed not just on their business performance, but also on their ability to develop local managers. ABB believed that management must continuously scout for, identify and keep track of internal talent. High-potential staff at ABB were identified through a performance appraisal system. Then, they were prepared for higher positions or greater responsibility by providing them with the necessary training and promoting them to more challenging positions as early as possible. Upper-level managers were also instructed to support and coach newly promoted managers. The company reported potential local managers to its corporate headquarters in Zurich.

Although most companies embraced the goal of localisation of managers and tried to implement it, ABB went one step further by systematically collecting and reporting data to monitor local performance. Its HR department in the Beijing holding company had to provide management with a monthly report which detailed the development of HR in the company, such as the training and promotion of local staff, and also positions available in the company. It also had to complete a monthly international expatriate assignment form, explaining to its regional headquarters why certain positions were filled by expatriates rather than by local Chinese. This reporting system provided feedback on how well the company was implementing its goal, and also served as a reminder of the pace and urgency of the localisation programme.

ABB achieved some tangible success with this programme. At its China holding company in early 1997, there were three local Chinese divisional managers (compared with none a year earlier), five local Chinese departmental managers and 20 local Chinese segmental managers. At its joint ventures, the company in 1997 had nearly 100 local Chinese divisional managers, departmental managers and segmental managers. By the year 2000, it had only 70 expatriate managers instead of the projected 250.

Source: Lasserre and Ching (1997).

SKILLS DEVELOPMENT

Global managers' skills are a combination of the *organisational roles* they have to fulfil and some key *individual characteristics*.

Roles

Bartlett and Ghoshal (1992) have identified three main global managers' roles:

(a) Business managers operate in *global business units* and 'further global scale efficiency and competitiveness'. Their task 'requires not only the perspectives to recognize opportunities and risks across national and functional boundaries but also the skills to coordinate activities and link capabilities across those barriers'. Their skills are a combination of *strategic thinking, organisational design, resource allocation* and *co-ordination*.

(b) Country managers operate in *local subsidiaries*. Their role is to meet local customer needs, to defend their market position and to satisfy local government requirements. Their skills are a combination of *entrepreneurship, competitive and market intelligence collection* and *local resource acquisition*.

(c) Functional managers sit at *corporate or regional headquarters*. Their primary role is to be an *organiser* and *co-ordinate worldwide learning*. They make sure that technologies and best practices are transferred across businesses and countries. 'Using informational networks, they create channels of communicating specialized information and repositories for specialised knowledge.'

During their career, global managers will normally experience all three roles in different locations and businesses. In case of conflict, it helps to create an attitude of mutual understanding and conflict resolution if one knows that during one's own career path, one is likely to be in the position of the other party at some time.

Individual skills

The set of managers' individual skills most frequently cited in research involves eight facets[9]:

(a) *Professional*: strong mastery of business knowledge in the relevant field (marketing, technology, finance, operations)
(b) *Cultural*: ability to respect and deal with cultural difference and avoid stereotyping
(c) *Negotiating*: ability to balance conflicting objectives with internal and external parties
(d) *Relational*: ability to relate easily with other people and show empathy
(e) *Leadership*: ability to set objectives, organise and motivate subordinates
(f) *Intellectual*: ability to balance global objectives with local realities
(g) *Courage* and *determination*
(h) *Flexibility* in moving from one role to another.

Mini-Example 12.3 shows how Percy Barnevick, the former CEO of ABB, described the characteristics he expected from global managers in his company.

Mini-Example 12.3 Characteristics of global managers

- Tough-skinned
- Fast on their feet
- Good technical and commercial backgrounds
- Ability to lead
- Open minds: respect of other ways of doing things
- Patience
- Stamina
- Humility
- Respect for other cultures
- Work experience in two or three countries
- Incisive
- Ability to sort out the debris of cultural excuses
- Generous
- People developers

Source: Kets de Vries (1994).

Developing skills through job rotation and training

Global skill development, known also as 'global leaders development', mixes career management with formal training, facilitating skills acquisition as well as coaching in the various global roles that managers are likely to play during their careers. Figure 12.9 shows how a global oil company has orchestrated the development of its international managers.

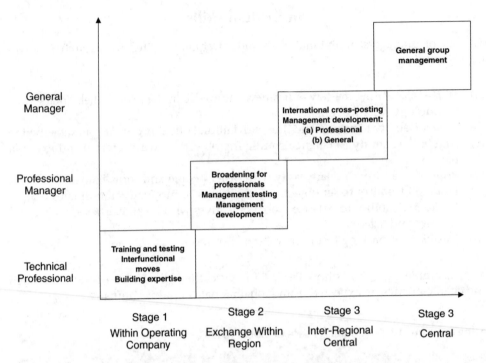

Figure 12.9 Global management development in a global oil company

In management seminars at various levels, global firms make sure that a mix of country managers, global managers and functional managers of various nationalities participate, favouring the expansion of a 'networking culture.'

SUMMARY AND KEY POINTS

1. There are four main issues of global HRM:
   - *Global human resource wheel*: personnel management and proportion of global/ local managers
   - *Expatriate management*: career management of global managers
   - *Localisation*: need to recruit and motivate local personnel
   - *Global skill development*: need to develop skills appropriate for global management.
2. There are two types of managers in global firms:
   - *Global managers*: career evolves by successive cross-border appointments
   - *Local managers*: career evolves within a country subsidiary.
3. Global human resource wheel (see table below).

	Multi-domestic design	Global design
Number of global managers	Small	Large
Proportion of local personnel	High	Low
Proportion of temporary detachments	Relatively less	Relatively more
Can local personnel join the global manager group?	No	Yes

4. Expatriate management

  ▪ There are two types of *nationals*:
    – Third-country nationals (TCN)
    – Parent-country nationals (PCN)

  ▪ Expatriate *challenges* – four main aspects:
    – *Job*
      (a) Inability of manager to adapt
      (b) Inability of manager's partner/family to adapt
    – *Local insertion*
      (a) Preparation
      (b) Culture shock
      (c) Political/social skills
      (d) Local acculturation (process by which group members from one culture adapt to the culture of the other group)
    – *Family*
      (a) Adaptation
      (b) Education
    – *Career*
      (a) Selection
      (b) Rotation
      (c) Re-entry

  ▪ Expatriate *failure*:
    – Measured by *recall rate* (proportion of assigned personnel who fail to complete their predetermined contract)
    – Main causes:
      (a) Inability of manager to adapt
      (b) Inability of manager's partner/family to adapt
      (c) Family-related problems
      (d) Manager's personality or emotional immaturity
      (e) Manager's inability to cope with responsibility
      (f) Manager's lack of technical competence
      (g) Manager's lack of motivation

  ▪ Reasons for expatriation *success*:
    – Recognition of cross-borders assignments by corporate headquarters
    – Corporate support/understanding given to expatriate personnel

  ▪ Four expatriate *attitudes* (four 'Fs'):
    – *Flight*: expatriates preserve own cultural identities, isolate themselves and avoid socialising with local community
    – *Fight*: expatriates criticise host countries, claim superiority of their own cultures and avoid socialising with locals
    – *Follow*: expatriates willing to embrace local culture and assimilate, gradually lose connection with global headquarters

     – *Fit*: cosmopolitans who can immerse themselves into the local culture and simultaneously preserve their own cultures

■ Expatriate *policy*:
- *Strategic – transfer policies* can:
  - (a) Fill position
  - (b) Develop manager
  - (c) Develop organisation
- *Selection and preparation*:
  - (a) *Choice* of expatriates: identifying people with: tolerance for ambiguity; behavioural flexibility; goal orientation; sociability and interest in other people; empathy; ability to be non-judgemental; meta-communication skills
  - (b) *Preparation* of expatriates: clearly communicated career plan to avoid re-entry problems; cultural and logistical preparation for the employee/ family (e.g. pre-assignment trips); assessment centres to provide tailored training after comparing current with required skills
- *Compensation*: additional compensation for the difference in living conditions, prices and burden on family (e.g. hardship allowance)
- *Tenure*
  - (a) *Duration*: company policy or function of time needed to learn business rules and build effective business relationships, depending on 'contextual hardship' of the country
  - (b) Optimal tenure length is determined by the combined effect of the expatriates' local impact on business results (which *increases* over time) and the benefits of global integration (which *decreases* over time)
- *Support*: mentoring, communication and assurance that the staff are not 'forgotten'
- *Career follow-up*: proactive international career management process to ensure staff have a desirable job after the overseas posting and to avoid 'repatriation problems'.

5. Localisation:

■ Localisation is *important*:
  - (a) Can build/maintain personal and business contacts without the potential problems caused by language barriers
  - (b) Local staff better qualified for business development which requires local sensitivity/knowledge
  - (c) Reduces expensive expatriate costs
  - (d) Allows a company to reap the benefits of implementing a 'think globally, act locally' policy
  - (e) Shows commitment to the country, which can be of concern to local government and/or people

■ *Concerns*:
  - (a) *Recruitment*: scarcity of local talent favours local instead of international firms
  - (b) *Retention*: loyalty of local staff may be hard to secure and companies can encourage loyalty through good career prospects and 'fair treatment' instead of financial compensation

      (c) *Career management*: local staff need career management and equal opportunity to become 'global managers' with an absence of a 'glass ceiling' for local staff

      (d) *Performance evaluation/cultural difference*: dilemma of implementing a standardised approach while taking cultural differences into account

      (e) *Reward practices*: awareness of importance of rewards on private lives and social standing.

6. Global skill development:

- Three main roles of global managers:
  - *Business* managers operate in global business units:
    - (a) Possess ability to co-ordinate activities and link capabilities
    - (b) Role is to increase global-scale efficiency/competitiveness
  - *Country* managers who operate in local subsidiaries:
    - (a) Possess skills of entrepreneurship, capacity to build local resources and collect competitive intelligence
    - (b) Role is to meet local customer needs, defend market position and satisfy local governments' requirements
  - *Functional* managers who operate at corporate or regional headquarters:
    - (a) Have informational networks
    - (b) Role is to organise/co-ordinate worldwide learning and transfer technologies and best practices

- Global skills
  - *For individual*:
    - (a) Professional
    - (b) Cultural
    - (c) Negotiating
    - (d) Relational
    - (e) Leadership
    - (f) Intellectual
    - (g) Courage and determination
    - (h) Flexibility
  - *Skill development*:
    - (a) Job rotation
    - (b) Ongoing training.

Learning assignments

1 What are the relative advantages and disadvantages of having a high proportion of global managers to local ones?

2 What are the main difficulties that expatriate managers are confronted with when assigned to an emerging country?

3 What are the main problems of short expatriate assignments?

4 One of the main problems global firms are confronted with in countries such as China is the turnover of local managers. How can this be prevented?

5 What will be the key content of a management programme designed to train managers to become 'country managers'?

Key words

- Acculturation
- Career plan
- Compensation
- Expatriates
- Global leaders development
- Global managers
- Local managers
- Mentoring
- Missions
- Retention
- Roles
- Skills
- Tenure

Web resources

<http://expat.ft.com/ft/gx.cgi/ftc?pagename = View&c = Collection&cid = IXLVQANC4DC>
Financial Times' section on expatriates.

<http://www.cio.com/forums/global/management.html>
Globalisation Research Centre – Managing a global enterprise.

<http://www.ipma-hr.org/>
A link to the International Personnel Management Association.

<http://www.mckinseyquarterly.com/category_archive.asp?tk = 86032::&L3 = 29>
McKinsey Quarterly – Leadership.

<http://www.mckinseyquarterly.com/category_archive.asp?tk = 86032::&L3 = 31>
McKinsey Quarterly – Talent.

Notes

1. This case study is an adaptation of Doz (1999); the names of the company and of participants have been changed as the present adaptation is not a precise replication of the original case.
2. Lasserre *et al.* (1997).
3. This definition is from F. Rieger and D. Wong-Rieger, 'The Application of Acculturation Theory to Structuring and Strategy Formulation in International Firms', a research paper quoted in Tung (1988, pp. 125–44).
4. Steward Blacke and Gregersen (1999, p. 4).
5. Rottenberg (1999).
6. Stahl (2001, pp. 206–7).
7. Davies *et al.* (1995, pp. 207–14).
8. Hsieh, Lavoie and Samek (1999, pp. 93–101).

9. Bartlett and Ghoshal (1992, pp. 124–32); the skills quoted below are from this article.
10. Adler and Bartholomew (1992, pp. 52–65); Mendenhall (2001, pp. 1–17).

References and further reading

Books and articles

Adler, Nancy and Susan Bartholomew, 'Managing Globally Competent People', *The Academy of Management Executive*, 6, 1992, pp. 52–65.

Bartlett, Christopher and Sumantra Ghoshal, 'What is a Global Manager?', *Harvard Business Review*, September–October 1992, pp. 124–32.

Blacke, J. Steward and Hal Gregersen, 'The Right Way to Manage Expatriates', *Harvard Business Review*, March–April 1999, p. 4.

Davies, H., T.K.P Leung, S.T.K. Luk, and Y.H. Wong, 'The Benefit of *Guanxi*: The Value of Relationships in Developing the Chinese Market', *Industrial Marketing Management*, 24, 1995, pp. 207–14.

Doz, Yves L., 'Ciba-Geigy Management Development', INSEAD Case Study, no. 11/1999-1153, 1999.

Edstrom, A. and J. Galbraith, 'Transfer of Managers as a Coordination and Control Strategy in Multinational Organizations', *Administrative Science Quarterly*, June 1977.

Evans, Paul, Vladimir Pucik and Jean-Louis Barsoux, *The Global Challenge: Frameworks for International Human Resources Management*. New York: McGraw-Hill, 2002.

Hsieh, Tsun-yan, Johanne Lavoie and Robert A.P. Samek, 'Think Global, Hire Local', *McKinsey Quarterly*, 4, 1999a, pp. 93–101.

Hsieh, Tsun-yan, Johanne Lavoie and Robert A.P. Samek, 'Are You Taking Your Expatriate Talent Seriously?', *McKinsey Quarterly*, 3, 1999b, pp. 71–83.

Kets de Vries, Manfred, 'Percy Barnevick and ABB', INSEAD Case Study 05/94-4308, 1994.

Lasserre, Philippe and Poy-Seng Ching, 'Human Resource Management in China and the Localization Challenge', *Journal of Asian Business*, 13(4), 1997, pp. 85–99.

Lasserre, Philippe, Lyman Porter, Gordon Redding and Pamela Steward, *Managing International Assignments in Asia: Individual and Organizational Challenge*. Boston, MA: The International Consortium for Executive Education, 1997.

Mendenhall, Mark E., 'New Perspectives on Expatriate Adjustment and its Relationship to Global Leadership Development', in M. Mendenhall, T. Kühlman and Günter Stahl, (eds), *Developing Global Leaders*. Westport, CT: Quorum Books, 2001, pp. 1–17.

Parsons, Andrew J., 'Nestlé: The Visions of Local Managers', *McKinsey Quarterly*, 2, 1996, pp. 5–29.

Quelch, John A. and Helen Bloom, 'The Return of the Country Manager', *McKinsey Quarterly*, 2, 1996, pp. 31–43.

Rieger, F. and D. Wong-Rieger, 'The Application of Acculturation Theory to Structuring and Strategy Formulation in International Firms', quoted in Rosali Tung, 'American Expatriates: From Neophytes to Cosmopolitans', *Journal of World Business*, 33(2), 1988, pp. 125–44.

Rosenweig, Philip M., 'Colgate-Palmolive: Managing International Careers', Harvard Business School Case Study 9-394-184, 1994.

Rottenberg, Stephanie, 'Prepare for the Overseas Trip', *Harvard Management Update*. Boston, MA: Harvard Business School Publishing, U9904C, 1999.

Sutari, Vesa and Christelle Tornikoski, 'The Challenge of Expatriate Compensation: The Sources of Satisfaction and Dissatisfaction Among Expatriates', *International Journal of Human Resource Management*, 12, 2001, pp. 389–94.

Stahl, Günter, 'Using Assessment Centers as Tools for Global Leadership Development: An Exploratory Study', in M. Mendenhall, T. Kühlman and Günter Stahl (eds), *Developing Global Leaders*. Westport, CT: Quorum Books, 2001, pp. 198–201.

Tung, Rosalie, 'Expatriate Assignments: Enhancing Success and Minimizing Failure', *The Academy of Management Executive*, 1, 1987, pp. 117–25.

Tung, Rosalie, 'American Expatriates: From Neophytes to Cosmopolitans', *Journal of World Business*, 33(2), 1988a, pp. 125–44.

Tung, Rosalie, *The New Expatriates: Managing Human Resources Abroad*. Cambridge, MA: Ballinger, 1988b.

Journal

International Journal of Human Resource Management, Routledge, United Kingdom <http://figaro. catchword.com/rpsv/catchword/routledg/09585192/contp1-1.htm>.

13

Global financial management

The world of global finance has been evolving quite dramatically since 1980. Alongside traditional financing instruments like international promissory notes that existed in the Middle Ages, a vast array of facilities has been opened to firms operating across borders, ranging from hedging techniques to cross-border listing and swaps. Firms operating globally face several challenges related to the management of their cash flows, the cost of their capital and their exposure to risks. The domain of international finance is vast, and cannot be fully analysed within this chapter; a list of specialised references is given at the end (p. 376). We shall address some key issues in global financial management, but the discussion will be limited to managerial issues and will avoid the technical examples that more specialised books often provide.[1]

Four central global financial management issues are discussed in this chapter (Figure 13.1):

- **Currency risk**: exposure and hedging: how to protect oneself against currency fluctuation
- **Project finance**: how to evaluate international investments, and how to finance them
- **Capital structure**: how to take advantage of global financial market to raise equity and deal with debt
- **Trade finance**: the traditional instruments of financing exports/ imports of goods.

At the end of the chapter one should be able:

- To understand the nature of the risks generated by currency fluctuations
- To understand the hedging techniques available to manage currency fluctuations

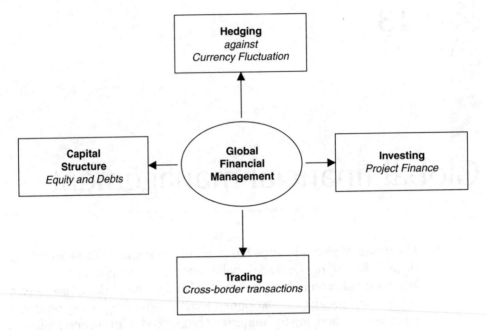

Figure 13.1 Key issues in global financial management

- To compute the cash flow of an international project and assess its economic return using either the Adjusted Present Value (APV) method or the Cost of Capital Adjustment (CCA) method
- To understand the benefits of cross-listing
- To understand the benefits and pitfalls of raising debt internationally
- To understand the mechanics and know-how of the various instruments of trade finance for global companies.

HEDGING AGAINST CURRENCY FLUCTUATIONS

The most prevalent feature of international finance is that *currencies fluctuate in value against each other*. Figure 13.2 shows the fluctuation of four major global currencies: the US dollar, the euro, the yen and the pound sterling.

Companies operating globally are by definition exposed to currency fluctuations. Their economic value can be affected in three ways:

- Their competitive advantage can deteriorate or be enhanced owing to the direct or indirect impact of change in currencies values. This is a **strategic exposure** that translates into a change in *future cash flow potential*.

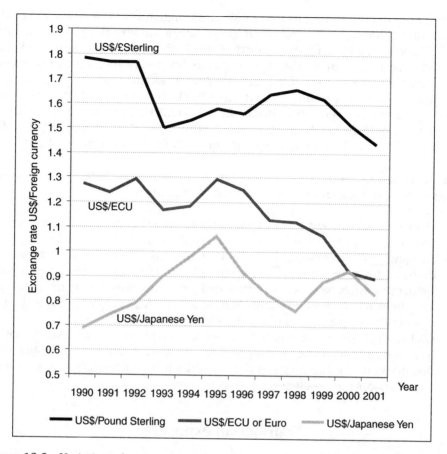

Figure 13.2 Variation of major currencies against the US$, 1990–2001, yearly average

Source: Federal Reserve Bank of the United States

- The short-term cash flow resulting from existing financial or commercial commitments can be affected positively or negatively. This is a **transaction exposure**.
- The reported valuation of assets and liabilities of global firms is also affected by currencies variations that in turn may affect the market perception and ultimately the market value of firms. This is the **translation exposure**.

Strategic exposure

Currency fluctuations may have a direct and indirect effect on companies' competitive advantages by increasing their costs to an uncompetitive level or by giving competitors with weakened currencies a sudden competitive edge. This type of exposure is most significant in products or services that serve price-sensitive customers, which is the case for most commodities. But even in differentiated products or services, like aero-engines or cars, a sharp increase in one country's currency value may lead to strategic disadvantage. In early 2001, Nissan was considering exiting from manufacturing its new small car in England because of the high value of the pound sterling. The group felt at a strategic disadvantage in maintaining manufacturing facilities in the country. Global firms are better positioned than domestic players to deal with strategic exposure because of their diversified market portfolio. They can also relocate production facilities, although it implies a lot of flexibility in resources transfer for effective implementation, and this may affect their reputation as responsible citizens in the countries from which they exit. In practice, it is difficult to take drastic action of this type without being certain of the *structural weakness* of a currency, which can be difficult to predict, as Figure 13.2 shows.

Hedging against this type of exposure is a matter of strategic product and geographic *positioning* and *global deployment of productive assets:*

- Hedging with strategic product positioning consists of developing products (or services) for price-insensitive market segments though *differentiation*
- Hedging with geographical positioning consists in *balancing sales and production* within exchange zones; a pure global company whose revenues and productive assets were evenly distributed across the dollar zone, the euro zone and the yen zone would be sheltered, to a large degree, against the damaging competitive consequences of currency variations
- Global deployment of productive assets would consist of *sourcing* either in-house or from external suppliers in low-cost countries like China that, despite its strong currency position, is still a low-cost manufacturing base for a large number of products.

Transaction exposure

Transaction exposure is the risks that currency fluctuations impose on existing contractual engagements and that may result in unexpected losses. This occurs when a company borrows in a given currency to finance a productive asset that generates revenues in another currency. This also occurs when a company operating in a given country has signed a sales or supply contract that will be billed and paid in the future in a different currency. The positive or negative variation of the exchange rate will induce transaction gains or transaction losses. Obviously, transaction losses can damage company wealth while transaction gains give a speculative profit. Confronted with the probability of such gains or losses, the company can take two positions – a *speculative* attitude, betting on the probability that there will be a transaction gain, or a *hedging* perspective, making sure as soon as the contact is signed the company will receive/pay a certain amount in its own currency whatever the exchange rate variation. There are several *hedging techniques* that can be used to guard against currencies variation. The most frequent ones are: forward contracts, future contracts, swap contracts and options. Other techniques such as *leading and lagging* or *netting* can also be used but they are not considered as 'hedging' in the sense that there is still a certain degree of uncertainty. Appendix 13.1 (p. 352) gives a full numerical example of the main hedging techniques with a practical example of a US champagne importer.

Hedging techniques

(a) **Forward contracts** consist of buying at a fixed future date a fixed quantity of a given currency at a fixed exchange rate (the *forward rate*). A European importer of Japanese goods will buy forward yen in order to be certain of paying his Japanese supplier at a known exchange rate. The same European who exports to the United States will sell the US dollars he will receive as payment at a fixed exchange rate. An alternative method that produces exactly the same results is for the exporter to borrow euros, transform them into yen for the amount needed at the prevailing known rate of exchange on the day of the order. The yen are placed in a yen money market account and, at the date of the settlement, are used to pay the Japanese supplier; the interest gained is used to pay the interest due on the euro borrowing. The company will have to bear only the interest differential between the yen and the euros, which is exactly how the forward rate is calculated. In case of the exporter to the United States, the company will borrow dollars and transform them into euros, put the euros in a money market account and, when it receives the money from the customer, use the dollars to pay back the loan; the interest gained on the euros pays the interest on the dollar loan. Forward contracts are the most common hedging techniques used by corporations.

(b) **Future contracts** are similar to forward contracts but they are standard financial instruments traded in *futures markets* such as London, Chicago or Singapore. They have a given size and a given expiry date.

(c) **Options** are contracts in which one buys the right to sell (*put* option) or buy (*call* option) a currency at a given exchange rate (the *strike* price) at the end of a maturity period. If at the end of the period the spot rate of the currency varies unfavourably, then one will not exercise one's right. This option has a price (the *option premium*).

(d) **Currency swaps** contracts are contracts intermediated by a swap bank that matches long-terms loans issued by two companies in their respective currency zones for use in the other company currency zone. Company X borrows in currency A to be used in country B with loan repayment generated in currency B, while company Y borrows in currency B to be used in country A with loan repayment generated in currency A. The two companies can swap their loan. Assuming a perfect symmetry of the two loans, which the swap bank can arrange, there is a perfect hedging for company X and Y. The swap contracts are good hedging techniques for long term-currency exposures.

Non-hedging techniques

Two other common forms of reducing transaction exposures are *leading and lagging* or *netting*:

(a) **Leading and lagging** is a technique by which one can collect receivables early (*leading*) if they are nominated in 'soft' currencies and delay (*lagging*) collection of receivables nominated in 'hard' currencies. Similarly, one would try to delay (lagging) payment of payables nominated in 'soft' currencies and accelerate payment of payables nominated in 'hard' currencies.

(b) **Netting** is a technique used by treasurers of global firms that have centralised cash management for subsidiaries that trade with each other. Only the *net cash balance* resulting from the forecast inter-trade movement in their respective currencies is actually transformed and hedged into the currency that has a creditor position. If a German factory is planning to sell 1 million euros of components to a Singaporean company and the Singaporean factory is expected to sell 3 million Singapore dollars of finished products, the German factory will actually hedge Singapore $650,000, which represents the net position at the rate of S$1.54 per euro at the time of the plan. This reduces the amount of currency exposed and the hedging costs. There are actually two different netting systems: *bilateral* netting (netting between pairs of subsidiaries) and *multilateral* netting (netting of all transactions and transfer of the net to a central centre).

Translation exposure

This type of exposure reflects the effects that change in currency values have on the financial statements of global firms, and therefore on their *profits* and *book valuation*. There are several techniques used to adjust income statements and balance sheets for currency fluctuations. The two main methods are the *monetary/non-monetary* method and the *current* method. An example of those methods is presented in Appendix 13.2 (p. 357). In practice, this type of exposure has relevance only to the extent that the economic source of value creation and valuation, the *cash flow*, is affected by difference in reported translations. This may be the case concerning the tax consequences of currency fluctuation. Accounting standards require that translation exposure be reported, but market valuation is affected only to the extent to which reporting translation exposure reveals the strategic and transaction risks to which the firm is exposed.

PROJECT FINANCE

International project finance deals with the *valuation* and the *financing* of productive investments (different from financial portfolio investments) in different countries from that of the investor. In a global firm, one may have a multitude of configurations of international investments. A Swiss-based pharmaceutical firm may use a French subsidiary to implement a project in China jointly with a German subsidiary because it may relate to a product in which the French subsidiary has global responsibilities and for which the German engineering subsidiary has competences in building plants. Project finance may concern greenfield wholly-owned investments, acquisitions or joint ventures. The two key issues in project finance are: How to value them? How to finance them?

Project valuation

As in any economic valuation, the value of an investment for an investor is equal to the value of *future cash flows discounted with the weighted average cost of capital minus the discounted value of debts.* The only complexities that an international investment generates are the strategic and transaction currency exposures and the country risks. As far as currency fluctuations are concerned, hedging techniques can possibly transform uncertainties into certainty in cash flow valuation, but what about country risks and currency risks when hedging is not available? There are two fundamental approaches for taking this type of risk into consideration: adjusting the cash flows or adjusting the cost of capital:

1. *Cash flow adjustment,* also known as **adjusted present value (APV)**, is a technique in which
    (a) specific downside adverse risks are identified
    (b) their impact on the cash flow is calculated
    (c) probability of their occurrence is determined
    (d) cash flows are adjusted using the probabilistic distribution
    (e) cash flows are translated into the investor's currency using Purchasing Power Parity (PPP)differences as a proxy for currency fluctuations
    (f) cash flows are discounted using the investor's cost of capital.

Appendix 13.3 (p. 361) gives a simplified example of this method, considered the most appropriate by financial theorists.

2. *Cost of capital adjustments* is applied to the cost of capital by introducing a premium risk to the cost of equity. Professor Donald Lessard from MIT (1996) argues that adjusting the risk premium by introducing a **'country beta'** to the cost of capital is more appropriate in case of investments in emerging countries when risks are not diversifiable.

Project Financing

There are two sources of project financing

1. *Generic financing* provided by the corporation that uses its global equity and debt financing capabilities
2. *Specific equity or debt financing* provided by various financial institutions.

Specific **equity project financing** is usually provided for projects in emerging countries by development banks. Equity for projects in industrialised market economies is financed through normal market mechanisms; either public (stock exchange), private (venture capital) or directly by the corporation using its global financing capabilities. The major development banks that provide equity financing are listed in Appendix 13.4 (p. 368).

Debt project financing is provided by banking institutions, development banks, government aid, or suppliers' credits. When provided by banks or suppliers' credits, debt financing is backed by *credit risk insurance.* When projects are structured as joint ventures, financing can also come from local institutions and governments.

GLOBAL CAPITAL STRUCTURE

The major financing issue for a global company is to decide where to generate equity and debt financing, and in what proportion. The overall objective is to minimise the cost of capital in order to enhance the *value-creation capabilities* of the company. When the cost of capital of a company decreases, the value of the company increases. Finance theory tells us that the cost of capital, both equity and debt, is a function of macroeconomic factors as well as the systematic risk[2] (non-diversifiable) incurred by the company. Finance theory makes a distinction between *unsystematic* risks (that can be diversified) and *systematic* risks (that cannot be diversified). Unsystematic risks can be reduced by diversification; a global firm reduces its unsystematic risks by having a portfolio of investments across countries, but cannot avoid the inherent risks of investing in a particular country owing to the political and economic situation of that country (systematic risks). Since in a global economy different countries have different macroeconomic outlooks and different risk profiles, and different institutions to manage them, one can expect the cost of capital to be different from country to country, giving an opportunity to optimise one's portfolio of financial sources in order to minimise cost. This creates the possibility of **cross-listing** and international bond issues.

In a pure global world in which free trade and free movement of capital, persons and goods as well as market-based institutions prevailed, such international portfolio optimisation would not exist: there would be one single capital market. The capital markets would be *integrated* and raising money in the United States, in Europe or Japan would cost the same. But since the world is not fully global, at least in the early twenty-first century, capital markets are still different in their structure, costs and risks, and are *fragmented*. Fragmentation can be observed in two ways. First, one can compare the cost of capital between countries. Academic researchers have found that the cost of capital has historically differed but has tended to converge, at least in the industrialised world (Mini-Example 13.1). Correlations between returns on various stock markets show high positive correlations (Table 13.1) except in Japan, which shows nearly zero correlation with the rest of the world. The Japanese stock market, during the period of the analysis, was not integrated.

Mini-Example 13.1 Academic research on international differences in the cost of capital

- McCauley and Zimmer (1994) found that there were different costs of capital between Japan, Germany, the United States and the United Kingdom for the period between 1978–92.
- A study by René Stulz (1999) found that the effect of globalisation on the decrease in cost of capital is significant but small. For globalisation to reduce the cost of capital, the shareholder base has to become truly global.

Source: McCauley and Zimmer (1994); Stulz (1999).

Table 13.1 Summary statistics of monthly returns for some stock markets, 1986–2001, correlation coefficients

Stockmarket	WORLD	AUS	BEL	CAN	FRA	GER	HK	ITA	JAP	NL	SWE	SW	UK
WORLD													
AUS	0.92												
BEL	0.95	0.91											
CAN	0.96	0.86	0.83										
FRA	0.99	0.89	0.92	0.96									
GER	0.98	0.91	0.95	0.93	0.98								
HK	0.86	0.95	0.81	0.81	0.83	0.84							
ITA	0.94	0.77	0.90	0.90	0.95	0.94	0.67						
JAP	−0.03	0.02	−0.15	0.01	−0.07	−0.12	0.04	−0.12					
NL	0.98	0.94	0.97	0.92	0.96	0.98	0.87	0.92	−0.13				
SWE	0.97	0.85	0.86	0.97	0.97	0.96	0.81	0.92	0.02	0.93			
SW	0.97	0.93	0.98	0.88	0.94	0.97	0.85	0.91	−0.16	0.99	0.90		
UK	0.98	0.93	0.98	0.91	0.96	0.98	0.85	0.92	−0.14	0.99	0.92	0.99	
US	1.00	0.90	0.95	0.95	0.99	0.98	0.83	0.95	−0.11	0.98	0.96	0.97	0.98

Source: Monthly MSCI stock market returns in US$ is from DataStream, August 1986–July 2001.

Cross-listing

Cross-listing occurs when a firm lists its equity shares on one or more foreign stock exchanges besides its home-country exchange. There are many reasons for a company to cross-list. Four proposed benefits are:

- Cross-listing allows a company to reach a *wider investor base,* which can potentially boost demand and hence liquidity for the company shares. Increased demand for a company's stock may increase the share price, which can lower a company's cost of capital.
- Cross-listing creates a *secondary* market for the company's shares and establishes recognition of the company in a new capital market, thus paving the way for the firm to source new equity or debt capital from local investors as demands dictate.
- Cross-listing has the secondary effect of *projecting the company's name and its products* in the foreign country where it is listed.
- By widening the investor base through cross-listing, there is a potential benefit of protection from a *hostile takeover* of the firm.

Cross-listing also raises some concerns. The company incurs cost in order to comply with the disclosure and listing requirements required by the foreign exchange and regulatory authorities. Secondly, volatility of the stock in one stock market can affect the volatility of the same stock selling in another stock market. Cross-listing also provides an easy means for foreign investors to purchase a company's stock, which can potentially lead to a foreign investor challenging the domestic control of

Table 13.2   Country distribution of overseas listing for various stock exchanges, 1998

Country	Foreign companies hosted (F)		Total domestic listings (D)		Ratio (F)/(D)
	Sample*	FIBV**	At home	Abroad	
Argentina	0	0	131	18	0.00
Australia	41	60	1,162	115	0.04
Belgium*–Brussels	98	122	146	35	0.67
Canada–Toronto	37	49	1384	264	0.03
France–Paris	150	183	914	73	0.16
Germany–Frankfurt	185	208	741	122	0.25
Ireland	13	21	79	73	0.16
Israel–Tel-Aviv	0	1	661	88	0.00
Italy	4	4	239	37	0.02
Japan–Tokyo	60	52	1,838	209	0.03
Mexico	0	4	191	31	0.00
Netherlands–Amsterdam	149	144	212	140	0.70
New Zealand	25	61	122	24	0.21
Sweden–Stockholm	17	18	258	48	0.07
Switzerland	168	193	232	33	0.72
UK–London	409	466	1,957	177	0.21
USA–NYSE/Nasdaq	615	893	7,555	425	0.08

Notes: *Sample = Sample of 2,248 listings studied in the source paper.
**FIBV = International Federation of Stock Exchanges.
Source: Sarkissian and Schill (2000).

the company. Table 13.2 summarises country distribution of overseas listings (1998) for various stock exchanges.

International bond market

The international bond market is another way in which multinationals can source new debt capital. When markets are imperfect, international financing can lower the firm's cost of capital – for instance, eurobond financing is usually cheaper than domestic bond financing.

- The international bond market consists of *foreign bonds and eurobonds*, which compete with domestic bonds for funding
- A *foreign bond issue* is offered by a foreign borrower and the foreign bond issue is denominated in the local currency of the buyer of the bonds
- A *eurobond issue* is denominated in a foreign currency to the buyer, a German borrower issues a dollar-denominated bond to investors in the United Kingdom, for instance
- A *global bond issue* is an offering by a single borrower to investors in North America, Europe and Asia.

Table 13.3 is a summary of various types of bond instruments.

Table 13.3 Types of international bonds

Types of bonds	Brief description	Payoff at maturity
Straight fixed rate	▪ Fixed annual coupon payment as a percentage of face value of the bond	Currency of issue
Floating-rate note	▪ Coupon payments which are indexed to some reference, such as three-month US dollar LIBOR*	Currency of issue
Convertible bond	▪ Allows investors to exchange bond for a predetermined number of equity shares of the issuer	Currency of issue or conversion to equity shares
Bonds with equity warrants	▪ Straight fixed-rate bonds with an additional call option that allows bondholder to purchase equity shares under specified conditions	Currency of issue
Zero-coupon bond	▪ Sold at discount from face value ▪ No coupon payments over its life	Currency of issue
Dual-currency bond	▪ Straight fixed-rate bonds issued and paid coupon in one currency but repay principal in another currency	Dual currency
Composite currency bond	▪ Denominated in currency basket instead of single currency	Composite currency of issue

Note: * LIBOR = London Inter Bank Offering Rate .

Benefits of raising debt globally

Global bond offerings enlarge the borrower's opportunities for financing at reduced cost, because with increased liquidity in global bonds, investors are willing to accept lower yields. With an increased pool of investors, global bonds also promote sources of financing.

Concerns of raising debt globally

A company may need to satisfy additional security regulations (for example, information disclosure) required by overseas regulatory bodies.

International bond market credit ratings

Moody's Investors Service and Standard & Poor's (S&P) provide *credit ratings* on various types of international bonds. Bond issues are classified into categories based upon the creditworthiness of the borrower. Potential bond ratings include investment grade, speculative grade or a grade which indicates a default risk.

Ratings providers assess the company's default probability based on current information and details of debt obligation. The ratings reflect only creditworthiness (not exchange rate uncertainty) and they are the result of an analysis of three factors:

- Likelihood of default and compliance with timely payment of interest and principal repayment
- Nature and provision of debt obligation
- Protection afforded by, and relative position of, obligation in the event of bankruptcy, reorganisation or other arrangement under the laws of bankruptcy and other laws affecting creditors' rights

There is a disproportionate percentage of international bonds which have high credit ratings when compared to domestic bonds. This can be explained by the fact that the eurobond market is accessible only to firms that have good credit ratings and reputation.

TRADE FINANCE

In addition to the classic financial facilities that exporters and importers can obtain in their respective countries from their banks, financing international trade can take three forms:

1. *Documentary credit* that benefits the exporters of goods
2. *Credit facilities* offered to importers and exporters by export credit agencies that also mitigate the risks of exporters.
3. *Counter-trade* deals that ease the cash outflow of exporters.

Documentary credit

For exporters of goods, the most traditional method of trade finance is the documentary credit represented in Figure 13.3. The principle is that an importer of goods mandates his bank to issue a letter of credit that guarantees the exporter that they will be paid on reception of shipping documents, establishing proof that the goods have been actually delivered to the transport company. The exporter can ask the importer's bank, through his own bank, to accept a *time draft* for the amount of the contract by issuing a *Bank Acceptance* (B/A). The exporter can discount this acceptance, known as a *bank acceptance*. Figure 13.3 gives a step-by-step simplified view of this process. There is a large variety of terms regulating the transactions and delineating the respective responsibilities of the exporters and the importers. Those terms, known as *Incoterms*, are defined by the International Chambers of Commerce (ICC) based in Paris.

Export credit agencies

Exporters, and sometimes importers, of goods can benefit from credits granted through export credit agencies such as the Eximbank (Export–Import Bank) backed by the Federal Credit Insurance Association (FCIA) in the United States, the ECGD (Export Credits Guarantee Department) in the United Kingdom or the Compagnie Française du Commerce Exterieur (COFACE) in France.

These agencies will either provide credits directly or facilitate the granting of credits from banks or from the exporter's bank to importers by covering political risks and commercial risks up to a certain percentage of the contract.

In addition, these institutions may grant facilities to exporters to obtain *pre-financing* of their exports in contracts of long duration.

Appendix 13.5 (p. 373) has a list of export credit agencies in different OECD Member Countries.

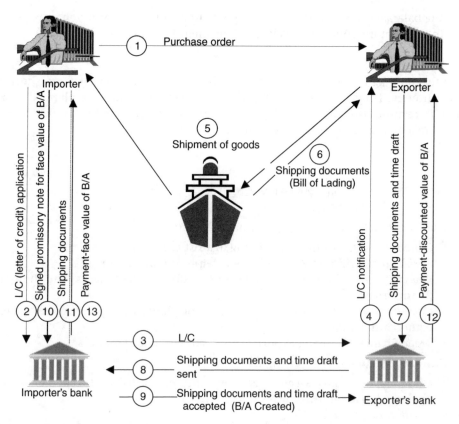

Figure 13.3 Documentary credit in international trade

Note: B/A=Bank acceptance.

Counter-trade

Counter-trade is another way of financing international transactions. It eases the pain for importers who have to find cash in hard currencies to pay for their imports. The principle of counter-trade is that the buyer pays the total or part of the contract in products or services. Counter-trade can take three main forms[3]:

- *Barter* trade, the most direct form of counter-trade. The exporter is paid in products coming from the importer's country.
- *Buy-back* contracts, in which the supplier of equipment agrees to buy part of the output of the exporter's facilities. In this case, there is cash outlay on both sides but the importer recoups his investment from the cash generated by the sales of products. A variant of buy-back is known as *counter-purchase* contracts, in which the products sold to the exporters come from a third party.
- *Bilateral clearing agreements*, which exist at government level when two governments agree to trade and the debit and credit of the trade are registered in an account whose balance is cleared at the end of an agreed period. In some cases,

the balance can be 'sold' to a third party that can use it for purchasing goods in the debtor's country. This last arrangement is known as *switch trade*.

Counter-trade agreements mostly involve developing countries that are short of hard currency. They were a common practice at the time of the state-planned economies in communist countries until the early 1990s, and have tended to decrease in importance with the liberalisation of markets.

SUMMARY AND KEY POINTS

1. There are five key issues in global financial management:
   - *Currency risk*: exposure and hedging against currency fluctuations
   - *Cash management*: how to optimise receipts and disbursements
   - *Project finance*: how to evaluate international investments and how to finance them
   - *Capital markets*: how to take advantage of global financial market to raise equity and handle debts
   - *Trade finance*: financing exports/imports of goods and services.

2. Currency fluctuations and hedging:
   - Currency fluctuations can affect the economic value of companies which operate globally in three ways:
     - *Strategic exposure*:
       (a) Change in competitive advantage of a company in terms of future cash flow owing to increased/decreased costs arising from changes in currency values
       (b) Global firms better positioned to deal with strategic exposures because of their diversified market portfolio and abilities to relocate production facilities
       (c) Hedging techniques include:
           (i) Hedging with *strategic product positioning*: developing products/ services for price-insensitive markets through differentiation
           (ii) Hedging with *geographical positioning*: balancing sales and production assets within exchange zones
           (iii) *Sourcing in low-cost countries*, e.g. countries with relatively low wages despite having strong currencies
     - *Transaction exposure*:
       (a) Positive or negative changes in short-term cash flows owing to existing financial or commercial commitments
       (b) Hedging techniques include:
           (i) *Forward contracts*: buying at a fixed future date a fixed quantity of a given currency at a fixed exchange rate (the forward rate); most common hedging technique used by corporations
           (ii) *Future contracts*: similar to forward contracts but standard financial instruments traded in recognised future markets

       (iii) *Options*: contracts allowing one to sell (put option) or buy (sell option) a currency at a given exchange rate (the strike price) at the end of the maturity period

       (iv) *Currency swaps*: when one company borrows in currency X but repays in currency Y and another company borrows in currency Y but repays in currency X; the two companies can swap their loans through a bank

  (c) Non-hedging techniques:

    (i) *Leading and lagging*:

  (a) For payments, a company would try to collect receivables early (leading) if they are nominated in 'soft' currencies and delay (lagging) the collection of receivables nominated in 'hard' currencies

  (b) For receipts, a company would try to pay early (leading) if they are nominated in hard currencies and delay (lagging) payments nominated in 'soft' currencies

    (ii) *Netting*:

  (a) Allows treasurers of global firms which have centralised cash management to hedge net cash position for any currency that has a creditor position

  (b) Types of netting system – *bilateral netting*, netting between pairs of subsidiaries; multilateral netting, netting of all transactions and transfer of the net to a central account

- *Translation exposure*:

  (a) Currency movement affects valuation of assets/liabilities of global companies and this can affect market perception and hence, market value of the firm

  (b) There are two main methods of adjusting financial statements for currencies fluctuations:

    (i) *Monetary/non-monetary* method: monetary assets are translated at the exchange rate prevailing on the date of the balance sheet; non-monetary assets are translated at the historic rate, i.e. the rate prevailing at the date they were entered in the balance sheet

    (ii) *Current* method: all balance sheet assets/liabilities are translated at the exchange rate on the balance sheet date; the income statement accounts can be translated either at the exchange rate at the date when the revenues and expenses are incurred or at the average exchange rate of the period; translation gains or losses are reported in a separate equity account of the parent company's balance sheet.

3. Project finance – international project finance deals with the valuation and financing of productive investments in countries that are not the investor's countries:

  ■ *Project valuation* – two approaches are available to take into account country risks and currency risks which are not diversifiable:

  - *Cash flow adjustments* (Adjusted Present Value, APV) involves the following four steps:

    (a) Specific downside risks are identified, their impact on the cash flow is calculated and the probability of their occurrence is determined

      (b) Cash flows are adjusted using probabilistic distribution

      (c) Cash flows are then translated into the investor's currency using Purchasing Power Parity (PPP) differences as a proxy for currency fluctuations

      (d) Cash flows are discounted using the investor's cost of capital.

    – *Cost of capital adjustments* (CCA) which introduces a premium risk to the cost of equity; adjusting the risk premium by introducing a 'country beta' to the cost of capital is argued to be more appropriate in case of investments in emerging countries where risks are not diversifiable

- *Specific project financing*:
  - *Equity project financing*:
    - (a) For *developing countries*, equity project finance is usually provided by development banks
    - (b) For *industrialised market economies*, equity project finance is usually provided by development banks
  - *Debt project financing* – provided by banking institutions, development banks, government aid or supplier credits; when provided by banks or supplier credits, debt financing is backed by credit risk insurance.

4. Global capital structure:

- Capital markets can be either integrated or fragmented:
  - *Integrated* capital markets means that raising money in any country comes at the same cost
  - *Fragmented* capital markets means that capital markets still differ in their structure, costs and risk:
    - (a) Fragmentation can be observed in:
      - (i) Correlation between the movements of one country's stock exchange against an index of all stock exchanges in the world (the world index); this measures the relative riskiness of different stock markets (like a country stock market 'beta')
      - (ii) Difference in cost of capital (debts and equity) in different countries
    - (b) With the different macroeconomic outlooks of different countries and different risk profiles, cost of capital can differ in different countries, which allows companies to benefit through:
      - (i) Cross-listing
      - (ii) International bond issues
- *Cross-listing*
  - Advantages include:
    - (a) Reaching wider investor base which can boost demand and liquidity of company shares
    - (b) Creating a secondary market for the company's shares and establishing name recognition in a new capital market
    - (c) Projecting the company's name and products in the foreign country where it is listed
    - (d) Potential benefit of protection from hostile takeover with a widened investor base
  - Disadvantages include:

(a) Costs incurred in compliance with disclosure/listing requirements of foreign exchange
(b) Volatility of the stock in one stock market can affect volatility of the stock in another
(c) Foreign investors can easily purchase a company's stock and challenge the domestic control of the company
- ■ International bond issues
  - – Benefits:
    (a) Means of financing at lower cost
    (b) Promotes diversified investor base
    (c) Dual currency bond assists parent company to finance its overseas subsidiaries' operation – the parent company can pay off the periodic coupon payment at local currency of the parent company but principal repayment by foreign subsidiaries is in foreign currency
  - – Potential disadvantages – company may need to satisfy additional security regulations (for example, information disclosure) required by overseas regulatory bodies.

5. Trade finance:
- ■ *Documentary credit*: an importer of goods mandates their bank to issue a letter of credit that guarantees that the exporter will be paid at reception of shipping documents establishing the proof that goods have been actually been delivered to the transport company
- ■ Credit facilities offered by *export credit agencies* to importers and exporters
- ■ *Counter-trade* deals that ease the cash outflow of exporters; in counter-trade, the buyer pays the total or part of the contract in products or services – mostly used by developing countries that are short of hard currency:
  - – *Barter trade*: exporter is paid in products coming from the importer's country
  - – *Buy-backs*: supplier of equipment agrees to buy part of the output of the exporter's facilities; a variant of buy-back is counter-purchase contracts in which the products sold to the exporters come from a third party
  - – *Bilateral clearing agreements*: governmental level when two governments agree to trade and the debit and credit of the trade is registered in an account whose balance is cleared at the end of the agreed period.

Appendix 13.1   Hedging exposure to currency risk – a champagne example[4]

We assume that a US wine distributor has just signed a contract with a French company for the delivery of 450 cases of champagne. The contract calls for the payment of FRF600,000 when delivery takes place in three months' time. As soon as the contract is signed, the distributor is exposed to exchange rate risk because the dollar cost of the champagne will not be known until dollars are exchanged for FRF600,000 at the exchange rate that will prevail in three months' time. We say that the distributor's *contractual, or transaction, exposure* is FRF600,000.

STRATEGIC EXPOSURE

Each time our US distributor places an order for champagne from France, he enters a contract to deliver French Francs to the French champagne exporter and is immediately exposed to a foreign exchange risk. If the distributor's business is to sell French champagne, his exposure to foreign exchange risk is not limited to the outstanding contracts with his French suppliers. Future purchases of champagne will generate continuous exposure to the volatility of the USD–French Franc exchange rate. This exposure to future exchange rate changes is an example of an *operating exposure.*

Importers (or exporters) of foreign goods and services are not the only firms subject to operating exposure. A firm that has only domestic operations can also be exposed to changes in exchange rates. Consider a US distributor of champagne made in the United States. If the value of the French Franc decreases relative to the USD (you get more Francs for a Dollar), the US distributor of the French-produced champagne can keep the same margin by selling his champagne at a lower price and, in the process, take market share from the distributor of US-made champagne.

TRANSACTION EXPOSURE

Our US distributor of French champagne currently has a contractual exposure of FRF600,000, which will remain outstanding for the next three months. As the FRF/USD exchange rate varies during that period of time, the *dollar value* of the FRF600,000 will change. There are many ways the distributor can hedge this exchange rate risk – that is, protect himself against currency fluctuations. He can choose among the many *hedging techniques* commonly used to reduce or eliminate the exchange rate risk associated with the purchase of raw materials, the sale of goods, the purchase of assets, or the issuance of debt when they are denominated in a foreign currency. These techniques use instruments available in the financial markets, such as forward, futures and option contracts.

As an alternative to forward contracts, the US distributor of the French champagne can use currency futures contracts. *Currency futures contracts*, or simply *currency futures*, are similar to forward contracts except that they have a standard contract size and a standard delivery date. Currency futures are traded every day on organised futures markets, such as the International Monetary Exchange (IMEX) in New Jersey, the London International Financial Futures Exchange (LIFFE), and the Singapore International Monetary Exchange (SIMEX).

THE CURRENCY FUTURES HEDGE

If our champagne distributor wants to use currency futures contracts to hedge his exposure to French Francs, he will have to have three-month futures contracts worth FRF600,000. Because currency futures contracts and forward contracts are similar instruments, the futures hedge should have the same overall effect as the forward hedge. However, there will be some differences.

- First, the other party in the futures contract is not a bank, but is instead the clearing corporation. The distributor, through his broker, will have to *buy* French Francs futures and then *sell* them later. If, in the meantime, the French Franc appreciates (depreciates) relative to the US dollar, the distributor will make a profit (loss) from his futures trade. But, if the franc appreciates (depreciates) relative to the dollar, he will also have to disburse more (fewer) dollars to buy, in the spot market, the FRF600,000 needed to pay his supplier. The profit (loss) made in the futures market will compensate for the increase (decrease) in the amount of dollars needed to buy the FRF600,000 in the spot market.
- Second, because the size and the maturity of the futures contracts are standardised, it is not always possible *perfectly* to hedge transaction exposure using a futures contract. For example, if the distributor decides to buy French Franc futures contracts on the Chicago Mercantile Exchange (CME), he will have to buy contracts with a unit size of FRF500,000. If he buys one contract, he will hedge only FRF500,000, leaving FRF100,000 'unhedged'. If he buys two contracts for a total of FRF1,000,000, he will 'over-hedge' his exposure by FRF400,000. Moreover, the distributor will have to decide on the maturity date of the futures contract. The only four expiration dates for a futures contract are the last Wednesday of March, June, September and December. Suppose the champagne supplier wants to be paid by the end of May? The distributor will buy June futures contracts because their expiration date is closest to the end of May. Then, he will *sell* the futures contracts at the end of May. However, he will still be exposed to exchange rate risk because he cannot know at the time the contract is bought what the price of the June futures contracts will be at the end of May. Suppose the supplier agrees to wait until 1 July to be paid and the distributor chooses to hedge with June futures? In this case, the distributor will be exposed to the USD/FRF exchange rate volatility between the last Wednesday of June (when the June futures contracts expire) and 1 July.
- Finally, the distributor will have to place a *margin* with a broker. Also, the daily marking to market may trigger margin calls if the USD/FRF futures exchange rate goes down. In this situation, the distributor would have to make additional cash payments until the futures contracts expire.

To summarise, a futures hedge has some disadvantages that are not present in a forward hedge. A futures hedge is more complicated, it does not completely eliminate exchange rate risk and it requires intermediary cash payments. These drawbacks are particularly significant for our distributor of champagne who may rightly prefer to hedge his contractual exposure with forward contracts. However, there are features of the futures market which, in some circumstances, cause corporations to hedge with futures rather than with forward contracts. A small firm without any established reputation, or a firm that does not enjoy a high credit standing, may find it convenient to use futures contracts because no credit check is required before trading in the futures market.

HEDGING WITH OPTION CONTRACTS

Suppose our distributor hedges his exposure to the French Franc by buying French Francs forward at FRF/USD6.25. Regardless of whether the French franc appreciates or depreciates during the hedging period, the US dollar cost of the champagne will be $96,000 (FRF600,000 divided by FRF/USD6.25). If the French Franc appreciates, the hedge will have accomplished its purpose – that is, it will have protected the distributor against an increase in the value of the French Franc. But if the French Franc depreciates, the distributor would have been better off if he had not hedged with forwards because he would then have benefited from the decrease in the value of the French Franc. Indeed, it is always the case that a forward hedge protects a firm from unfavourable exchange rate movements but prevents it from benefiting from *favourable changes* in the exchange rate. Does a hedging technique exist that insulates the distributor from an appreciation of the French Franc but allows him to benefit from its depreciation? The answer is 'yes' and the technique is the *currency option hedge*.

THE CURRENCY OPTION HEDGE

If our distributor of champagne decides to hedge his French Franc exposure with options, he will buy a three-month French Franc *call* option. This will give him the right to buy French Francs at a fixed exchange rate (the *exercise rate*). He is not obliged to exercise the option, and he will not do so if the exchange rate is unfavourable. For example, if the spot rate of the French Franc in three months' time is lower than the exercise rate of the option, the distributor will not exercise his option and, instead, will buy the necessary Francs in the spot market. On the other hand, if the spot rate is higher than the exercise rate, he will exercise his option to get the Francs at a lower rate. The option hedge provides a flexibility that is absent in a forward or futures hedge. However, this flexibility comes with a price, which is the price of the option.

To illustrate, suppose the distributor can buy from his bank a three-month French Franc European call option at $0.005 per Franc, with an exercise rate of 16 cents per Franc. This means (1) the distributor must now pay the bank $0.005 per Franc, or $3,000 for FRF600,000 ($0.005 multiplied by 600,000 Francs) and (2) in three months, the distributor can buy 600,000 French Francs from the bank at 16 cents per franc for a total of $96,000 ($0.16 multiplied by 600,000 francs). Whether or not the distributor will exercise the option in three months depends on the USD/FRF spot exchange rate prevailing at that time. Table 13A.1 examines four cases corresponding to the following exchange rates in three months: FRF/USD6.00, FRF/USD6.15, FRF/USD6.25 and FRF/USD6.40.

If the exchange rate is FRF/USD6.00 (USD/FRF0.1667), the distributor will exercise his option because he will be able to buy at 16 cents what is worth 16.67 cents. He will get the FRF600,000 for $96,000 ($0.16 multiplied by FRF600,000) from the bank (the seller of the option) and pay his supplier of champagne. However, the option cost is $3,000, so the total cost of the champagne will be $99,000 ($96,000 plus $3,000). If the exchange rate is FRF/USD6.15 (USD/FRF0.1626), he will also exercise his option and the total cost of the champagne will remain at $99,000. If the exchange rate is FRF/USD6.25 (USD/FRF0.16) – that is, if it is equal to the exercise rate – there is no longer any incentive for the distributor to exercise the

Table 13A.1 Comparison of currency option costs for four exchange rates

Spot rate in three months' time USD/FRF	FRF/USD	Exercise USD/FRF	Will option be exercised?	Dollar amount paid for FRF600,000	Cost of option	Total cost
6.00	0.1667	0.16	Yes	$96,000	$3,000	$99,000
6.15	0.1626	0.16	Yes	$96,000	$3,000	$99,000
6.25	0.16	0.16	No	$96,000	$3,000	$99,000
6.40	0.1563	0.16	No	$93,750	$3,000	$96,750

In the monetary/non-monetary method, monetary assets and liabilities are translated at the exchange rate on the date of the balance sheet, and the non-monetary assets are valued at the rate when they were entered in the balance sheet.

option because he can get the FRF600,000 in the spot market at the same exchange rate. For any USD/FRF exchange rate higher than the exercise rate of 16 cents per franc (or for any FRF/USD exchange rate *lower* than FRF/USD6.25), the distributor will exercise his option and the total cost of the champagne will be $99,000.

If the exchange rate is FRF/USD6.40 (USD/FRF0.1563), the distributor will not exercise his option to buy at 16 cents what is worth only 15.63 cents. He will buy the FRF600,000 in the spot market at FRF/USD6.40 for a total cost of $93,750 (FRF600,000 divided by FRF/USD6.40) and pay his supplier. However, because he paid $3,000 for the option, the total cost of the champagne will be $96,750 ($93,750 plus $3,000). For any USD/FRF spot rate lower than the exercise rate of 16 cents per franc (or for any FRF/USD exchange rate *higher* than FRF/USD6.25), the distributor will let the option expire without exercising it and exchange dollars for francs at the spot rate. And the lower the USD/FRF exchange rate, the lower the dollar cost of the champagne.

Figure 13A.1 shows the net result of the option hedge for the distributor for a wide range of spot rates in three months. The hedge accomplishes the dual goal of (1) protecting the distributor from an appreciation of the French Franc by setting an upper limit to the dollar amount he will have to pay for the champagne ($99,000), and (2) allowing him to benefit from a depreciation of the French Franc. If the French Franc rises above the exercise rate (the FRF/USD rate drops below 6.25), the distributor will exercise his right to buy French francs at that rate; thus, he limits the dollar cost of the FRF600,000 to $99,000, the amount he will pay the bank ($96,000) when exercising the option plus the cost of the option ($3,000). However, if the French Franc falls below the exercise rate (the FRF/USD rate rises above 6.25), the distributor will not exercise his option. The dollar cost of the FRF600,000 will be equal to FRF600,000 multiplied by the spot rate in three months' time plus the $3,000 cost of the option.

WHICH HEDGING TECHNIQUE TO CHOOSE?

Before deciding which technique to use in hedging a currency exposure created by a particular transaction, a manager must first decide *if a hedge is needed at all*. A hedge is not needed if another business unit belonging to the firm has a currency exposure that is the opposite of the one created by the transaction. However, a business unit manager is not usually informed of the size and timing of the currency exposure of other business units. This is the reason why large firms engaging in foreign trade have a centralised foreign currency management group that constantly monitors the firm's *net exposure* on a currency-by-currency basis and makes the required hedging decisions. Having all the business units' currency exposures consolidated and managed by a central unit prevents the multiplication of unnecessary and costly hedges.

Contractual exposure: FRF600,000 to be paid in three months' time
Three-month call option price: USD/FRF0.005
Exercise price: $0.16 per franc or FRF/USD6.25

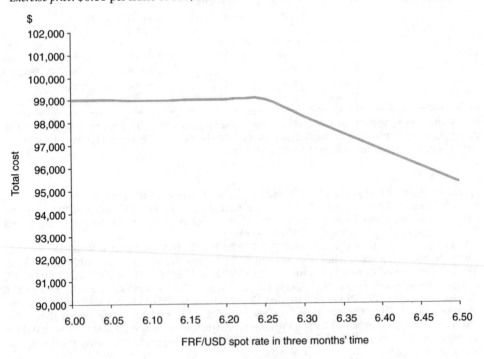

Figure 13A.1 The option hedge for the US champagne distributor

Currency risk exposure can be further reduced using a procedure known as *leading* and *lagging*. This process consists of timing the cash inflows and outflows from the different foreign business units so as to minimise the firm's overall exposure to exchange rate risk. For example, if a US company has to make a payment in Japanese yen, it can ask its Japanese subsidiary – assuming it has one – for an early payment of the same amount of yen on any of the subsidiary's outstanding debt to the parent company. This procedure is known as *leading*. If the parent is owed money denominated in yen, it can delay the payment of some of its debt to the subsidiary until that money is received. This procedure is called *lagging*.

What hedging technique should our champagne distributor use? We have shown that a forward hedge is preferable to a futures hedge for eliminating his FRF600,000 exposure. What about an option hedge? Figure 13A.1 shows the net dollar cost of the FRF600,000 when using either the forward hedge or the option hedge for different spot rates in three months. The difference in the outcomes of the two hedging techniques is clear. With a forward hedge, the net cost is $96,000 regardless of the prevailing spot rate in three months. Furthermore, the distributor knows that cost when he enters the contract. With an option hedge, the net cost depends on the spot rate in three months, with the cost limited to $99,000. Thus, the choice depends on the distributor's opinion of future changes in the USD/FRF spot rate. If he strongly believes the French Franc will depreciate in the following three months, he may consider that the extra cost of the option hedge – if it turns out the French Franc appreciates – is not large enough to dissuade him from taking a chance. However, if he has no strong opinion about future currency movements, he may prefer the certainty of the forward hedge to the uncertain outcome of the costlier option alternative.

Appendix 13.2 Translating financial statements: monetary/non-monetary method and current method[5]

THE MONETARY/NON-MONETARY METHOD

In the **monetary/non-monetary method**, monetary assets, such as cash and accounts receivable, and monetary liabilities, such as accounts payable, accrued expenses, and short-term and long-term debts, are translated at the exchange rate prevailing on the date of the balance sheet. The non-monetary items, such as inventories and fixed assets, are estimated using the rate prevailing at the date they were entered on the balance sheet – the *historical rate*. The logic of this approach is that monetary assets and monetary liabilities are contracted amounts that would be redeemed at a rate that is likely to be closer to the rate prevailing on the date of the balance sheet than to the historical rate. The average exchange rate of the reporting period is used to translate the income statement accounts, except for those accounts related to the non-monetary items, such as depreciation expenses, which are translated at the same rate as the corresponding balance sheet item. Any gain or loss from translating balance sheet accounts is reflected in the income statement and, as a result, affects reported earnings.

The top part of Table 13A.2 shows how the balance sheet accounts at year-end 1997 of the French subsidiary of Uncle Sam's Bagel are translated into USD according to the monetary/non-monetary method. Two possible values are shown for the exchange rate, USD/FRF0.15 and USD/FRF0.165 where USD refers to the US Dollar and FRF refers to the French Franc. The dollar value of cash, trade receivables, trade payables and financial debt is obtained by multiplying their French Franc value by the exchange rate that prevailed on 31 December 1997. The dollar value of inventories and fixed assets is the same regardless of the exchange rate at year-end 1997 because, as non-monetary assets, their value is determined by the exchange rate on the date when they were recorded in the balance sheet, not on the date of the balance sheet. The dollar value of the subsidiary owners' equity, which is the difference between the dollar value of its assets and that of its liabilities, depends on the exchange rate at the end of the year. It will be $25 million if the exchange rate is USD/FRF0.15 and $21.250 million if the exchange rate is USD/FRF0.165. The difference, $3.750 million, is the difference between the

Table 13A.2 Monetary/non-monetary translation method, applied to the balance sheet of the French subsidiary of Uncle Sam's Bagel on 31 December, 1997, figures in thousands

	Value in French Francs (FRF)	Value in U.S. dollars (USD) Exchange rate on 31 December, 1997		Change in U.S. dollars
		USD/FRF 0.15	USD/FRF 0.165	
Assets				
Cash	50,000	50,000×0.15 = 7,500	50,000×0.165 = 8,250	+750
Accounts receivable	100,000	100,000×0.15 = 15,000	100,000×0.165 = 16,500	+1,500
Total monetary assets	150,000	22,500	24,750	+2,250
Inventories	100,000	16,500	16,500	–
Property, plant and equipment	250,000	46,000	46,000	–
Total non-monetary assets	350,000	62,500	62,500	–
Assets	**500,000**	**85,000**	**87,250**	**+2,250**
Liabilities				
Short-term debt	75,000	75,000×0.15 = 11,250	75,000×0.165 = 12,375	+1,125
Accounts payable	75,000	75,000×0.15 = 11,250	50,000×0.165 = 12,375	+1,125
Long-term debt	250,000	250,000×0.15 = 37,500	250,000×0.165 = 41,250	+3,750
Total monetary liabilities	400,000	60,000	66,000	+6,000
Owners' Equity	***100,000***	***25,000***	***21,250***	***−3,750***
−(Assets-Liabilities)				
Liabilities & Owners' Equity	**500,000**	**85,000**	**87,250**	**+2,250**

change in the value of the monetary liabilities and the change in the value of the monetary assets ($6 million *less* $2.250 million). Note, however, that owners' equity changes in the opposite direction to the change in the exchange rate – it *decreases* when the exchange rate *increases* from USD/FRF0.15 to USD/FRF0.165. This is not surprising because as long as monetary liabilities are larger than monetary assets, an *appreciation* of the foreign currency (the USD cost of one French Franc increase) will increase the dollar value of the firm's liabilities relative to that of its assets, thus reducing the dollar value of its owners' equity. For most firms, the value of monetary liabilities is greater than the value of monetary assets, so an *appreciation* of the foreign currency will usually result in a *translation loss* when using the monetary/non-monetary method. A *depreciation* of the foreign currency will result in a *translation gain*.

THE CURRENT METHOD

In the **current method**, known as FASB (Financial Accounting Standards Board) 52, *all* the balance sheet assets and liabilities are translated at the exchange rate on the balance sheet date. The income statement accounts can be translated either at the exchange rate at the date when the revenues and expenses are incurred or at the average exchange rate of the period. To avoid large variations in reported earnings, which may be caused by large fluctuations in the exchange rate, translation gains or losses are reported in a *separate equity account* of the parent balance sheet. The logic behind the current method approach is that it does not distort the structure of the balance sheet as the monetary/non-monetary method does, because all the assets and liabilities are affected proportionally by changes in exchange rates.

Table 13A.3 shows how the balance sheet accounts of the French subsidiary of Uncle Sam's Bagel are translated according to the current method, using the same data as in Table 13A.2 where the monetary/non-monetary method is applied. When the exchange rate increases from USD/FRF0.15 to USD/FRF0.165, the value of *all* the French subsidiary's assets and liabilities increases by the same proportion as the exchange rate (10 per cent). As a result, owners' equity also increases by the same proportion, from $15 million to $16.5 million. Contrary to the previous method, the current method always shows a *translation gain* when the foreign currency *appreciates* and a *translation loss* when the foreign currency *depreciates*.

WHICH METHOD IS BETTER?

The difference between the monetary/non-monetary method and the current method comes from a different valuation of the *non-monetary assets*. The first method values them at the historical exchange rate, and the second values them at the current exchange rate. Which is the right approach? Neither approach is right because managing for value creation implies that the relevant value of a firm's assets is their *market value*, not their book value. Whichever method we use to translate the book value of assets from one currency to another, we always get book values, never market values.

Which method do most companies use? Most companies use the current rate method, simply because it is recommended by most accounting regulating bodies worldwide. Why do the regulating bodies favour the current method? Given that neither of the approaches presents a definitive advantage over the other, that their choice seems to be based on practical considerations. The current method is easier to apply, and also easier to understand. Another reason why the current method is preferred by most managers may be based on the

Table 13A.3 Current translation method, applied to the balance sheet of the French subsidiary of Uncle Sam's Bagel on 31 December 1997, figures in thousands

	Value in French Francs (FRF)	Value in US dollars (USD) Exchange rate on 31 December, 1997		Change in US dollars
		USD/FRF0.15	USD/FRF0.165	
Assets				
Cash	50,000	$50,000 \times 0.15 = 7,500$	$50,000 \times 0.165 = 8,250$	+1,250
Accounts receivable	100,000	$100,000 \times 0.15 = 15,000$	$100,000 \times 0.165 = 16,500$	+1,500
Inventories	100,000	$100,000 \times 0.15 = 15,000$	$100,000 \times 0.165 = 16,500$	+1,500
Property, plant and equipment	250,000	$250,000 \times 0.15 = 37,500$	$250,000 \times 0.165 = 41,250$	+3,750
Assets	**500,000**	**75,000**	**82,500**	**+7,500**
Liabilities				
Short-term debt	75,000	$75,000 \times 0.15 = 11,250$	$75,000 \times 0.165 = 12,375$	+1,125
Accounts payable	75,000	$75,000 \times 0.15 = 11,250$	$50,000 \times 0.165 = 12,375$	+1,125
Long-term debt	250,000	$250,000 \times 0.15 = 37,500$	$250,000 \times 0.165 = 41,250$	+3,750
Total monetary liabilities	400,000	60,000	66,000	+6,000
Owners' equity (assets –liabilities)	**100,000**	**15,000**	**16,500**	**+1,500**
Liabilities and owners' equity	**500,000**	**75,000**	**82,000**	**+7,500**

In the current method, all assets and all liabilities are translated at the exchange rate on the date of the balance sheet.

difference in the treatment of gains or losses from translation adjustments. The monetary/non-monetary method includes them in the computation of reported income, but the current method does not. Because most managers' performance measures are derived from reported income, it may make sense to account for the impact of changes in exchange rates (over which managers have little control) separately from other sources of gain or loss.

Appendix 13.3   Surf'n Zap project valuation[6]

The net present value (NPV) rule is used to select investment projects that create value and reject those that destroy value. The objective of *value maximisation* applies to any management decision, so the NPV rule is also applicable to the decision to invest in a foreign country. However, there are two new factors that must be taken into account here. First, the project's future cash flows are usually denominated in a foreign currency with an exchange rate that may fluctuate; second, there is the risk that the cash flows may be affected by changes in local regulations governing foreign investments, a risk we refer to as 'country risk' or 'political risk'. These complications make the NPV rule more difficult to apply.

We take the example of Surf'n Zap, a US manufacturer of a small remote control device, called Zap Scan, that can automatically show selected programmes on a TV set at regular and brief intervals of time. After a successful entry in the US market, the firm wants to export the device to Europe and has to decide where to locate its regional distribution centre. The choice is between Switzerland and Zaragu, two countries with significantly different political risks.

SURF'N ZAP CROSS-BORDER ALTERNATIVE INVESTMENT PROJECTS

To export Zap Scan to Europe, Surf'n Zap needs to set up a distribution centre there. After an extensive search for the most convenient location, the choice was reduced to two countries, Switzerland and Zaragu. Both countries are located in the centre of Europe and from a logistical point of view, neither one appears superior to the other. However, while investing in Switzerland would not carry any country risk, Zaragu has recently been the subject of unfavourable articles in the press. Analysts are concerned that the country's monetary situation may deteriorate in the future and that the earnings from the subsidiaries of foreign companies located in Zaragu may soon be subject to a 'foreign' tax in addition to the regular corporate tax. The local currency is the Swiss Franc (CHF) in Switzerland and the zaragupa (ZGU) in Zaragu. Financial data on the alternative projects' cash flows are presented in Table 13A.4.

The cost of acquiring and refurbishing a building plus the project's start-up costs are estimated at CHF25 million for the Swiss alternative and at ZGU230 million for the Zaragu alternative. It is expected that the investment will last five years, at which time digital TV sets with incorporated zapping devices will make Zap Scan obsolete. The annual cash flows in Table 13A.4 are *net of all local and US taxes*. It is estimated that the building can be sold for CHF20 million or ZGU250 million (after taxes) at the end of the fifth year.

The inflation rate in Switzerland has been remarkably stable in the past, at about 2 per cent a year, and it is not expected to behave differently during the next few years. In Zaragu, the

Table 13A.4 Cash flows, the Zap Scan project, million

	Switzerland alternative (CHF)	Zaragu alternative (ZGU)
Initial cash outlay	25.0	230
Annual cash flows		
Year 1	4.0	50
Year 2	4.8	60
Year 3	5.0	65
Year 4	5.1	70
Year 5	5.2	75
Liquidation value in Year 5	20.0	250
Current annual inflation rate	2%	10%
Current spot exchange rate	CHF/USD1.1	ZGU/USD10

inflation rate has continuously increased during the recent past. It is now at 10 per cent a year and is expected to stay at this level for the foreseeable future. In the United States, the inflation rate is expected to average 3 per cent a year for the next five years.

The current spot exchange rates are CHF/USD1.1 and ZGU/USD10. Finally, the rate of return required by Surf'n Zap from its distribution centres in the United States is 10 per cent. Furthermore, Surf'n Zap requires that the NPV for all projects be estimated in USD.

The NPV of the Swiss alternative

To compute the NPV of the Swiss alternative of the Zap Scan project, we need to estimate both the project's expected cash flows and its cost of capital in USD. The project's cash flows, taken from Table 13A.4, are shown in the first row of Table 13A.5. To convert these Swiss Franc cash flows into their USD equivalents, we need to forecast the year-end USD/CHF spot rate for the next five years. We can use the purchasing power parity (PPP) relation to predict these future spot rates.

As indicated in (13A.1) in Mini-Example 13A.1, the PPP relation relates the expected changes in the spot exchange rates to the expected inflation rates in the home country and the foreign country.

The inflation rates in the United States and in Switzerland are expected to be 3 per cent and 2 per cent, respectively, in the near future, so we can use these values for the expected inflation rates $E(i_h)$ and $E(i_f)$ in (13A.1). To find the expected value of the year-end USD/CHF spot exchange rate for years 1–5, we start with the current spot exchange rate of USD/CHF0.9091 (1 divided by CHF/USD1.1). We then solve (13A.1) successively for each year using the expected spot rate from the previous year.

For year 1:

$$E(S^1_{USD/SFR}) = USD/SFR\,0.9091 \times \frac{1+0.03}{1+0.02} = SFR/USD\,0.9180$$

For year 2:

$$E(S^2_{USD/SFR}) = USD/SFR\,0.9180 \times \frac{1+0.03}{1+0.02} = SFR/USD\,0.9270$$

Table 13A.5   Expected cash flows from the Swiss alternative, the Zap Scan Project

Timing	Initial	End of year 1	End of year 2	End of year 3	End of year 4	End of year 5
Expected cash flows in million Swiss francs (CHF)						
Annual cash flow	(25.0)	4.0	4.8	5.0	5.1	5.2
Cash flow from liquidation						20.0
Total cash flow	(25.0)	4.0	4.8	5.0	5.1	25.2
Estimation of the USD/CHF spot rate using PPP (13A.1)						
Swiss expected inflation rate (%)		2	2	2	2	2
US expected inflation rate (%)		3	3	3	3	3
Current exchange rate: USD/CHF	0.9091					
Expected future spot rate: USD/CHF		0.9180	0.9270	0.9361	0.9453	0.9545
Expected cash flows in million US dollars (USD)						
Total cash flow (USD)	(22.727)	3.672	4.450	4.681	4.821	24.053
Net present value at 10% = USD6.034 million						

The result of this calculation for years 1–5 is shown in Table 13A.5. The expected USD value of the project's cash flows is obtained by multiplying the Swiss Franc cash flows by the expected exchange rates.

To compute the project's NPV we need to estimate the *cost of capital*. Surf'n Zap requires a return of 10 per cent from its distribution centres in the United States. Should the firm use the same cost of capital for the Swiss alternative or should it use a higher one to account for exchange rate risk – that is, for the probability that the future USD/CHF exchange rate may be

Mini-Example 13A.1   Calculating expected exchange rates using the PPP relation

The **purchasing power parity (PPP)** relation says that exchange rates should adjust so that the same basket of goods will cost the same in different countries. It is based on the following premise: If the price of goods increases faster in one country than in another because the inflation rate is higher in the first country than in the second, then the exchange rate between the two countries should move to offset the difference in inflation rates and, consequently, the difference in prices. More formally, according to the PPP relation:

Expected future spot rate = current spot rate

$$\times \frac{1 + \text{Expected inflation rate in the home country}}{1 + \text{Expected inflation rate in the foreign country}}$$

If $S^0_{h/f}$ is the current spot rate and $E(S^1_{h/f})$ is the expected future spot rate in one year, both expressed in units of the home currency per unit of the foreign currency, and if $E(i_h)$ and $E(i_f)$ are the expected inflation rates for next year at home and in the foreign country, respectively, then:

$$E(S^1_{h/f}) = S^0_{h/f} \times \frac{1 + E(i_h)}{1 + E(i_f)} \qquad (13A.1)$$

different from the expected one? The risk that matters to investors is not the *total* risk of the investment but only the portion of the risk that cannot be reduced or eliminated by diversification. If we assume the portfolios of Surf'n Zap shareholders include either shares of foreign companies or shares of US firms with international business activity, we can assume that the shareholders have already eliminated the portion of the Zap Scan project risk associated with the USD/CHF exchange rate volatility. In this case, no premium should be added to the domestic (US) cost of capital to account for the exchange rate risk. What if Surf'n Zap shareholders are not diversified internationally? In this case, the Swiss project gives them the opportunity to become diversified, albeit indirectly. As a consequence, the risk of their portfolio of assets would be *reduced*, which would imply a *lower* required rate of return for the project.

Using a cost of capital of 10 per cent and the project's expected cash flows in Table 13A.5, we can now estimate the project's NPV in million USD:

$$NPV_{Switzerland} = -USD22.727 + \frac{USD3.672}{1+0.1} + \frac{USD4.450}{(1+0.1)^2} + \frac{USD4.681}{(1+0.1)^3}$$
$$+ \frac{USD4.821}{(1+0.1)^4} + \frac{USD24.053}{(1+0.1)^5}$$

$$NPV_{Switzerland} = USD6.034 \text{ million}$$

The NPV is positive, so the Swiss project would create value for Surf'n Zap investors. But would the Zaragu project create more value?

The NPV of the Zaragu alternative

The procedure for estimating the expected value of the Zaragu project's cash flows is the same as the one we used for the Swiss alternative. We estimate the USD value of the project's expected future cash flows and then discount these cash flows at the project's cost of capital. The PPP relation is again used to estimate the year-end USD/ZGU spot rates for the next five years, using the expected inflation rates in the United States and Zaragu. The cash flows in zaragupas are converted into their USD equivalents using the predicted spot rates. The results of our estimation are shown in Table 13A.6.

Table 13A.6 Expected cash flows for the Zaragu alternative without country risk, the Zap Scan Project

Timing	Initial	End of year 1	End of year 2	End of year 3	End of year 4	End of year 5
Expected cash flows in million zaragupas (ZGU)						
Annual cash flow (ZGU)	(230)	50	60	65	70	75
Cash flow from liquidation (ZGU)						250
Total cash flow (ZGU)	(230)	50	60	65	70	325
Estimation of the USD/ZGU spot rate using PPP (13A.1)						
Zaragu expected inflation rate (%)		10	10	10	10	10
United States expected inflation rate (%)		3	3	3	3	3
Current exchange rate: USD/ZGU	0.1000					
Expected future spot rate: USD/ZGU		0.0936	0.0877	0.0821	0.0769	0.0720
Expected cash flows in million US dollars (USD)						
Total cash flow (USD)	(23)	4.680	5.262	5.335	5.383	23.400

Net present value at 10% = USD7.818 million

If we assume for a moment that there is no country risk in the Zaragu alternative, there is no need to adjust the project cost of capital for exchange rate risk. Thus, *in the absence of country risk*, the project cost of capital in the Zaragu alternative is 10 per cent, the same as the rate used for similar projects in the United States or Switzerland. Using the USD denominated cash flows from Table 13A.6, the NPV of the Zaragu alternative is:

$$NPV_{Zaragu}^{w/o\ country\ risk} = -USD23 + \frac{USD4.680}{1+0.1} + \frac{USD5.262}{(1+0.1)^2} + \frac{USD5.3365}{(1+0.1)^3}$$
$$+ \frac{USD5.3830}{(1+0.1)^4} + \frac{USD23.400}{(1+0.1)^5}$$
$$NPV_{Zaragu}^{w/o\ country\ risk} = USD7.818\ million$$

However, as mentioned earlier, the project will be exposed to country risk because there is some probability that the authorities in Zaragu will impose a 'foreign' tax on the project's earnings. To account for this risk, most firms systematically add a risk premium to their domestic cost of capital. We disagree with this procedure, for three reasons. First, if we assume that shareholders have already eliminated the country risk by holding a well-diversified portfolio of assets, we do not need to make any adjustment at all. Second, there is no rational way to estimate the size of the risk premium for the particular risk that needs to be taken into account. For example, should the Zaragu alternative be 1, 2 or 10 per cent? No one knows. Third, simply adding an arbitrary 'fudge' factor to the domestic cost of capital may lead to complacency and prevent managers from thoroughly assessing the impact of country risk on the project.

We suggest that any adjustment for country risk should be made on the project's *expected cash flows* rather than on the cost of capital. An expected cash flow is just a weighted average of the values that the cash flow can take in the future, where the weights are the probability that the cash flow will actually take these values. Thus, we can adjust these cash flows to reflect the likelihood of expropriation. If this is done, there is no need to adjust the cost of capital. Furthermore, the estimation of the expected cash flows forces managers to make a thorough analysis of country risk and its impact on the project.

Suppose that after a careful analysis of economic trends in Zaragu, we estimate that there is a 20 per cent probability that a monetary crisis will occur at some time during the project's life. Should such a crisis erupt, we can expect the project's earnings to be subjected to a 'foreign' tax. When such a tax was imposed in the past, the tax rate was always 25 per cent. There is no reason to expect that the rate will be different during the next monetary crisis, so we can apply the same rate to the project. To avoid cumbersome computations, we also assume that the project's *earnings*, which will be subjected to the 'foreign' tax, represent, each year, 90 per cent of the project's operating cash flows in the absence of 'foreign' tax. (Taxes are paid on earnings not cash flows.)

Table 13A.7 presents the detailed computation of the project's expected cash flows, taking into account the risk that the 'foreign' tax will be imposed on the project. The first section of the exhibit shows the cash flows in the absence of tax taken from Table 13A.6.

We now present the computation of the operating cash flows net of the 'foreign' tax, if the tax is imposed, and then show the computation of the project's expected cash flows, taking into account the probability that the project will be subjected to the tax. If the probability of taxation is 20 per cent during the life of the project, the project's *expected* cash flows are the cash flows net of the 'foreign' tax multiplied by 20 per cent plus the cash flows without the tax multiplied by 80 per cent, because there is 20 per cent chance that the first outcome will occur and 80 per cent chance that the second will occur. The last part of the exhibit shows the dollar value of the expected cash flows, using the same expected future exchange rates as in Table 13A.6. The NPV of the project, obtained by discounting the cash flows at the 10 per cent cost of capital, is:

$$NPV_{Zaragu}^{with\ country\ risk} = -USD23 + \frac{USD4.471}{1+0.1} + \frac{USD5.024}{(1+0.1)^2} + \frac{USD5.096}{(1+0.1)^3}$$
$$+ \frac{USD5.139}{(1+0.1)^4} + \frac{USD23.151}{(1+0.1)^5}$$
$$NPV_{Zaragu}^{with\ country\ risk} = USD6.930\ million$$

Table 13A.7 Expected cash flows for the Zaragu alternative with country risk, the Zap Scan Project

Timing	Initial	End of year 1	End of year 2	End of year 3	End of year 4	End of year 5
Expected cash flows in the absence of a 'foreign' tax on the project's earnings, in million zaragupas (ZGU)						
Annual cash flow (ZGU)	(230)	50	60	65	70	75
Cash flow from liquidation (ZGU)						250
Total cash flow (ZGU)	(230)	50	60	65	70	325
Expected operating cash flows in the presence of a 'foreign' tax on the project's earnings, in million zaragupas (ZGU)						
Project's earnings (90% of cash flow) (ZGU)		45.000	54.000	58.500	63.000	67.500
'Foreign' tax (25% of earnings) (ZGU)		11.250	13.500	14.625	15.750	16.875
Annual operating cash flow net of tax (ZGU)	(230)	38.750	46.500	50.375	54.250	58.125
Expected cash flows in million zaragupas (ZGU)						
Probability that the earnings will be taxed (%)		20	20	20	20	20
Annual operating cash flow (ZGU)	(230)	0.2 × 38.750 +0.8 × 50.000 =47.750	0.2 × 46.500 +0.8 × 60.000 =57.300	0.2 × 50.375 +0.8 × 65.000 =62.075	0.2 × 54.250 +0.8 × 70.000 =66.850	0.2 × 58.125 +0.8 × 75.000 =71.625
Cash flow from liquidation						250
Total cash flow	(230)	47.750	57.300	62.075	66.850	321.625
Expected cash flows in million US dollars (USD)						
Expected spot rate: USD/ZGU	0.1	0.0936	0.0877	0.0821	0.0769	0.0720
Total cash flow (USD)	(23)	4.471	5.024	5.096	5.139	23.151
Net present value at 10% = USD6.930 million						

The NPV with country risk is USD888,000 lower than without country risk ($7.818 million *less* $6.930 million), an 11 per cent reduction in value. The difference in NPV between the Zaragu and Swiss alternative is USD896,000 ($6.930 million *less* $6.034 million) and is in favour of the Zaragu alternative. Then, should the distribution centre be located in Zaragu? The answer depends on how confident we are in the assumptions we used to reach our conclusion.

We made two critical assumptions that could have a significant impact on our result. The first is that the PPP relation holds between the US Dollar and the two foreign currencies. The second is that the probability assessment of the imposition of a 'foreign' tax on the project is reliable. More generally, the second assumption refers to the probability that a portion or all of a project's cash flows accruing to the foreign parent will be expropriated and the form this expropriation will take. The only realistic way to improve our confidence in our analysis of the project is to do a *sensitivity analysis* that will show how responsive the project's NPV is to changes in the assumptions. Scenarios can be developed using percentage deviations from the PPP combined with different forms of expropriation that can be expected from the country in which the project is to be located. Only then can a decision be made that fully accounts for the project's risk.

In the relatively simple case of the Zap Scan project, the sensitivity analysis can be aimed at the responsiveness of the project's NPV to changes in the probability of having the project subject to a 'foreign' tax. Repeating the same computations as in Table 13A.7, we estimated the project's NPV with a range of probabilities from zero to 50 per cent. The results are reported in Table 13A.8. The probability for which the NPV of the Zaragu project is the same as the NPV of the Swiss project (USD6.034 million), approximately 40 per cent. This probability is twice the expected one of 20 per cent. The difference is large enough to decide that, despite the presence of some country risk, the Zap's Scan project should be located in Zaragu rather than in Switzerland.

Table 13A.8 Net present value for the Zaragu alternative as a function of the probability of the project being subjected to the 'foreign' tax, the Zap Scan Project

Probability that the project will be subjected to the 'foreign' tax (%)	0	10	20	30	40	50
Project NPV (USD million)	7.814	7.373	6.930	6.489	6.047	5.605

Appendix 13.4   Development banks providing project equity financing

Name of Development Bank	Details of funding available
Asian Development Bank (ADB) <www.adb.org>	ADB's traditional modes of financing include equity investments Equity may include preferred stock, convertible loans, and other forms of mezzanine financing *Eligibility for ADB assistance* To be eligible for ADB assistance, the proposed investment should be in the private sector of a DMC* and owned by local or foreign private sector entities An enterprise owned jointly by private interests and the government of the DMC may be eligible for ADB assistance, provided the majority of its equity is privately owned and it is controlled by private investors *Sale of ADB equity investment* ADB intends to divest its shareholdings at a fair market price once the objective of its investment is considered achieved In general, ADB will prefer to sell its shares to nationals of the host country to broaden local ownership and further develop local capital markets *DMC = Developing Member Country
CDC Capital Partners (formerly Commonwealth Development Cooperation (CDC)) <http://www.cdcgroup.com/>	CDC Capital Partners provides equity capital to businesses in the emerging markets, especially poorer countries As a medium to long-term investor which ultimately aims to realise its investments in consultation with its partners, the following constitutes key elements of CDC Capital Partners' investment policy: ■ It seeks to establish a partnership with sponsors to acquire, expand or restructure a business ■ It invests primarily in equity or equity-related finance and can arrange the provision of debt finance ■ It may co-sponsor and invest during the due diligence or bid stage of a potential business ■ It looks to invest from US$0.5 million–US$60 million in any one investment

CDC Capital Partners is on track to becoming a Public Private Partnership (PPP) – essentially a joint venture between UK government and the private sector in order to mobilise greater investment into emerging markets

Agence Française de Développement (AFD)
<http://www.afd.fr/english/>

Private sector financing is provided by Proparco, a member of the European economic interest group EDFI, which unites the 12 European financial institutions that finance the private sector
Proparco invests in enterprises in the form of equity, medium and long-term loans, including subordinate loans, and guarantees
In the Overseas departments and territories, it engages only in long-term investments
The investments may involve financing of projects promoted by start-up companies, development programmes, privatisation or restructuring
Proparco also executes specific financing provided by the International Finance Corporation (IFC) and the European Investment Bank (EIB)
The Group also invests long-term in the overseas departments through two vehicles:

– A regional development corporation, the Société de Développement Economique de la Réunion (Sodere) makes equity or quasi-equity investments in SMEs
– Proparco can make equity investments (shares and participating loans) in companies of a certain size

Proparco's investments are always minority shareholdings
They are intended for transfer to other shareholders, or sale on the financial market in the case of negotiable securities, after an average period of six years when the company has reached a sustainable level of maturity
That is why, when the investment is made, the project's internal rate of return must be at least 15 per cent in order to ensure a reasonable return on the capital invested and thus facilitate the liquidity of the shares held

European Bank for Reconstruction and Development (EBRD)
<http://www.ebrd.com>

The EBRD exists to foster the transition towards open market oriented economies and to promote private and entrepreneurial initiative in the countries of Central and Eastern Europe (CEE) and the Commonwealth of Independent States (CIS) committed to applying to principles of market economics
EBRD provides project-specific direct financing for private sector activities, restructuring and privatisation, or financing of infrastructure that supports these activities

ERBD projects
Each project is assessed according to the appropriate country strategy and certain guidelines apply for any EBRD project:

- The EBRD funds up to 35 per cent of the total project cost for a greenfield project or 35 per cent of the long-term capitalisation of an established company
- Significant equity contributions from other investors are required, in particular from industrial sponsors in the case of greenfield projects or new joint ventures, where special technical and management skills are needed; in such cases, industrial sponsors are expected to have a majority shareholding or adequate operational control
- Typical private sector projects are based on no more than two-thirds debt financing and at least one-third equity
- Additional funding by other co-financiers is typically required
- Equity from sponsors need not be exclusively in cash but can be in the form of equipment, plant machinery, etc.

As a guideline, the standard minimum involvement for the Bank is €5 million, though this may be reduced if the project has fundamental benefits for the country

Table *(Continued)*

Name of Development Bank	Details of funding available
	Equity finance In order to support privatisation and restructuring of medium-sized enterprises, the EBRD uses a number of equity financing instruments known collectively as 'early-stage equity' funds Two such instruments developed by the EBRD are Special Restructuring Programmes (SRPs) and Post-Privatisation Funds (PPFs) While most of the SRPs and PPFs are in the 'start-up' phase, several of the funds moved into the 'investment phase' in 1997 PPFs are designed to provide equity and management assistance, mainly to formerly state-owned firms that have been wholly or partially privatised by mass privatisation or individual auction schemes These funds seek minority stakes in enterprises, with the fund manager taking a proactive role in developing the company through board representation and support for the enterprise's management SRPs, in contrast, target enterprises requiring more comprehensive restructuring support before being viable for access to market-based financing on acceptable commercial terms **Equity finance for SME (also called 'equity window')** EBRD has established links with a variety of financial intermediaries to provide financing for projects that are too small to be funded directly. This allows the Bank to support SMEs Equity finance will be available to SMEs through privately managed investment funds in the region The EU and the EBRD have each contributed €25 million to the equity window, which will invest in private equity funds focused on SMEs The size of the fund is expected to range between €10 and €15 million on average, and maximum financing per investee will be restricted to €1 million for a minority stake To take account of the higher risks and costs involved in managing equity funds for SMEs, the EU contribution may be structured to provide appropriate incentives, such as an operating cost subsidy This is intended to overcome the private sector's reticence about SME investment Otherwise, SME funds will be structured on a case-by-case basis in line with business practice for private equity funds as well as local market conditions **Eligibility criteria and investment policy of SME funds** All accession countries are eligible for the establishment of an SME fund These funds could cover a region within one country, or a whole country when this is deemed manageable The Bank will seek to share the resources of the equity window evenly among accession countries Investment funds committed in their investment policy to focusing on SMEs, according to the EU definition of SMEs, will be eligible for equity funding Other requirements for investment under the SME funds are that: ▪ The target SMEs should be incorporated and operate in an accession country ▪ Only private, unlisted enterprises are eligible, regardless of ownership (domestic, foreign or joint venture) ▪ The maximum size of investment is capped at €1 million

SME funds will be allowed to use the full range of equity and quasi-equity instruments
SME funds will, as a matter of policy, hold minority positions in their investee companies, with a minimum stake of 10 per cent and a maximum of 49 per cent
The average shareholding is expected to be between 25 and 49 per cent
The fund managers will secure rights enabling them to exercise appropriate corporate governance over the SME portfolio

European Commission (EC) <http://europa.eu.int/comm/secretariat_general/sgc/aides/forms/regio07_en.htm >	Most funding granted by the EU is not paid by the European Commission direct but through the national and regional authorities of the Member States That holds for assistance under the Common Agricultural Policy (CAP) and most grants awarded under structural policy financial instruments (European Regional Development Fund (ERDF), European Social Fund (ESF), European Agricultural Guidance and Guarantee Fund (AGGF) and the Financial Instruments for Fisheries Guidance (FIFG)), which accounts for the bulk of EU aid in money terms The European Commission (EC) gives grants direct to recipients (public or private bodies – firms, interest groups, etc. – and private individuals in certain cases) for the implementation of other common policies in areas such as R&D, the environment, consumer protection and information, training and education It also awards direct grants for the application of the EU's external policies Projects under different categories have varying eligibility and percentage funding provided by the EC, e.g. maximum funding provided by EC could be set from 35 per cent–100 per cent
International Finance Corporation (IFC) <www.ifc.org>	IFC (an affiliate of the World Bank) provides equity finance for private companies operating in emerging economies It provides equity investments based on project needs and anticipated returns IFC is never the largest single shareholder and is considered a passive investor Its equity investment is usually maintained for 8–15 years and is considered a long-term investor IFC also provides a full range of quasi-equity finance, including convertible debentures, subordinated loans, loans with warrants and other instruments These products are provided, whenever necessary, to ensure that a project is soundly funded In order to receive funding, a project must meet IFC's investment guideline: – the project must be in the private sector – it must be technically sound – it must have a good prospect of being profitable – it must benefit the local economy – it must be environmentally sound (i.e. meet the IFC's stringent environmental standards) IFC financing is generally limited to no more than 25 per cent of project cost IFC also provides equity financing to commercial financial institutions which lend to local businesses for working capital, trade finance, project finance, venture capital and equipment leasing
Japan International Cooperation Agency (JICA) <www.jica.go.jp/english>	The development co-operation programme is intended to contribute to autonomous economic development in developing countries by providing financial and technical support on a governmental basis for development projects implemented by Japanese private companies in these countries

Table *(Continued)*

Name of Development Bank	Details of funding available
	Of the various types of development project implemented by Japanese private companies in developing countries, this co-operation programme is concerned primarily with projects that contribute to social development and the development of agriculture, forestry, mining and industry
	Having assessed the public benefits, technical and economic risks, profitability and experimental features of a project, the funds required for implementation are made available under long-term, low-interest conditions
	Types of project
	Investment and financing
	Financing is provided over the long term and at low rates of interest to:
	1. Japanese corporations implementing development projects in developing countries, and
	2. Japanese corporations which finance local corporations implementing development projects
	Projects eligible for financing and investment are:
	░ Projects involving the provision and upgrading of related facilities are intended to deal with situations where development projects have already received loans, guarantees of obligations or financing from other government bodies
	Experimental projects
	An experimental project is a type of development project that cannot be realised unless combined with technical improvements and development
	Experimental projects include cultivation of crops, livestock breeding, forestation, development of unused timber resources, excavation, screening and refining of non-ferrous minerals such as limestone, rock phosphate and rock salt, and construction of low-cost housing
United States Agency for International Development (USAID) <http://gopher.in fo.usaid.gov/>	USAID works to support long-term and equitable economic growth and advance US foreign policy objectives by supporting:
	░ Economic growth and agricultural development;
	░ Global health; and
	░ Conflict prevention and developmental relief
	USAID typically works in countries committed to achieving sustainable development but which lack the technical skills or resources necessary to implement policies and programmes that will accomplish these results.
	It provides assistance in four regions of the world, sub-Saharan Africa; Asia and the Near East; Latin America and the Caribbean and Europe and Eurasia
	An example of the USAID Equity Finance Program is the Trans-Balkan SME Equity Finance Program
	This provides equity and quasi-equity financing in combination with active business assistance and trade linkages to SMEs in the former Yugoslavia and neighbouring Balkan states
	Investments generally range between $100,000 and $500,000 per transaction

Appendix 13.5   Official export credit agencies of OECD Member Countries

Country	Agency	Link
Australia	Export Finance and Insurance Corporation	EFIC
Austria	Oesterreichische Kontrollbank AG	OeKB
Belgium	Office National du Ducroire/Nationale Delcrederedienst	ONDD
Canada	Export Development Corporation	EDC
Czech Republic	Export Guarantees Development Corporation	EGAP
	Czech Export bank	CEB
Denmark	Eksport Kredit Fonden	EKF
Finland	Finnvera Oyj	Finnvera
	FIDE Ltd.	FIDE
France	Compagnie française d'Assurance pour le commerce extérieur	COFACE
	Direction des Relations Economiques Extérieures (Ministère de l'Economie)	DREE
Germany	Hermes Kreditversicherungs-AG	HERMES
Greece	Export Credit Insurance Organization	ECIO
Hungary	Magyar Exporthitel Biztosító Rt.	MEHIB
Italy	Sezione Speciale per l'Assicurazione del Credito all'Esportazione	SACE
Japan	Export–Import Insurance Department	EID/MITI
	Japan Bank for International Cooperation	JBIC
Korea	Korea Export Insurance Corporation	KEIC
	The Export–Import Bank of Korea	Korea Eximbank
Mexico	Banco National de Comercio Exterior, SNC	Bancomext
Netherlands	Nederlandsche Credietverzekering Maatschappij NV	NCM
Norway	The Norwegian Guarantee Institute for Export Credits	GIEK
Poland	Korporacja Ubezpieczén Kredytów	KUKE
Portugal	Companhia de Seguro de Créditos, SA	COSEC
Spain	Compañía Española de Seguros de Crédito a la Exportación, S.A.	CESCE

Appendix *(Continued)*

Country	Agency	Link
	Compañía Española de Seguros y Reaseguros de Crédito y Caucíon, SA	CESCC
	Secretaría de Estado de Comercio (Ministerio de Economía)	SEC
Sweden	Exportkreditnämnden	EKN
Switzerland	Export Risk Guarantee	ERG
United Kingdom	Export Credits Guarantee Department	ECGD
United States	Export–Import Bank of the United States	Exim Bank

Other

Country	Site	Link
France	Coface Scrl	SCRL
Germany	Gerling Credit Insurance Group	GCIG
Hong Kong	Hong Kong Export Credit Insurance Corporation	HKEC
India	Export–Import Bank of India	Eximbankindia
Indonesia	Asuransi Ekspo Indonesia	ASEI
	PT Bank Ekspor Indonesia (Persero)	BEI
Israel	Israel Foreign Risks Insurance Corporation Ltd	IFTRIC
	Israel Discount Bank	Discount Bank
Italy	Societa Italiana Assicurazione Credit SpA	EULER-SIAC
Malaysia	Malaysia Export Credit Insurance Berhad	MECIB
New Zealand	EXGO	EXGO
Oman	Export Credit Guarantee Agency, Oman Development Bank	ECGA
Singapore	ECICS Credit Insurance Ltd	ECICS
Slovenia	Slovene Export Corporation, Inc.	SEC
South Africa	Credit Guarantee Insurance Corporation of Africa	CGIC
Sri Lanka	Export Credit Insurance Corporation	SLECIC
United Kingdom	EULER Trade Indemnity plc	EULER
United States	Overseas Private Investment Corporation	OPIC

International organisations

Organisation	Link
Asian Development Bank	ADB
Asia Pacific Economic Cooperation	APEC
European Union	EU
European Bank for Reconstruction and Development	EBRD
European Investment Bank	EIB
Inter-American Development Bank	IADB
International Monetary Fund	IMF
Multilateral Investment Guarantee Agency	MIGA
United Nations	UN
World Bank	WB
Banks for International Settlements	BIS

Source: <http://www.oecd.org/ech/act/xcred/ecas.htm>.

Learning assignments

1 What are the three types of risk that a global company is exposed to as a consequence of currency fluctuations ?

2 On 14 January 2002 it was announced that the US carrier Jetblue would buy 10 Airbus 320 for US$500 million. The planes were to be delivered over four years (two in 2002, two in 2003, three in 2004 and 2005). Airbus incurs 70 per cent of its cost in euros. What can Airbus Industrie do to cover its currency fluctuation risks?

3 Why are most major British global companies in favour of joining the eurozone?

4 What are the benefits and problems for a Japanese firm being listed on the New York Stock Exchange?

5 Why is the Adjusted Present Value (APV) method preferred to the Cost of Capital Adjustment (CCA) method in valuing international projects?

6 How can a company deal with strategic exposure?

7 What is a letter of credit?

8 Why are correlation coefficients between stock market returns so high (Table 13.1, p. 343)?

9 What type of global financial management tools would a global firm have used to counteract the adverse impacts of the 1997 Asian Crisis?

10 The central finance function is one of the central corporate functions of a conglomerate. Do you foresee a trend towards the formation of a global swapping bank account? What are the pros and cons of implementing such a financial tool?

11 Can companies take advantage of favourable exchange or tax rates and make purchases in different currencies/countries?

12 Name six commodity products which have forward and futures trades. Can you think of a commodity product not related to natural resources which has forward and futures trades?

13 When a global company originates from a country which may not have a sound financial system (e.g. Korea), should its overseas offices/subsidiaries hedge their local currencies against the currency of the head office or hedge it against a foreign currency (e.g. US$), which is less prone to attack from international finance companies (IFCs)?

14 Why do you think the Japanese stock market, in Table 13.1 (p. 343), was not correlated to other markets?

Key words

- Adjusted Present Value country risk (APV)
- Country stock market beta
- Cross-listing
- Currency swaps
- Documentary credit
- Export credit agencies
- Forward contracts
- Future contracts
- Hedging
- Leading and lagging
- Netting
- Options
- Project valuation
- Strategic exposure
- Transaction exposure
- Translation exposure

Web resources

<http://www.derivativesweek.com/>
Derivatives Week covers all aspects of global derivatives markets including interest rate, equity, commodity and foreign exchange derivatives.

<http://www.euromoney.com/index.html>
Euromoney covers international finance, capital markets and banking, it also contains a country section, which shows economy, debt, equity and currency factors for any of the 33 countries listed online.

<http://www.euroweek.com/New_EW/>
Euroweek provides information on the global capital markets spanning Asia, the Middle East, Europe, Africa and the Americas.

<http://www.isfmagazine.com/>
The *Journal of International Securities Finance* is a publication which focuses on international debt and equity financing via stock lending, repossession and swaps.

<http://www.oecd.org/ech/act/xcred/ecas.htm>
A list of official export credit agencies of OECD Member Countries.

<http://www.projectfinancemagazine.com/contents/publications/pf/>
Contains project finance news and a *Project Finance Global Directory* which lists, by business activity and geographic location, the contact details for companies, their teams and specific personnel.

Notes

1. See Eun and Resnick (2001); Hawawini and Viallet (2001).
2. Finance theory makes a distinction between *unsystematic* risks (that can be diversified) and *systematic* risks (that cannot be diversified). Unsystematic risks are those that a company can diversify though portfolio investments. A global firm reduces its unsystematic risks by having a portfolio of investments across a country, but cannot avoid the inherent risks of investing in a particular country owing to the particularities of that country (systematic risks).
3. See Hennart (1989, pp. 243–70).
4. This example is reproduced from chapter 13 in Hawawini and Viallet (1999). Reproduced with permission.
5. Ibid.
6. Ibid.

References and further reading

Ammer, J. and Jianpoing Mei, 'Strategic Returns to International Diversification', *European Financial Management*, 1(1), 1996.

Bailey, Warren, Peter Y. Chung and Jun-koo Kang, 'Foreign Ownership Restrictions and Equity Price Premiums: What Drives the Demand for Cross-Border Investments?', *Journal of Financial and Quantitative Analysis*, 34(4), 1999, pp. 489–511.

Eun, Cheol S. and Burce G. Resnick, *International Finance Management*, 2nd edn. New York: McGraw-Hill.

Giddy, Ian, *Global Financial Markets*. Lexington, MA: D.C. Heath, 1994.

Hawawini, Gabriel and Claude Viallet, *Finance for Executives: Managing for Value Creation*. Cincinnati, OH: South Western Publishing, 1999.

Hennart, Jean-François, 'Some Empirical Dimensions of Counter Trade', *Journal of International Business Studies*, 21(4), 1989, pp. 243–70.

International Finance Corporation, *Project Finance in Developing Countries: Lessons from Experience*, 7, 2001.

Lessard, Donald, 'Incorporating Country Risks in the Valuation of Offshore Projects', *Journal of Applied Corporate Finance*, 9(3), 1996.

McCauley, Robert and Steven Zimmer, 'Exchange Rates and International Differences in the Cost of Capital', in Y. Amihud and R. Levich (eds) *Exchange Rates and Corporate Performance*. Burr Ridge, NY: Irwin, 1994.

Sarkissian, Sergei and Michael J. Schill, 'The Overseas Listing Decision: New Evidence of Proximity Preference', Working Paper Series, McGu University and University of Virginia, 2000.

Solnik, Bruno, *International Investments*. Reading, MA: Addison-Wesley, 1996.

Stulz, Réne M., 'Globalization of Equity Markets and the Cost of Capital', NYSE Working Paper, 99-02, February 1999.

Part III

Broad issues in globalisation

Part III, Broad Issues in Globalisation, is particularly concerned with some recent *technological and social developments* that affect global firms as well as the challenges of the future.

Chapter 14   Globalisation and the Internet

Chapter 14 focuses on the emergence of the Internet as a tool enhancing the global managerial capabilities of firms. It discusses the promise of the Internet as well as its limitations for globalisation. It ends by looking at the organisational and cultural consequences of becoming 'web-enabled'.

Chapter 15   The Social responsibility of the global firm

Chapter 15 describes the environmental and social issues associated with globalisation and the work of global firms: corruption, environment protection, child labour and human rights being among the topics covered.

Chapter 16   Global trends

Finally, Chapter 16 reviews some of the salient trends that can be anticipated in the future and that may affect the development of global firms. The chapter ends by presenting some future scenarios as well as some future global organisational designs.

14

Globalisation and the Internet

The combination of broadband capabilities, connectivity, standard languages (html, xml), wireless communication and portability have given birth to the digital age and its most pervasive manifestation: the Internet. The Internet is a global network connecting millions of computers across the world, exchanging data, opinions, information and news using a common architecture, the Internet Protocol (IP). The network is also known as the World Wide Web (WWW) or the 'Web'. In essence, the Internet is a global tool since it has abolished physical distance for the transmission of data, images and sounds and it has standardised the transmission protocol as well as the machine software, making it possible for any computer in the world to be part of network and to 'talk' to other computers. In 2000, Forrester Research, a company specialised in analysis of the Internet businesses, published a series of reports predicting 'Global eCommerce Approaches Hypergrowth' with a significant slice of that growth coming from cross border transactions.[1] The report predicted that by the year 2004, e-commerce would reach US$6.7 trillion as compared to US$647 million in 2000, and that 18 per cent of world exports would be done via the World Wide Web. In this chapter, the terms 'Web', 'Net' or 'Internet' will be used interchangeably. More recent figures show that e-commerce will reach US$12.8 trillion by 2006[2], (Figure 14.1). The usage of the Internet is spreading all over the world (see Figure 14.2). The Internet is at the root of the so-called 'new economy' that flourished from 1995 to 2000 but that experienced a slump during the year 2001.

In this chapter, we will look first at the *business Internet space*, defining the players as well as the different types of e-transaction. Then we will look at the effect of the Internet on globalisation, from both a theoretical and a practical point of view, and at the contribution it is making towards global management.

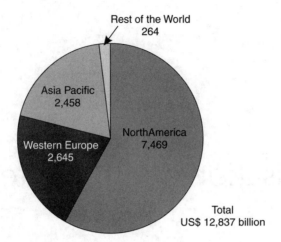

Figure 14.1 Forecast of online trade by 2006

Source: Forrester Research (2001).

At the end of the chapter one should be able:

- To define the business Internet space and its importance for the global business
- To show how the Internet has contributed to globalisation
- To show how the Internet can enhance firms' global capabilities.

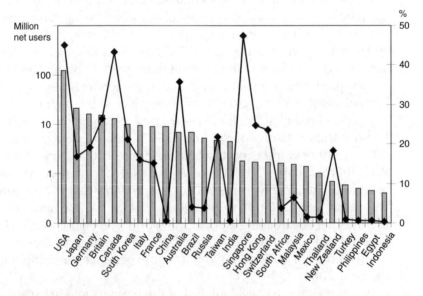

Figure 14.2 Internet users in 2000

Note: The bars show the number of users while the line shows the percentage of the population who were net users.

Source: *Asiaweek*.

THE BUSINESS INTERNET SPACE

The business Internet space can be defined in two ways:

(a) By the various *players* that use it to conduct their business or who provide services and equipment to the net users
(b) By the type of *transactions activities* taking place through the Internet.

The players

One can distinguish three major categories of players:

- The traditional companies of the so-called 'old economy' also called '**bricks and mortar**', that offer physically produced products and services with 'real' assets. These companies use the net for selling, buying, partnering and internal management through their Internet (open to the general public) or intranet (secured sites internal to the company) websites or extranet (secured websites external to the company)
- The 'pure plays' or the '**dotcom companies**' that have been created to enable web transactions and whose products and services essentially organise transactions, serve as e-commerce intermediaries and provide software platforms. Among those players one can find:

    - The **e-commerce** companies selling or organising sales to customers (B2C: Business-to-Consumers), trade among companies (B2B: Business-to-Business) or among customers (C2C: Customers-to-Customers). Well-known examples are Amazon.com (B2C retailer), e-bay (C2C auctioneer), E-Trade (B2C investment), Autobyline (B2C car dealership), Freemarket on line (B2B procurement).
    - The **intermediaries** providing tools for transactions: E-payment, security, domain names, search engines, etc.
    - The **browsers** such as Yahoo! or AltaVista.

- The traditional companies providing physical products or services to the two previous types of players:

    - Internet Service Providers (ISPs) providing access to the Web: AOL, most of the traditional telecom operators
    - Traditional software vendors and application service providers (ASPs), selling or supporting software: Oracle, SAP, IBM
    - Web hosting and maintenance: Exodus Communication, acquired in 2002 by Cable and Wireless, a UK global telecommunication operator
    - Consulting firms advising companies about Internet applications and development: Accenture, Gartner, Forrester
    - Content providers: Reuters, Time Warner, media companies
    - Equipment providers: CISCO, Nortel, Lucent, and Alcatel.

Figure 14.3 gives a pictorial representation of the Internet space.

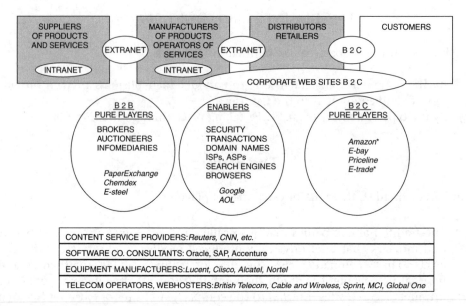

Figure 14.3 Players in the Internet space

Note: *Amazon and E-Trade are no longer pure plays.

Types of transactions

When one looks at the type of transactions on the Web, one has to distinguish three types:

- *Commercial transactions external to the firms:* E-commerce (selling), e-procurement (buying)
- *External relational transactions* other than buying and selling: E-partnering (co-ordinating, information-sharing, R&D with partners)
- *Internal relations:* E-management (planning and control, data base-sharing, recruiting, training, administration).

TRANSACTING THROUGH THE INTERNET: THE WEB-ENABLED COMPANY

The **web-enabled company** not only sells through the Internet but engages in a multitude of external and internal transactions so that the whole management processes are linked together, as in Figure 14.4. The best example of a web-enabled company is CISCO, which achieves more than 80 per cent of its sales on the Web but also carries most of its internal processes, its procurement and partner relationships through the Internet (see Mini-Example 14.1).

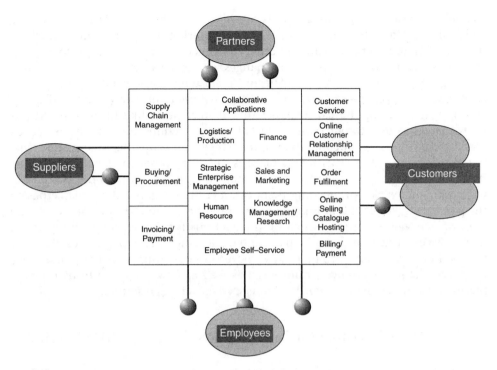

Figure 14.4 The web-enabled company

Source: *SAP*

Mini-Example 14.1 CISCO Systems

Founded in 1984 by a group of computer scientists from Stanford University, CISCO Systems has established itself as the world leader in networking technology. Its products include: routing and switching, voice and video over the Internet Protocol (IP), optical networking, wireless, storage, security and broadband products. CISCO has evolved as global company and is present in 68 countries. In 2001, its turnover was US$22 billion and it employed 20,000 people. In addition to being a very innovative firm in technological products and application, CISCO has pioneered the use of the Internet for sales and procurement as well as for internal management and partnering with its contract manufacturers, software developers and distributors. According to John Chambers, the company's Chairman and CEO, CISCO has achieved cost savings and increased customer satisfaction from their Internet-based applications – in 2001, such cost savings amounted to US$1 billion. Global results can be consolidated in half a day and all employees over the world use the HR Internet platform to settle their expenses as well as study e-learning modules. CISCO has established 24 'Networking Academies' in least developed countries to train and develop Internet-related skills.

Source: CISCO, *Annual report*, 2001, available on line at <http://www.cisco.com/>

The majority of transactions amounts are business-to-business. Firms are buying and selling online either directly or using **B2B marketplaces** or e-Hubs[3] in which they network to other companies in order to deliver complete solutions to customers. Those marketplaces can be Exchanges or Aggregators like e-steel, Paper-Exchange, Altra, Chemdex or CapitalStream. To illustrate how it works, we will take the example of a customer – say, a farmer – who is willing to buy newly hatched chicks and animal food. She/he can connect to a market place like Farmscom <http://www.eharvest.com/> to purchase products through auctions and also the associated services like financing, documentation, insurance, surveying, packaging and transportation (Figure 14.5). This marketplace is linked to other marketplaces that are linked to other individual producers or marketplaces. In Figure 14.5, the farmer who is buying chicks for breeding them can identify several of these marketplaces: the poultry marketplace that is going to organise the auction for the chicks, the agri marketplace that is going to organise the auctions for animal food, the financial marketplace, the insurance marketplace and the logistics marketplace. Several players will be linked electronically including 'old economy' companies (crop and chick producers, banks, insurances, transports) as well as new economy firms (marketplaces, auctioneers, digital security verifiers, credit ratings intermediaries, etc.).

THE CONTRIBUTION OF THE INTERNET TO GLOBALISATION

The Internet is, by design, a *global network*. It can be seen as an additional driver to globalisation, but not a revolutionary one. As it was discussed in Chapter 1, globalisation has been enhanced and fostered by political, technological, sociological and competitive factors. The additional contribution that the Internet brings to the

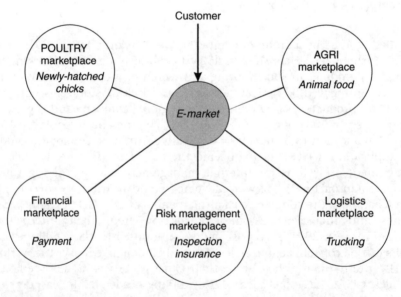

Figure 14.5 Example of an e-marketplace: B2B transactions imply the integration of several marketplaces

Source: Forrester Research (2000).

globalisation trend is the enhanced capability to decouple physical activities from the information exchange needed to support them. Evans and Wurster (2000) have argued that the Internet breaks the traditional **reach versus richness** trade-off. (see Mini-Example 14.2) and, as a consequence, fosters the ability of companies to organise transactions and transfer data beyond national boundaries in real time. The Internet is a *facilitator to globalisation*.

Mini-Example 14.2   Reach versus richness trade-off

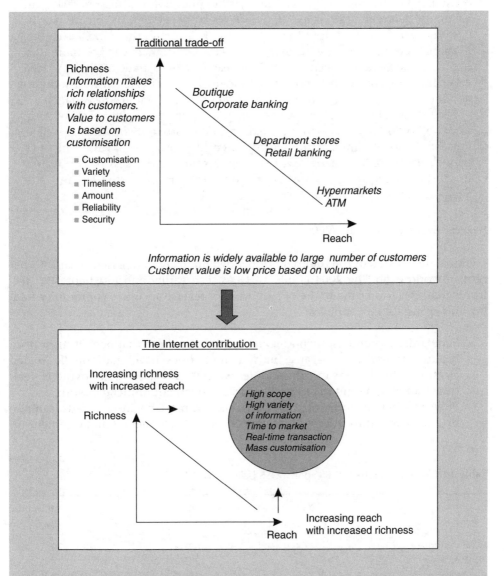

Evans and Wurster (2000) argue that, traditionally, economic activities are constrained by the difficulty of simultaneously achieving intense exchange of information (richness) with a large number of people (reach). Economic entities

Mini-Example 14.2 *(Continued)*

have therefore to choose between *volume* (reach) and *quality* of relationships (richness). If a company wants to increase its volume and reach a larger number of people, it has to reduce the amount of information it will exchange with the customers and therefore standardise its product and customers interactions. Hypermarkets that can handle large number of customers provide no (or little) assistance to customers, for example. On the other hand, when one wants to customise a product or service, one need to exchange rich information with customers, but there is a limit to the amount of customers that one can handle. A specialised boutique giving expert advice to customers cannot handle as many customers as a supermarket. This reach/richness trade-off has induced companies to choose between two fundamental strategic positions: high-volume, low-cost *standardised products/services* or low-volume *differentiation.*

The Internet, because of its standard platform and connectivity, and because of its ability to carry very rich information in the form of text, video as well as voice and data, permit a certain degree of customisation for a vast number of people, therefore increasing reach without sacrificing richness. It is possible, for instance, to work at a distance with suppliers or customers and still exchange customised information.

Source: Evans and Wurster (2000).

Global trade through the Internet is growing and likely to represent nearly 18 per cent of world export by 2004 (Table 14.1) As seen earlier and in Chapter 9, electronic marketplaces facilitate the organisation of reverse auctions, commodity trading and aggregation of supplies:

■ Standardised products, such as commodities, are those that benefit most from Internet transactions because most commodities have traditionally traded electronically. Traders in commodities were already used to anonymous, real-time transactions and the Internet adds a convenient unified network.

■ Progressively semi-customised products, such as metal-engineered parts, can also find their way into the e-marketplaces because once there is an agreement on

Table 14.1 Global Internet B2B exports, US$ billion

	2000	2004	% of Total Exports (%)
Western Europe	22.4	691.5	20
North America	14.8	385.2	22.7
Asia Pacific	5.8	218.9	12.1
Rest of the World	1.1	70.3	~10
Total	44.1	1,365.9	18

Source: Forrester Research (2000).

technical specifications, reverse auctions can be organised for their procurement, as mentioned in Chapter 9.

- George Yip (2000) predicted that the Internet would increase the globalisation of markets, reinforce global cost reduction, foster global competition and weaken governments' barriers open trade (see Table 14.2).

However, in spite of its global enhancement capabilities, Internet transactions across borders are subject to potential limitation owing to regulatory and socio-technical/cultural factors:

(a) *Cross-border regulatory restrictions*, such as customs duties and VAT taxes still apply to physical transfer of goods transacted on the Net
(b) *Local legislations*, as for instance the insistence of certain governments to restrict the access to certain Web sites: a well-publicised example was provided by the experience of Yahoo! with the French anti-racist legislation (see Mini-Example 14.3)
(c) *Socio-technical and cultural factors*, such as the propensity of customers to accept online payment, attitude towards electronic trade versus direct face-to-face relationships which may hamper/foster the development of e-business.

Table 14.2 Effects of the Internet on globalisation

Market globalisation	- Increases global commonality in customer needs and tastes (facilitates customised standardisation and strengthens appeal of global brands: Barbie online) - Enables global customers and global channels (facilitates global sourcing) - Supports global marketing (enhances global brands and standardises search) - Makes global products more rapidly visible
Cost reduction	- Exploits differences in country costs and facilitates competition from low-cost small-scale campanies from emerging markets - Enhances global sourcing (see Chapter 9) - Speeds up global logistics - Reduces product development costs
Foster global competition	- Makes competitive comparisons easier - Increases the number of potential global suppliers by reverse auctions - Puts new rivals in the global competitive arena
Weaken government barriers to open trade	- Makes it easier for customers to by-pass customs and tax levies - Puts pressure on government to harmonise standards and policies - Gives customers more incentives to lobby their governments to align with more customers - Friendly regulations

Source: Yip (2000).

Mini-Example 14.3 Yahoo! and anti-racist legislation in France

In November 2000, a French court ruled that Yahoo! should block French users from viewing and buying Nazi memorabilia on its American auction site, in accordance with French anti-racist regulation. The implication of the judgement was that Yahoo!'s parent in the United States, and not only the French subsidiary, should make sure that access to Nazi objects auctions to French citizens should be banned. Yahoo! counter-attacked by asking the US court to declare that this decision could not be enforced in the United States because it violates the First Amendment of the American constitution and that US citizens were not obliged to follow French rules outside France. A US district court followed this argument, and decided that Yahoo! was not bound by the French judgement. Two French human rights groups appealed the decision. This series of events generated a polemic about the right of governments to regulate a 'global' medium such as the Internet. Some analysts saw the French decision as a dangerous one for the future of the Web, others argued that the Internet had to follow local rules.

As Jack Goldsmith, a Professor of Law at the University of Chicago, wrote in the *Financial Times* commenting on the Yahoo!–French court dispute: 'Confusion begins with the metaphor of the Internet as a 'borderless medium'. It is no more a borderless medium than the telephone, the telegraph, postal service, facsimile or smoke signal. All of these media facilitate transactions by someone in 'real space' in one nation with someone in 'real space' in another nation. When French citizens are on the receiving end of an offshore communication that their government deems harmful, France has every right to take steps within its territory to check and redress the harm.'

Sources: Press reports. Jack Goldsmith in *Financial Times*, 27 November 2000.

As Companies such as Yahoo!, Amazon.com or e-Bay have discovered, globalising their business is not so different than for traditional 'bricks and mortar' companies. It implies the development of local alliances, acquisitions and an adaptation of the product offering to local conditions (see Mini-Example 14.4).

Mini-Example 14.4 How do dotcom companies globalise?

Internet companies, known as 'dotcoms', follow a classical pattern of international expansion in order to get a global reach. They invest in countries and set up subsidiaries, acquire local players or enter into strategic alliances. Following are examples of the globalisation of dotcom firms.

- **StarMedia Network, Inc.** is an Internet media company targeting Spanish- and Portuguese-speaking markets worldwide. The company's network consists of 14 branded Internet properties, which include Star-Media, a portal for Spanish and Portuguese speakers: Latinred, a Spanish language online community; Zeek!, an online directory of Portuguese language online sites; Adnet, a Mexican Web directory; Openchile, a comprehensive Chilean directory and guide; Batepapo, a Brazilian chat portal; Guia Sp, Guia Rj and Guia Nacidade, Brazilian metropolitan Web directories; Panoramas, a Chilean guide for Santiago; Paisas.com and Yoinvito, online Colombian city guides, and Periscopio, an information portal for Spanish speakers worldwide. The company also operates StarMedia Mobile, its wireless division. The company headquarters is based in New York and is listed on the NYSE. The company grew by acquisition and internal development. It encounters the same problems of global efficiency versus local responsiveness as any other global firm (in this case, a regional one).

- **Yahoo! Inc.** is a global Internet communications, commerce and media company that offers a comprehensive branded network of services. The company's principal offering, <www.yahoo.com>, is an online navigational guide to the Web. The company also provides online business and enterprise services designed to enhance the productivity and Web presence of Yahoo!'s clients. Yahoo! has offices in Europe, Asia Pacific, Latin America, Canada and the United States. The company has developed 24 international online properties in 13 languages. During 2000, the company launched Yahoo! Argentina, Yahoo! India and Yahoo! Canada en Français. Yahoo! Get Local offers extensive information for all 50 states, 219 metropolitan areas and more than 30,000 counties and cities in the United States. In January 2002, the company acquired Cade?, a Brazilian search engine, from StarMedia Network, an integrated Media and Business Solutions company targeting Spanish- and Portuguese-speaking audiences. Yahoo! Brazil and Cade will be integrated into a new property, providing individuals and businesses with the resources and services of Yahoo!'s global network, combined with the localised programming and expertise of both properties.

THE INTERNET AND GLOBAL FIRMS

Overall, the Internet was been seen during the heady days of the 'new economy' in 1999 and 2000 as a new business paradigm allowing firms to completely revolutionise the way of designing and implementing strategies.[5] This was fuelled by the hyperinflation of stock valuations, when any dotcom newcomer could challenge the market value of well-established centenarian 'bricks and mortar' players. The later burst of the market bubble showed that traditional business strategy models are still valid, even in virtual space.[6]

For the global or globalising firms, the Internet provides a tool to manage internal and external linkages, to run business processes more efficiently, enhancing their **cross-border management capabilities:**

- Real-time communication over all locations with various media: video, text, and data
- Ability to get customer interactions, requests and feedback and to consolidate customer data

- Ability to serve as a platform for a global knowledge management system
- Ability to reach new sets of suppliers through electronic global procurement
- Ability to identify and communicate with customers in low-density locations.

In order to do this they need to develop several types of **web-enabling capabilities**:

- Partnering capabilities:

  - The ability to form partnerships and to activate them in real time
  - The ability to share information with partners so that the transaction can be executed automatically
  - The ability to make deals instantaneously

- A *'no secret' management system*: in order to make decisions quickly, the various internal processes of the company have to share information (in fact, automatically) horizontally
- *Decision-making*: an ability to make important decisions, such as pricing, at increased speed and, on some occasions in real time, implying a very strong decentralisation of authority
- *Feedback*: to collect and consolidate feedback from customers, interpret it, disseminate it and adapt the responses to local conditions
- *IT*: to develop an IT platform and telecoms network that can work in a seamless way
- *Internal implications*: in order to participate in the Web economy, firms are not only cataloguing their products on the Web and organising 'clicking' sales, as currently done on most of the B2C Internet sites, but have to completely rethink their managerial systems, structures and cultures. Table 14.3 summarises these internal implications.

Table 14.3   Organisational requirements for e-business

Internal requirements	Consequences
Transparency	▪ Integrity and consistency of information ▪ Clear data and procedures
Sharing culture	▪ Horizontal as well as vertical exchange of information ▪ External partners have access to data-bases ▪ No 'silos'
Process integration	▪ All management processes are compatible with each other to facilitate information flow
Pooled co-ordination	▪ Ability to have different departments working together instantaneously instead of sequentially ▪ Ability to bundle different parameters in real time ▪ Sequential co-ordination too time-consuming
Real-time commitment	▪ Ability to make decisions quickly ▪ No time for hierarchical checking
Horizontal processes	▪ Hierarchical communications and decision processes inefficient

Table 14.4 Internet managerial culture versus Asian managerial culture

Internet culture	Typical Asian corporate culture
Transparency	▣ Partial, and multiple information
	▣ Lack of clear procedures
Sharing culture	▣ Vertical information sharing
	▣ Clannic retention
Process integration	▣ 'Siloed' processes
Pooled co-ordination	▣ Top-down processes, otherwise sequential processes
Real-time commitment	▣ Several checks, vertically organised
Horizontal processes	▣ Hierarchical

Those organisational attributes may sometime **conflict with local cultures.** Table 14.4 contrasts Internet cultural requirements with typical Asian corporate cultures.

The challenge for the global firm is to overcome these cultural differences among their employees, suppliers, customers and partners to make Web transactions effective.

SUMMARY AND KEY POINTS

1. Business Internet space is defined by the various *players* involved in Internet-related business and by the type of *transactions* taking place through it:
   - Players:
     - Traditional companies 'old economy' or 'bricks and mortar'
     - 'Pure plays' or 'dotcom companies':
       - (a) E-commerce companies.
       - (b) Intermediaries
       - (c) Portals and browsers
     - Traditional companies providing physical products/services
   - Transactions:
     - *Commercial transactions external to the firms*: E-commerce (selling), e-procurement (buying)
     - *External relational transactions* other than buying and selling: e-partnering (co-ordinating, information-sharing, R&D with partners, etc.)
     - *Internal relations*: E-management (planning and control, data base-sharing, recruiting, training, administration, etc.).

2. The Web-enabled company not only sells but engages in external and internal transactions through the Internet:
   - The majority of the transactions are business-to-business (B2B).
   - Firms use e-marketplaces or e-hubs that can be B2B exchanges, aggregators or auctioneers.

3. The Internet constitutes an additional driver to globalisation thanks to its reach and richness capabilities:
   - *Reach* is the ability to access a large number of people in real time owing to a standard platform and connectivity
   - *Richness* is the ability to carry a high level of information in the form of text, video and voice.

4. Standardised products and semi-customised products benefit most from Internet transactions.

5. The Internet:
   - Increases globalisation of markets
   - Increases global costs reduction
   - Fosters global competition
   - Weakens governments' barriers to open trade.

6. Limitations to the globalisation of the Internet:
   - Cross-border regulatory restrictions
   - Local legislation
   - Socio-technical/cultural factors.

7. The Internet provides a management tool that enhances global cross-border management capabilities:
   - Partnering capabilities:
   - A 'no secret' management system
   - Ability to make important decisions in 'real time'
   - Ability to collect and consolidate feedback from customers
   - Ability to develop an IT platform and telecoms network that can work in a seamless way
   - Ability to rethink completely managerial systems, structures and cultures.

8. Cultural differences can restrain Internet capabilities: the challenge for the global firm is to overcome those cultural differences among their employees, suppliers, customers and partners to make Web transaction effective.

Learning assignments

1 Based on your personal experience on surfing the Web, give concrete examples of its reach and richness capabilities.
2 Go to the Dell website in the country where you are located and try to configure your laptop with a keyboard that is not used in your country (for instance, a French keyboard if you are in the United States). What do you observe? What conclusions can you draw about the Internet as a global tool?
3 Why do you think Business-to-Consumer (B2C) transactions are less likely to develop on the Internet, both domestically and globally?
4 Do you know of any other cases similar to the Yahoo!/French dispute over anti-racist legislation? What are the pros and cons of government regulations of Internet traffic?
5 What are the benefits and constraints of global e-learning platforms (education programs on the Internet)?
6 Why does e-business demand horizontal processes and pooled co-ordination (see Table 14.3, p. 392)?
7 Give a example of a global Web application in a firm you know.
8 E-bay is a virtual auctioneer. How can it globalise its activities?

Key words

- Bricks and mortar
- Browsers
- Business-to-Business (B2B) marketplaces
- Conflict with local culture
- Cross-border management capabilities
- Dotcom companies
- E-commerce
- Intermediaries
- Reach versus richness
- Web-enabled company
- Web-enabling capabilities

Web resources

\<http://www accenture.com/\>
The Web site of a leading IT and strategy consulting firm.

\<http://www.business2.com\>
A general information Web-based magazine on Internet-related issues.

\<http://www.forrester.com/\>
Specialised in research about the Internet and the 'new economy'.

\<http://www.gartner.com/\>
Research about the Internet and the 'new economy'.

\<http://www.strategy-business.com/\>
Web site of a publication published by Booz Allen & Hamilton a global business organisation.

\<http://www.news.com/\>
Newsletter about technology, computers and media news.

Notes

1. Sanders (2000a, 2000b).
2. Sharrard (2001).
3. Lief (1999); Kaplan and Sawney (2000, pp. 97–103); Truong (2000a).
4. Booz Allen & Hamilton (1999).
5. Coltman *et al.* (2001, pp. 57–86); Porter (2001, pp. 63–78); Subramanian and Adner (2001, pp. 44–53).
6. Truong (2000b).

References and further reading

Booz Allen & Hamilton, *Competing in the Digital Age: How the Internet Will Transfer Global Business*. New York: EIU, 1999.

Cairncross, Frances, *The Death of Distance: How the Communications Revolution Will Change Our Lives*. London: Orion Business Books, 1997.

Coltman, Tim, Timothy Devinney, Alopi Latukefu and David Midgley, 'Revolution, Evolution, or Hype?', *California Management Review*, 44(1), 2001, pp. 57–86.

De Meyer, Arnoud, Soumitra Dutta and Sandeep Srivastana, *The Bright Stuff: How Innovative People and Technology Can Make the Old Economy New*. London: Financial Times/Prentice-Hall, 2002.

Dutta, Soumitra and Sandeep Srivastana, *Embracing the Net: get.competitive*. London: FT. com, Financial Times, 2001.

Economist, The, 'E-Management', *Special Survey*, 11 November 2000.

Evans, Philip and Thomas Wurster, *Blown to Bits*. Boston, MA: Harvard Business School Press, 2000.

Hartman, Amir and John Sifonis, *Net Ready: Strategies for Success in the Net Economy*. New York: McGraw-Hill, 2000.

Kaplan, Steven and Mohanbir Sawney, 'E-Hubs: The New Marketplaces', *Harvard Business Review*, May–June 2000, pp. 97–103.

Liautaud, Bernard and Mark Hammond, *e-Business Intelligence: Turning Information into Know-ledge into Profit*. New York: McGraw-Hill, 2000.

Lief, Varda, 'Net Market Places Grow Up', *The Forrester Report*, December 1999. Forrester Research, Inc., 400 Technology Square, Cambridge, MA 02239; also available at <http://www.forester.com>.

Porter, Michael, 'Strategy and the Internet', *Harvard Business Review*, March–April 2001, pp. 63–78.

Sanders, Matthew, 'Global eCommerce Approaches Hypergrowth', *The Forrester Brief*, 18 April 2000a. Forrester Research, Inc., 400 Technology Square, Cambridge, MA 02239; also available at <http://www.forrester.com>.

Sanders, Matthew, 'Sizing Global Online Exports', *The Forrester Report*, November 2000b. Forrester Research, Inc., 400 Technology Square, Cambridge, MA 02239; also available at <http://www.forrester.com>.

Sharrard, Jeremy, 'Global Online Trade Will Climb to 18 per cent of Sales', *The Forrester Brief*, 21 December 2001. Forrester Research, Inc., 400 Technology Square, Cambridge, MA 02239; also available at <http://www.forrester.com>.

Subramanian, Rangan and Adner, Ron, 'Profits and the Internet: Seven Misconceptions', *MIT Sloan Management Review*, Summer 2001, pp. 44–53.

Truong, David, 'E-Business Networks', *The Forrester Report*, April 2000a. Forrester Research, Inc., 400 Technology Square, Cambridge, MA 02239; also available at <http://www.forrester.com>.

Truong, David, 'Brokered Partner Integration', *The Forrester Report*, April 2000b. Forrester Research, Inc., 400 Technology Square, Cambridge, MA 02239; also available at <http://www.forrester.com>.

Yip, George S., 'Global Strategy in the Internet Era', *Business Strategy Review*, 11(4), 2000, pp. 1–14.

15

The social responsibility of the global firm

Globalisation has had, and still has, deep social, *political and environmental consequences*. The effects of globalisation on society and general welfare are often challenged on the ground that globalisation tends to widen the gap between the rich and the poor and encourages, supports or generates practices that are detrimental to the well-being of the world population, particularly in developing countries. Global companies, as the agents of globalisation, are the front-line targets of critics who blame them for misconduct in a vast array of domains, ranging from global warming, pollution, corruption, encroachment on human rights, child labour and vivisection. This chapter tries to address some of the issues that global companies face in dealing with the societies in which they operate, with a particular emphasis on the kind of 'ethical' dilemma that firms and global managers have to confront in their worldwide operations. Most of those ethical and societal issues are not limited to global enterprises: a purely domestic firm can be confronted with corruption or environmental pollution; this chapter does not pretend to give an exhaustive coverage of business ethics in general, it concentrates only on those related to global operations. Figure 15.1 shows the four main categories of social and ethical issues facing global companies.

At the end of the chapter one should be able:

- To understand the causes and effects of corruption in business
- To understand the role that a global company can play in fighting corruption
- To be able to participate in the formulation of environmental friendly policies

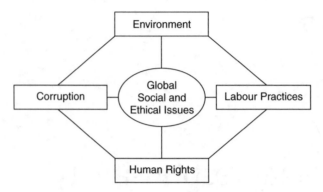

Figure 15.1   Social and ethical issues and the global firm

- To understand the social responsibility of global firms in maintaining appropriate practices with regard to child labour, human rights and labour conditions
- To understand the role of global non-government organisations (NGOs).

GLOBAL COMPANIES AND CORRUPTION

Corruption can be simply defined as 'the abuse of public office for private gain'.[1] This definition applies to public officials as well as employees of private companies who receive a personal benefit (a *bribe*) in the form of a cash or non-cash advantage (such as car, family travel or the employment of a relative) and, in return, give a preferential advantage to the donor. Transparency International (TI), a non-governmental organisation (NGO, see below) regularly publishes two indices: the Corruption Perception Index (CPI) and the Bribe Payers' Index (BPI). The CPI is a score that relates the perceptions of corruption in different countries as seen by business, academics and risk analysts. It represents a compilation of different surveys. The BPI ranks the leading exporting countries in terms of the degree to which their companies are perceived to be paying bribes abroad. This index is based on extensive interviews done by Gallup International Association of senior executives, bankers, lawyers and accountants.

Table 15.1 gives the 2001 Corruption Perception Index and the BPI computed in 1999.

The Chairman of Transparency International, at the launch of the results of the 2001 index, declared: 'There is no end in sight to the misuse of power by those in public office and corruption levels are perceived to be as high as ever in both developed and developing worlds'.[2]

The industries in which corruption is most acute are: public works contracts and construction, arms and defence, power (including petroleum and energy), mining, telecoms, aerospace and banking. Although the practice of corruption is not limited

Table 15.1   Corruption indices

Corruption Perception Index (CPI) (From 0 = Highly Corrupt to 10 = Highly Clean)			Bribe Payers' Index (BPI) (From 0 = High Level of Bribery to 10 = Negligible)		
Low corruption					
1	Finland	9.9	1	Sweden	8.3
2	Denmark	9.5	2	Australia	8.1
3	New Zealand	9.4	3	Canada	
4	Iceland	9.2	4	Austria	7.8
	Singapore				
6	Sweden	9.0	5	Switzerland	7.7
7	Canada	8.9	6	Netherlands	7.4
8	Netherlands	8.8	7	United Kingdom	7.2
9	Luxembourg	8.7	8	Belgium	6.8
10	Norway	8.6	9	Germany	6.2
			10	United States	
High corruption					
82	Tanzania	2.2	11	Singapore	5.7
83	Ukraine	2.1	12	Spain	5.3
84	Azerbaijan	2	13	France	5.2
	Bolivia				
	Cameroon				
	Kenya				
88	Indonesia	1.9	14	Japan	5.1
	Uganda				
90	Nigeria	1	15	Malaysia	3.9
91	Bangladesh	0.4	16	Italy	3.7

Sources: Transparency International <http:///www.transparency.org>. The CPI Index refers to corruption in the public sector.

to global enterprises, their visibility and power give them a particular responsibility to, as well as a great impact on, the societies in which they operate.

There is vigorous debate about the exact limits of corruption (When does it start?), its origin (Why?) its real effect (Is corruption having a negative effect?) and its practice (How is corruption activated?).

When gifts become bribes, where does corruption start?

It is current practice in some countries to offer gifts as recognition of friendship and relationships.[3] The border between a bribe and a gift is frequently ambiguous, but the common rule would be to consider as gift a present offered openly whose content can be disclosed in the person's professional and social environment. Gifts can also be offered to communities (school sponsoring, donation to communities, etc.) the rule still being that it can be openly offered. Beyond the frontiers of transparency, the land of bribery begins.

In the United States the Foreign Practice Act of 1977 that exposes American executives to criminal sanctions strictly forbids bribery. Such legislation does not exist in other countries although the Convention on Combating Bribery on Foreign Public Officials in International Business Transactions adopted by the OECD on 21 November 1997 has been ratified by nearly 30 countries. This convention prohibits the use of bribes, states that criminal sanctions should be applied to the persons engaged in bribery, and recommends that tax deductibility of bribes not be permitted.[4] The OECD convention, however, has a lower dissuasive power than the American Foreign Practice Act.

Causes and effects of corruption

The causes of corruption are diverse[5], and belong to five main categories:

1. *Administrative resource allocation*: when transparent market mechanisms are substituted by administrative authorisation and distribution. Price controls, multiple exchange rates, subsidies and administrative authorisations granted without competitive bidding are mechanisms that induce corruption.
2. *Lack of institutional checks and balances and information*: absent or powerless public audit, single source of power without right of appeal, cowed legal system.
3. *Insufficient funding of public services*: leading to low remuneration of public officials relative to private sector, lack of proper financing of political parties or undersupply of public goods for hospitals, transport and schools.
4. *Social and cultural factors*: such as a societal division along ethnic and linguistic lines leading to nepotism.
5. *Natural resources*: abundant natural resources are also an incentive for bribery.[6] This is more prevalent in developing countries; as Figure 15.2 shows, there is a positive correlation between GDP *per capita* and the CPI. Countries that formerly had a planned economy score lower on the scale.

Several studies converge to demonstrate the adverse effects of corruption on the economy.[7] The effects are both direct and indirect.

Direct effects

We can list three in particular:

(a) It *discourages domestic and foreign indirect investment* because of the additional cost burden on projects: it amounts to another *hidden tax*. If India could reduce its corruption level to Singapore's level, the effect on foreign investment would be the same as a reduction of corporate tax rate by 22 per cent.[8] Corruption thus hampers economic growth.
(b) It *skews public capital expenditure* in favour of new equipment as opposed to maintenance and operational expenditures. It also discriminates against educational and health expenditures that are less amenable to bribery.
(c) It *reduces the productivity of public investments* and reduces the *collection of taxes*.

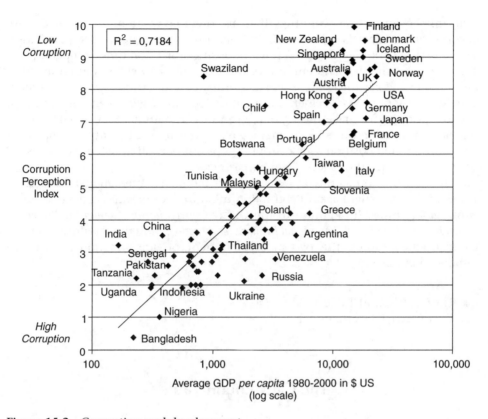

Figure 15.2 Corruption and development

Indirect effects

Two are common:

(a) *Reduction in work productivity* as a result of demotivation
(b) *Dislocation of social fabric.*

Although some economists have argued that corruption facilitates transactions in inefficient markets and therefore is a form of 'grease, speeding the wheels of commerce',[9] the negative effects are overwhelmingly dominant.

THE PRACTICE OF CORRUPTION AND THE ROLE OF GLOBAL COMPANIES

Contradicting the statement made by the Chairman of Transparency International that corruption is increasing, not decreasing, many companies, despite the damaging, economic and social effects, engage in bribery to obtain contracts.

Companies coming from countries that are themselves 'immune' from corrupt practices bribe officials or executives from other countries. This paradoxical behaviour[10] is attributed to competitive necessities ('If I don't my competitor will do and my shareholders and employees will lose out') as well as cultural justifications ('In Rome do as the Romans do'). Performance and rewards systems that focus entirely on economic achievements also induce local managers to engage in corrupt practices in order to 'make the figures', even in corporations that officially assert a global code of ethics. As a result, many global firms implicitly put their managers in a schizophrenic position. The distribution of bribes is often delegated to a third party such as an agent or a joint venture partner.

In the late 1990s some firms, as well as private and public international institutions, created platforms to fight against corruption and introduce practical codes of conduct within global firms. In addition to the OECD *Convention on Combating Bribery of Foreign Public Officials in International Business Transactions*, and the US Foreign Practice Act mentioned earlier, the two most prominent private and non-government initiatives have been:

- The Caux Round Table[11]
- Transparency International.[12]

The Caux Round Table

Founded in 1986, the Caux Round Table is a network of senior business leaders from both the industrialised and the developing nations who recognise that business must take a leadership role in developing a more fair, free and transparent society, leading to greater world prosperity and sustainability of resources. The Caux Round Table meets annually at Mountain House, Caux, Switzerland and initiates global conferences of business leaders and government officials. These act as a catalyst and promote their *Principles for Business*, including among other things an objective of fighting against corruption. Mini-Example 15.1 reproduces the set of anti-corruption measures adopted at the Singapore meeting in September 2000.

Transparency International

Transparency International (TI) is an international NGO based in London organised in national chapters in 77 countries. The stated mission is 'to curb corruption by mobilising a global coalition to promote and strengthen international and national integrity systems.' Its activities consist of distributing information about corrupt practices and ways to fight against them. It has launched an annual awards programme to honour individuals and organisations around the globe that are making a difference in ending corruption. The goal is to give greater recognition to the efforts of journalists, civil society workers, activists, government and corporate whistleblowers who work to investigate and unmask corruption, often at great

Mini-Example 15.1   Caux Round Table: anti-corruption measures, 2000

Anti-Corruption Measures

The following measures are offered to all firms, wherever situated, and whatever their lines of business. The Measures were presented at the Caux Round Table Global Dialogue September 2000 in Singapore. The Caux Round Table commends them for consideration by business corporations.

1. Disclose publicly and make widely known its endorsement of the Anti-Corruption Measures.
2. Establish a clearly articulated written policy prohibiting any of the firm's employees from paying or receiving bribes and 'kickbacks'.
3. Implement the policy with due care and take appropriate disciplinary action against any employee discovered to have made payments in violation of the policy.
4. Provide training for employees to carry out the policy, and provide continuing support, such as help lines, to assist employees to act in compliance with the firm's policy.
5. Record all transactions fully and fairly, in accordance with clearly stated record-keeping procedures and accounting controls, and conduct internal audits to assure that all payments made are proper.
6. Report annually on the firm's bribery and corruption policy, along with a description of the firm's experiences implementing and enforcing the policy.
7. Have the annual report in step six above audited either by an independent financial auditor or an independent social auditor, or both.
8. Require all agents of the firm to affirm that they have neither made nor will make any improper payments in any business venture or contract to which the firm is a party.
9. Require all suppliers of the firm to affirm that they have neither made nor will make any improper payments in any business venture or contract to which the firm is a party.
10. Establish a monitoring and auditing system to detect any improper payments made by the firm's employees and agents.
11. Report publicly any solicitations for payments whenever such reporting will not lead to harsh reprisals of material consequences to the company or its employees (or report privately to a monitoring organisation, such as Transparency International or a social auditor).
12. Establish a system to allow any employee or agent of the firm to report any improper payment without fear of retribution for their disclosures.

Source: <www.cauxroundtable.org/anti-corruption measures.htm>.

personal risk. The Integrity Awards also seek to encourage those whose example provides leadership in the global anti-corruption effort. It publishes the CPI and the BPI as well as a Global Corruption Report. It gives free access to a Corruption On-Line Research and Information System and its national chapters implement a large variety of activities to inform about and fight against corruption. In a recent (Pope, 2000) book, TI draws 32 lessons that constitute a source of inspiration and guide for action.

Other anti-corruption initiatives

Four other organisations have issued guidelines and regulations to prevent corrupt practices:

- The **International Chambers of Commerce** in 1977 issued the *Rules of Conduct on Bribery*.
- The **UN General Assembly** in 1996 adopted a *Declaration against Corruption and Bribery* calling for the elimination of tax deductions for bribes and for the exchange of information among member countries.
- The **World Bank** in 1995 issued *procurement guidelines* in order to prevent corruption in projects financed by the Bank.
- The **Council of Europe** in 1994 created a Multidisciplinary Group on Corruption and in 1997 issued the *Guiding Principles for the Fight against Corruption* and in 1999 a *Criminal Law Convention on Corruption*.

Despite all this effort, there is still a long way to go before bribery disappears, but global firms and global executives are under increasing public scrutiny and the most progressive firms have made considerable progress in the implementation of ethical behaviour.

GLOBAL COMPANIES AND ENVIRONMENTAL PROTECTION

In 1984, a gas leak at a pesticide plant of Union Carbide in Bhopal, India, killed more than 2,000 people. This event was the starting point of a vast global public opinion movement that puts in question the role of multinational corporations (MNCs) with respect to the environment. Since then the activities of firms in the extractive and energy industries (oil, mining, forestry), biotechnology and agro business (genetically modified organisms), chemical, pulp and paper, are permanently challenged on the ground that they are contributing to the degradation of the environment. Mini-Example 15.2 lists nine corporate causes of environmental crisis, as noted by Corpwatch, a Californian-based anti-globalisation group.

Mini-Example 15.2   Corporations at the root of the environmental crisis

Destruction of the ozone layer
Production of chlorofluorocarbons (CFCs), the most serious ozone depletors, and 'CFC-lite' substitutes – HCFCs and HFCs – two chemical replacements that are either harmful to the ozone or potent global warming gases.

A handful of chemical corporations produce and distribute the hazardous pesticide methyl bromide – considered today to be the leading threat to the ozone layer.

Global warming
According to the UN, the influence of transnational corporations extends over roughly 50 per cent of all emissions of greenhouse gases. This includes about half of the oil production business, virtually all of the production of road vehicles, most chlorofluorocarbon production, and significant portions of electricity generation and use.

Persistent organic pollutants
Annual world production of synthetic organic chemicals has skyrocketed from one million tons in 1930 to seven million in 1950 to sixty-three million in 1970, to 500 million tons in 1990. At current rates, by the year 2000, the world will produce more than a billion tons of synthetic-organic chemicals every year.

Used to create pesticides, synthetic fibers, plastics, pulp and paper, detergents and more, the production of these chemicals also makes tremendous amounts of waste. For instance, roughly two-thirds of all hazardous waste produced in the United States comes from chemical corporations.

Radioactive waste
The nuclear industry, along with corporations servicing the military–industrial complex, especially nuclear weapons contractors, have created some of the worst toxic problems the planet has ever seen.

Mining
Global corporations such as Rio Tinto Zinc, Kobe Steel and Broken Hill Properties dominate the pollution-intensive mining, refining and smelting of metals such as platinum, aluminium and copper.

High costs of high-tech
The production of computers carries with it a set of negative ecological and social impacts. For instance, when the Intel corporation produces just one six inch silicon wafer from which its Pentium chip is cut, it also creates by-products that include 25 pounds of sodium hydroxide, 2,840 gallons of wastewater and 7 pounds of hazardous waste.

Mini-Example 15.2 *(Continued)*

- **Unsustainable agriculture**

  Corporations control virtually every step of the food production and distribution system, which is riddled with ecologically unsustainable practices.
- Just twenty chemical companies account for the sales of over 90 per cent of all the world's pesticides. These agricultural chemicals are responsible for tens of thousands of deaths, and at least a million more farm worker poisonings every year.

  Chemical giants such as Shell, Monsanto, Mitsubishi and Novartis now control many of the world's genetic seed stocks, as well as much of the agricultural biotechnology industry – which presents a new series of potential environmental problems.

  Global giants such as Phillip Morris, United Fruit, Pepsico, Cargill, Unilever and Nestlé oversee vast portions of international agricultural production and trade. In fact, transnationals either directly or indirectly command 80 per cent of the land around the world that is cultivated for export crops such as bananas, tobacco and cotton. Such agro-export 'development' patterns regularly displace farmers producing food for local consumption, pushing them into situations where they must over-exploit the environment to survive.

- **Deforestation**

  While a number of factors contribute to deforestation, timber transnationals such as MacMillan Bloedel, Mitsubishi and Georgia Pacific play a central role. Indeed, commercial timber harvests have increased by 50 per cent between 1965 and 1990.

- **Over-fishing**

  Once a way of life for millions of families and coastal communities, fishing has become big business.

  Highly-mobile, high-tech, large-scale factory fishing fleets owned by corporations such as Spain's Pescanova, Japan's Taiyo, South Korea's Dong Won, and the United States' Arctic Alaska/Tyson Foods roam the world's oceans, indiscriminately plundering the biological diversity of the seas, overstepping the limits of marine ecosystems and wiping out traditional fishing communities.

  According to UN Food and Agriculture Organization (FAO) figures, nearly 70 per cent of the world's conventional fish stocks are either fully exploited, severely over-taxed, declining or recovering. 'This situation' says the FAO, is globally non-sustainable and major ecological and economic damage is already visible.

Source: <http://www.corpwatch.org/FeatureTheCorporatePlanetFactSheet#2.htm>.

Integrating environmental policies into business strategies

Confronted with such criticisms, some firms have developed policies and practices designed to integrate environmental issues in their business strategies. Forest

Reinhart at the Harvard Business School (1999) found that those environmental strategies were based on three inter-related developments:

(a) Design and implementation of **information systems**, both internal and external, in order to understand the environmental impact of products over their entire life cycle as well as the concerns and expectations of customers, employees, environmentalists, international institutions and governments. Such information is complemented by proactive communication such as the yearly publication of the *Shell Report: People, Planet and Profit*, in which the company documents the actions that it has taken to meet its economic, environmental and social responsibility.[13]

(b) Design and implementation of incentives **systems** devoted to fostering environmental performances, such as tying bonuses to good environmental practice.

(c) Contribution to **environmental institutions**, such as the *Global Compact* (see Mini-Example 15.3), the *World CSR*, which groups different organisations like the Business Impact, The Center for Corporate Citizenship at Babson College, The Prince of Wales Business Leader Forum (PWBLF), CSR Europe and Business Impact.

Mini-Example 15.3   The Global Compact

At the World Economic Forum, Davos, on 31 January 1999, UN Secretary-General Kofi A. Annan challenged world business leaders to 'embrace and enact' the Global Compact, both in their individual corporate practices and by supporting appropriate public policies. These principles cover topics in **human rights, labour** and **environment**.

Human rights

The Secretary-General asked world business to adopt two principles:

Principle 1: support and respect the protection of international human rights within their sphere of influence; and
Principle 2: make sure their own corporations are not complicit in human rights abuses.

Labour

The Secretary-General asked world business to uphold four principles:

Principle 3: freedom of association and the effective recognition of the right to collective bargaining;
Principle 4: the elimination of all forms of forced and compulsory labour;
Principle 5: the effective abolition of child labour;
Principle 6: the elimination of discrimination in respect of employment and occupation.

Environment

The Secretary-General asked world business to do three things:

Principle 7: support a precautionary approach to environmental challenges;
Principle 8: undertake initiatives to promote greater environmental responsibility;
Principle 9: encourage the development and diffusion of environmentally friendly technologies.

The Global Compact Network

Nearly 300 companies from all regions of the world have pledged support of the Global Compact and are implementing the nine principles.

International Inter-Sectoral Business Associations
International Chambers of Commerce (ICC)
International Organization of Employers (IOE)
World Business Council on Sustainable Development (WBCSD)
Prince of Wales Business Leaders Forum (PWBLF)
Business for Social Responsibility (BSR)
Caux Round Table
Conference Board
CSR Europe
Instituto Ethos
Rotary International
Young Entrepreneurs
International Sectoral Business Associations
International Federation of Consulting Engineers (FIDIC)
International Fertilizer Industry Association (IFA)
International Petroleum Industry Environmental Conservation Agency (IPIECA)
International Road Transportation Union (IRU)
International Council of Chemical Associations (ICCA)
Global Mining Initiative (GMI)
Labour
The International Confederation of Free Trade Unions (ICFTU), with approximately 134 million members.
International Federation of Chemical, Energy, Mine and General Workers' Unions (ICEM)
Union Network International (UNI)
Trade Union Advisory Committee to the OECD (TUAC)
Civil Society Organizations Human Rights:
Amnesty International
Human Rights Watch
Lawyers Committee for Human Rights

Environment:
World Wide Fund for Nature (WWF)
The World Conservation Union (IUCN)
World Resources Institute
International Institute for Environment and Development
Conservation International
Development, Others:
Regional International Networking Group
Global Reporting Initiative (GRI)
Transparency International
The Save the Children Alliance
SA 8000
Global Sullivan Principles
The Copenhagen Centre
European Business Campaign 2005 for CSR
International Center for Alcohol Policies (ICAP)
Academic Institutions
Numerous leading think tanks from around the world.
National Associations
Ethos
Fundação Abrinq pelos Direitos da Criança
Entreprises pour l'Environnement

The activities and roles of the Global Compact are challenged by militant organisations like Corpwatch on the grounds that:

- Corporate influence at the UN is already too great. Corporate lobby groups working directly and through national governments have weakened environmental agreements and influenced important regulatory documents affecting health and safety.
- Such partnerships set a dangerous precedent towards partial privatisation/commercialization of the UN system.
- The UN's positive image is vulnerable to being sullied by corporate criminals – while corporations can 'blue wash' their image by wrapping themselves in the UN's flag symbolizing peace, human rights, and dignity.
- The partnerships have no provision to keep the corporations accountable for their behaviour – such as a monitoring or enforcement mechanism – which allows companies to declare their allegiance to UN principles without making a commitment to follow them.
- Even civil society groups participating in the Global Compact like Amnesty International and Human Rights Watch have serious reservations about the lack of monitoring and enforcement provisions.
- The International Chambers of Commerce – which represents the interests of the world's largest corporations – insists that it will only support the Compact if monitoring and enforcement are left out.

Sources: <http://www.unglobalcompact.org/and http://www.corpwatch.org>.

GLOBAL CORPORATIONS AND LABOUR PRACTICES

Global executives are often confronted with the issue of procuring components, materials or services in countries that do not respect normal labour practices. The most significant are the utilisation of school-aged children as workers, the non-respect of acceptable working hours and working conditions, forced labour, the exploitation of legal and illegal immigrants or the obstruction or elimination of trade-unions.

Child labour is the most publicised and the one that provokes a typical ethical dilemma (see Mini-Example 15.4 for examples). In a thought-provoking article, Martha Nichols (1993) explained the dilemma as the choice between respecting a code of ethics and cancelling an order to a supplier employing young children, and therefore accepting the consequences of depriving their families of much needed income and putting the children back on the street, or accepting the order knowing that children are working to fulfil it.[14]

Mini-Example 15.4 Child labour and the global firm

Soccer balls[15]

By the mid-1990s, Sialkot, located in the Punjab province of Pakistan, was the centre for the production of customised, high-quality sporting goods and surgical equipment: 25,000 jobs were involved in those activities. Soccer ball production and export of 35 million balls accounted for US$45 million in 1995. Since the stitching of soccer balls is labour-intensive, children were used to perform this task. In Pakistan, it was estimated that 3.6 million children were employed as labourers; one-third earning wages, the remaining being engaged as family helpers for agricultural tasks.

- In the mid-1990s, child labour cases were brought to public opinion via television reports and news magazines. This drew attention to soccer ball production. Reebok, a leading sporting goods global firm, implemented its own policy in order to abolish child labour. Reebok's policy was (1) to buy finished goods from a child labour-free factory to which stitching is brought out of the home, (2) to set up a monitoring programme, (3) to start an educational programme. David Husselby, Programme Director of Save the Children Fund's UK office in Islamabad, came to Sialkot and served as a catalyst to facilitate dialogue between the industry and the International Labour Organisation (ILO). This resulted in a Sialkot Partnership to End Child Labour that induced a agreement with the Sporting Goods Manufacturers' Association in Atlanta in 1997. The Atlanta Agreement stated that:
- Stitching centers were to be established which would bring the work out of households
- Workers would be systematically registered in order to check for age
- Alternative educational programmes would be created for children

- Rewards, warnings and penalties were set up to encourage vendors who did not use child labour
- Members of the World Federation of Sporting Goods would favour vendors who did not use child labour.

The programme was a success from the point of view of child labour in the soccer ball industry but it had some indirect negative effect such as the fact that by taking the work out of household, Punjabi women could not work in the factory for religious reasons. Other industries, like carpets or brickeries, were still employing children and some of the children that went out of stitching, a relatively flexible job, moved to a more hazardous work.

Nike[16]

In 1988, the Asian–American Free Labour Association (AAFLA, a branch of the AFL–CIO trade union) found that Nike, the sporting goods company, used contractors in Indonesia who were breaking Indonesian labour laws and paying workers below-subsistence wages. The author of the AAFLA report, denouncing those practices, initiated a public campaign that reached the media. Nike's reaction was to deny any responsibility. During the 1990s, the name of Nike was consistently mentioned as a company using contractors who exploited workers in Indonesia or used children in Pakistan. By 1996–7 the anti-Nike campaign had large visibility in the media and on American campuses where students organised protests. Nike adopted a defensive approach, hiring Ernst & Young to audit their foreign operations as well as asking Andrew Young, an African American, ex-mayor of Atlanta to produce a report. Those attempts were criticized on methodological grounds. In May 1998 Phil Knight, Nike's CEO, admitted that 'Nike products has become synonymous with slave wages, forced overtime and arbitrary abuse'. He announced a series of reforms: raising the minimum age of workers to 18 for shoes and 16 for apparels, adopting clean air standards based on the US standards in all factories, expanding the monitoring program, expanding educational programs for workers and making micro loans available to workers. Nike worked to bring apparel manufacturers to join the Apparel Industry Partnership task force created by President Clinton in order to reach an agreement on labour standards to be accepted by all competitors.

Sources: Crawford, Cadot and Traça (1999); Burns and Spar (2000).

GLOBAL COMPANIES AND HUMAN RIGHTS

The final set of issues that global corporations have to confront is their direct or indirect involvement in human rights abuses. This happens when global firms operate in countries whose political regimes use methods of enforcement that do not respect the principles of the Universal Declaration of Human Rights (UDHR) as adopted by the United Nations. This includes arbitrary detention, execution of political dissidents, non-respect of legal procedures for trials of opponents, deportation of population, use of military forces for civilian unrest, rapes or tortures by security forces or by factions in civil wars, etc. Global firms can be involved directly, when human rights abuses are committed, to protect their operations or indirectly when their activities contribute to maintaining political regimes involved in human rights abuse. Mini-Example 15.5 gives a sample of some cases of global firms associated with human rights abuses.

Mini-Example 15.5 Global firms and human rights: a sample

Oil companies in Myanmar[17]

Unocal and its partner, Total of France (SLORC), are building a natural gas pipeline from the Andaman Sea through the rainforests of southern Burma into Thailand. This represents the country's largest foreign investment. According to a report by Earth Rights International, a human rights watchdog group, SLORC has secured development by forcing members of the Karen and Mon ethnic groups to work on pipeline-related infrastructure, military bases and heliports. The pipeline has become the target of intense lobbying by international human rights groups.

Furthermore, according to a four-year investigation by Paris-based Geopolitical Drug Watch, the Myanmar Oil and Gas Enterprise (MOGE), Unocal's other partner, 'is the main channel for laundering the revenues of heroin produced and exported under the control of the Burmese army'.

Oil companies in Nigeria[18]

The 1995 execution of Ken Saro Wiwa, the Nigerian environmental and democracy activist, galvanised protests around the role of Royal Dutch Shell and other oil companies in the Niger Delta

Nigerian security forces have beaten, detained, or even killed people who were involved in protests over oil company activities and individuals who have called for compensation for environmental damage. Victims include youths, women, children and traditional leaders. In some cases, the abuse occurs after oil companies have requested that security forces intervene. A Human Rights Watch report charges that multinational oil companies are complicit in abuses committed by the Nigerian military and police because they fail to condemn them publicly and to intervene with the Nigerian government to help ensure that they do not recur. In many cases, Human Rights Watch found that the oil companies had made no effort to learn what was done in their name by abusive local security forces, seeking to keep oil flowing in the face of local objections.

Enron in India[19]

Leading Indian environmental activists and representatives of villagers' organ-isations opposing a power plant project by a subsidiary of the Enron Develop-ment Corporation in India, the Dabhol Power Corporation (DPC), have been subjected to beatings and repeated short-term detention. In many cases, they have been detained for periods ranging from several days to two weeks with-out being produced before a magistrate as required under Indian law. During mass arrests at demonstrations in villages surrounding the project site, protesters have been beaten with canes (lathis) or otherwise assaulted by the police, in some cases sustaining severe injuries. Police have also tear-gassed peaceful demonstrations. Police have frequently used laws providing for preventative detention to arrest demonstrators in anticipation of protests, sometimes under suspicion of violence.

Exxon in Indonesia[20]

The International Labor Rights Fund, representing villagers in the Aceh prov-ince in Indonesia, sued Exxon Mobil Corp. in a US federal court, accusing the company of complicity in human rights abuses committed by state security forces that protected its large natural gas field. The suit contests that Exxon Mobil looked the other way as the military terrorised Acehnese villagers. Officials from Exxon Mobil rejected and categorically denied that it was in any way involved with human rights abuses.

Sources:
<www.moles.org/ProjectUnderground/drillbits>; Drillbits & Tailings (15 December, 1996).
<http://www.hrw.org/research>; Oil Companies Complicit in Nigerian Abuses, Lagos, (23 February, 1999).
<http://www.hrw.org/reports/1999/enron/>; The Enron Corporation Corporate Com-plicity in Human Rights Violations Summary and Recommendations (January 1999).
Neela Banerjee, 'US Lawsuit Snares Exxon', *International Herald Tribune* (Friday 22 June, 2001).

According to Amnesty International Secretary General Pierre Sané (2000), there are five reasons why business should care about human rights.

1. 'The first one is the moral argument. We do not need to convince managers and boardrooms that the amputation of children's limbs in Sierra Leone in order to terrorize a population and win a war is wrong, or that the gang rape of women by Serb soldiers in Kosovo is evil, or that the killing of civilians in East Timor or Chechnya is to be condemned. These acts are wrong, insidious. They have been prohibited internationally'.
2. 'The second argument is the legitimacy of human rights. They have been codified in treaties ratified by governments. Peoples the world over are struggling to hold

their governments accountable for the implementation of international law. Believe me, if a free ballot was upheld globally today, overwhelmingly people will say they want their human rights, all their human rights'.

3. 'The third argument is that it is in the interest of business to see human rights protected. The rule of law protects investments by guaranteeing political stability. An educated and healthy population increases economic productivity. A company tarnished by controversies around human rights violations can see its reputation destroyed and its profitability threatened'.

4. 'Fourthly, companies and more specifically, Multinational Corporations, have secured for themselves freedoms to operate which has given them enormous power to affect the lives of people but with power comes responsibility'.

5. 'Finally, the Universal Declaration of Human Rights (UDHR) calls upon all organs of society to protect and promote human rights. The ILO conventions protect the rights of the workers. Other conventions place direct responsibility on companies to act in accordance with international human rights law'.

Amnesty International proposes a checklist of conduct principles for global firms to adopt (see Mini-Example 15.6).

Mini-Example 15.6   Human rights principles for companies: a checklist[21]

Company Policy on Human Rights

All companies should adopt an explicit company policy on human rights that includes public support for the Universal Declaration of Human Rights (UDHR). Companies should establish procedures to ensure that all operations are examined for their potential impact on human rights, and safeguards to ensure that company staff are never complicit in human rights abuses. The company policy should enable discussion with the authorities at local, provincial and national levels of specific cases of human rights violations and the need for safeguards to protect human rights. It should enable the establishment of programs for the effective human rights education and training of all employees within the company and encourage collective action in business associations to promote respect for international human rights standards.

Security

All companies should ensure that any security arrangements protect human rights and are consistent with international standards for law enforcement. Any security personnel employed or contracted should be adequately trained. Procedures should be consistent with the United Nations (UN) Basic Principles on the Use of Force and Firearms by Law Enforcement Officials and the UN Code of Conduct for Law Enforcement Officials. They should include measures to prevent excessive force, as well as torture or cruel, inhuman or degrading treatment. Companies should develop clear rules for calling in or contracting with state security forces and for not hiring security personnel who have been responsible for serious human rights violations. Any complaint about security procedures or personnel should be promptly and independently investigated. Companies which supply military security or police products or services should take stringent steps to prevent those products and services from being misused to commit human rights violations.

Community engagement

All companies should take reasonable steps to ensure that their operations do not have a negative impact on the enjoyment of human rights by the communities in which they operate. This should include a willingness to meet with community leaders and voluntary organizations to discuss the role of the company within the broader community. Companies should work cooperatively with organizations, which promote human right.

Freedom from discrimination

All companies should ensure that their policies and practices prevent discrimination based on ethnic origin, sex, colour, language, national or social origin, economic status, religion, political or other conscientiously held beliefs, birth or other status. This should include recruitment, promotion, and remuneration, working conditions, customer relations and the practices of contractors, suppliers and partners. It should include measures to deal with sexual or racial harassment, and to prohibit national, racial or religious hatred.

Freedom from slavery

All companies should ensure that their policies and practices prohibit the use of chattel slaves, forced labour, bonded child labourers or coerced prison labour. This should include ensuring that suppliers, partners or contractors do not use such labour.

Health and safety

All companies should ensure that their policies and practices provide for safe and healthy working conditions and products. The company should not engage in or support the use of corporal punishment, mental or physical coercion, or verbal abuse.

Freedom of association and the right to collective bargaining

All companies should ensure that all employees are able to exercise their rights to freedom of expression, peaceful assembly and association, as well as a fair means of collective bargaining without discrimination, including the right to form trade unions and to strike. Companies have a responsibility to ensure such rights for their employees even if such rights are not protected in a particular country's national law. Companies should take steps to ensure that suppliers, partners or contractors do not infringe such rights.

Mini-Example 15.6 *(Continued)*

Fair working conditions

All companies should ensure just and favourable conditions of work, reasonable job security and fair and adequate remuneration and benefits. This should include provision for an adequate standard of living for employees and their families. Companies should take steps to ensure that suppliers, partners or contractors do not infringe such rights.

Child labour

Companies shall not engage in or support the use of child labour as defined by applicable national laws and relevant international standards.

Monitoring human rights

All companies should establish mechanisms to monitor effectively all their operations' compliance with codes of conduct and international human rights standards. Such mechanisms must be credible and all reports must periodically be independently verifiable in a similar way to the auditing of accounts or the quality of products and services. Other stakeholders such as members of local communities in which the company operates and voluntary organizations should have an opportunity to contribute in order to ensure transparency and credibility.

Sources:
- *United Nations Universal Declaration of Human Rights (UDHR), Preamble* Organization for Economic Cooperation and Development (OECD), *Guidelines for Multinational Enterprises.*
- *UN Code of Conduct for Law Enforcement Officials,* UDHR Articles 3, 5, and 9.
- *UP Basic Principles on the Use of Force and Firearms by Law Enforcement Officials.*
- *Principles Governing Conventional Arms Transfers of the Organization for Security Cooperation in Europe.*
- *UDHR Articles 21, and 26,* International Labour Organization (ILO), *Tripartite Declaration of Principles Concerning Multinational Enterprises and Social Policy.*
- *UDHR Article 2, ILO Conventions 100,111, and 165.*
- *UDHR Article 4, ILO Convention 29,105, and 138.*
- *UDHR Article 3, ILO Convention 155.*
- *UDHR Articles 20, and 23, ILO Conventions 87, 98, and 135.*
- *UDHR Articles 23, and 24, ILO Convention including 95 and 131 (on wages), 14 and 4006 (on weekly rest), and 132 (on holidays with pay).*
- *ILO Conventions 138,146.*
Reproduced with the permission of Amnesty International Publications, 1 Easton Street, London, WCIX ODJ, United Kingdom (http://www.amnesty.org)

SOCIAL RESPONSIBILITY AND GLOBAL FIRMS: AN ON-GOING CHALLENGE

We have described the most salient issues concerning the social responsibilities of global firms. The list is not exhaustive and every day new cases appear; firms are often taken off guard and have to try to react and adjust their policies. Some adopt a very defensive attitude, but soon realise that it does not work. A multiple dialogue between governments, NGOs, international institutions, the media and public opinion and industry associations has been going on since the 1990s and will progressively align corporate strategies and human dignity (see Figure 15.3 on the Global Ethical Web). The 'ethical dimension' has now reached the financial markets with the development of socially responsible investing (SRI) in which investors select companies that are considered as socially responsible.[22] However, as the case of corruption demonstrates, improvement is slow and regressive behaviour can still be exhibited, such as the refusal by the US government, on behalf of American industrialists, to sign the 1997 Kyoto Treaty on the reduction of carbon dioxide emissions. New ethical debates arise daily, as in the cases of bio-ethics, genetically modified (GM) organisms or the right of pharmaceutical companies to limit the development of alternative HIV drugs in developing countries. More and more, global firms are being held accountable for impacts that were traditionally the domain of government and this looks likely to be one of the most challenging tasks for the future.

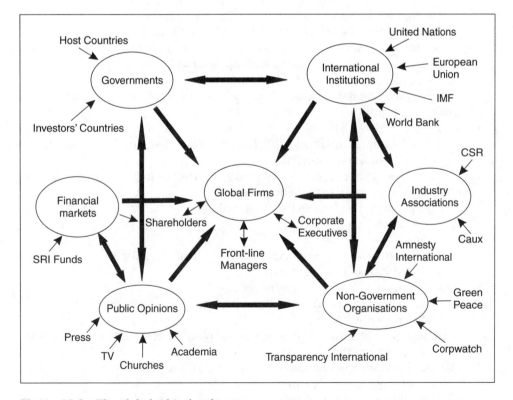

Figure 15.3 The global ethical web

Note: The list of organisations is not exhaustive.

SUMMARY AND KEY POINTS

1. There are four main categories of social and ethical issues facing global companies:
    - Corruption
    - Environmental
    - Human rights
    - Labour practices

    The challenge ahead is how global companies handle an increasing responsibility for social issues that were traditionally the domain of governments.

2. Corruption:
    - *Definition*: Corruption can be defined as the abuse of public office for private gain; a gift can be offered openly but a bribe cannot
    - Two *indices* relate to corruption:
        - *Corruption Perception Index (CPI)*: a score which relates the perception of the degree of corruption businesses, academics and risk analysts
        - *Bribe Payers' Index (BPI)*: ranks the different exporting countries in terms of the degree to which their companies are perceived to be paying bribes abroad
    - There are five *causes* of corruption:
        - *Administrative resource allocation*: when administrative authorisation and distribution replaces transparent market mechanisms
        - *Lack of institutional checks*, balances and information
        - *Inadequate funding* of public services leading to relatively low remuneration of public servants and under-supply of public goods
        - *Social and cultural factors* leading to nepotism
        - *Abundance of natural resources* leading to discrimination in funds allocation
    - *Effects* of corruption:
        - *Direct*:
            (a) Discourages domestic and foreign investments owing to additional cost burden on projects
            (b) Skews public capital expenditure in favour of new equipment instead of operating existing equipment
            (c) Reduces the productivity of public investments and reduces tax collection
        - *Indirect*:
            (a) Decreased work productivity through demotivation
            (b) Dislocation of social fabric
    - Global companies *engage in bribery* because of:
        - Need to keep up with competitors' practices
        - Cultural justifications
        - Result of an incentive system which emphasises economic achievements
    - *Anti-corruption* measures:
        (a) Disclose publicly and make widely known the company's endorsement of anti-corruption measures
        (b) Establish a clearly articulated written policy prohibiting employees from paying/receiving bribes

(c) Implement policies with due care and take disciplinary action for any violations
(d) Provide training and support to employees to carry out the policy
(e) Maintain full and proper accounting records, subject to periodic internal audit review
(f) Report annually on firm's bribery and corruption policy and describe the company's experience in its enforcement; the annual report should be independently audited.
(g) Require all agents/suppliers to affirm that they have neither made nor will make any improper payments
(h) Establish a monitoring and auditing system to detect any improper payments made by firm's employees/agents
(i) Report publicly any solicitation for payments
(j) Establish a system for employees/agents to report any improper payment without fear of retribution.

3. Environmental issues:
   - Types of *environmental crisis*:
     - Destruction of ozone layer
     - Global warming
     - Persistent organic pollution
     - Radioactive waste
     - Environmental pollution
     - Deforestation
     - Over-fishing
   - Interrelated development which facilitates incorporation of environmental strategies in *business strategies*:
     - Implementation of *information system* to understand the environmental impact of company's products over their entire life cycle; complement the information system with a *communication system*
     - Implement an *incentive system* to promote company's environmental performance
     - Contribute to environmental institutions.

4. Human rights:
   - Global firms' involvement:
     - Direct involvement: human rights invoked by global companies to protect their operations
     - Indirect involvement: contributions to political regimes are involved in human rights abuse
   - Principles for global firms:
     - Formulate company policy on human rights
     - Security arrangements should protect human rights and be consistent with international standards of law enforcement
     - Be involved in community that promotes human rights
     - Company policy should not approve discrimination, slavery or child labour practices
     - Provide safe and healthy working conditions and products

- All employees should have the freedom to associate with and right to join collective bargaining mechanisms
- Mechanisms should be established to monitor a company's compliance with international human rights standards.

5. Labour practices – what to do when global companies procure in countries which do not respect normal labour practices, such as using child labour.

6. Companies face four main categories of social/ethical issues:

   ▪ Corruption
   ▪ Environmental
   ▪ Human rights
   ▪ Labour practices

How can global companies handle their increasing responsibility for social issues that were traditionally the domain of governments?

Learning assignments

1 What are the main causes of corruption?
2 What corrupt practices involving global firms have you heard of?
3 What dilemma may a country manager face when confronted by a request to solicit a bribe to obtain a major contract?
4 What policies should a global firm implement to prevent corrupt practices?
5 How can corporate policies be designed to contribute to global environment protection?
6 What should the country managers do if a local supplier in a developing country is employing 12-years-old labour?
7 Should a global company pull out of Myanmar, a country well known for human rights abuses by the military power?
8 Draw a global ethical web for a pharmaceutical company engaged in anti-HIV drug production?
9 What are SRI funds? Select an SRI fund and track its evolution as compared to the general evolution of the stock market.

Key words

▪ Bribe
▪ Child labour
▪ Corruption
▪ Environmental crisis
▪ Ethics
▪ Human rights
▪ Socially responsible investment (SRI)
▪ Transparency International

Web resources

<http://www.corpwatch.org/trac/index.html>
Corpwatch's Globalization and Corporate Rule web site, which covers the institutions that are the agents of globalisation.

<http://www.mckinseyquarterly.com/category_editor.asp?tk= 86032::9&L2=9>
McKinsey Quarterly – Environment.

<http://www.wbscd.ch>
The World Business Council for Sustainable Development web site.

<http://www.un.org/>
The UN web site containing human rights, economic and social development information.

Notes

1. The definition is from Transparency International <http://www.transparency.org>
2. Press Release from Transparency International, Paris, 27 June 2001.
3. Fadiman (1986, pp. 4–12).
4. See the OECD web site at <http://www.oecd.org//daf/nocorruption>
5. See Mauro (1997); Tanzi (1998).
6. Leite and Weiman (1999).
7. Besides the IMF papers cited earlier, there is a series of World Bank reports showing the negative effects of corruption available at <http://wbln0018.worldbank.org/research / workpapers.nsf/>
8. The calculation is from Wei (1998).
9. Kaufmann and Shang-Jin Wei (1999).
10. See Hess and Dunfee (2001).
11. <http://www.cauxroundtable.org>
12. <http://www.transparency.org>
13. The Shell report is available at <http://www.shell.com/shellreport>
14. Speech given by Amnesty International Secretary General Pierre Sané at the Energy Conference 2000, Sanderstolen, Norway, 2 February 2000; available at <http://amnesty-usa.org/business/globalisationandHR.htm>
15. Crawford, Cadot and Traça (1999).
16. Burns and Spar (2000).
17. <www.moles.org/ProjectUnderground/'Drillbits and Tailings'>, 15 December 1996.
18. <http://www.hrw.org/research>; 'Oil Companies Complicit in Nigerian Abuses', Lagos, 23 February 1999.
19. <http://www.hrw.org/reports/1999/enron/>; 'The Enron Corporation Complicity in Human Rights Violations Summary and Recommendations', January 1999.
20. Banerjee (2001).
21. Amnesty International, *Human Right Principles or Companies*, AI index number ACT 70/001/1998, Amnesty International Publications, 1 Easton Street, London, WCIX ODJ, 1998. Also available at <http://www.amnesty.org>
22. See <www.sustainability-index.com>

References and further reading

Banerjee, Neela, 'US Lawsuit Snares Exxon', *International Herald Tribune*, 22 June 2001.

Burns, Jennifer L. and Debora L. Spar, 'Hitting the Wall: Nike and International Labor Practices', Harvard Business School Case 9-700-047, 2000.

Crawford, Robert, Olivier Cadot and Daniel Traça, 'Soccer Balls: Made by Children for Children? Child Labor in Pakistan', INSEAD Case Study 12/1999-4865, 1999.

Dunchin, Faye and Glenn-Marie Lange, *Our Common Future*. Oxford: Oxford University Press, 1994.

Fadiman, Jeffrey A., 'A Traveller's Guide to Gifts and Bribes', *Harvard Business Review*, July–August 1986, pp. 4–12.

Hess, David and Thomas Dunfee, 'Fighting Corruption: A Principled Approach', Wharton School Working Paper, 2001.

Kaufmann, Daniel and Shang-Jin Wei, Does 'Grease Money' Speed up the Wheels of Commerce, *National Bureau of Economic Research*, NBER Working Paper No. w7093, April 1999.

Kolk, A., R. van Tulder and Carlijn Welters, 'International Codes of Conduct and Corporate Social Responsibility: Can Transnational Corporations Regulate Themselves?', *Transnational Corporations*, 8(1), 1999, pp. 143–80.

Leite, Carlos and Jens Weiman, 'Does Mother Nature Corrupt Natural Resources? Corruption and Economic Growth', IMF Working Paper, WP/99/85, July 1999.

Mauro, Paolo, 'Why Worry About Corruption?', *Economic Issues*, 6, Washington, DC: IMF, 1997.

Nichols, Martha, 'Third-World Families at Work: Child Labor or Child Care?', *Harvard Business Review*, January–February 1993, pp. 2–10.

OECD, *No Longer Business as Usual*, OECD Publication, Paris 2000.

OECD, *Sustainable Development*, OECD Publication, Paris 2001.

Pope, Jeremy, 'Confronting Corruption: The Elements of a National Integrity System', *TI Source Book 2000*. London: Transparency International, 2000; available at the TI web site as a free-of-charge download.

Reinhart, Forest L., *Down to Earth: Applying Business Principles to Environmental Management*. Boston, MA: Harvard Business School Press, 1999.

Tanzi, Vito, 'Corruption Around the World: Causes, Consequences, Scope and Cure', *International Monetary Fund Staff Paper*, 559, 1998.

Van Tulder, R. and A. Kolk, 'Multinationality and Corporate Ethics: Codes of Conduct in the Sporting Goods Industry', *Journal of International Business Studies*, 32(2), 2001.

Wei, Shang-Jin, 'Corruption in Economic Development: Beneficial Grease, Minor Annoyance or Major Obstacle?', Harvard University and National Bureau of Economic Research Working Paper, 1998.

16

Global trends

In July 2001 in Genoa, Carlo Giuliani, an anti-globalisation protester at the G8 meeting, was killed during a clash with the police. This event came after a series of protests had taken place in many 'global' meetings at Seattle, Prague, Nice and Davos. At the same time, an international meeting was held in Bonn to agree on the practical measure to implement the Kyoto 1997 Treaty aiming at reducing global carbon dioxide emissions by 5.2 per cent of 1990 levels by 2012. Unfortunately, the United States, the largest producer of carbon dioxide, refused in 2001 to implement the Kyoto Agreement. On 11, September 2001 a terrorist suicide attack, in the name of a Jihad (holy war) destroyed the New York Twin Towers and part of the Pentagon in Washington, killing more than 3,000 people. Those almost contemporaneous events show that the road toward globalisation is paved with many hurdles.

Throughout the previous chapters, it has been assumed that globalisation is ineluctable, and most corporations are building strategies based on that assumption. The past 30 years have evolved in that direction. If one looks at the future, however, the pursuit of globalisation seems one likely scenario, but not the only one.

This last chapter is devoted to describing some of the most salient trends that are likely to affect firms' global strategic management. Many of the issues described are conjectural and incomplete. When one looks at the future one has to identify the ideological, social, demographic, political and scientific developments that affect the world of economics and business. Some of those are already visible today; some others are hidden or are present only in the form of 'weak signals'. Several organisations have projected future scenarios: all come up with three possible images – a globalised world, a fragmented world and an intermediate world in which globalisation is partially achieved.

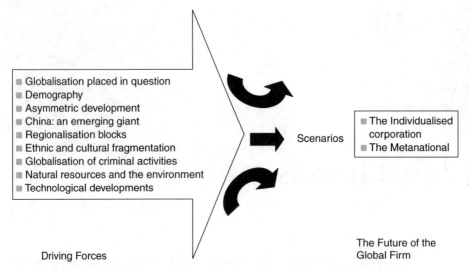

Figure 16.1 Global driving forces and the global corporation

Figure 16.1 shows how this last chapter is organised. First some of the most significant driving forces will be briefly described. Then we shall summarise the most well-known scenarios. Finally, we will look at the emerging theories of *global management*.
At the end of the chapter one should be able:

▪ To understand the arguments in favour and against globalisation
▪ To appreciate the major trends in the global economy
▪ To contribute to the building of future scenarios

DRIVING FORCES

Globalisation placed in question

From a historical perspective, the globalisation phenomena experienced at the end of the twentieth century were not new. Some economic historians have observed that at the end of the nineteenth century the world was more 'global' than it is today. Obviously, the state of affairs was different: global powers such as Britain, France or the United States were globalised because of their colonial influence. Trade barriers were limited and people, money and goods moved easily across borders. Nationalism, epitomised by the First and Second World Wars, provoked protectionism and restriction of exchange. The post-war technological, political and economic factors described in Chapter 1 reintroduced globalisation and generated new management paradigms. But at the dawn of the twenty-first century, while globalism seems to be triumphant some dissonant voices are increasingly putting in question the concept of a borderless, free market, monocultural world. This dialectic tension between the zealots and the dissidents dominates the background of any future scenarios.

The zealots' point of view is best represented by a quotation from a report published by the US National Intelligence Council (NIC) entitled *'Global Trends 2015: A Dialogue about the Future with Non Government Experts'*[1]:

'The networked global company will be driven by rapid and largely unrestricted flows of information, ideas, cultural values, capital, goods and services, and people: that is, globalization. This globalized economy will be a net contributor to increased political stability in the world in 2015, although its reach and benefits will not be universal. In contrast to the Industrial Revolution, the process of globalization is more compressed. Its evolution will be rocky, marked by chronic financial volatility and a widening economic divide.

The global economy, overall, will return to the high levels of growth reached in the 1960s and early 1970s. Economic growth will be driven by political pressures for higher living standards, improved economic policies, rising foreign trade and investment, the diffusion of information technologies, and an increasingly dynamic private sector. Potential brakes on the global economy – such as sustained financial crisis or prolonged disruption of energy supplies – could undo this optimistic projection.

Regions, countries and groups feeling left behind will face deepening economic stagnation, political, ethnic, ideological, and religious extremism, along with the violence that often accompanies it. They will force the United States and other developed countries to remain focused on "old-world" challenges while concentrating on the implications of "new-world" technologies at the same time.'

Dissentient voices are expressed more and more in the countries that have benefited the most from globalisation – the OECD countries – and their point of view can be the best represented by a quotation from Rodrik (1997).

'First, reduced trade barriers and investment accentuate the asymmetry between the groups that can cross international borders (directly or indirectly via outsourcing, owners of capital, skilled workers, professionals) and those that cannot (semi-skilled and unskilled) can be substituted by other cheaper workers. This undermines the social fabric in the developed world.

Second, globalization engenders conflicts within and between nations over domestic norms and the social institutions that embody these. (Pension funds, social security, values and culture…)

Third, globalization has made it increasing difficulty for governments to provide social insurance. The welfare state is under attack.

The question therefore is how the tension between globalization and the pressure for socialization of risks can be eased. If the lesson is not managed intelligently and creatively, the danger is that domestic consumers in favor of open markets will ultimately erode to the point where a generalized resurgence of protectionism becomes a serious possibility.'

More radical views are obviously expressed by militant groups. Below is an extract from a talk given by Walden Bello, a representative of Corpwatch, during demonstrations in Melbourne against the World Economic Forum[2]:

'What is **deglobalization**?

I am not talking about withdrawing from the international economy. I am speaking about reorienting our economies from production for export to production for the local market;

– about drawing most of our financial resources for development from within rather than becoming dependent on foreign investment and foreign financial markets;

– about carrying out the long-postponed measures of income redistribution and land redistribution to create a vibrant internal market that would be the anchor of the economy;

– about de-emphasizing growth and maximizing equity in order to radically reduce environmental disequilibrium;

– about not leaving strategic economic decisions to the market but making them subject to democratic choice;

– about subjecting the private sector and the state to constant monitoring by civil society;

– about creating a new production and exchange complex that includes community cooperatives, private enterprises, and state enterprises, and excludes TNC [transnational corporations];

– about enshrining the principle of subsidiarity in economic life by encouraging production of goods to take place at the community and national level if it can be done so at reasonable cost in order to preserve community.

We are speaking, in short, about re-embedding the economy in society, rather than having society driven by the economy.'

This anti-globalisation view has been gaining support in the early twenty-first century in places and among populations that had traditionally pushed for and benefited from it.

Demography

By the year 2015 the world population is expected to reach 7.4 billion (it was 5.6 billion in 1995). As seen in Table 16.1, the increase in world population comes from the developing world of Asia, Africa and Latin America. The age pyramid in the industrialised countries of North America, Europe and Japan will shift toward aging people; that will create pressures on health care, social services and pensions management.

One can expect an increase in cross-border migration as well as intense urbanisation. It is forecast that half the world population will live in urban areas,[3] leading to the development of **megacities** of more than 10 million people: Beijing, Shanghai, Calcutta, Mumbai, Karachi, Dhaka, Jakarta, Cairo, Lagos, Mexico, São Paolo, Buenos Aires, Tokyo, New York and Los Angeles.

Table 16.1 World population, 1995 and 2015, million people

	1995	2015
China	1,204.9	1,470.2
India	916.5	1210.3
Developing Asia	893.8	1221.2
Total Asia	3,015.2	3,901.7
Latin America	489.0	645.7
Russia and Eastern Europe	407.7	413.5
Middle East and Africa	927.1	1505.8
USA	263.1	308.5
Japan	125.6	130.7
Europe, Australasia, Canada	436.6	463.6
Total World	5,664.3	7,369.5

Source: Maddison (1998).

Asymmetric development

Figure 16.2 shows the income gap between the rich and the poor countries. Although according to the World Bank the number of people living below the poverty level of 1.08 dollars a day stagnated at around 1.2 billion during the last decade of the twentieth century, the evolution has been unequal. In East Asia, the number

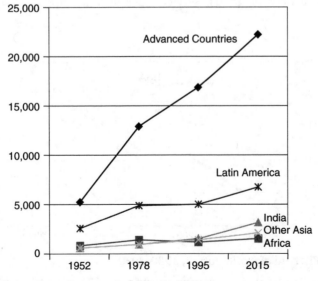

Figure 16.2 The global income gap, 1952–2015

Source: Maddison (1998).

of people below the poverty level has decreased, but it has increased in South and Central Asia, Latin America and Africa.[4]

This unequal development is a factor of instability that can generate conflict and ultimately disrupt global trade and investments.

China: an emerging giant

Since 1979 China's GDP growth rate has averaged 9.33 per cent per year, compared with a world average of 3.3 per cent. If computed in Purchasing Power Parity (PPP) terms, China's share of world output was 3.4 per cent in 1980 and 11.5 per cent in 2001. Assuming a growth differential of 4 per cent with the United States, China would catch up with the United States by 2020 (see Figure 16.3).

China has aggressively rebuilt its industrial base thanks to a massive import of foreign technology. The state-owned sector has progressively modernised. Some Chinese firms – such as Haier in appliances, Legend in computers or Shanghai Industrial Automotive Corporation – can make a pretence of becoming global players in their respective industries. If China continues its political and financial reforms, it will become a global economic and political power, and its corporations will challenge established global firms.

Regionalisation

An alternative to globalisation is **regionalisation**. The argument put forward by Professor Alan Rugman to announce the 'end of globalisation' (2000) projects that instead of a free flow of goods, services, people and capital across the world,

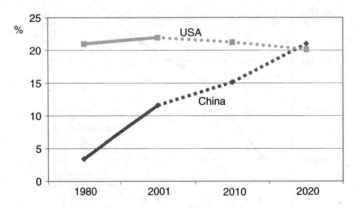

Figure 16.3   PPP share of world output, 1980–2020

Note: The projection assumes an average growth rate of 7 per cent for China, 3 per cent for the United States and 3.5 per cent for the World.
Source: IMF Statistics, May 2001.

regional 'fortresses' may emerge as the dominant form of economic structure.
Table 16.2 lists the various forms of such regional agreements.

Table 16.2 Regional agreements

Region	Regional agreement	Countries involved	Content
Europe	EU (European Union) (ex-EEC and EC)	Austria, Belgium, Denmark, Finland, France, Germany, Greece, Holland, Ireland, Italy, Luxemburg, Spain, Sweden, United Kingdom, Portugal	Created in 1957 as European Economic Community (EEC) by the Treaty of Rome by six countries Enlarged in 1974 and 1997 to 15 members More countries from Central Europe will join before 2010 Single Market (SEM) since 1992: free movement of people, goods, capital Single currency, the euro, since 2002 for 12 countries (United Kingdom, Denmark, Sweden excluded) Beyond economic integration the EU has political integration ambitions
Latin America	MERCOSUR (Mercado Common del Sur)	Argentina, Bolivia, Brazil, Chile, Paraguay, Uruguay	Created by the Treaty of Asunción in 1991 Aims at establishing a common market
North America	NAFTA (North American Free Trade Agreement)	Canada, Mexico, United States	Created in 1992 Aims at establishing a common market
South East Asia	ASEAN (Association of South East Asian Nations)	Brunei, Indonesia, Laos, Malaysia, Myanmar, Philippines, Thailand, Vietnam	Created in 1967 Initial objective was to promote regional stability Progressively transformed into economic co-operation Aims at implementing an ASEAN Free Trade Area (AFTA)
Asia-Pacific	APEC (Asia Pacific Economic Co-operation)	21 countries from Asia, North and South America and Australia New Zealand	Created in 1989 Begun as an informal dialogue group promoting open trade and practical economic co-operation Goal is to advance Asia-Pacific economic dynamism and sense of community
North Africa	MAU (Maghreb Arab Union)	Algeria, Libya, Mauritania, Morocco, Tunisia	Created in 1989 Aims at establishing a common market

Table 16.2 (*Continued*)

Region	Regional agreement	Countries involved	Content
Southern Africa	SADC (Southern African Development Community)	Angola, Botswana, Democratic Republic of Congo, Lesotho, Malawi, Mauritius, Mozambique, Namibia, South Africa, Seychelles, Swaziland, Tanzania, Zambia, Zimbabwe	Created 1979 and expanded in 1992 to harmonise economic development among the countries of Southern Africa

Ethnic and cultural fragmentation

An increased search for *communal identity* – religious, ethnic or linguistic – is expected to develop alongside, or against, globalisation. Manifestations of such movements have been experienced in the Balkans, in Chechnya, in Mexico, in Indonesia, China, Corsica, and Spain.

Huntington (1997) has argued forcefully that future conflicts will be primarily rooted in cultural differences, and will thus occur between different 'civilisations'.[5] The terrorist attacks of 11 September 2001 in the United States gives some credence to this thesis.

The globalisation of criminal activities

Illicit criminal activities are increasingly crossing borders: drug trafficking, prostitution, smuggling, 'cybercrimes' or illegal immigration are the most frequent and increasing criminal global activities, as well as global terrorism.

Natural resources and the environment

According to a scenario developed by the US NIC (2000):

'Contemporary environmental problems will persist and in many instances grow over the next 15 years (2000–2015)...Environmental issues wil become mainstream issues in several countries, particularly in the developed world. The main future environmental concerns are water supply, global warming and deforestation. Those three issues are those that were mentioned as the major emerging issues according to a survey conducted by the Scientific Committee on Problems of the Environment of the International Council for Science among 200 scientists in 50 countries' (UNEP, 1999)

▪ **Water supply**. It is anticipated that 'by 2015 nearly half of the world population will live in countries with less than 1,700 cubic meters of water *per capita* per year, a water-stressed situation' (National Intelligence Council, 2000). According to the UN Environment Programme, if the trend continues this proportion will grow to two-thirds of the world's population by 2025 (UNEP, 1999). In the developed countries the price of water is likely to increase considerably, and in the developing world water disputes may degenerate into armed conflicts.

▪ **Global warming**. Global emissions of CO^2 were 23,900 million tonnes in 1996, four time the level of 1950 (Figure 16.4). Without proper control of the 'greenhouse effect', the emission of CO^2 and other gases threatens to raise the average temperature of the globe, inducing sea-level rise and other natural disasters. Industries are the major producers of CO^2 and without proper control the whole ecology of the planet may be disrupted.

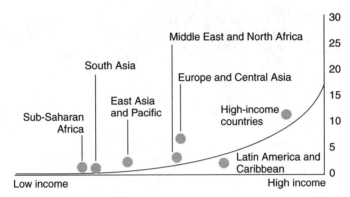

Figure 16.4 Industrial CO^2 emissions, 1998, metric tons *per capita*

Source: OECD, IMF, World Bank, UN (2000).

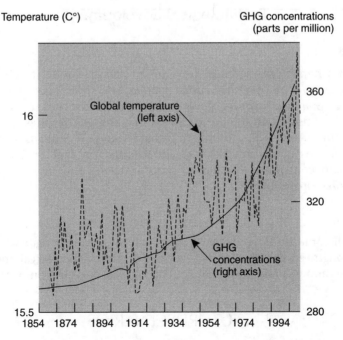

Figure 16.5 Global temperatures and concentration of GHG gases, 1854–1994

Source: OECD (2001).

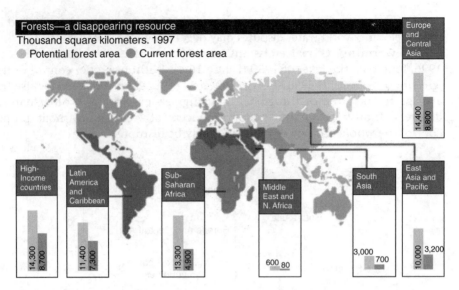

Figure 16.6 Deforestation

Source: OECD, IMF, World Bank, UN (2000).

● **Deforestation** (Figure 16.6). The progressive cutting of forests without a proper renewal creates droughts and desertification.

Technological developments

The Internet

As seen in Chapter 14, Internet technology can theoretically create the basis for the development of *global virtual marketplaces* that make national borders irrelevant. In practice, however, governments need the means to control the physical flow of goods as well to control access to websites. Despites its technological capacities, the future of the Internet's global usage still depends on political will. Electronic means of communication and transaction will nevertheless become pervasive and contribute to a faster, more efficient and more effective way to manage global operations.

Biotechnology

The other major technological development will come from genetic sciences. Genetic decoding, engineering and 'cloning' will make inroads in medical and agricultural applications, and will raise some fundamental ethical and environmental issues.

FUTURE SCENARIOS

The technique of **scenario** building is used to picture potential images of the future (Wack, 1985a, 1985b). Scenarios are built upon contrasted configurations of key socio-economic and political drivers. The configurations are based on expert opinion. Two–four possible futures are pictured – most scenarios contain two or three extreme representations and a middle one. Table 16.3 summarises four scenarios: Global Trends 2015[6] is published by the US National Security Agency, the Millennium Project[7] is organised by the United Nations University, the Global scenarios 1998–2020 are prepared by Shell Corporation[8] and 'Which World?' is prepared by Allen Hammond, a Director of Strategic Analysis at the World Resources Institute (1998). Appendix 16.1 (p. 441) gives a more detailed description of the Global Trends 2015 scenarios.

Table 16.3 Four global scenarios

Name of project and origin	Alternative scenarios	Brief description
Global Trends 2015 (National Intelligence Council – 2000)	▓ **Inclusive globalisation**	A virtuous circle develops among technology, economic growth, demographic factors and effective governance, which enables a majority of the world's people to benefit from globalisation
	▓ **Pernicious globalisation**	The majority of the world's population fails to benefit from globalisation The global economy splits into three: growth continues in developed countries; many developing countries experience low or negative *per capita* growth, resulting in a growing gap with the developed world; the 'black' economy grows dramatically
	▓ **Regional competition**	Regional identities sharpen in Europe, Asia and the Americas There is an uneven diffusion of technologies Regional economic integration in trade and finance increases
	▓ **Post-polar world**	Economic and political tensions with Europe grow, the US–European alliance deteriorates Asia is generally prosperous and stable
Global Exploratory Scenarios, 1998 State of the Future (Glen and Gordon, 1999)	▓ **Cybertopia**	The explosive growth of Internet-accelerated globalisation in all forms Explosive growth in international activity Developing countries make remarkable progress Government involvement is low, communications are vibrant, security is high
	▓ **The rich get richer**	While the poorer countries in Africa and Asia run into a plethora of problems, the richer countries experience a period of robust GNP growth Government involvement is low, communications are vibrant, security is low Globalisation goes on
	▓ **A passive mean world**	Isolation prevails, government involvement is high, communications are stagnant, security is high Population growth outpaces job growth in most regions, and the concomitant unemployment and under-employment produces pressure on economic systems and fosters political unrest

Table 16.3 (Continued)

Name of project and origin	Alternative scenarios	Brief description
	■ **Trading places**	Loss of Western industrial leadership in key sectors, growing Asian economic and political power, and structural economic problems in the United States set the US economy on a downward slope. Government involvement is low, communications are vibrant, security is low. Globalisation goes on
Global Scenarios 1998–2020 (Shell Oil, 1998)	■ **The new game**	Existing institutions and organisations successfully adapt to the new and evolving complexities. The Kyoto Agreement works. By 2020, a new global system is in place. Global corporations continuously reinvent themselves.
	■ **People power**	Values are changing. A fragmented world. Unequal development
Which World?: Scenarios for the 21st Century (Allen Hammond 1998)	■ **Market world**	The free market prevails, economic reform, privatisation and deregulation continue. Globalisation is achieved and transnational corporations are the core players of this world
	■ **Fortress world**	Widespread social instability, rising conflict and return to protectionism
	■ **Transformed world**	A world in which social, environmental, economic and political issues are harmoniously managed

THE FUTURE OF GLOBAL CORPORATIONS

Academic and consulting research on the future roles, capabilities and organisation of global firms is all based on the fundamental assumption that globalisation is progressing and that global firms are the main vectors of that 'progress'. The main focus of organisational and strategic thinkers is to imagine and craft the organisation of the future as more innovative or 'revolutionary'[9] in order to lead, and adapt to, the changes brought by global competition. One can distinguish two major models or 'blueprints' for the future global firm: the **individualised corporation** model and the **metanational** model.

The individualised corporation

'The individualized corporation' is a terminology suggested by Ghoshal and Bartlett (1997). Based on the example of some leading global firms such as Canon, ABB or 3M, the authors argue that the future organisational form is best described by a *portfolio of three key processes*, embodied into a *new organisational model* in which *new management competencies and roles* are redefined:

- The *key processes* are: the entrepreneurial process, the integration process and the renewal process (Figure 16.7)

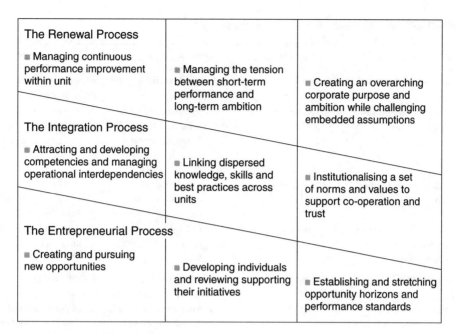

Figure 16.7 Portfolio of processes

Source: Ghoshal and Bartlett (1997, p. 201).

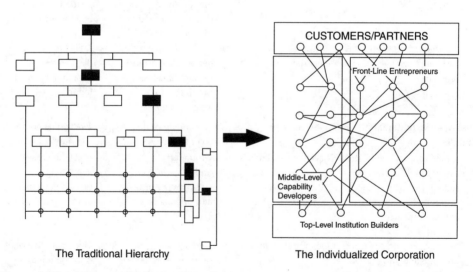

Figure 16.8 A new organisational model

Source: Ghoshal and Bartlett (1997, p. 205).

- The *new organisational model* is based on a network of relationships as opposed to the traditional hierarchical structure (Figure 16.8)
- The *new management roles* are: the operating-entrepreneurial role of front-line managers, the management-developer of senior and middle-level managers and the top-level institutional builder of top leaders (Table 16.4).

Table 16.4 Management competencies for new roles

Role/Tasks	Attitude/Traits	Knowledge/Experience	Skills/Attitudes
Operating-entreprenial	*Results-oriented competitor*	*Detailed operating knowledge*	*Focuses energy on opportunities*
▪ Creating and pursuing opportunities	▪ Creative, intuitive	▪ Knowledge of the business's technical, competitive and customer characteristics	▪ Ability to recognise potential markets and make commitments
▪ Attracting and utilising scarce skills and resources	▪ Persuasive, engaging	▪ Knowledge of internal/external resources	▪ Ability to motivate and drive people
▪ Managing continuous performance improvement	▪ Competitive, persistent	▪ Detailed understanding of the business	▪ Ability to sustain organisational energy around demanding objectives
Management-Developers	*Peoples-oriented integrator*	*Broad organisational experience*	*Focuses energy on opportunities*
▪ Reviewing, developing, supporting individuals and their initiatives	▪ Supportive, patient	▪ Knowledge of people as individuals and understanding how to influence them	▪ Ability to delegate, develop, empower
▪ Linking dispersed knowledge/skills	▪ Integrative, flexible	▪ Understanding of interpersonal dynamics among diverse groups	▪ Ability to develop relationships and build teams
▪ Managing short-term and long-term pressures	▪ Perceptive, demanding	▪ Understanding means –ends relationships linking short-term priorities and long-term goals	▪ Ability to reconcile differences while maintaining creative tensions
Top-level institutional builders	*Institution-visionary*	*Understanding company in its context*	*Understanding company in its context*
▪ Challenging assumptions while setting stretching opportunities horizons and performance standards	▪ Challenging, stretching	▪ Grounded understanding of the company, its business and operations	▪ Ability to create an existing, demanding work environment
▪ Building a context of co-operation and trust ▪ Creating an overarching, sense of corporate purpose and ambition	▪ Open-minded, fair ▪ Insightful, inspiring	▪ Understanding of the organisation as a system of structures, processes and culture ▪ Broad knowledge of different companies, industries and societies	▪ Understanding of the organisation as a system of structures, processes and cultures ▪ Ability to combine conceptual insight with motivational challenges

Source: Ghoshal and Bartlett (1997, pp. 221–2).

The metanational corporation was mentioned in Chapter 10. This form of global organisation proposed by Doz, dos Santos and Williamson (2002), is based on the assumption that in a globalised world competitive advantage is obtained at three levels:

1. The ability to *identify and access* new competencies, innovative technologies and lead market knowledge
2. The speed and the effectiveness with which companies can connect scattered pieces of knowledge and use them to create *innovative products and services*
3. The ability to optimise the efficiency of global sales, distribution, marketing and supply chains to *leverage those products, services and process innovations* across global markets rapidly and cost-effectively.

The traditional global firms were 'projectors', meaning that the source of their competitive advantage was to be found in their home countries, and their globalisation was to *project those advantages* internationally. The metanational corporation is a 'prospector', meaning that the source of their competitive advantage is to be able to prospect, tap and leverage knowledge *scattered across the world* in a speedy and efficient manner. Although the authors have not yet identified fully-fledged companies that correspond to the characteristics of their model, they found that companies like Nokia, the Finnish leader in mobile phones, or ST Microelectronics, a European microprocessor firm, are examples of metanationals in the making. The metanational firm has a dispersed internal and external network of design, production and customer relationship centres, each of which contributes to knowledge-creation and leverage. The concept of a 'centre' or 'home headquarters' disappears in this type of organisation – it is a *pure global firm within a global world*.

Both models are based on the form of a networked organisation that implies the co-ordinated combined effort of 'unbundled' business units (Hagel and Singer, 2001), some of them being 'internal' to a corporation (subsidiaries), some external (partners, suppliers, distributors), some in between (joint ventures, strategic alliances). The concept of the networked organisation is not new but it gained momentum during the 1980s and 1990s because of the restructuring of firms, the forming of global strategic alliances and the development of IT.

SUMMARY AND KEY POINTS

1. The significant *driving forces of globalisation* include:
   - ▪ Globalisation put in question:
     - – *Zealot* point of view:
       - (a) Globalisation will drive networked global company
       - (b) Globalised economy will increase political stability but reach and benefits will not be universal
       - (c) Globalisation process will evolve with financial volatility and a widening economic divide
       - (d) Potential brakes on global economy include sustained financial crisis or prolonged disruption of energy supplies

(e) Regions, countries and groups feel left behind will face deepening economic stagnation, political, ethnic, ideological and religious extremism

(f) Developed countries will be forced to focus on 'old-world' challenges while concentrating on the implications of 'new-world' technologies

- *Dissentient* point of view:

  (a) Reduced trade barriers and investment increases asymmetry between groups that can cross international borders and groups that cannot

  (b) Globalisation stimulates conflicts within and between nations over domestic norms and social institutions embodying them

  (c) Globalisation makes it increasingly difficult for governments to provide social insurance

  (d) How to ease tension between globalisation and pressures for socialisation to minimise the possibility of a generalised resurgence of protectionism?

- *Radical* point of view:

  (a) Re-embedding the economy in society instead of having society driven by the economy:

    (i) Obtain financial resources for development from within instead of foreign investment

    (ii) Implement measures of income and land redistribution

    (iii) De-emphasise growth and maximise equity

    (iv) Make strategic economic decisions subject to democratic choice

    (v) Subject private sector and state to constant monitoring by civil society

    (vi) Create a new production/exchange complex that includes community co-operatives, private enterprises, state enterprises but exclude TNCs

    (vii) Encourage production of goods at community/sub-national level

■ Demographic trends:
  - Increase in world population will come from developing world
  - Age pyramid in industrialised countries will shift towards aging people, increasing pressures on health care, social services and pension management
  - Increase in cross-border migrations and intense urbanisation will create megacities of more than 10 million people

■ Asymmetric development – the unequal development of people living below a certain poverty level will generate conflicts and ultimately disrupt global trade and investment

■ China (the emerging giant):
  - Projected to catch up with US GDP in PPP terms by 2020
  - Has built a large industrial base with progressively modernised state-owned enterprises
  - Likely to become a global economic and political power with corporations challenging established global firms

■ Regional blocks:
  - As alternative to globalisation, regional blocks emerging as the dominant form of economic structure

- Examples include EU, MERCOSUR, NAFTA ASEAN, APEC, MAU, SADC
⬛ Ethnical and cultural fragmentation – increased search for community identity (religious, ethnic, linguistic) which will develop against globalisation, as evidenced by the Balkans area
⬛ Global criminal activities – increasingly cross-border, e.g. drug trafficking
⬛ Natural resource and environment:
  - Environmental issues will become mainstream issues in the developed world
  - Main future concerns are water supply, global warming and deforestation
⬛ Technological developments:
  - *Internet:*   a global tool abolishing physical distance for multimedia transmission with usage spreading throughout the world; theoretically, Internet technology creates the basis for the development of global virtual marketplaces and makes borders irrelevant, in practice, governments still can control the physical flow of goods and access to websites
  - *Biotechnology:* genetic engineering will raise fundamental ethical and environmental issues.

2. There are four well-known scenarios:

⬛ *Global Trends 2015* (US National Security Agency):
  - Majority of the world's population benefit from globalisation ('inclusive globalisation')
  - Majority of people do not enjoy the benefits ('pernicious globalisation')
  - Regional economic integration ('regional competition')
  - Economic and political tension between United States and Europe, Asia generally prosperous and stable ('post-polar world')
⬛ *Millennium Project* (UN University):
  - Periods of explosive growth of Internet-accelerated globalisation ('Cyber-topia')
  - Richer countries experience a period of robust GNP growth ('The rich get richer')
  - Concomitant unemployment and under-employment produce pressure on economic system and fostered political unrest ('A passive mean world')
  - Loss of Western industrial leadership, growing Asian economic and political power and US economy on a downward slope ('Trading places')
⬛ *Global scenarios 1998–2020* (Shell Corporation):
  - Existing institutions and organisations successfully adapt to new and evolving complexities and global corporations continuously reinvent themselves ('The new game')
  - A fragmented world with changing values and unequal development ('People power')
⬛ *Which World?* (World Resources Institute):
  - Free market prevails with economic reforms, privatision and deregulation, globalisation achieved with transnational corporations as core players in the world ('Market world')
  - Widespread social instability with rising conflict and return to protectionism ('Fortress world')

- Social, environmental, economical and political issues are harmoniously managed ('Transformed world').

3. Emerging theories of global management with two major firm models:

- *Individualised corporation* with a portfolio of three key processes by which new management competencies and roles are defined:
  - Key processes are the entrepreneurial process, the integration process and the renewal process
  - The new organisational model is based on a network relationship instead of the traditional hierarchical structure
  - The new management roles are the operating-entrepreneurial role of front-line managers, the management-developer of senior and middle-level managers and the top-level institutional builder of top leaders
- *Metanational*
  - The networked organisation implies the co-ordinated combined effort of 'unbundled' business units, some 'internal' to a corporation (e.g. subsidiaries), some 'external' to a corporation (e.g. partners, suppliers, distributors) and some in between (e.g. joint ventures, strategic alliances)
  - Assumes competitive advantage is obtained at three levels:
    (a) Ability to identify and access new competencies, innovative technologies and lead market knowledge
    (b) Speed and effectiveness with which companies can connect scattered pieces of knowledge and use them to create innovative products and services
    (c) Ability to optimise the efficiency of global sales, distribution, marketing and supply chains to leverage those products, services and processes innovations across global market rapidly and cost-effectively.

Appendix 16.1   Four alternative global futures

In September–October 1999, the NIC initiated work on *Global Trends 2015* by co-sponsoring with the Department of State/Institute of National Resources (INR) and the Central Intelligence Agency's Global Futures Project two unclassified workshops on 'Alternative Global Futures: 2000–2015'. The workshops brought together several dozen government and non-government specialists in a wide range of fields.

The first workshop identified major factors and events that would drive global change through 2015. It focused on demography, natural resources, science and technology, the global economy, governance, social/cultural identities and conflict, and identified main trends and regional variations. These analyses became the basis for subsequent elaboration in *Global Trends 2015*.

The second workshop developed four alternative global futures in which these drivers would interact in different ways through 2015. Each scenario was intended to construct a plausible, policy-relevant story of how this future might evolve: highlighting key uncertainties, discontinuities and unlikely or 'wild-card' events, and identifying important policy and intelligence challenges.

SCENARIO ONE: INCLUSIVE GLOBALISATION

A virtuous circle develops among technology, economic growth, demographic factors and effective governance, which enables a majority of the world's people to benefit from globalisation. **Technological** development and diffusion – in some cases triggered by severe environmental or health crises – are utilised to grapple effectively with some problems of the developing world. Robust global **economic growth** – spurred by a strong policy consensus on economic liberalisation – diffuses wealth widely and mitigates many demographic and resource problems. **Governance** is effective at both the national and international level. In many countries, the state's role shrinks, as its functions are privatised or performed by public–private partnerships (PPPs), while global co-operation intensifies on many issues through a variety of international arrangements. **Conflict** is minimal within and among states benefiting from globalisation. A minority of the world's people – in sub-Saharan Africa, the Middle East, Central and South Asia, and the Andean region – do not benefit from these positive changes, and internal conflicts persist in and around those countries left behind.

441

SCENARIO TWO: PERNICIOUS GLOBALISATION

Global elites thrive, but the majority of the world's population fails to benefit from globalisation. **Population growth and resource scarcities** place heavy burdens on many developing countries, and migration becomes a major source of inter-state tension. **Technologies** not only fail to address the problems of developing countries but are also exploited by negative and illicit networks and incorporated into destabilising weapons. The global **economy** splits into three: growth continues in developed countries; many developing countries experience low or negative *per capita* growth, resulting in a growing gap with the developed world; and the 'black' economy grows dramatically. **Governance** and political leadership are weak at both the national and international level. Internal **conflicts** increase, fuelled by frustrated expectations, inequities and heightened communal tensions; Weapons of Mass Destruction (WMD) proliferate and are used in at least one internal conflict.

SCENARIO THREE: REGIONAL COMPETITION

Regional identities sharpen in Europe, Asia and the Americas, driven by growing political resistance in Europe and East Asia to US global preponderance and US-driven globalisation and each region's increasing preoccupation with its own economic and political priorities. There is an uneven diffusion of **technologies**, reflecting differing regional concepts of intellectual property and attitudes towards biotechnology. Regional **economic** integration in trade and finance increases, resulting in both fairly high levels of economic growth and rising regional competition. Both the state and institutions of regional **governance** thrive in major developed and emerging market countries, as governments recognise the need to resolve pressing regional problems and shift responsibilities from global to regional institutions. Given the preoccupation of the three major regions with their own concerns, countries outside these regions in sub-Saharan Africa, the Middle East and Central and South Asia have few places to turn for resources or political support. Military **conflict** among and within the three major regions does not materialise, but internal conflicts increase in and around other countries left behind.

SCENARIO FOUR: POST-POLAR WORLD

US domestic preoccupation increases as the US **economy** slows, then stagnates. Economic and political tensions with Europe grow, the US–European alliance deteriorates as the United States withdraws its troops, and Europe turns inward, relying on its own regional institutions. At the same time, national **governance** crises create instability in Latin America, particularly in Colombia, Cuba, Mexico and Panama, forcing the United States to concentrate on the region. Indonesia also faces internal crisis and risks disintegration, prompting China to provide the bulk of an *ad hoc* peacekeeping force. Otherwise, Asia is generally prosperous and stable, permitting the United States to focus elsewhere. Korea's normalisation and *de facto* unification proceed, China and Japan provide the bulk of external financial support for Korean unification, and the United States begins withdrawing its troops from Korea and Japan. Over time, these geostrategic shifts ignite long-standing national rivalries among the Asian powers, triggering increased military preparations and hitherto dormant or covert WMD programmes. Regional and global institutions prove irrelevant to the evolving **conflict** situation in Asia, as China issues an ultimatum to Japan to dismantle its nuclear programme and Japan – invoking its bilateral treaty with the United States – calls for US re-engagement in Asia under adverse circumstances at the brink of a major war. Given the priorities of Asia, the Americas and Europe, countries outside these regions are marginalised, with virtually no sources of political or financial support.

GENERALISATIONS ACROSS THE SCENARIOS

The four scenarios can be grouped in two pairs, the first contrasting the 'positive' and 'negative' effects of globalisation, the second contrasting intensely competitive but not conflictual regionalism and the descent into regional military conflict:

- In all but the first scenario, globalisation does not create widespread global co-operation. Rather, in the second scenario, globalisation's negative effects promote extensive dislocation and conflict, while in the third and fourth they spur regionalism.
- In all four scenarios, countries negatively affected by population growth, resource scarcities and bad governance fail to benefit from globalisation, are prone to internal conflicts and risk state failure.
- In all four scenarios, the effectiveness of national, regional and international governance and at least moderate but steady economic growth are crucial.
- In all four scenarios, US global influence wanes.

Source: NIC (2000).

Learning assignments

1 Why is globalisation increasingly being put in question?
2 Does globalisation increase the income gap?
3 If China becomes a global economic/political power, its corporations will challenge established global firms. How will this affect the global economy?
4 Why are the Internet and biotechnology the major technological trends likely to influence the future development of globalisation?
5 How will the 'global warming issue' affect the global economy?

Key words

- Asymmetric development
- Cybercrime
- Deglobalisation
- Global warming
- Individualised corporation
- Megacities
- Metanational
- Regionalisation
- Scenarios

Web resources

Pro-globalisation web sites

<http://www.wto.org>
The official website of the World Trade Organization (WTO).

<http://europa.eu.int/index.htm>
This website provides information on the EU's goal and policy.

<http://news.ft.com/news/worldnews/globaleconomy>
The *Financial Times'* news feature section on global economy.

<http://www.economist.com/about/about_globalagenda.cfm>
Global Agenda is a service on <Economist.com> which offers a concise analysis of the international issues and events.

<http://www.unctad.org>
The UN Commission on Trade and Development.

<http://www.imf.org>
The IMF website.

<http://www.odc.org>
The US Overseas Development Council website.

<http://www.oecd.org>
The OECD website.

Anti-globalisation websites

<http://www.southcentre.org/>
Collection of papers presented by the South Centre representing the 'South' countries.

<http://www.globalpolicy.org>
A critical view about the UN.

<http://www.wtowatch.org>
Critical views about the WTO.

<http://www.twnside.org.sg>
A Third World network based in Singapore.

Academic websites

<http://www.adelaide.edu.au/cies >
A collection of academic papers dealing with various globalisation issues.

<http://www.stern.nyu/~nroubini/>
From the Stern Business School.

<http://www.cid.harvard.edu/cidtrade >
Global Trade and Negotiation home page.

√<http://www.geocities.com/~acunu/millennium/sof/index.html>
This provides an annotated bibliography on scenarios.

Notes

1. National Intelligence Council (NIC) (2000, p.34); available at <http://www.odci.gov/cia/publications/pubs.html>
2. Bello (2000); available at <http://www.corpwatch.org/issues/wto/featured/2000/8-bello.html>
3. NIC (2000, p.20).
4. World Bank (2001).
5. Huntington (1997); the original article, 'The Clash of Civilizations?' (*Foreign Affairs*, Summer 1993, pp. 22–49), sparked a vigorous debate about a new 'civilisation paradigm', replacing the former division of the globe into the First (free world), Second (communist) and Third (developing) Worlds. (See comments in *Foreign Affairs*, September–October 1993, pp. 2–26, and Huntingdon's response, *Foreign Affairs*, November–December 1993, pp. 186–94.)
6. NIC (2000).
7. Glen, Jerome Theodore Gordon, *1998 State of the Future*. Washington, DC: American Council for the United Nations University, 1999.

8. Shell (1998); available at <http://www.shell.com>
9. Hamel (2000). The author is not centred on the issues of globalisation, but the book implicitly assumes that corporations will become more and more globalised.

References and further reading

Bello, Walden, 'The Struggle for a Deglobalized World', Focus on the Global South, September 2000; available at <http://www.corpwatch.org/issues/wto /featured/2000/8-bello.html>

Beneviste, Guy, *The Twenty-First Century Organization: Analyzing Current Trends – Imagining the Future*. San Francisco: Jossey-Bass, 1994 – two scenarios of the organisation in the twenty-first century.

Doremus, Paul N., William W. Keller, Louis W. Pauly and Simon Reich, *The Myth of the Global Corporation*. Princeton: Princeton University Press, 1998.

Economist, The, 'A Survey of Globalisation', 29 September–5 October 2001.

Doz, Yves L., José dos Santos and Peter Williamson, *From Global to Metanational: How Companies Win in the Knowledge Economy*. Boston, MA: Harvard Business School Press, 2002.

Friedman, Thomas L., *The Lexus and the Olive Tree: Understanding Globalization*. New York: Farrar, Strauss & Giroux, 1999.

Ghoshal, Sumantra and Christopher A. Bartlett, *The Individualized Corporation: A Fundamental Approach to Management*. New York: HarperCollins, 1997.

Glen, Jerome Theodore Gordon, *1998 State of the Future*. Washington, DC: American Council for the United Nations University, 1999.

Hagel, John III and Marc Singer, 'Unbundling the Corporation' *Harvard Business Review* 77(2) March/April 1999, pp. 133–44.

Hamel, Gary, *Leading the Revolution*. Boston, MA: Harvard Business School Press, 2000.

Hammond, Allen, '*Which World? Scenarios for the 21st Century*'. Washington, DC: Island Press, Shearwater Books, 1998.

Harvey, Michael, Mirolad Novicevic and Timothy Kiessling, 'Hypercompetition and the Future of Global Management in the Twenty First Century', *Thunderbird International Business Review*, 43(5), 2001, pp. 599–616.

Heilbroner, Robert, *21st Century Capitalism*. New York: W.W. Norton, 1993 – five scenarios of capitalism to the twenty-first century.

Huntington, Samuel P., *The Clash of Civilizations and the Remaking of the World Order*. London: Simon & Schuster, 1997.

Institute for the Future (IFTF), *1990 Ten Year Forecast*, Corporate Associates Program. Menlo Park, CA: IFTF, 1990 – three scenarios of the business environment to 2000, 2030 and 2050.

Laszlo, Ervin, *Vision 2020: Reordering Chaos for Global Survival*. New York, NY: Gordon & Breach, 1994 – world environment scenario to the twenty-first century.

Maddison, Angus, 'Chinese Economic Performance in the Long-Run', *OECD Development Centre Studies*, 1998.

Mitroff, Ian I., *Business Not as Usual: Rethinking Our Individual, Corporate, and Industrial Strategies for Global Competition*. San Francisco: Jossey-Bass, 1997 – four scenarios of US development into the twenty-first century.

National Intelligence Council (NIC), *Global Trends 2015: A Dialogue about the Future with Non Government Experts*, December 2000, p. 34; available at <http://www.odci.gov/cia/publications/pubs.html>

OECD, IMF, World Bank, UN, *A Better World for All*. Paris: OECD, 2000.

OECD, 'Policies to Enhance Sustainable Development'. Paris: OECD, 2001.

Saari, David J., *Global Corporations and Sovereign Nations: Collision or Cooperation?* Westport, CT: Quorum Books, 1999.

Rodrik, Dani, '*Has Globalization Gone too Far?*'. Washington, DC: Institute for International Economics, 1997.

Rugman, Alan, *The End of Globalization: A New and Radical Analysis of Globalization and What it Means for Business*. London: Random House, 2000.

Sheffield, Charles, Alonso Marceto, and Morton A. Kaplan (eds). *The World of 2044 – Technological Development and the Future of Society*. St. Paul, MN: Paragon House, 1994. A Global economy scenario to the year 2044.

Shell, *Global Scenarios 1998–2015*. London: United Kingdom: Shell; available at <http://www.shell.com>

UNEP, 'Global Environment Outlook'. CARY, NC; Oxford University Press, 1999, p. 4.

UN University, Millennium Project. ??: United Nations University, 19??; available at <http://www.geocities.com/~acunu/>

Wack, Pierre, 'Scenarios: Uncharted Waters Ahead', *Harvard Business Review*, September–October 1985a, pp. 73–89.

Wack, Pierre, 'Scenarios: Shooting the Rapids, *Harvard Business Review*, November–December 1985b, pp. 139–49.

White, James (ed.), *Global Climate Change: Linking Energy, Environment, Economy, and Equity*. New York: Plenum Press, 1992 – energy scenarios to the twenty-first century.

World Bank, *World Development Report 2000/2001: Attacking Poverty*. Washington, DC: World Bank, 2001.

Index of companies and organisations

Index of names

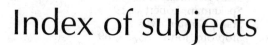

Index of subjects